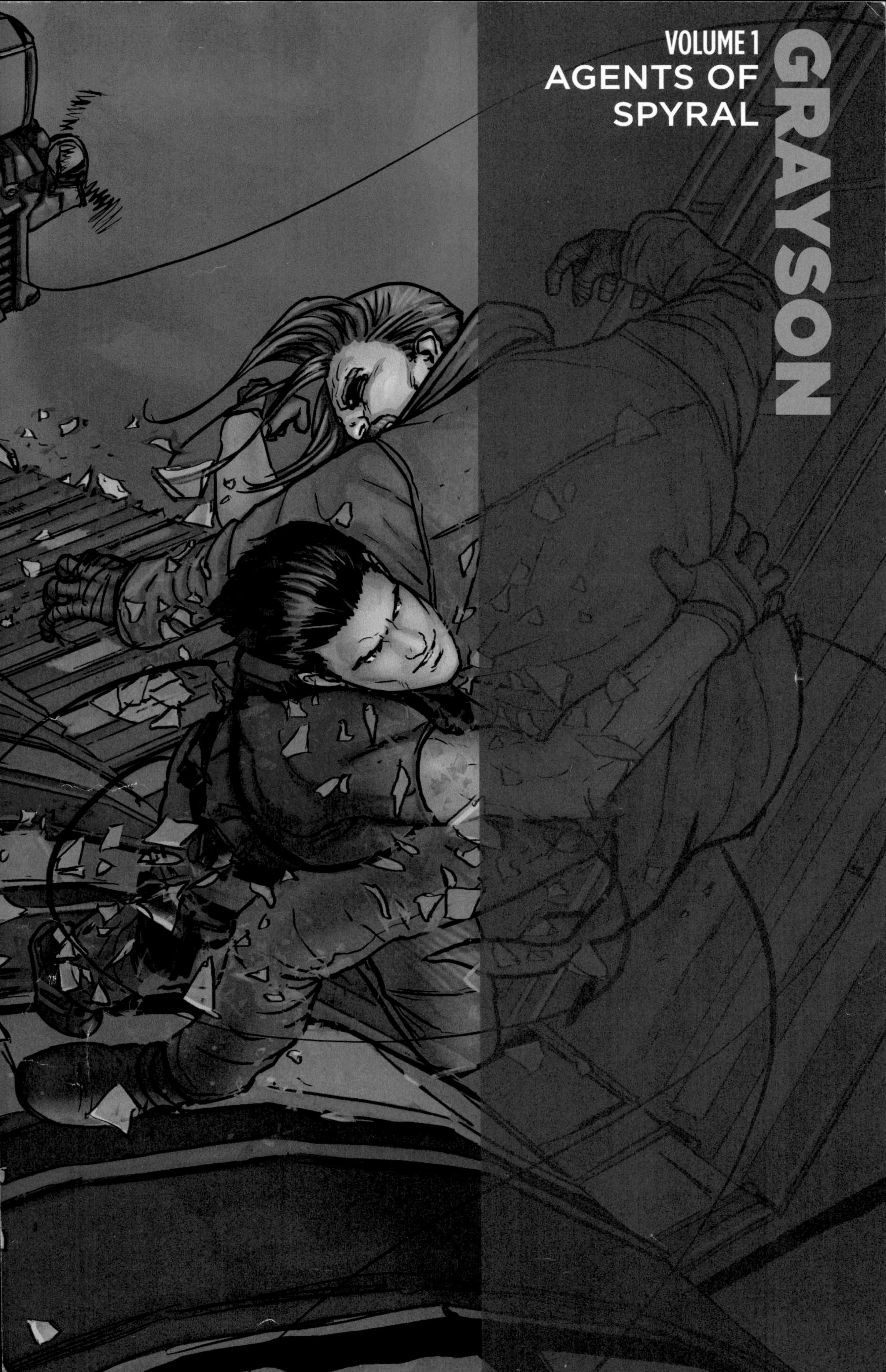

GRAYSON

VOLUME 1
AGENTS OF SPYRAL

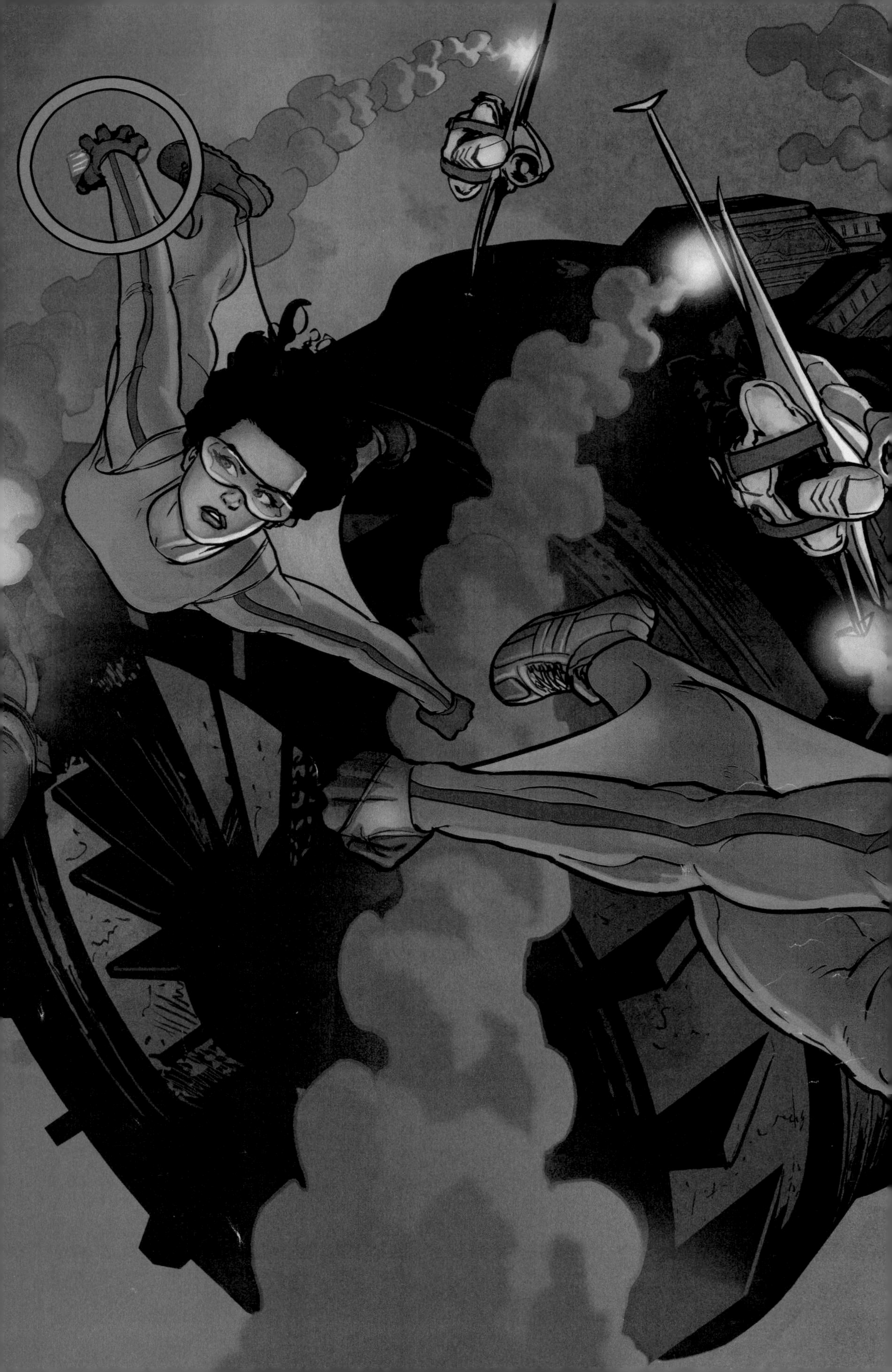

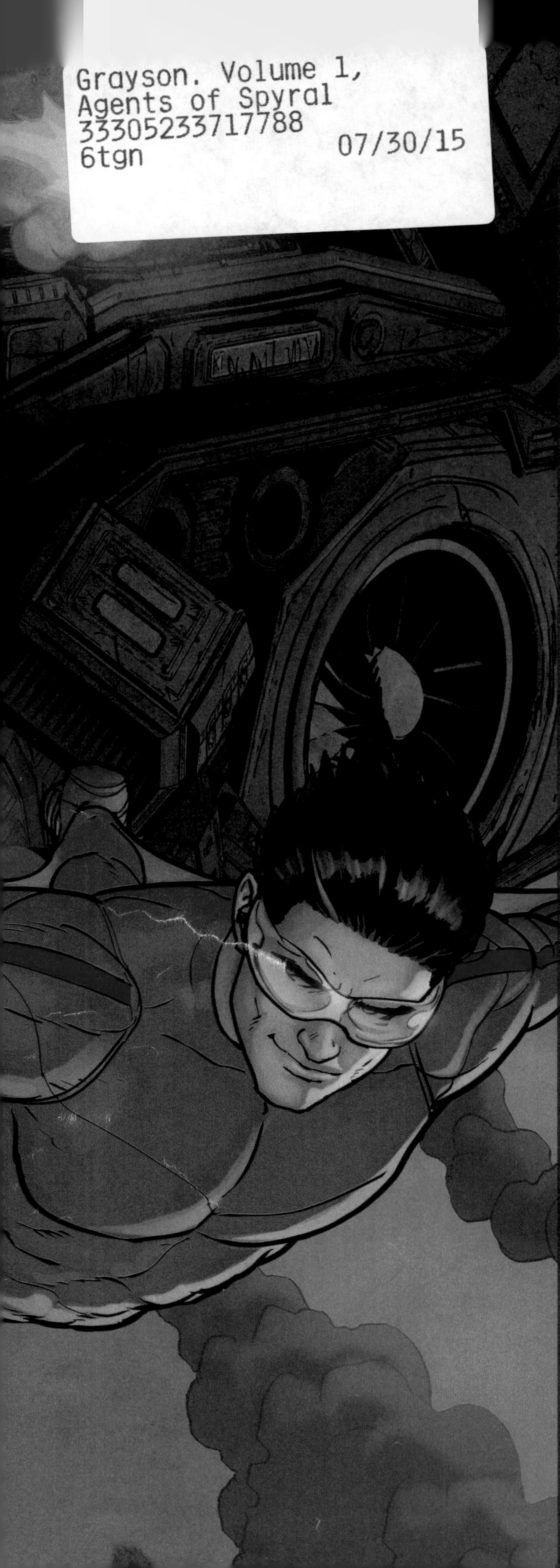

GRAYSON

VOLUME 1
AGENTS OF
SPYRAL

WRITTEN BY
TIM SEELEY
TOM KING

ART BY
MIKEL JANÍN
STEPHEN MOONEY
GUILLERMO ORTEGO
JUAN CASTRO

INKS BY
JONATHAN GLAPION

COLOR BY
JEROMY COX

LETTERS BY
CARLOS M. MANGUAL

COLLECTION COVER ARTIST
ANDREW ROBINSON

BATMAN CREATED BY
BOB KANE

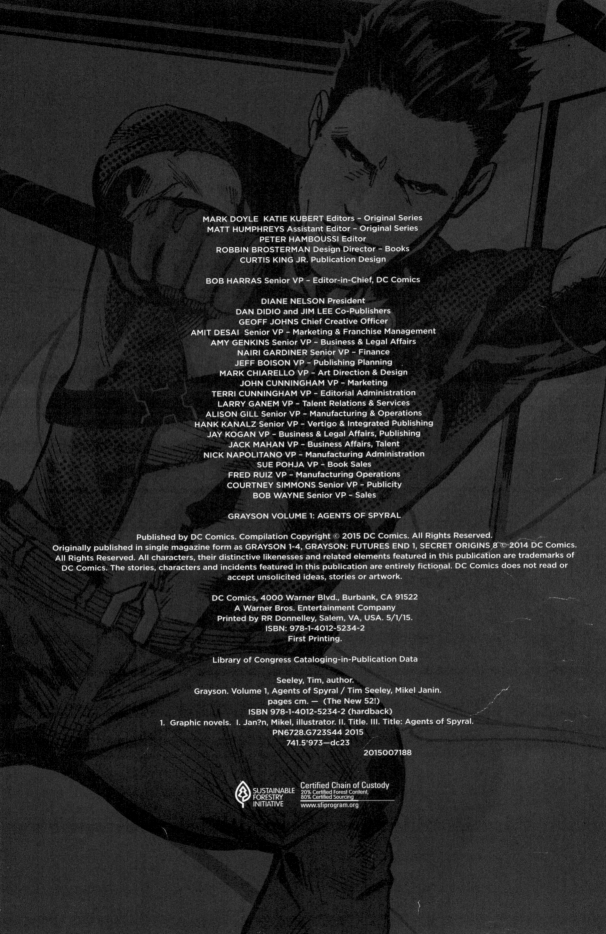

MARK DOYLE KATIE KUBERT Editors – Original Series
MATT HUMPHREYS Assistant Editor – Original Series
PETER HAMBOUSSI Editor
ROBBIN BROSTERMAN Design Director – Books
CURTIS KING JR. Publication Design

BOB HARRAS Senior VP – Editor-in-Chief, DC Comics

DIANE NELSON President
DAN DIDIO and JIM LEE Co-Publishers
GEOFF JOHNS Chief Creative Officer
AMIT DESAI Senior VP – Marketing & Franchise Management
AMY GENKINS Senior VP – Business & Legal Affairs
NAIRI GARDINER Senior VP – Finance
JEFF BOISON VP – Publishing Planning
MARK CHIARELLO VP – Art Direction & Design
JOHN CUNNINGHAM VP – Marketing
TERRI CUNNINGHAM VP – Editorial Administration
LARRY GANEM VP – Talent Relations & Services
ALISON GILL Senior VP – Manufacturing & Operations
HANK KANALZ Senior VP – Vertigo & Integrated Publishing
JAY KOGAN VP – Business & Legal Affairs, Publishing
JACK MAHAN VP – Business Affairs, Talent
NICK NAPOLITANO VP – Manufacturing Administration
SUE POHJA VP – Book Sales
FRED RUIZ VP – Manufacturing Operations
COURTNEY SIMMONS Senior VP – Publicity
BOB WAYNE Senior VP – Sales

GRAYSON VOLUME 1: AGENTS OF SPYRAL

DC Comics, 4000 Warner Blvd., Burbank, CA 91522
A Warner Bros. Entertainment Company
Printed by RR Donnelley, Salem, VA, USA. 5/1/15.
ISBN: 978-1-4012-5234-2
First Printing.

Library of Congress Cataloging-in-Publication Data

Seeley, Tim, author.
Grayson. Volume 1, Agents of Spyral / Tim Seeley, Mikel Janin.
pages cm. — (The New 52!)
ISBN 978-1-4012-5234-2 (hardback)
1. Graphic novels. I. Jan?n, Mikel, illustrator. II. Title. III. Title: Agents of Spyral.
PN6728.G723S44 2015
741.5'973—dc23
                                   2015007188

SUSTAINABLE
FORESTRY
INITIATIVE

Certified Chain of Custody
20% Certified Forest Content,
80% Certified Sourcing
www.sfiprogram.org

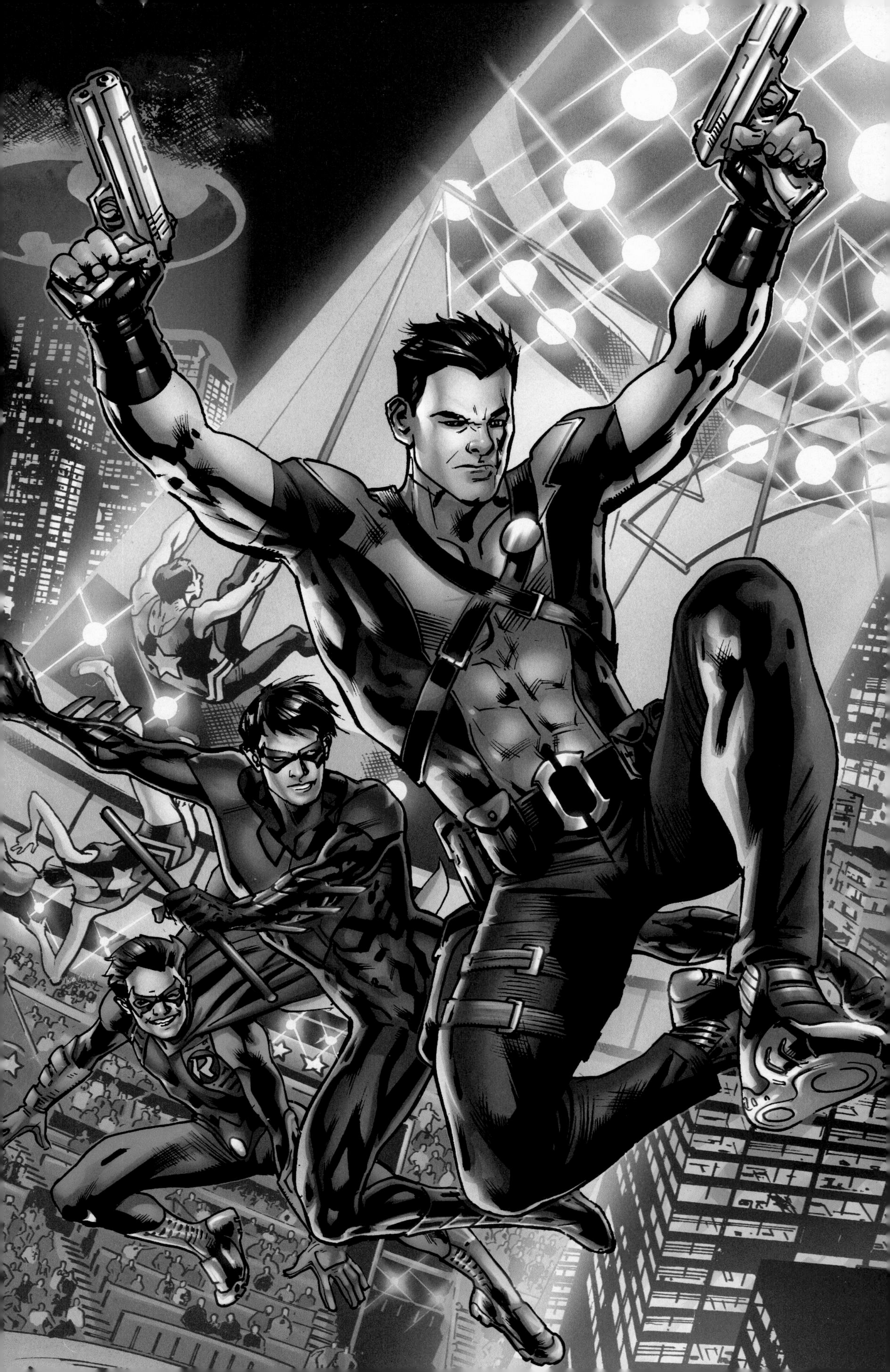

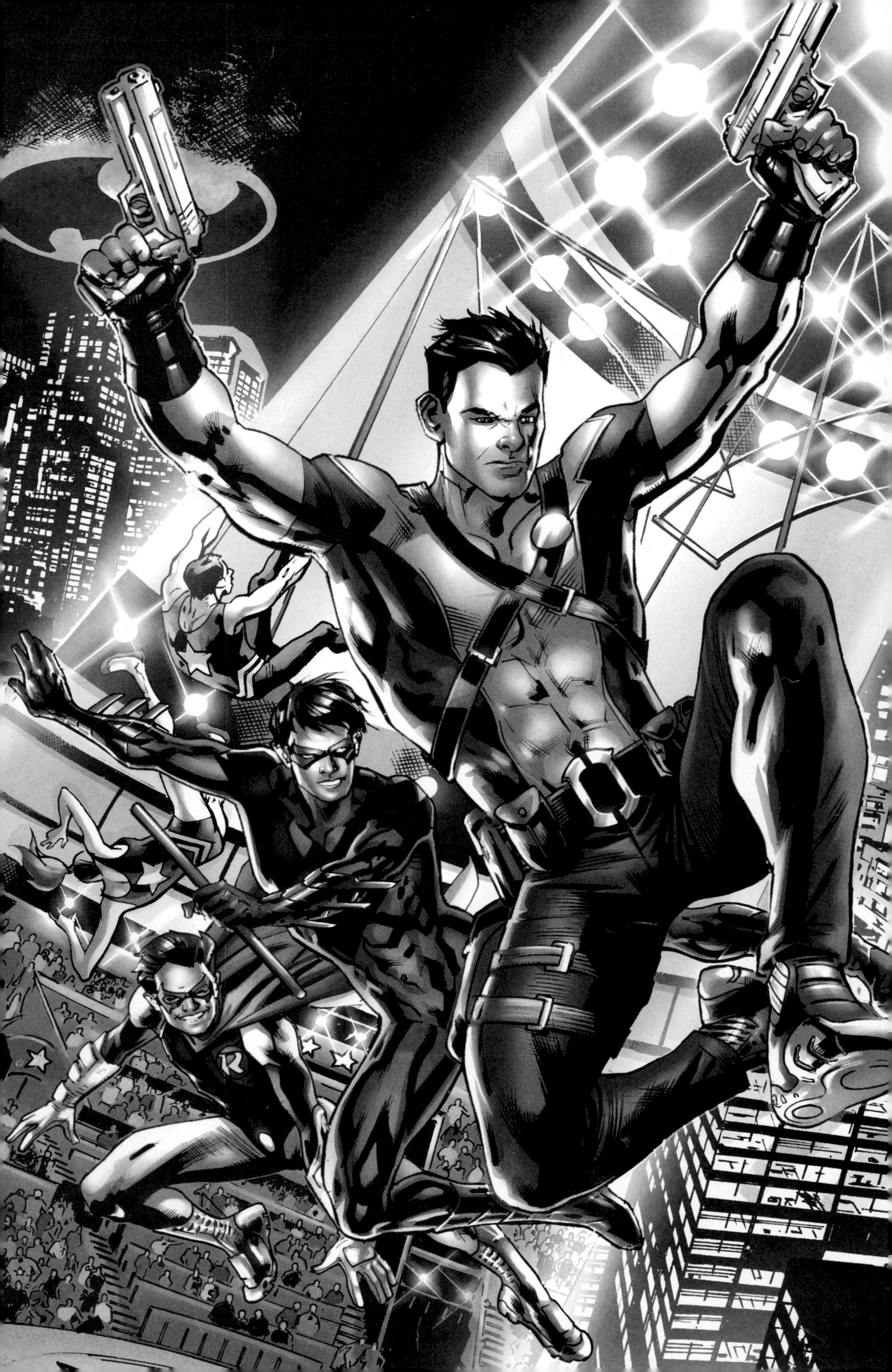

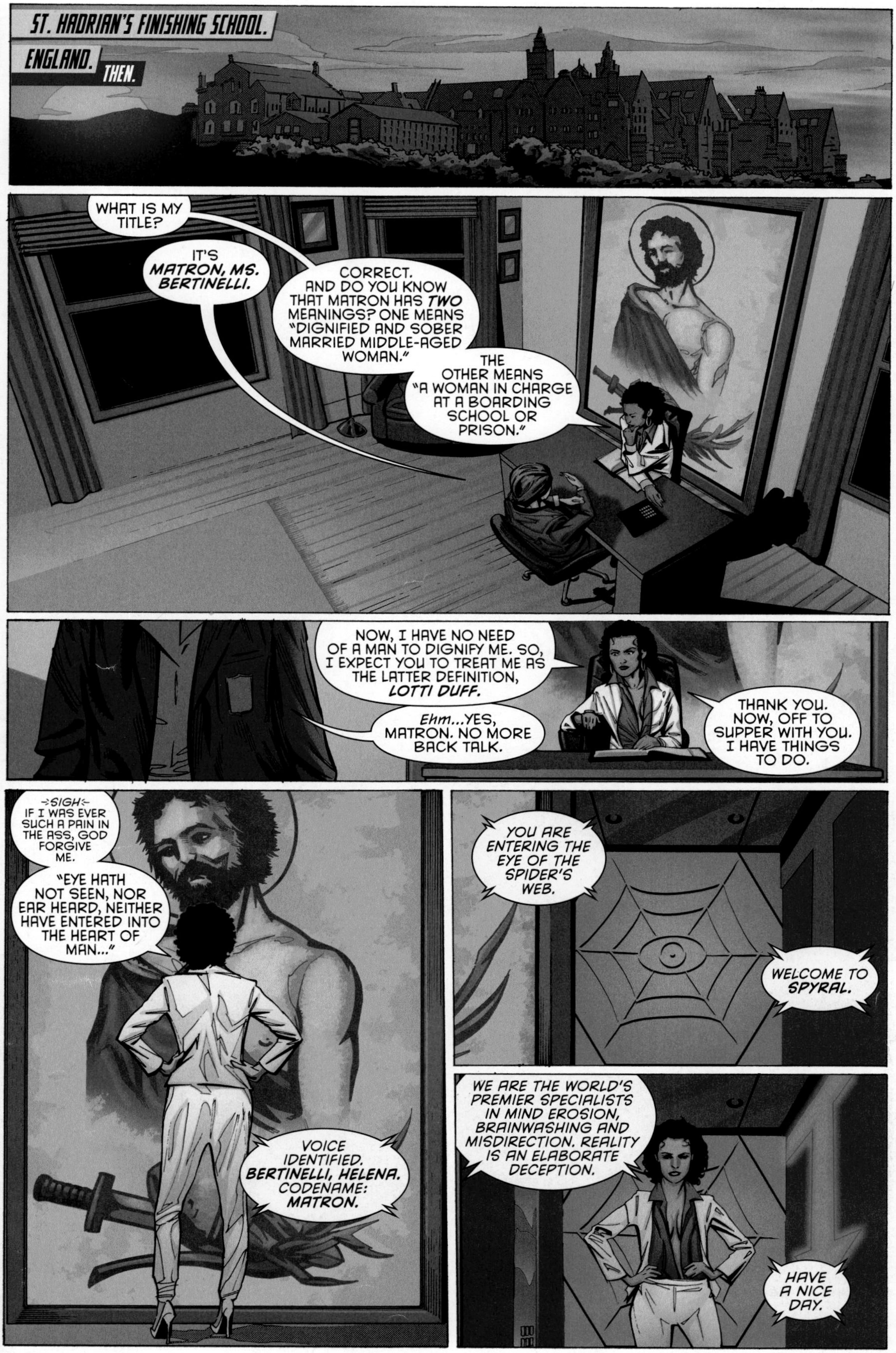
ST. HADRIAN'S FINISHING SCHOOL.
ENGLAND.
THEN.
WHAT IS MY TITLE?
IT'S MATRON, MS. BERTINELLI.
CORRECT. AND DO YOU KNOW THAT MATRON HAS TWO MEANINGS? ONE MEANS "DIGNIFIED AND SOBER MARRIED MIDDLE-AGED WOMAN."
THE OTHER MEANS "A WOMAN IN CHARGE AT A BOARDING SCHOOL OR PRISON."
NOW, I HAVE NO NEED OF A MAN TO DIGNIFY ME. SO, I EXPECT YOU TO TREAT ME AS THE LATTER DEFINITION, LOTTI DUFF.
Ehm...YES, MATRON. NO MORE BACK TALK.
THANK YOU. NOW, OFF TO SUPPER WITH YOU. I HAVE THINGS TO DO.
-SIGH- IF I WAS EVER SUCH A PAIN IN THE ASS, GOD FORGIVE ME.
"EYE HATH NOT SEEN, NOR EAR HEARD, NEITHER HAVE ENTERED INTO THE HEART OF MAN..."
VOICE IDENTIFIED. BERTINELLI, HELENA. CODENAME: MATRON.
YOU ARE ENTERING THE EYE OF THE SPIDER'S WEB.
WELCOME TO SPYRAL.
WE ARE THE WORLD'S PREMIER SPECIALISTS IN MIND EROSION, BRAINWASHING AND MISDIRECTION. REALITY IS AN ELABORATE DECEPTION.
HAVE A NICE DAY.

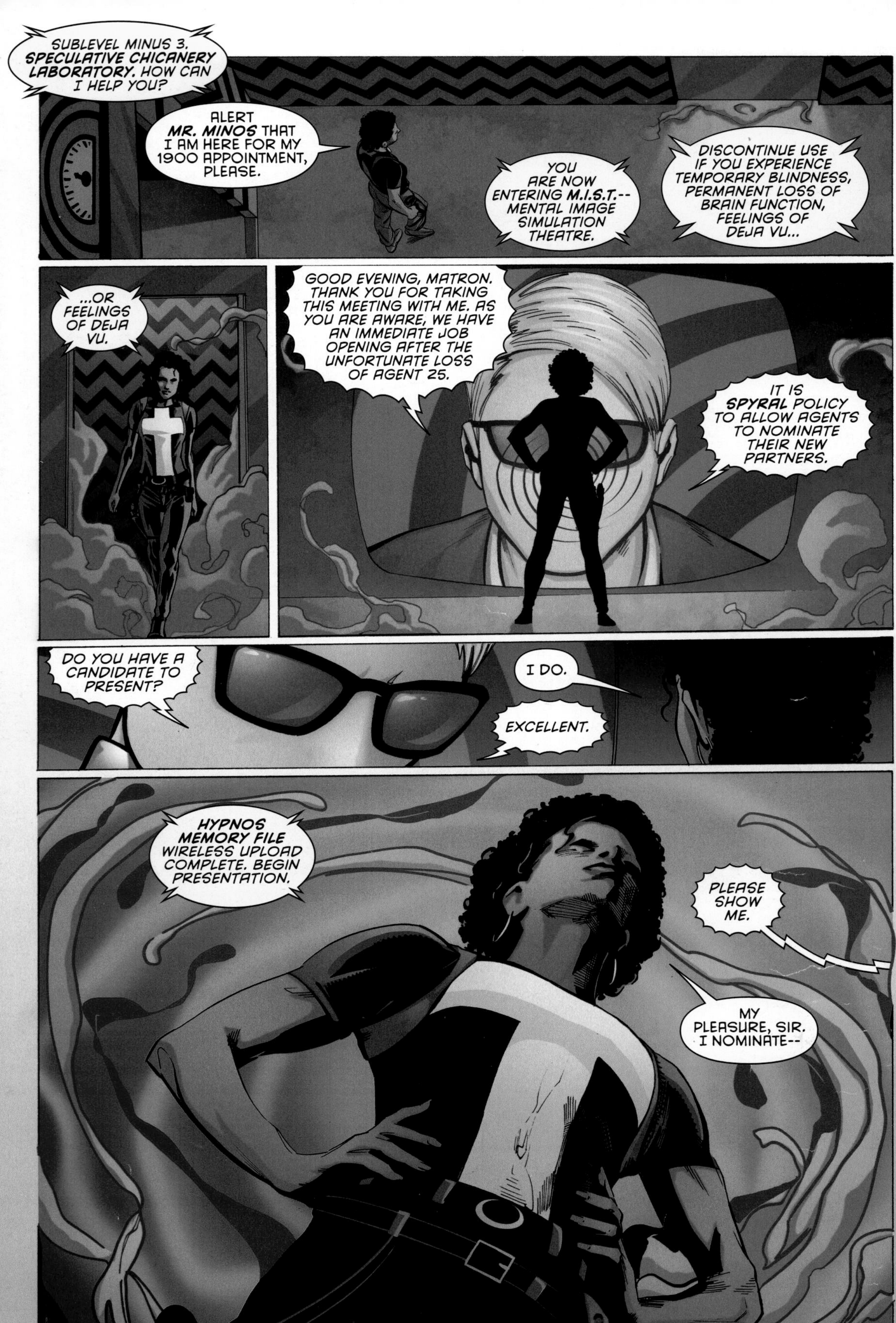
SUBLEVEL MINUS 3. **SPECULATIVE CHICANERY LABORATORY.** HOW CAN I HELP YOU?
ALERT **MR. MINOS** THAT I AM HERE FOR MY 1900 APPOINTMENT, PLEASE.
YOU ARE NOW ENTERING **M.I.S.T.**--MENTAL IMAGE SIMULATION THEATRE.
DISCONTINUE USE IF YOU EXPERIENCE TEMPORARY BLINDNESS, PERMANENT LOSS OF BRAIN FUNCTION, FEELINGS OF DEJA VU...
...OR FEELINGS OF DEJA VU.
GOOD EVENING, MATRON. THANK YOU FOR TAKING THIS MEETING WITH ME. AS YOU ARE AWARE, WE HAVE AN IMMEDIATE JOB OPENING AFTER THE UNFORTUNATE LOSS OF AGENT 25.
IT IS **SPYRAL** POLICY TO ALLOW AGENTS TO NOMINATE THEIR NEW PARTNERS.
DO YOU HAVE A CANDIDATE TO PRESENT?
I DO.
EXCELLENT.
HYPNOS MEMORY FILE WIRELESS UPLOAD COMPLETE. BEGIN PRESENTATION.
PLEASE SHOW ME.
MY PLEASURE, SIR. I NOMINATE--

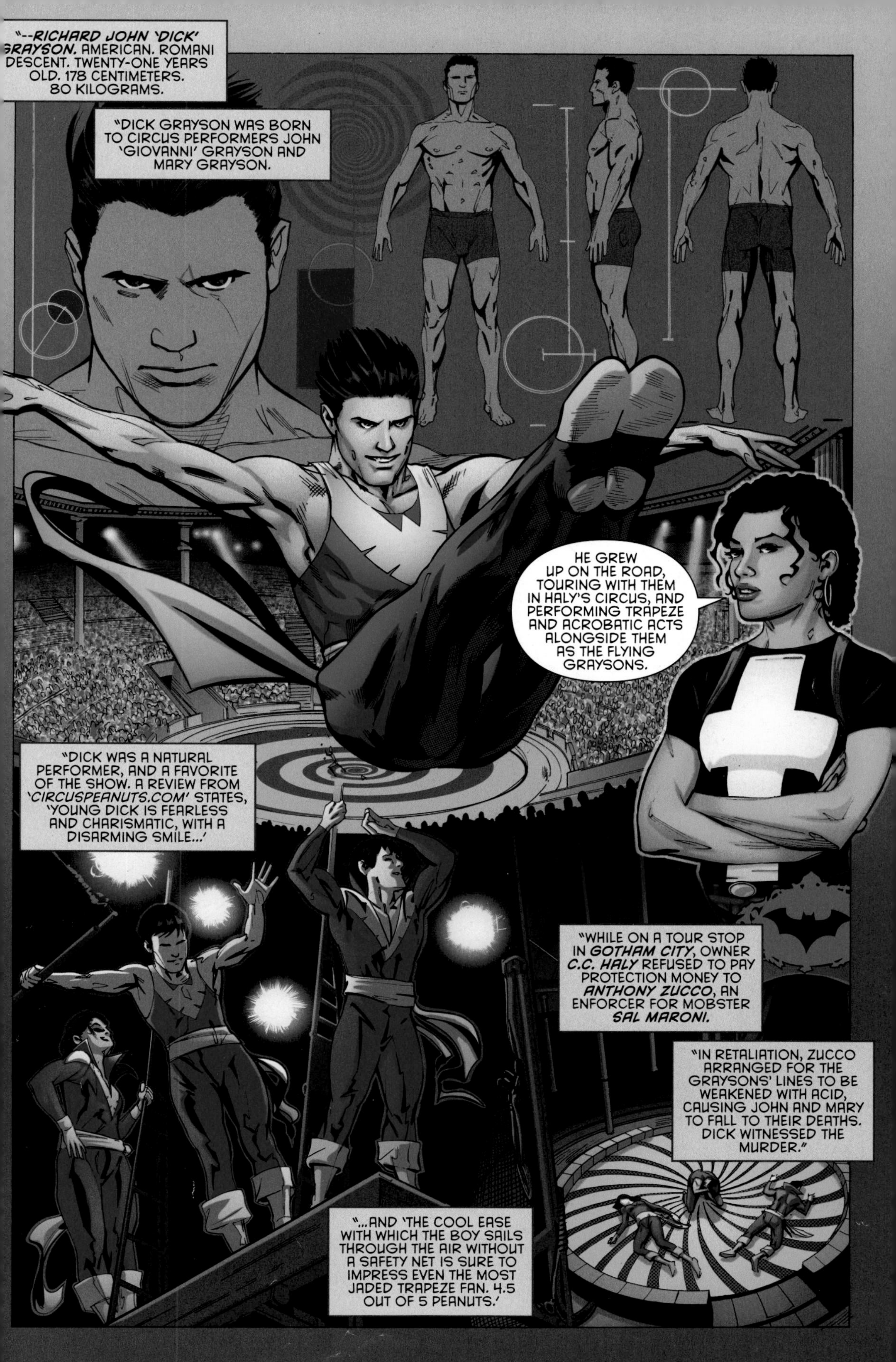
"--RICHARD JOHN 'DICK' GRAYSON. AMERICAN. ROMANI DESCENT. TWENTY-ONE YEARS OLD. 178 CENTIMETERS. 80 KILOGRAMS.
"DICK GRAYSON WAS BORN TO CIRCUS PERFORMERS JOHN 'GIOVANNI' GRAYSON AND MARY GRAYSON.
HE GREW UP ON THE ROAD, TOURING WITH THEM IN HALY'S CIRCUS, AND PERFORMING TRAPEZE AND ACROBATIC ACTS ALONGSIDE THEM AS THE FLYING GRAYSONS.
"DICK WAS A NATURAL PERFORMER, AND A FAVORITE OF THE SHOW. A REVIEW FROM 'CIRCUSPEANUTS.COM' STATES, 'YOUNG DICK IS FEARLESS AND CHARISMATIC, WITH A DISARMING SMILE...'
"...AND 'THE COOL EASE WITH WHICH THE BOY SAILS THROUGH THE AIR WITHOUT A SAFETY NET IS SURE TO IMPRESS EVEN THE MOST JADED TRAPEZE FAN. 4.5 OUT OF 5 PEANUTS.'
"WHILE ON A TOUR STOP IN GOTHAM CITY, OWNER C.C. HALY REFUSED TO PAY PROTECTION MONEY TO ANTHONY ZUCCO, AN ENFORCER FOR MOBSTER SAL MARONI.
"IN RETALIATION, ZUCCO ARRANGED FOR THE GRAYSONS' LINES TO BE WEAKENED WITH ACID, CAUSING JOHN AND MARY TO FALL TO THEIR DEATHS. DICK WITNESSED THE MURDER."

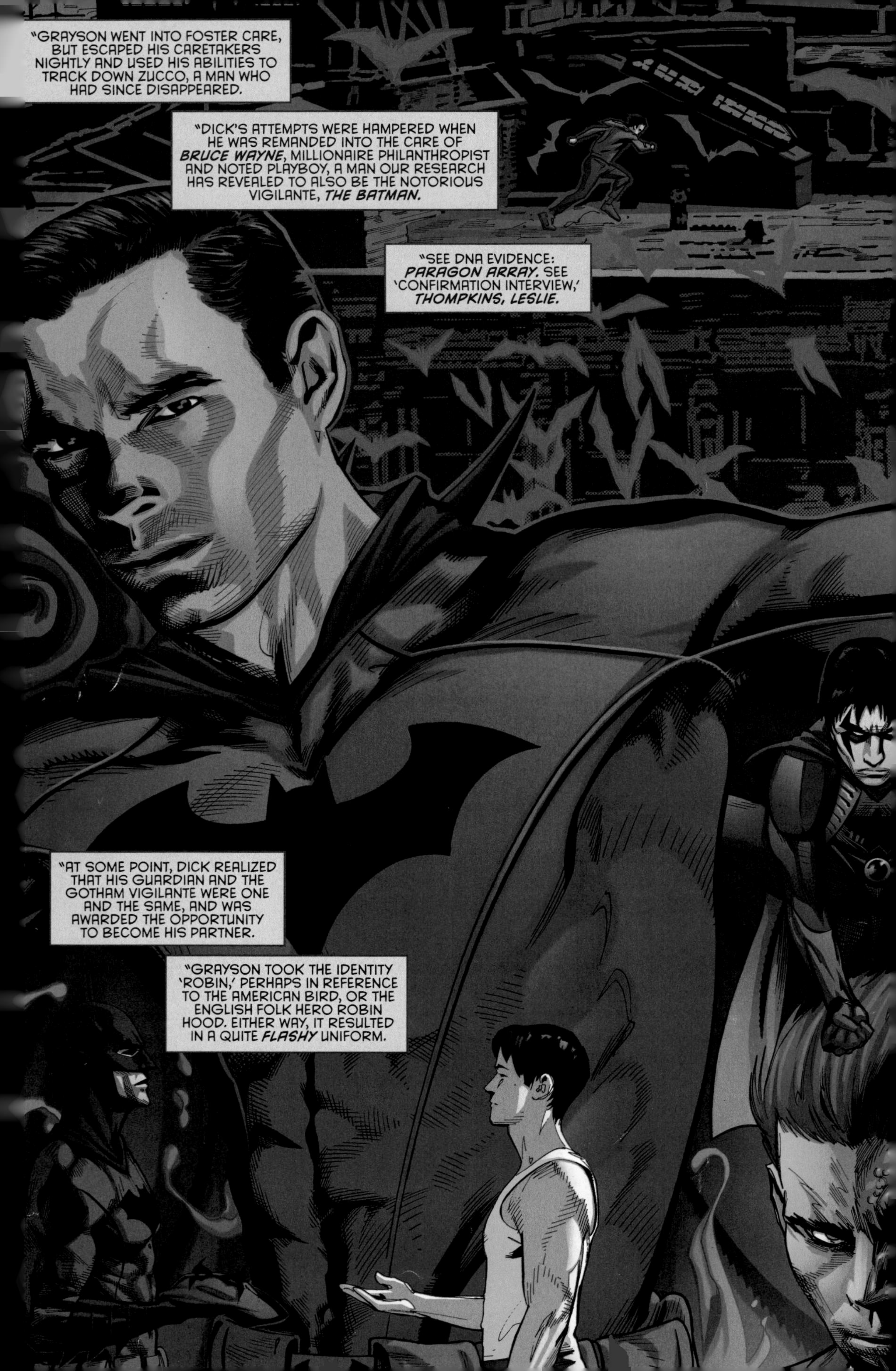
"GRAYSON WENT INTO FOSTER CARE, BUT ESCAPED HIS CARETAKERS NIGHTLY AND USED HIS ABILITIES TO TRACK DOWN ZUCCO, A MAN WHO HAD SINCE DISAPPEARED.
"DICK'S ATTEMPTS WERE HAMPERED WHEN HE WAS REMANDED INTO THE CARE OF *BRUCE WAYNE*, MILLIONAIRE PHILANTHROPIST AND NOTED PLAYBOY, A MAN OUR RESEARCH HAS REVEALED TO ALSO BE THE NOTORIOUS VIGILANTE, *THE BATMAN.*
"SEE DNA EVIDENCE: *PARAGON ARRAY.* SEE 'CONFIRMATION INTERVIEW,' *THOMPKINS, LESLIE.*
"AT SOME POINT, DICK REALIZED THAT HIS GUARDIAN AND THE GOTHAM VIGILANTE WERE ONE AND THE SAME, AND WAS AWARDED THE OPPORTUNITY TO BECOME HIS PARTNER.
"GRAYSON TOOK THE IDENTITY 'ROBIN,' PERHAPS IN REFERENCE TO THE AMERICAN BIRD, OR THE ENGLISH FOLK HERO ROBIN HOOD. EITHER WAY, IT RESULTED IN A QUITE *FLASHY* UNIFORM.

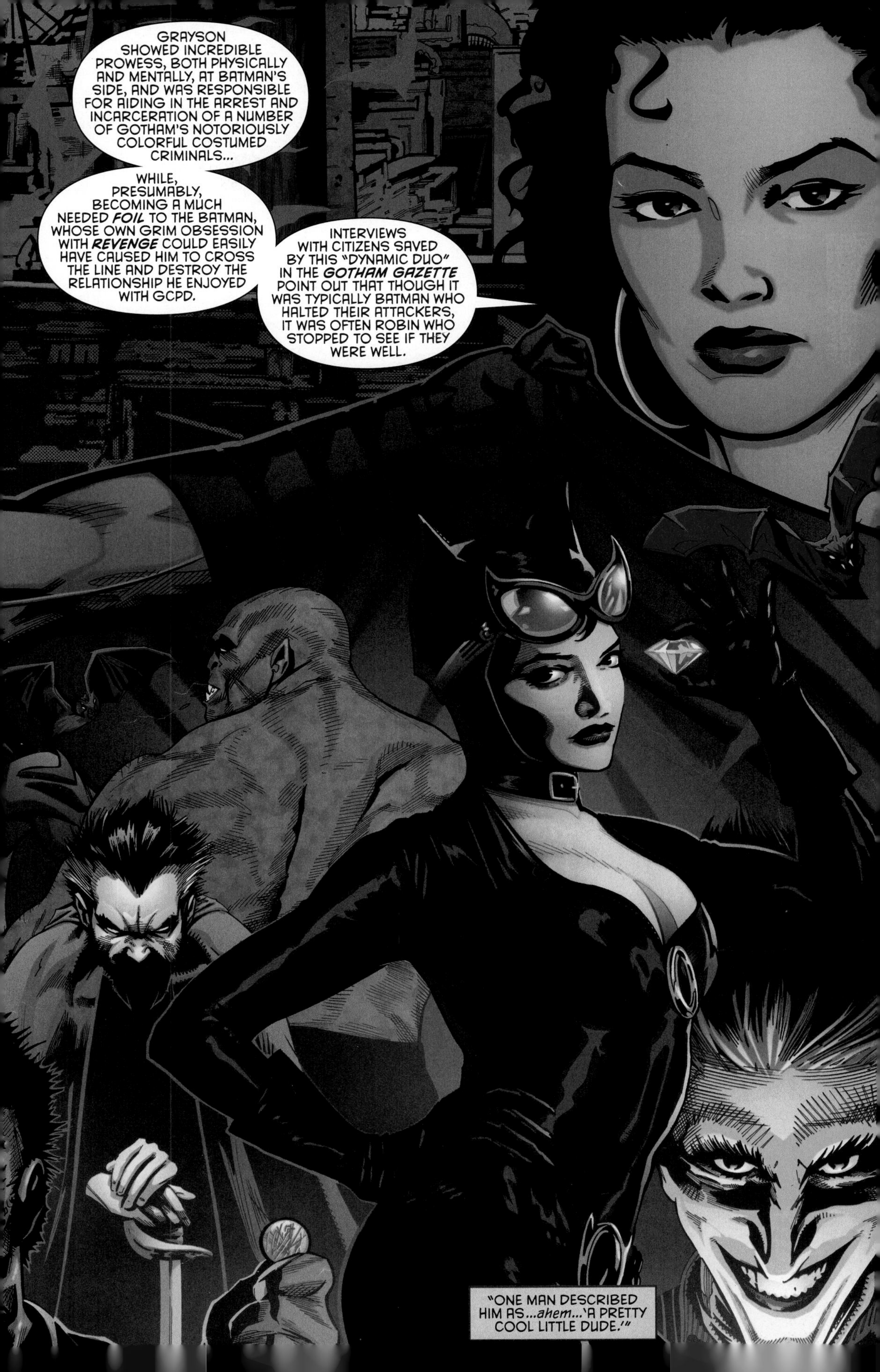
GRAYSON SHOWED INCREDIBLE PROWESS, BOTH PHYSICALLY AND MENTALLY, AT BATMAN'S SIDE, AND WAS RESPONSIBLE FOR AIDING IN THE ARREST AND INCARCERATION OF A NUMBER OF GOTHAM'S NOTORIOUSLY COLORFUL COSTUMED CRIMINALS...
WHILE, PRESUMABLY, BECOMING A MUCH NEEDED *FOIL* TO THE BATMAN, WHOSE OWN GRIM OBSESSION WITH *REVENGE* COULD EASILY HAVE CAUSED HIM TO CROSS THE LINE AND DESTROY THE RELATIONSHIP HE ENJOYED WITH GCPD.
INTERVIEWS WITH CITIZENS SAVED BY THIS "DYNAMIC DUO" IN THE *GOTHAM GAZETTE* POINT OUT THAT THOUGH IT WAS TYPICALLY BATMAN WHO HALTED THEIR ATTACKERS, IT WAS OFTEN ROBIN WHO STOPPED TO SEE IF THEY WERE WELL.
"ONE MAN DESCRIBED HIM AS...*ahem*...'A PRETTY COOL LITTLE DUDE.'"

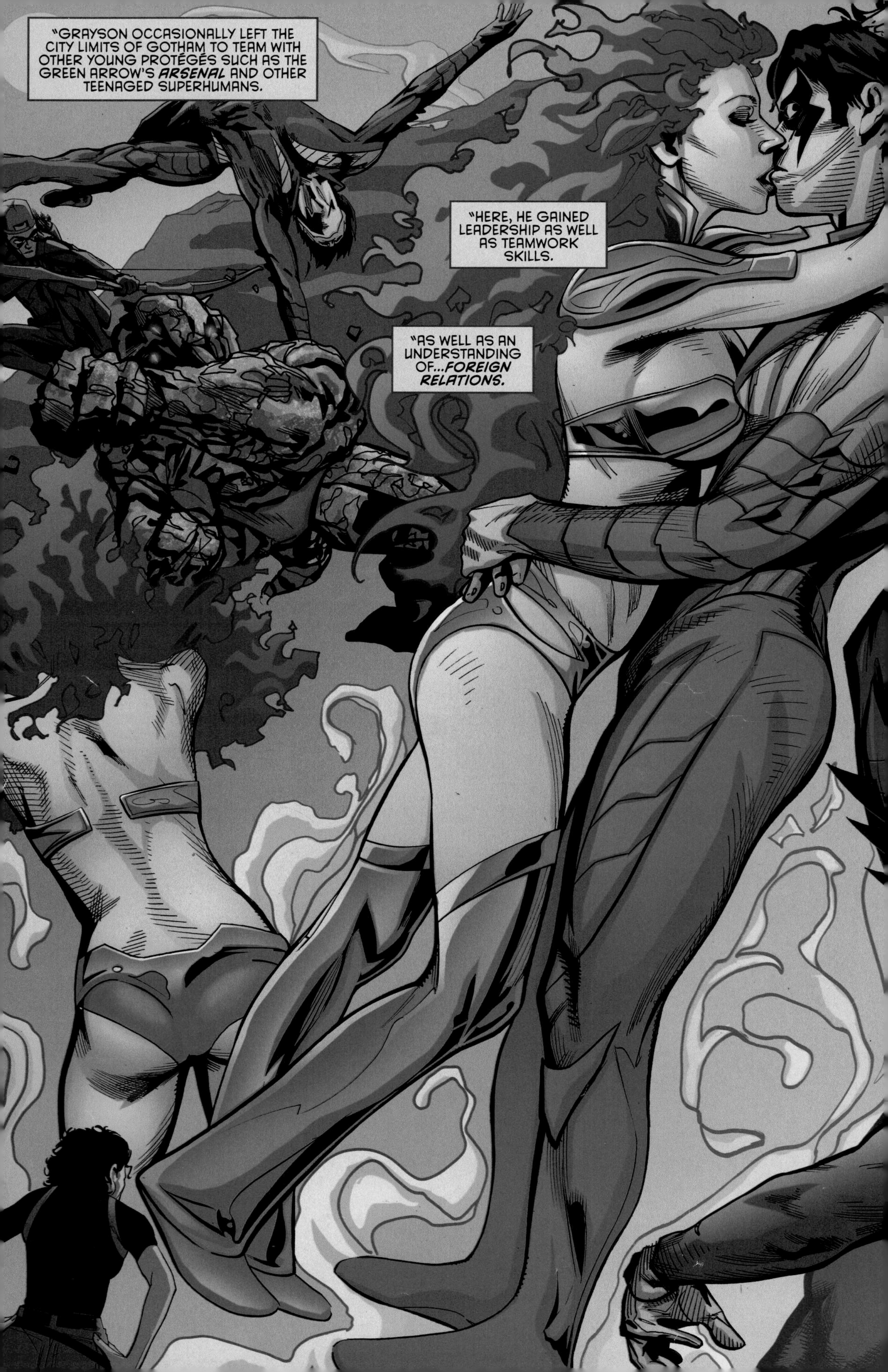
"GRAYSON OCCASIONALLY LEFT THE CITY LIMITS OF GOTHAM TO TEAM WITH OTHER YOUNG PROTÉGÉS SUCH AS THE GREEN ARROW'S *ARSENAL* AND OTHER TEENAGED SUPERHUMANS.
"HERE, HE GAINED LEADERSHIP AS WELL AS TEAMWORK SKILLS.
"AS WELL AS AN UNDERSTANDING OF...*FOREIGN RELATIONS.*

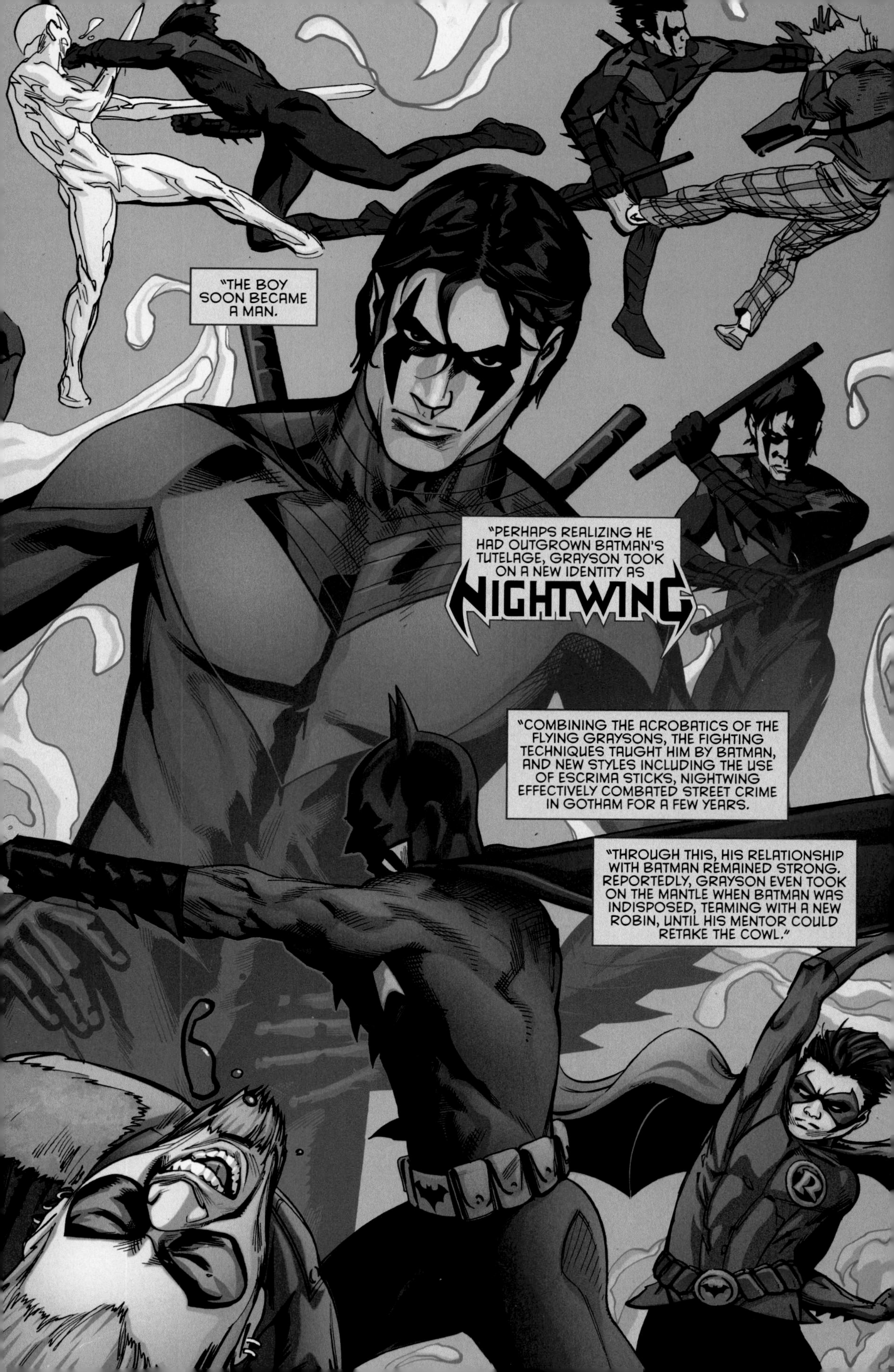
"THE BOY SOON BECAME A MAN.
"PERHAPS REALIZING HE HAD OUTGROWN BATMAN'S TUTELAGE, GRAYSON TOOK ON A NEW IDENTITY AS
NIGHTWING
"COMBINING THE ACROBATICS OF THE FLYING GRAYSONS, THE FIGHTING TECHNIQUES TAUGHT HIM BY BATMAN, AND NEW STYLES INCLUDING THE USE OF ESCRIMA STICKS, NIGHTWING EFFECTIVELY COMBATED STREET CRIME IN GOTHAM FOR A FEW YEARS.
"THROUGH THIS, HIS RELATIONSHIP WITH BATMAN REMAINED STRONG. REPORTEDLY, GRAYSON EVEN TOOK ON THE MANTLE WHEN BATMAN WAS INDISPOSED, TEAMING WITH A NEW ROBIN, UNTIL HIS MENTOR COULD RETAKE THE COWL."

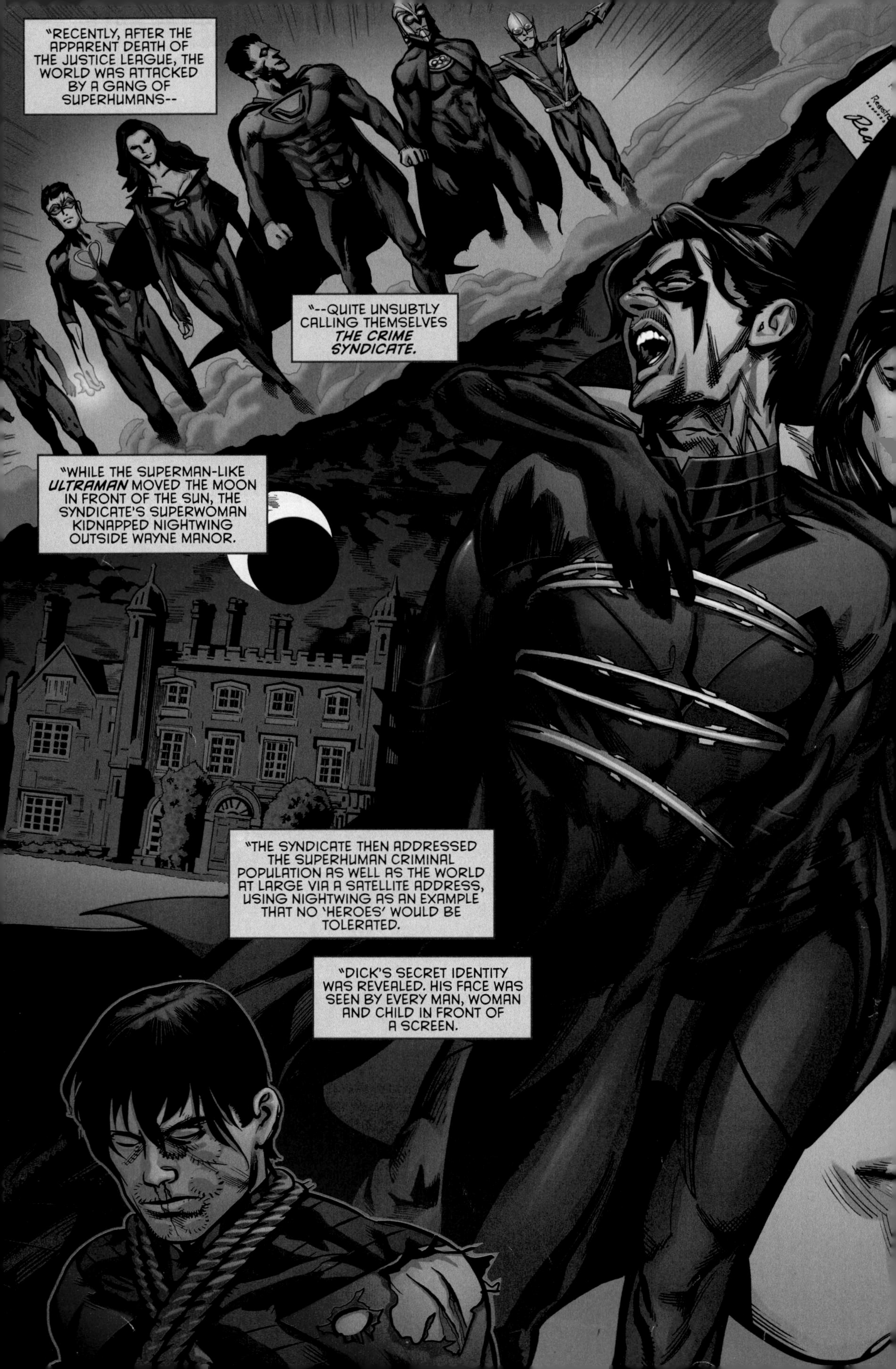
"RECENTLY, AFTER THE APPARENT DEATH OF THE JUSTICE LEAGUE, THE WORLD WAS ATTACKED BY A GANG OF SUPERHUMANS--
"--QUITE UNSUBTLY CALLING THEMSELVES THE CRIME SYNDICATE.
"WHILE THE SUPERMAN-LIKE ULTRAMAN MOVED THE MOON IN FRONT OF THE SUN, THE SYNDICATE'S SUPERWOMAN KIDNAPPED NIGHTWING OUTSIDE WAYNE MANOR.
"THE SYNDICATE THEN ADDRESSED THE SUPERHUMAN CRIMINAL POPULATION AS WELL AS THE WORLD AT LARGE VIA A SATELLITE ADDRESS, USING NIGHTWING AS AN EXAMPLE THAT NO 'HEROES' WOULD BE TOLERATED.
"DICK'S SECRET IDENTITY WAS REVEALED. HIS FACE WAS SEEN BY EVERY MAN, WOMAN AND CHILD IN FRONT OF A SCREEN.

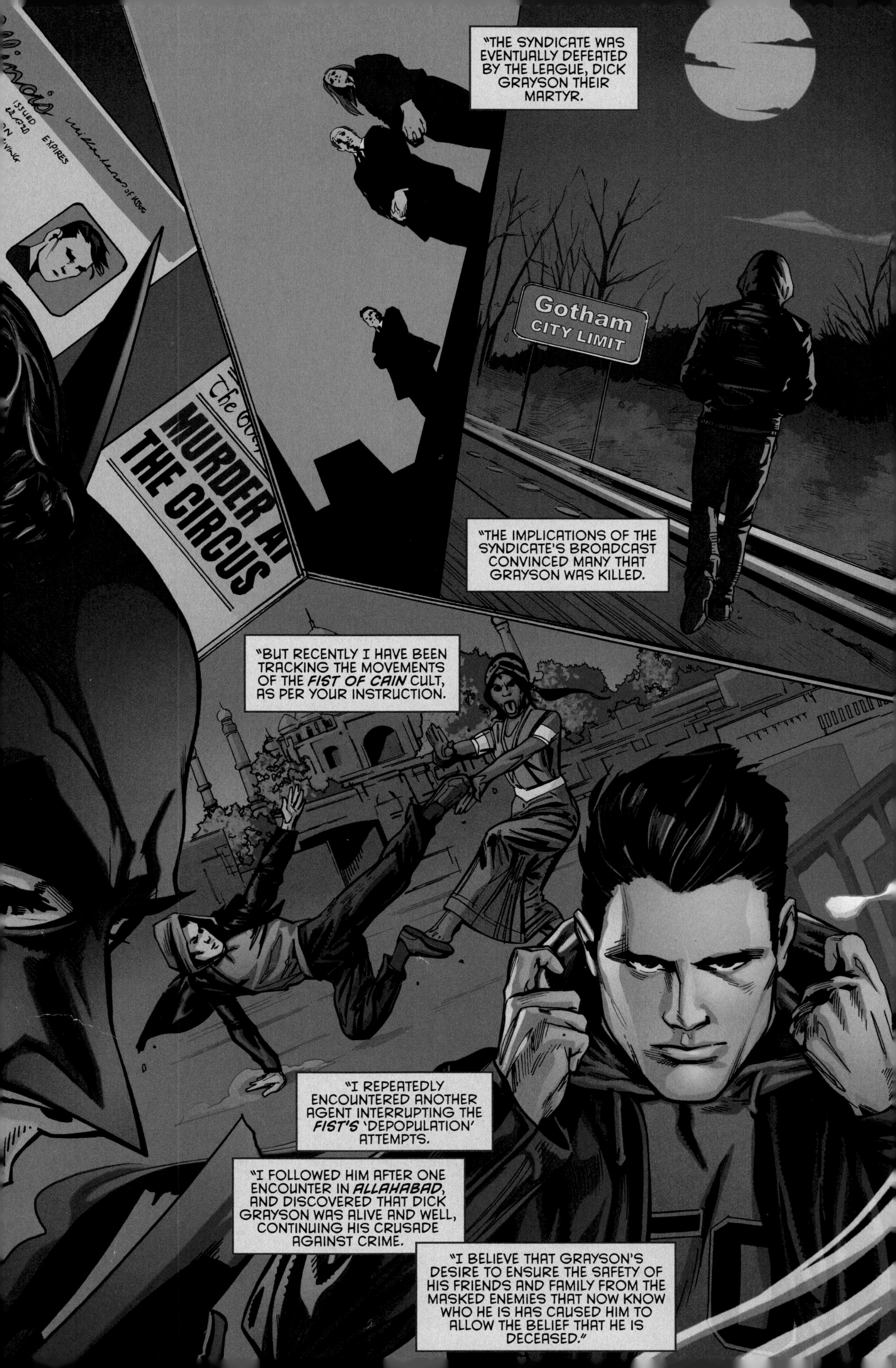
"THE SYNDICATE WAS EVENTUALLY DEFEATED BY THE LEAGUE, DICK GRAYSON THEIR MARTYR.
MURDER AT THE CIRCUS
Gotham CITY LIMIT
"THE IMPLICATIONS OF THE SYNDICATE'S BROADCAST CONVINCED MANY THAT GRAYSON WAS KILLED.
"BUT RECENTLY I HAVE BEEN TRACKING THE MOVEMENTS OF THE FIST OF CAIN CULT, AS PER YOUR INSTRUCTION.
"I REPEATEDLY ENCOUNTERED ANOTHER AGENT INTERRUPTING THE FIST'S 'DEPOPULATION' ATTEMPTS.
"I FOLLOWED HIM AFTER ONE ENCOUNTER IN ALLAHABAD, AND DISCOVERED THAT DICK GRAYSON WAS ALIVE AND WELL, CONTINUING HIS CRUSADE AGAINST CRIME.
"I BELIEVE THAT GRAYSON'S DESIRE TO ENSURE THE SAFETY OF HIS FRIENDS AND FAMILY FROM THE MASKED ENEMIES THAT NOW KNOW WHO HE IS HAS CAUSED HIM TO ALLOW THE BELIEF THAT HE IS DECEASED."

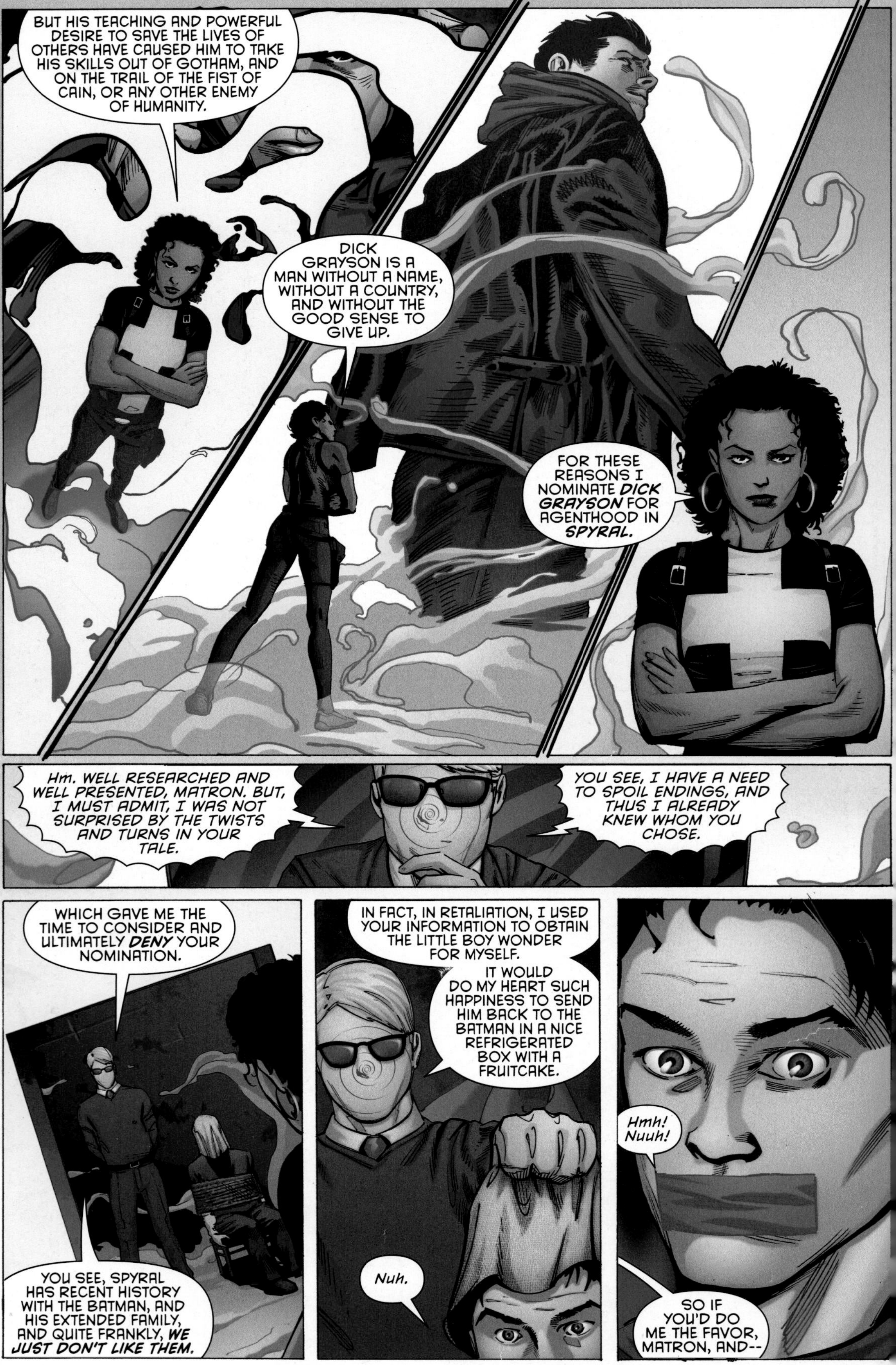

BUT HIS TEACHING AND POWERFUL DESIRE TO SAVE THE LIVES OF OTHERS HAVE CAUSED HIM TO TAKE HIS SKILLS OUT OF GOTHAM, AND ON THE TRAIL OF THE FIST OF CAIN, OR ANY OTHER ENEMY OF HUMANITY.
DICK GRAYSON IS A MAN WITHOUT A NAME, WITHOUT A COUNTRY, AND WITHOUT THE GOOD SENSE TO GIVE UP.
FOR THESE REASONS I NOMINATE *DICK GRAYSON* FOR AGENTHOOD IN *SPYRAL.*
Hm. WELL RESEARCHED AND WELL PRESENTED, MATRON. BUT, I MUST ADMIT, I WAS NOT SURPRISED BY THE TWISTS AND TURNS IN YOUR TALE.
YOU SEE, I HAVE A NEED TO SPOIL ENDINGS, AND THUS I ALREADY KNEW WHOM YOU CHOSE.
WHICH GAVE ME THE TIME TO CONSIDER AND ULTIMATELY *DENY* YOUR NOMINATION.
YOU SEE, SPYRAL HAS RECENT HISTORY WITH THE BATMAN, AND HIS EXTENDED FAMILY, AND QUITE FRANKLY, ***WE JUST DON'T LIKE THEM.***
IN FACT, IN RETALIATION, I USED YOUR INFORMATION TO OBTAIN THE LITTLE BOY WONDER FOR MYSELF.
IT WOULD DO MY HEART SUCH HAPPINESS TO SEND HIM BACK TO THE BATMAN IN A NICE REFRIGERATED BOX WITH A FRUITCAKE.
Nuh.
Hmh! Nuuh!
SO IF YOU'D DO ME THE FAVOR, MATRON, AND--

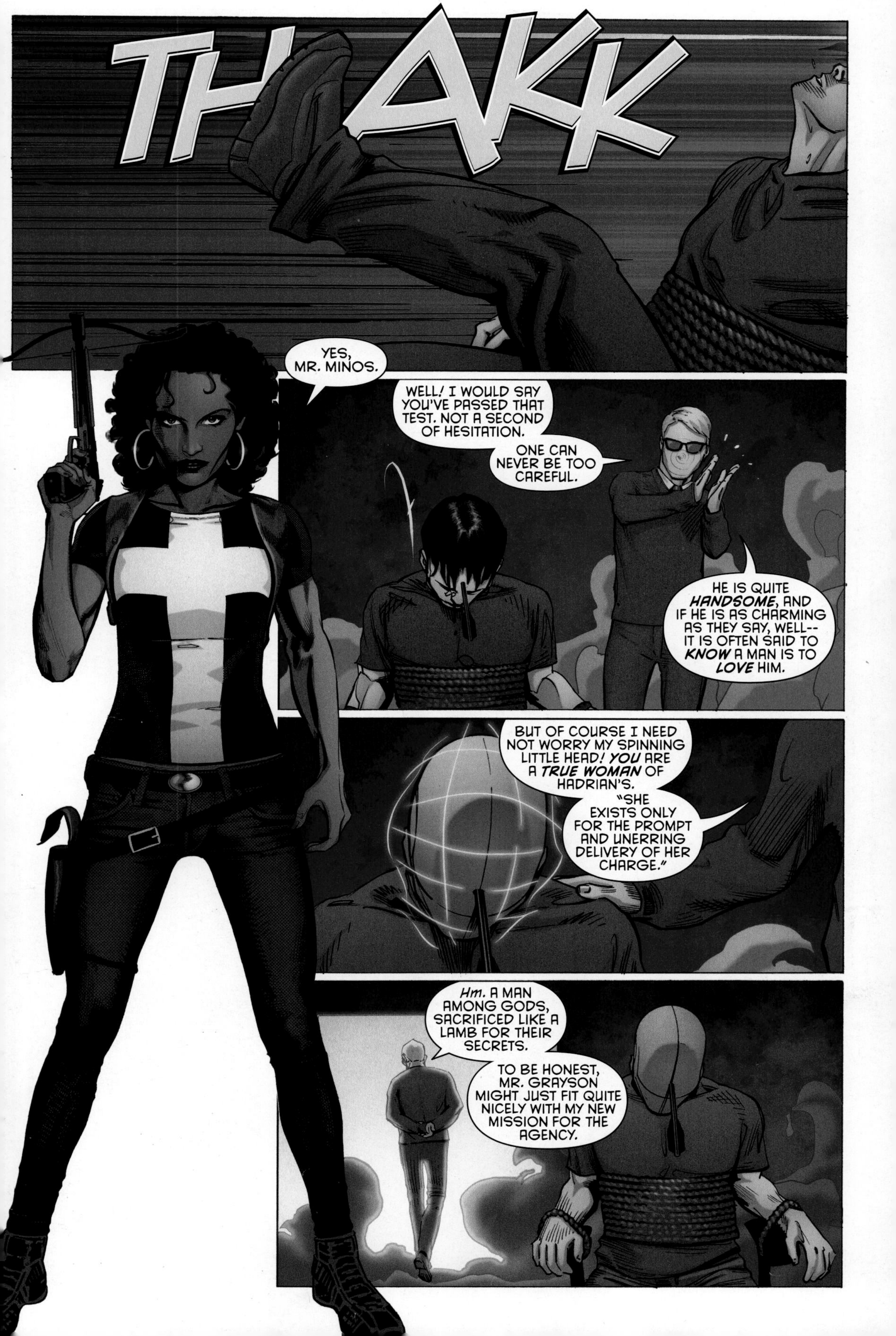
THAKK
YES, MR. MINOS.
WELL! I WOULD SAY YOU'VE PASSED THAT TEST. NOT A SECOND OF HESITATION.
ONE CAN NEVER BE TOO CAREFUL.
HE IS QUITE HANDSOME, AND IF HE IS AS CHARMING AS THEY SAY, WELL-- IT IS OFTEN SAID TO KNOW A MAN IS TO LOVE HIM.
BUT OF COURSE I NEED NOT WORRY MY SPINNING LITTLE HEAD! YOU ARE A TRUE WOMAN OF HADRIAN'S.
"SHE EXISTS ONLY FOR THE PROMPT AND UNERRING DELIVERY OF HER CHARGE."
Hm. A MAN AMONG GODS, SACRIFICED LIKE A LAMB FOR THEIR SECRETS.
TO BE HONEST, MR. GRAYSON MIGHT JUST FIT QUITE NICELY WITH MY NEW MISSION FOR THE AGENCY.

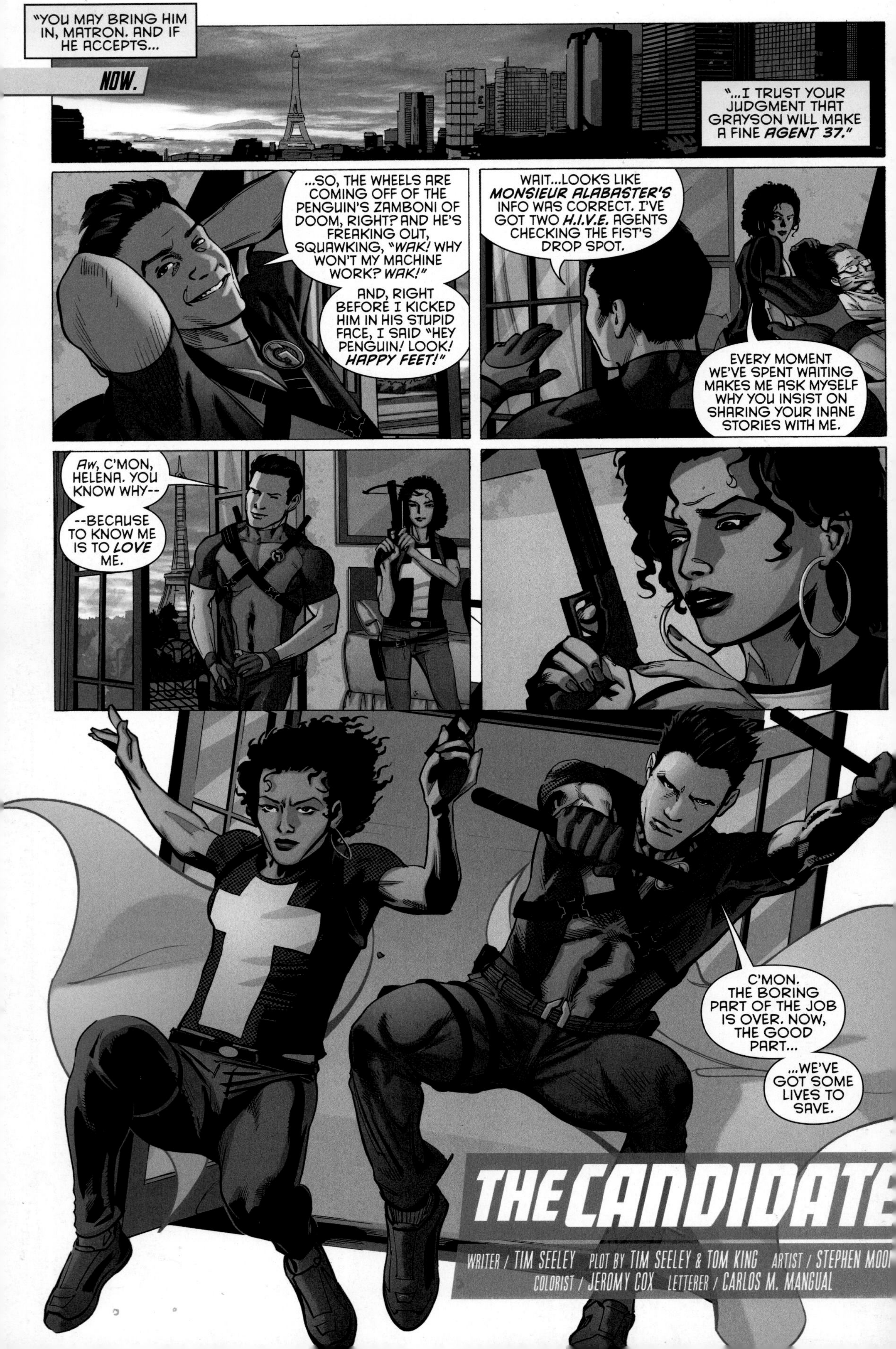
"YOU MAY BRING HIM IN, MATRON. AND IF HE ACCEPTS...
NOW.
"...I TRUST YOUR JUDGMENT THAT GRAYSON WILL MAKE A FINE AGENT 37."
...SO, THE WHEELS ARE COMING OFF OF THE PENGUIN'S ZAMBONI OF DOOM, RIGHT? AND HE'S FREAKING OUT, SQUAWKING, "WAK! WHY WON'T MY MACHINE WORK? WAK!"
AND, RIGHT BEFORE I KICKED HIM IN HIS STUPID FACE, I SAID "HEY PENGUIN! LOOK! HAPPY FEET!"
WAIT...LOOKS LIKE MONSIEUR ALABASTER'S INFO WAS CORRECT. I'VE GOT TWO H.I.V.E. AGENTS CHECKING THE FIST'S DROP SPOT.
EVERY MOMENT WE'VE SPENT WAITING MAKES ME ASK MYSELF WHY YOU INSIST ON SHARING YOUR INANE STORIES WITH ME.
AW, C'MON, HELENA. YOU KNOW WHY--
--BECAUSE TO KNOW ME IS TO LOVE ME.
C'MON. THE BORING PART OF THE JOB IS OVER. NOW, THE GOOD PART...
...WE'VE GOT SOME LIVES TO SAVE.
THE CANDIDATE
WRITER / TIM SEELEY PLOT BY TIM SEELEY & TOM KING ARTIST / STEPHEN MOO
COLORIST / JEROMY COX LETTERER / CARLOS M. MANGUAL

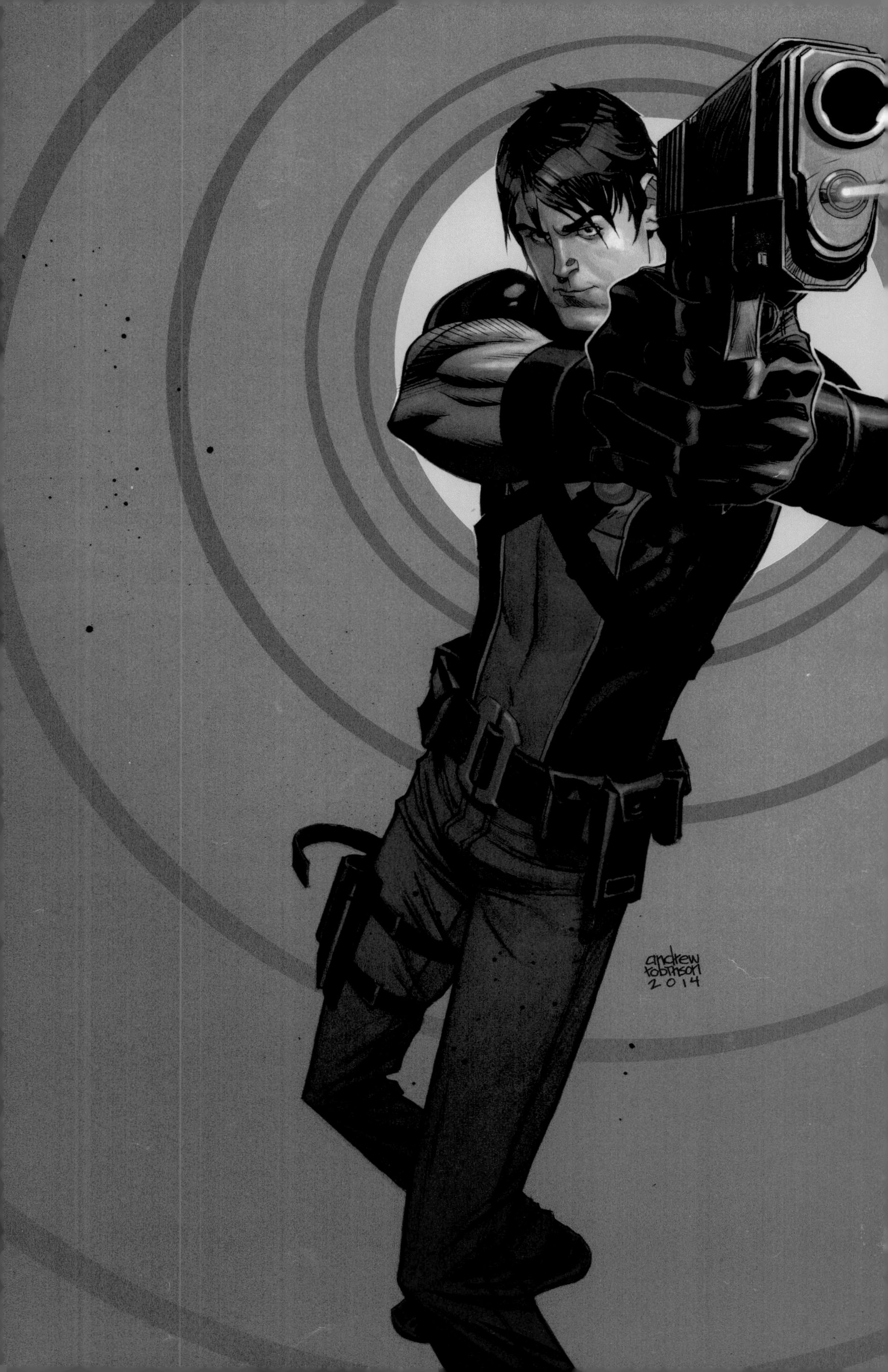
andrew robinson
2014

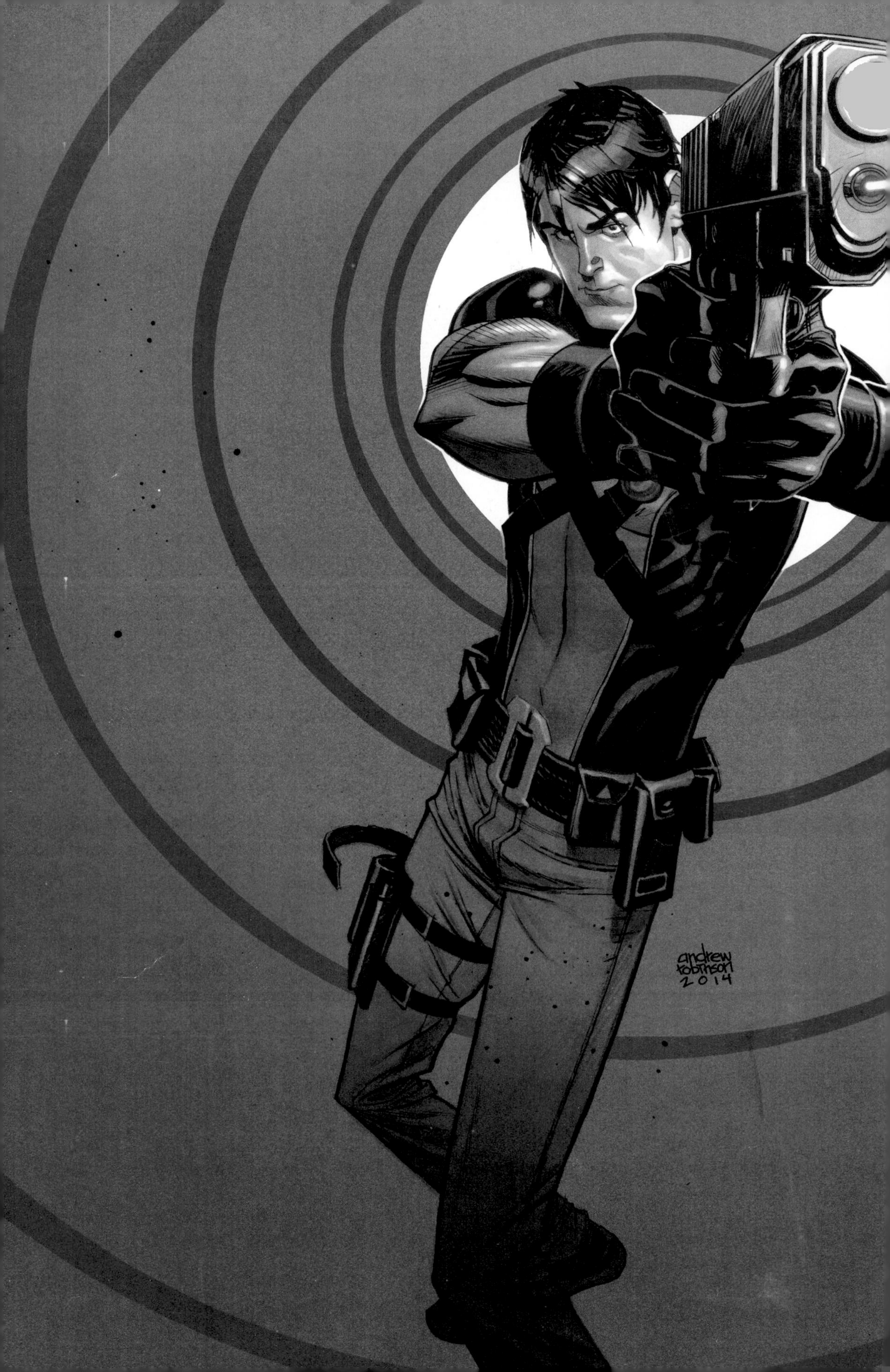
andrew robinson
2014

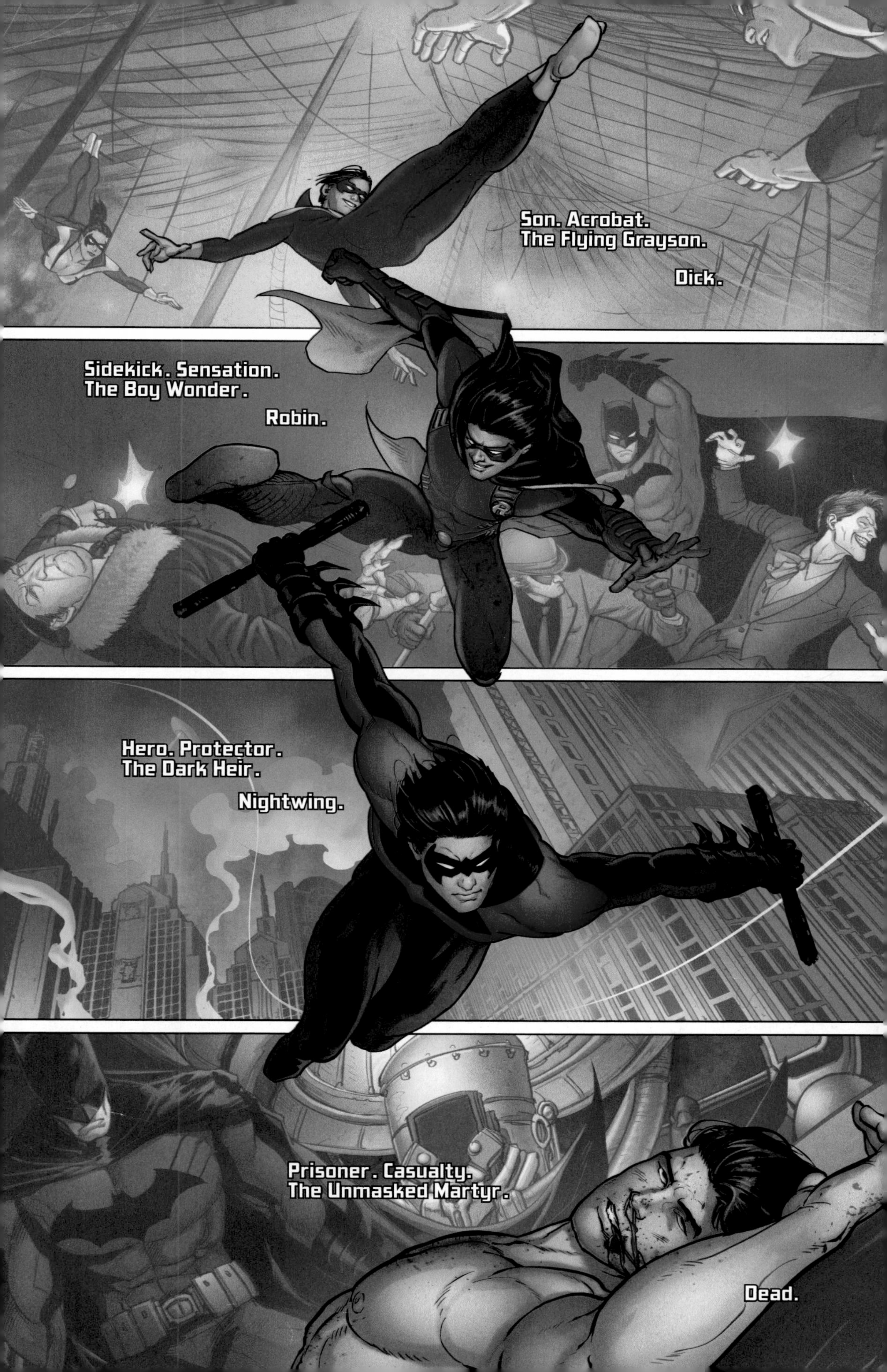

Son. Acrobat.
The Flying Grayson.
Dick.
Sidekick. Sensation.
The Boy Wonder.
Robin.
Hero. Protector.
The Dark Heir.
Nightwing.
Prisoner. Casualty.
The Unmasked Martyr.
Dead.

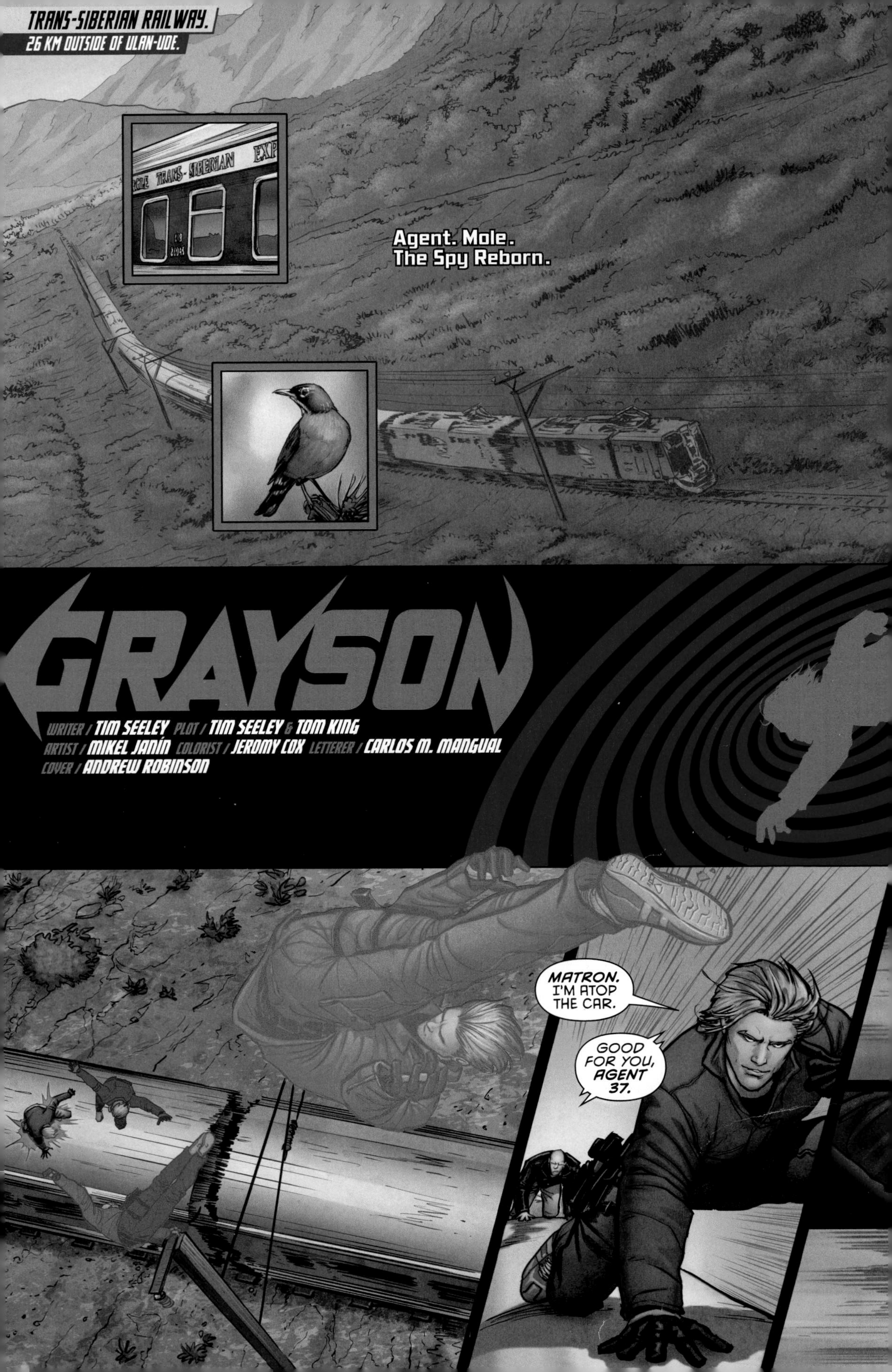
TRANS-SIBERIAN RAILWAY.
26 KM OUTSIDE OF ULAN-UDE.
TRANS-SIBERIAN EXP
Agent. Mole.
The Spy Reborn.
GRAYSON
WRITER / TIM SEELEY PLOT / TIM SEELEY & TOM KING
ARTIST / MIKEL JANÍN COLORIST / JEROMY COX LETTERER / CARLOS M. MANGUAL
COVER / ANDREW ROBINSON
MATRON. I'M ATOP THE CAR.
GOOD FOR YOU, AGENT 37.

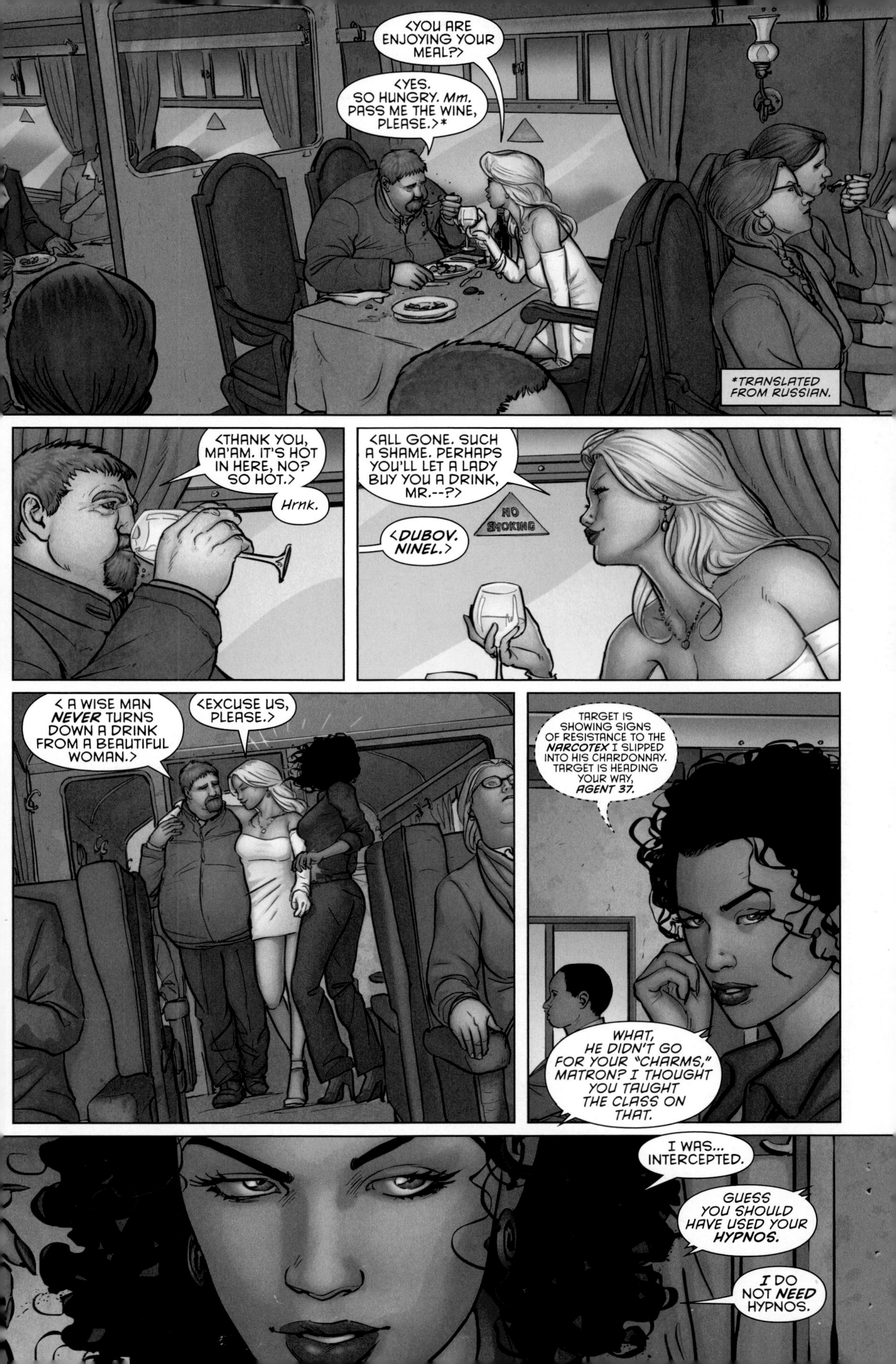

<YOU ARE ENJOYING YOUR MEAL?>
<YES. SO HUNGRY. *Mm.* PASS ME THE WINE, PLEASE.>*
*TRANSLATED FROM RUSSIAN.
<THANK YOU, MA'AM. IT'S HOT IN HERE, NO? SO HOT.>
Hrnk.
<ALL GONE. SUCH A SHAME. PERHAPS YOU'LL LET A LADY BUY YOU A DRINK, MR.--?>
NO SMOKING
<***DUBOV. NINEL.***>
< A WISE MAN ***NEVER*** TURNS DOWN A DRINK FROM A BEAUTIFUL WOMAN.>
<EXCUSE US, PLEASE.>
TARGET IS SHOWING SIGNS OF RESISTANCE TO THE ***NARCOTEX*** I SLIPPED INTO HIS CHARDONNAY. TARGET IS HEADING YOUR WAY, ***AGENT 37.***
WHAT, HE DIDN'T GO FOR YOUR "CHARMS," MATRON? I THOUGHT YOU TAUGHT THE CLASS ON THAT.
I WAS... INTERCEPTED.
GUESS YOU SHOULD HAVE USED YOUR ***HYPNOS.***
I DO NOT ***NEED*** HYPNOS.

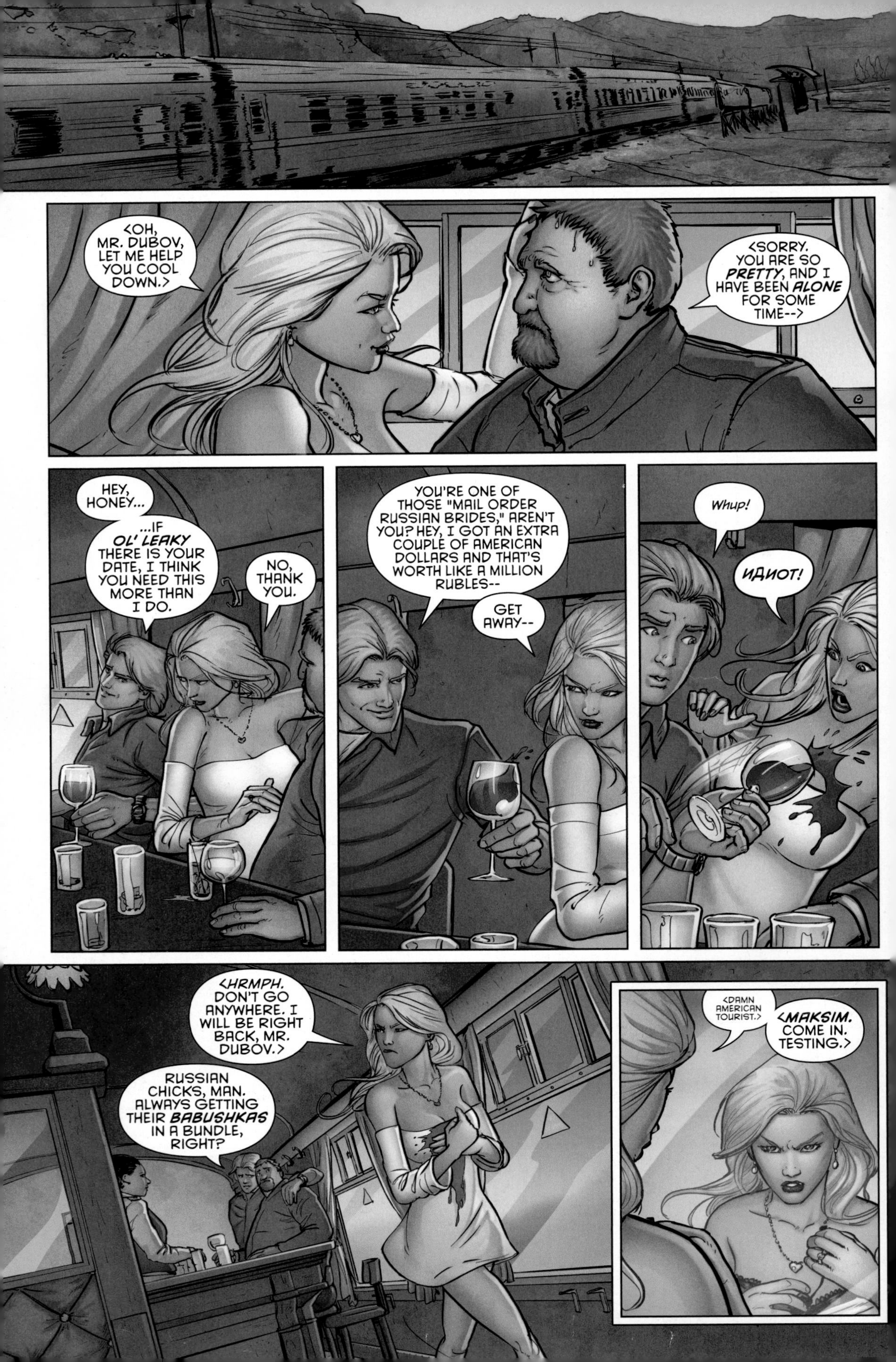
<OH, MR. DUBOV, LET ME HELP YOU COOL DOWN.>
<SORRY. YOU ARE SO PRETTY, AND I HAVE BEEN ALONE FOR SOME TIME-->
HEY, HONEY...
...IF OL' LEAKY THERE IS YOUR DATE, I THINK YOU NEED THIS MORE THAN I DO.
NO, THANK YOU.
YOU'RE ONE OF THOSE "MAIL ORDER RUSSIAN BRIDES," AREN'T YOU? HEY, I GOT AN EXTRA COUPLE OF AMERICAN DOLLARS AND THAT'S WORTH LIKE A MILLION RUBLES--
GET AWAY--
Whup!
ИДИОТ!
<HRMPH. DON'T GO ANYWHERE. I WILL BE RIGHT BACK, MR. DUBOV.>
RUSSIAN CHICKS, MAN. ALWAYS GETTING THEIR BABUSHKAS IN A BUNDLE, RIGHT?
<DAMN AMERICAN TOURIST.>
<MAKSIM. COME IN. TESTING.>

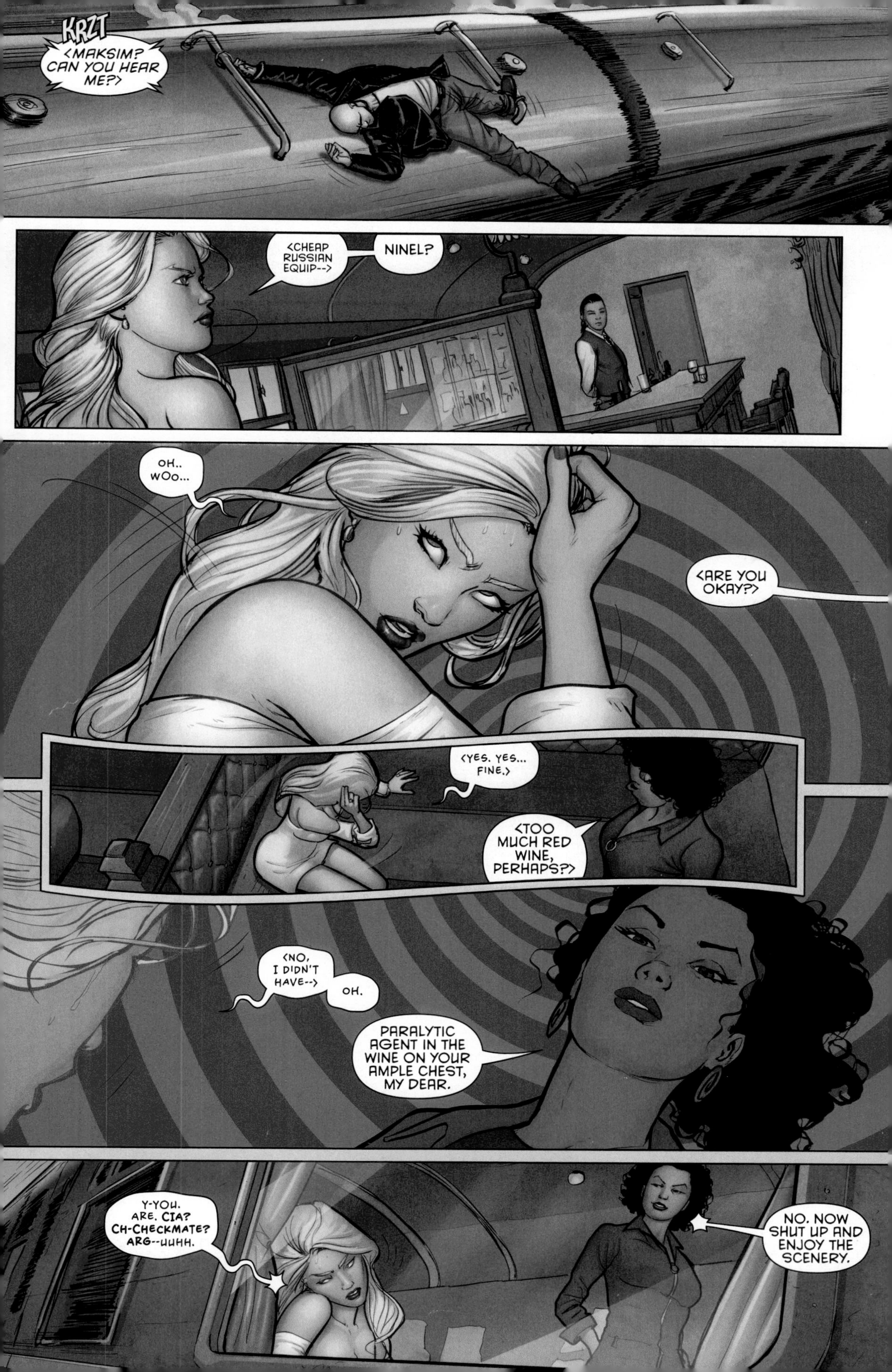
KRZT
<MAKSIM? CAN YOU HEAR ME?>
<CHEAP RUSSIAN EQUIP-->
NINEL?
OH.. WOo...
<ARE YOU OKAY?>
<YES. YES... FINE.>
<TOO MUCH RED WINE, PERHAPS?>
<NO, I DIDN'T HAVE-->
OH.
PARALYTIC AGENT IN THE WINE ON YOUR AMPLE CHEST, MY DEAR.
Y-YOU. ARE. CIA? CH-CHECKMATE? ARG--UUHH.
NO. NOW SHUT UP AND ENJOY THE SCENERY.

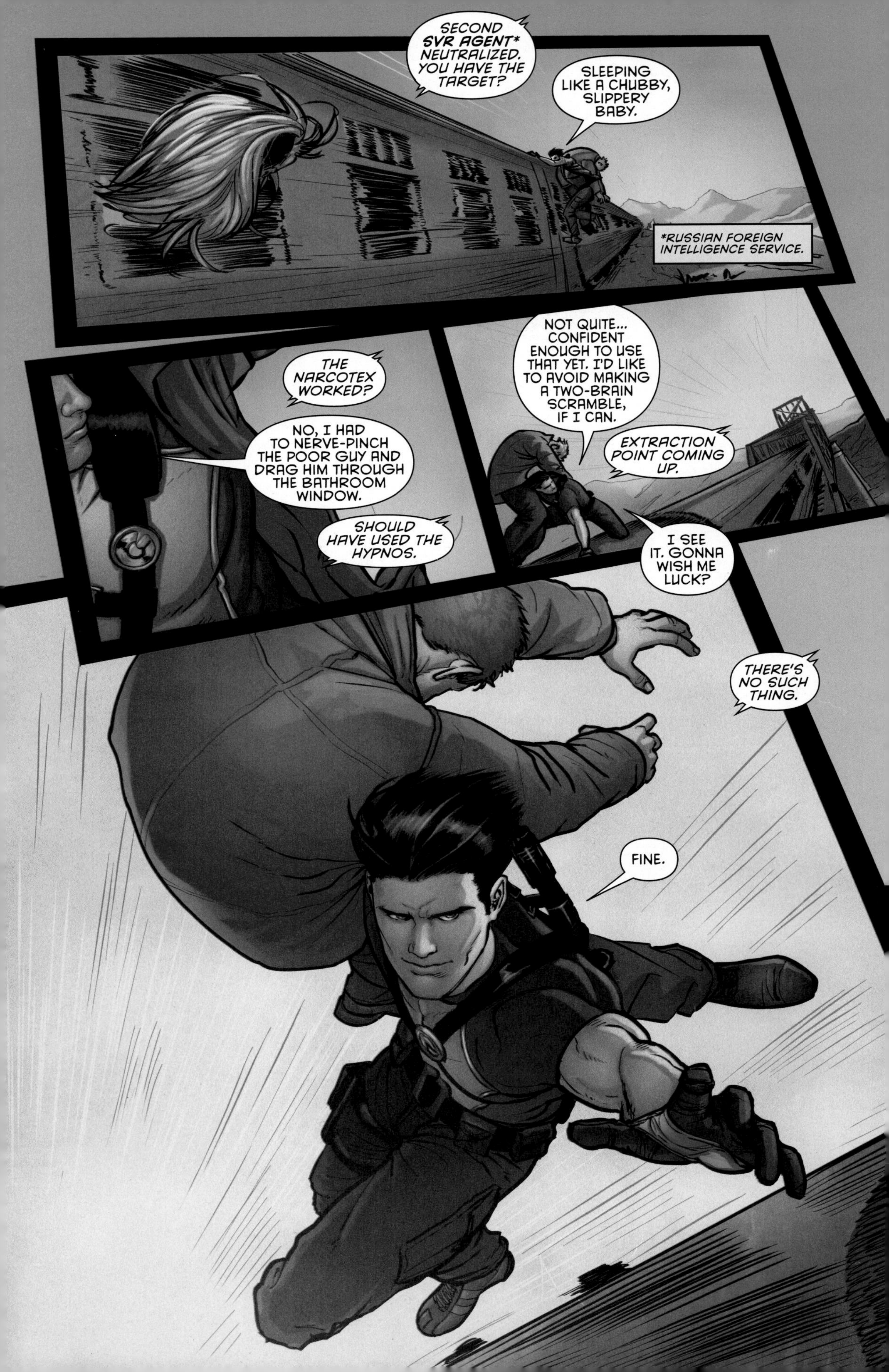
SECOND SVR AGENT* NEUTRALIZED. YOU HAVE THE TARGET?
SLEEPING LIKE A CHUBBY, SLIPPERY BABY.
*RUSSIAN FOREIGN INTELLIGENCE SERVICE.
THE NARCOTEX WORKED?
NO, I HAD TO NERVE-PINCH THE POOR GUY AND DRAG HIM THROUGH THE BATHROOM WINDOW.
SHOULD HAVE USED THE HYPNOS.
NOT QUITE... CONFIDENT ENOUGH TO USE THAT YET. I'D LIKE TO AVOID MAKING A TWO-BRAIN SCRAMBLE, IF I CAN.
EXTRACTION POINT COMING UP.
I SEE IT. GONNA WISH ME LUCK?
THERE'S NO SUCH THING.
FINE.

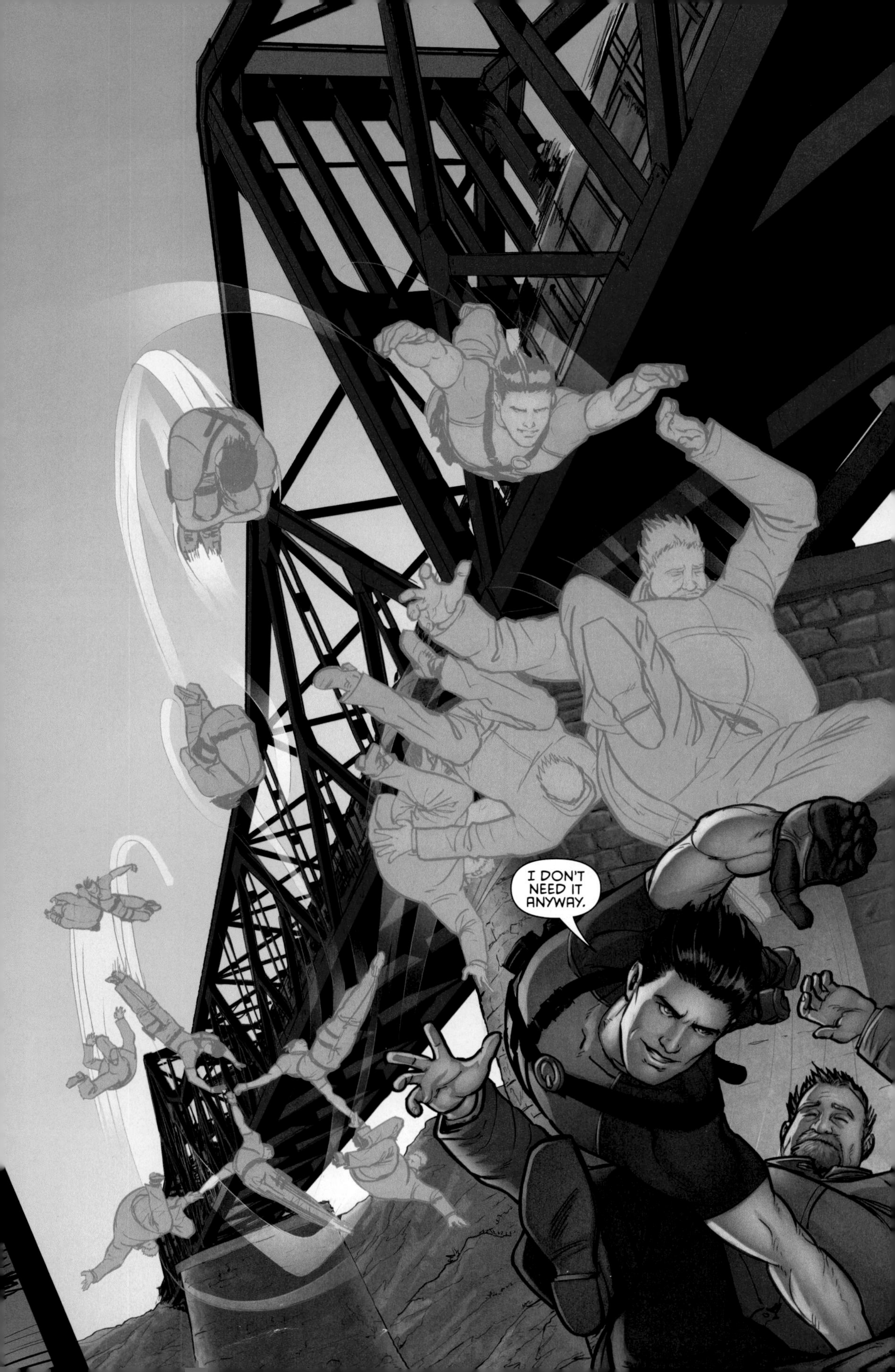
I DON'T NEED IT ANYWAY.

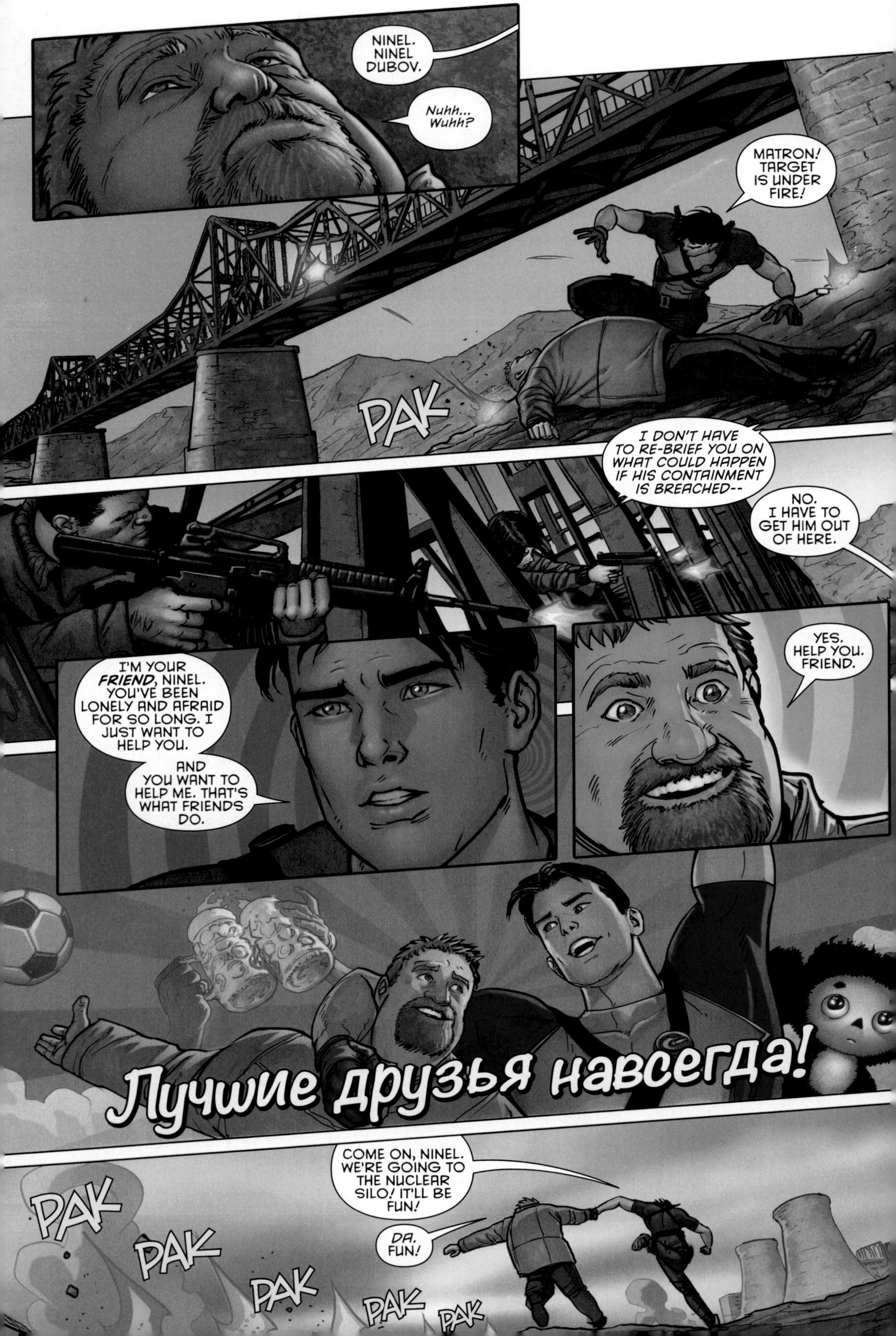
NINEL. NINEL DUBOV.
Nuhh... Wuhh?
MATRON! TARGET IS UNDER FIRE!
PAK
I DON'T HAVE TO RE-BRIEF YOU ON WHAT COULD HAPPEN IF HIS CONTAINMENT IS BREACHED--
NO. I HAVE TO GET HIM OUT OF HERE.
I'M YOUR FRIEND, NINEL. YOU'VE BEEN LONELY AND AFRAID FOR SO LONG. I JUST WANT TO HELP YOU.
AND YOU WANT TO HELP ME. THAT'S WHAT FRIENDS DO.
YES. HELP YOU. FRIEND.
Лучшие друзья навсегда!
COME ON, NINEL. WE'RE GOING TO THE NUCLEAR SILO! IT'LL BE FUN!
DA. FUN!
PAK
PAK
PAK
PAK
PAK

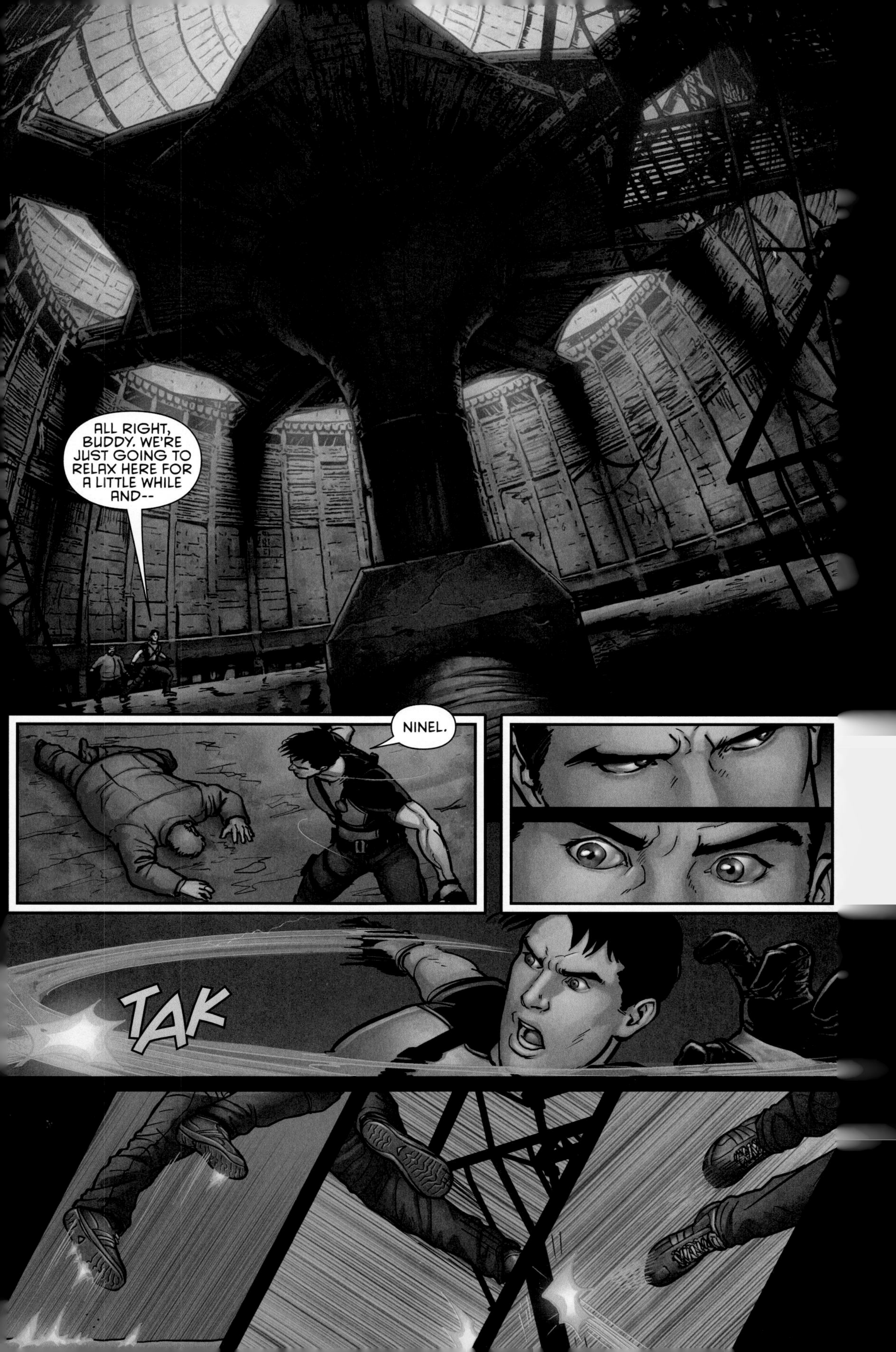
ALL RIGHT, BUDDY. WE'RE JUST GOING TO RELAX HERE FOR A LITTLE WHILE AND--
NINEL.
TAK

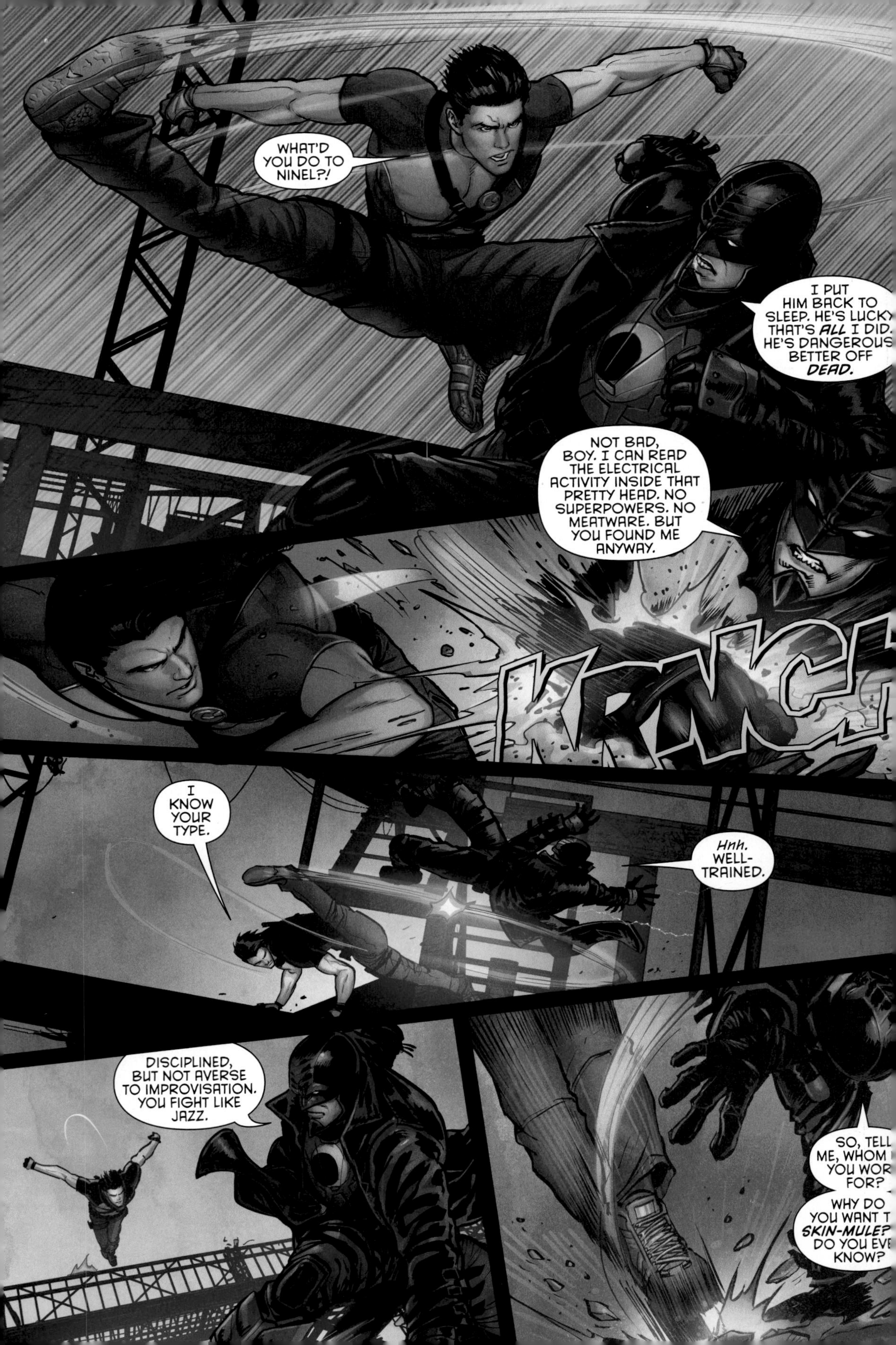
WHAT'D YOU DO TO NINEL?!
I PUT HIM BACK TO SLEEP. HE'S LUCKY THAT'S *ALL* I DID. HE'S DANGEROUS BETTER OFF *DEAD.*
NOT BAD, BOY. I CAN READ THE ELECTRICAL ACTIVITY INSIDE THAT PRETTY HEAD. NO SUPERPOWERS. NO MEATWARE. BUT YOU FOUND ME ANYWAY.
KRNCH
I KNOW YOUR TYPE.
Hnh. WELL-TRAINED.
DISCIPLINED, BUT NOT AVERSE TO IMPROVISATION. YOU FIGHT LIKE JAZZ.
SO, TELL ME, WHOM YOU WOR FOR?
WHY DO YOU WANT T *SKIN-MULE?* DO YOU EVE KNOW?

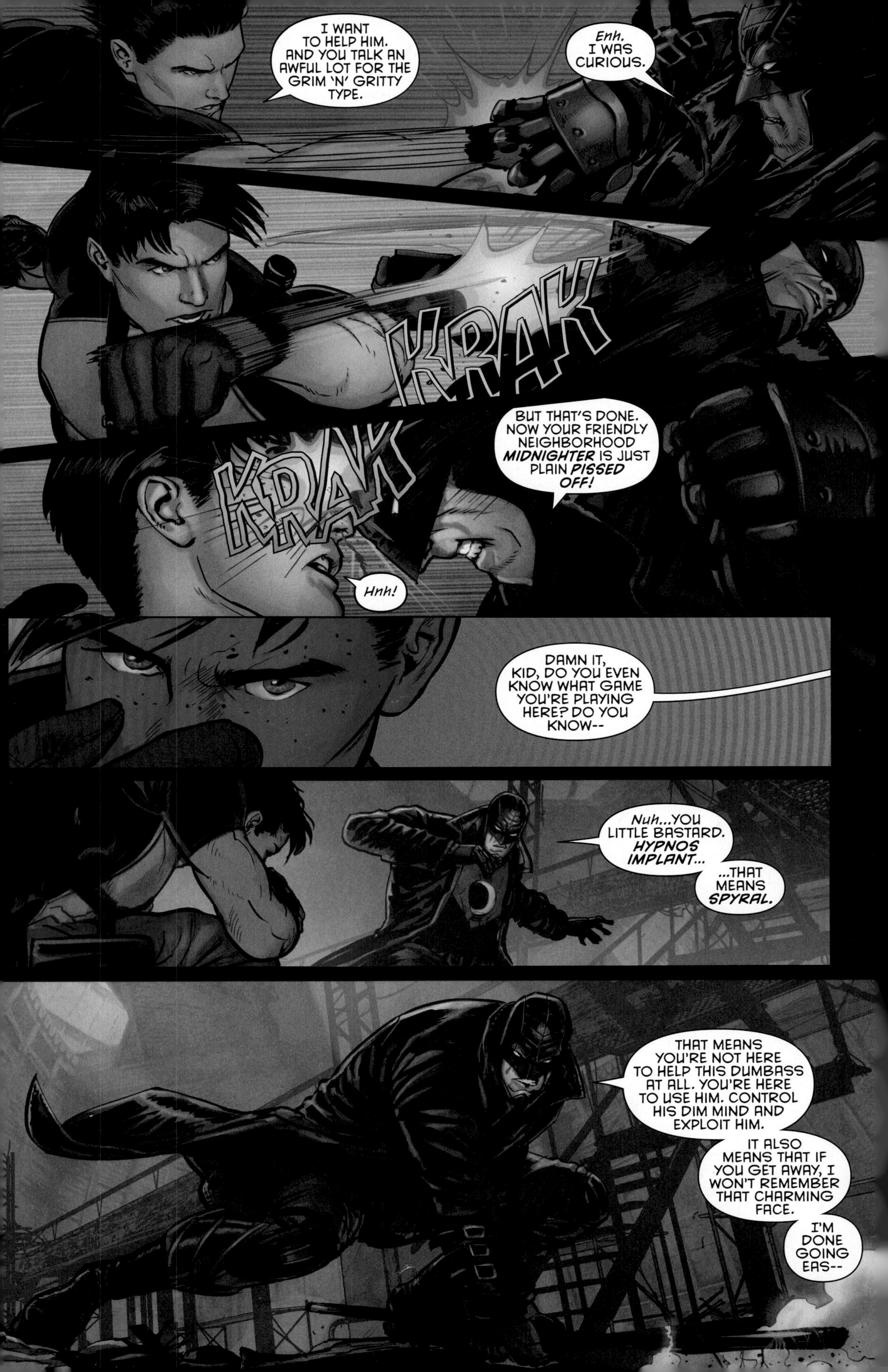
I WANT TO HELP HIM. AND YOU TALK AN AWFUL LOT FOR THE GRIM 'N' GRITTY TYPE.
Enh. I WAS CURIOUS.
KRAK
BUT THAT'S DONE. NOW YOUR FRIENDLY NEIGHBORHOOD MIDNIGHTER IS JUST PLAIN PISSED OFF!
KRAK
Hnh!
DAMN IT, KID, DO YOU EVEN KNOW WHAT GAME YOU'RE PLAYING HERE? DO YOU KNOW--
Nuh...YOU LITTLE BASTARD. HYPNOS IMPLANT...
...THAT MEANS SPYRAL.
THAT MEANS YOU'RE NOT HERE TO HELP THIS DUMBASS AT ALL. YOU'RE HERE TO USE HIM. CONTROL HIS DIM MIND AND EXPLOIT HIM.
IT ALSO MEANS THAT IF YOU GET AWAY, I WON'T REMEMBER THAT CHARMING FACE.
I'M DONE GOING EAS--

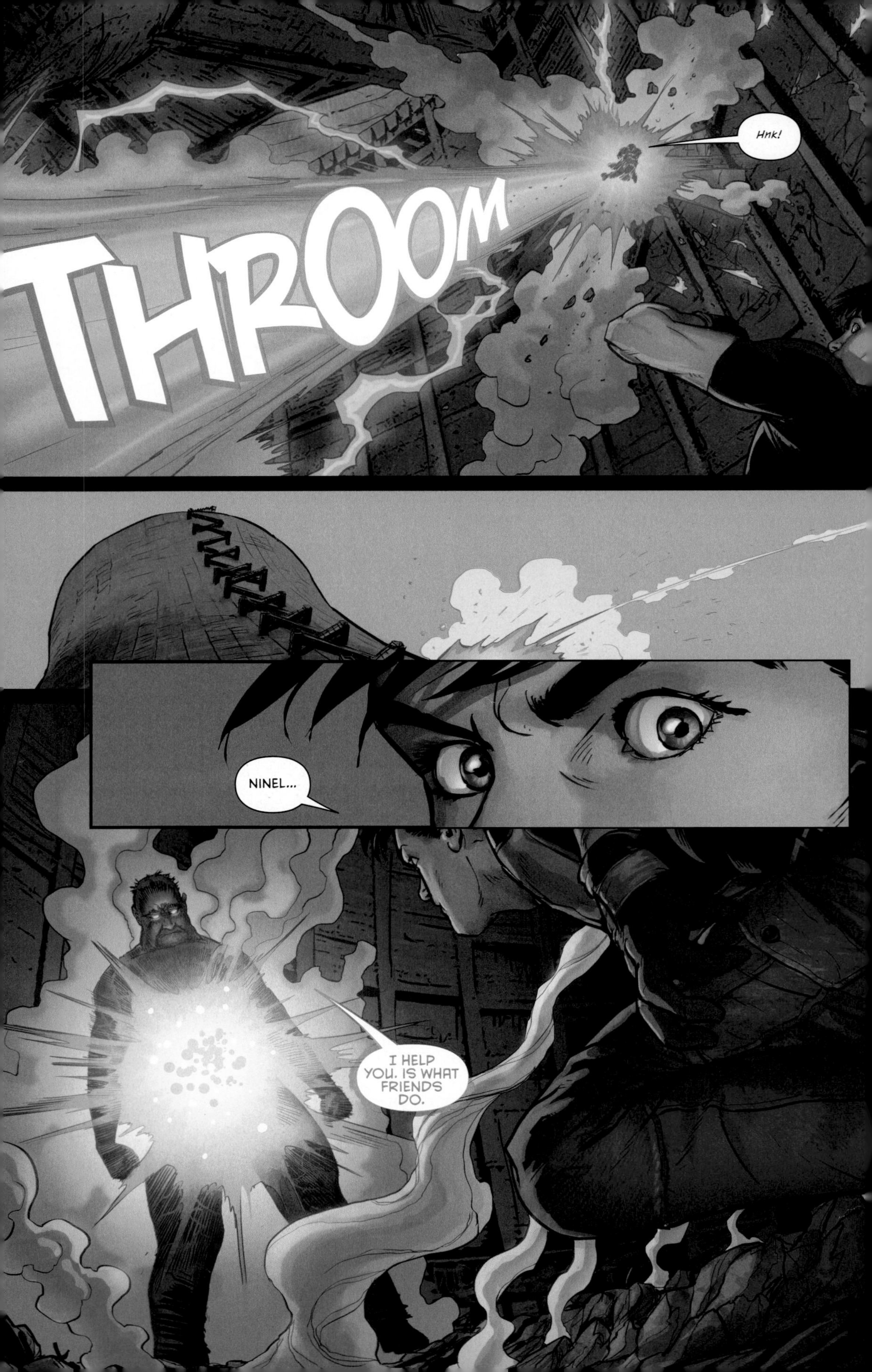
Hnk!
THROOM
NINEL...
I HELP YOU. IS WHAT FRIENDS DO.

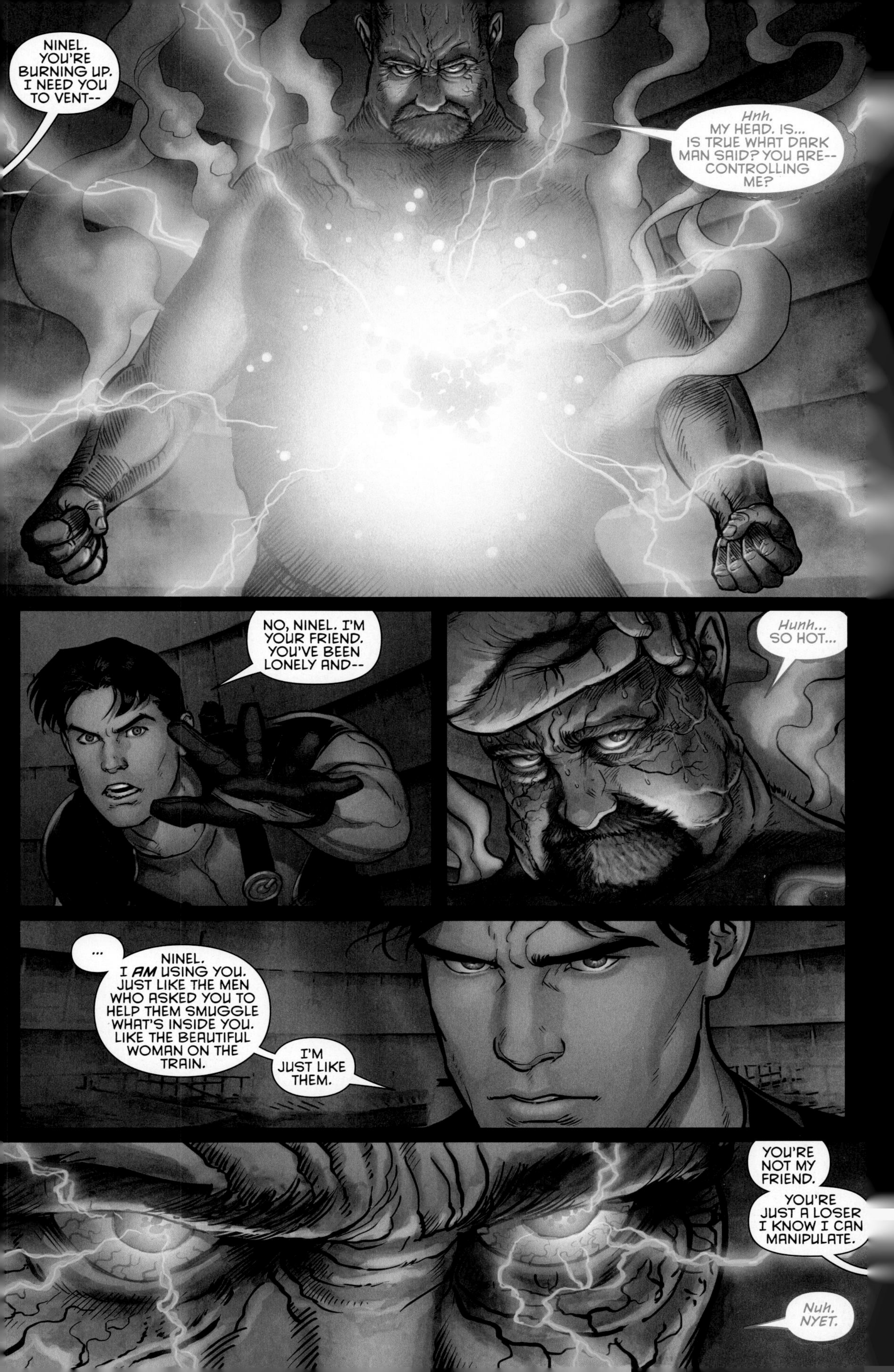
NINEL. YOU'RE BURNING UP. I NEED YOU TO VENT--
Hnh. MY HEAD. IS... IS TRUE WHAT DARK MAN SAID? YOU ARE-- CONTROLLING ME?
NO, NINEL. I'M YOUR FRIEND. YOU'VE BEEN LONELY AND--
Hunh... SO HOT...
...
NINEL. I ***AM*** USING YOU. JUST LIKE THE MEN WHO ASKED YOU TO HELP THEM SMUGGLE WHAT'S INSIDE YOU. LIKE THE BEAUTIFUL WOMAN ON THE TRAIN.
I'M JUST LIKE THEM.
YOU'RE NOT MY FRIEND.
YOU'RE JUST A LOSER I KNOW I CAN MANIPULATE.
Nuh. NYET.

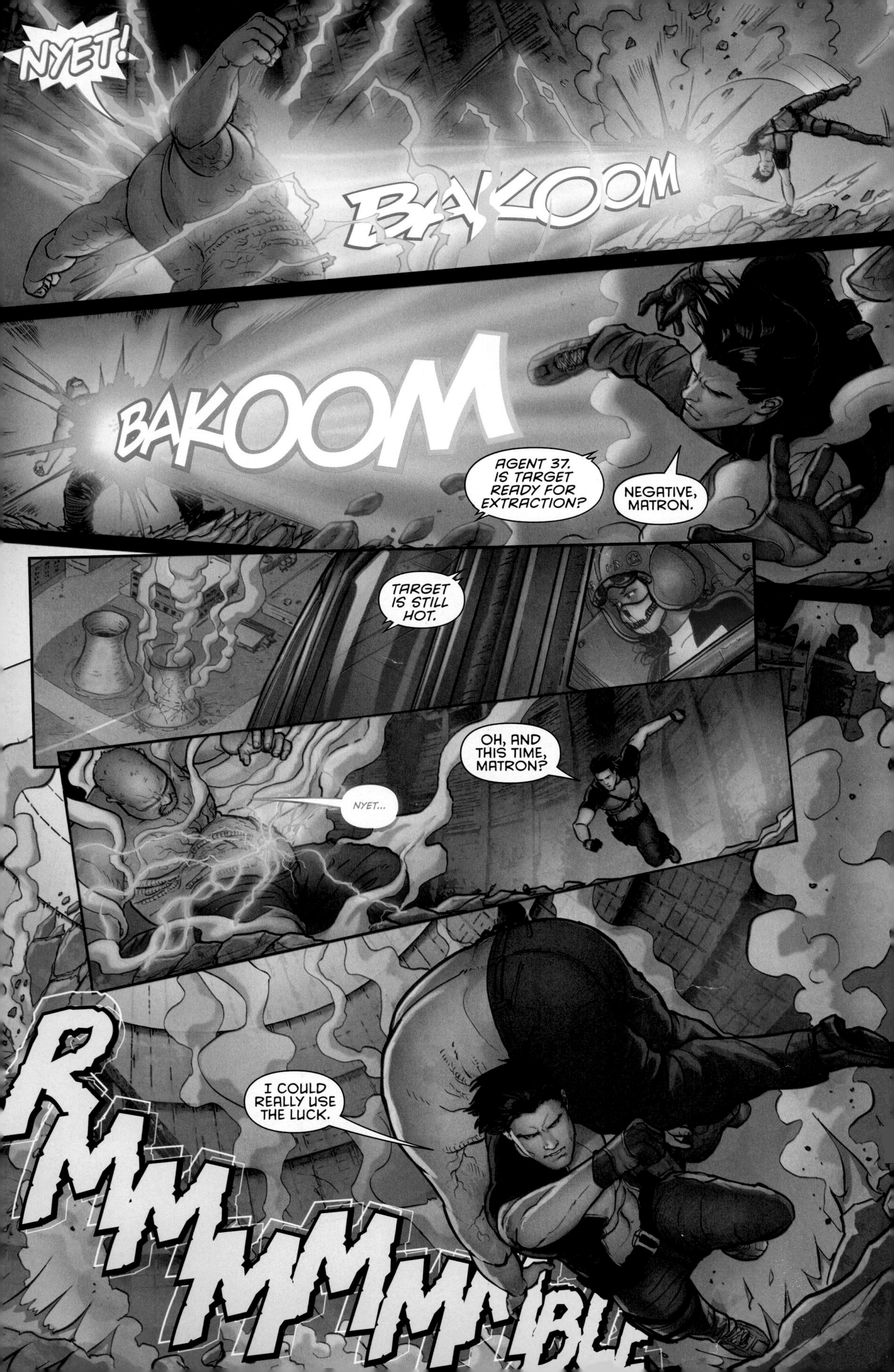
NYET!
BAKOOM
BAKOOM
AGENT 37. IS TARGET READY FOR EXTRACTION?
NEGATIVE, MATRON.
TARGET IS STILL HOT.
OH, AND THIS TIME, MATRON?
NYET...
I COULD REALLY USE THE LUCK.

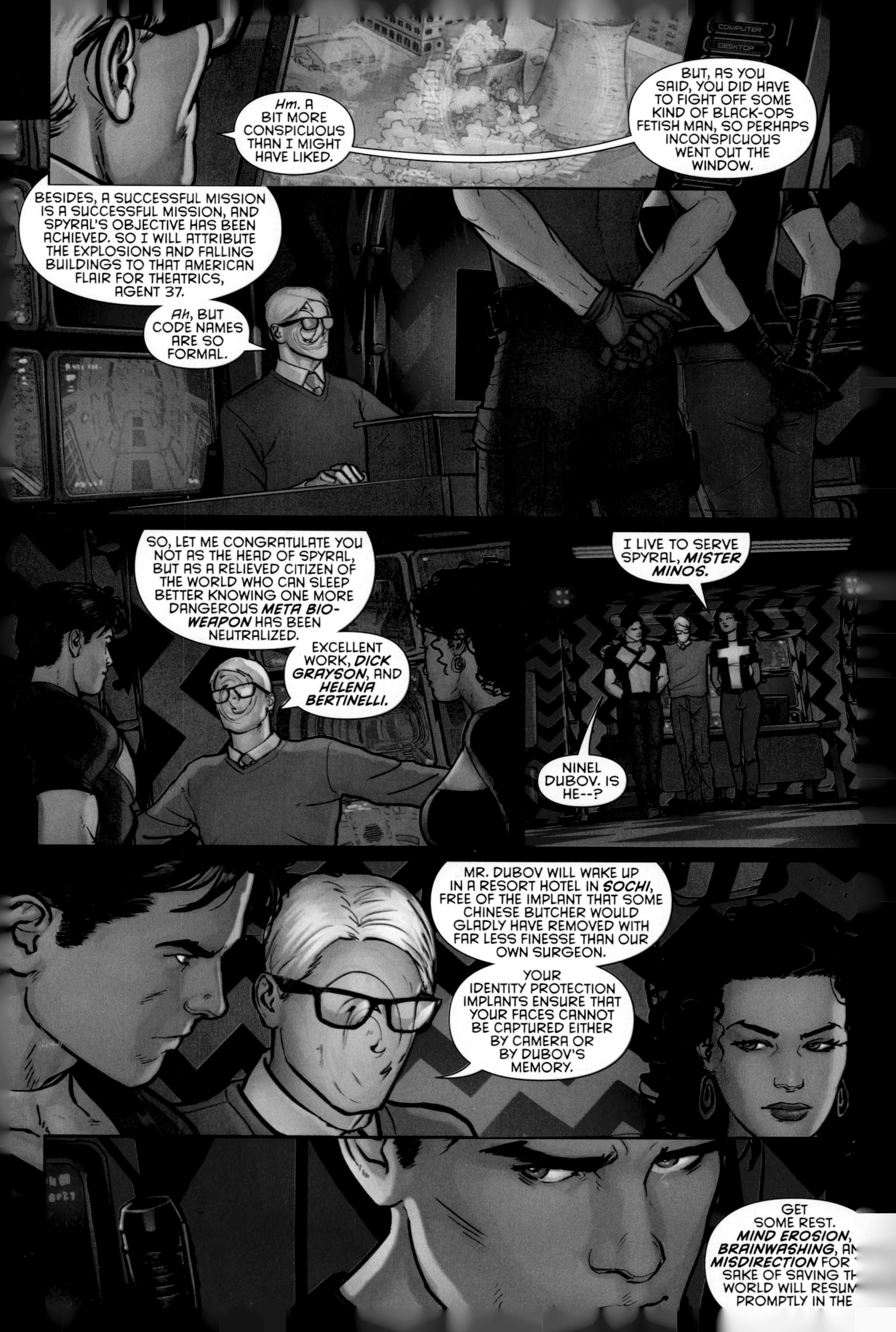
COMPUTER
DESKTOP
Hm. A BIT MORE CONSPICUOUS THAN I MIGHT HAVE LIKED.
BUT, AS YOU SAID, YOU DID HAVE TO FIGHT OFF SOME KIND OF BLACK-OPS FETISH MAN, SO PERHAPS INCONSPICUOUS WENT OUT THE WINDOW.
BESIDES, A SUCCESSFUL MISSION IS A SUCCESSFUL MISSION, AND SPYRAL'S OBJECTIVE HAS BEEN ACHIEVED. SO I WILL ATTRIBUTE THE EXPLOSIONS AND FALLING BUILDINGS TO THAT AMERICAN FLAIR FOR THEATRICS, AGENT 37.
Ah, BUT CODE NAMES ARE SO FORMAL.
SO, LET ME CONGRATULATE YOU NOT AS THE HEAD OF SPYRAL, BUT AS A RELIEVED CITIZEN OF THE WORLD WHO CAN SLEEP BETTER KNOWING ONE MORE DANGEROUS ***META BIO-WEAPON*** HAS BEEN NEUTRALIZED.
EXCELLENT WORK, ***DICK GRAYSON***, AND ***HELENA BERTINELLI.***
I LIVE TO SERVE SPYRAL, ***MISTER MINOS.***
NINEL DUBOV. IS HE--?
MR. DUBOV WILL WAKE UP IN A RESORT HOTEL IN ***SOCHI***, FREE OF THE IMPLANT THAT SOME CHINESE BUTCHER WOULD GLADLY HAVE REMOVED WITH FAR LESS FINESSE THAN OUR OWN SURGEON.
YOUR IDENTITY PROTECTION IMPLANTS ENSURE THAT YOUR FACES CANNOT BE CAPTURED EITHER BY CAMERA OR BY DUBOV'S MEMORY.
GET SOME REST. ***MIND EROSION***, ***BRAINWASHING***, AN ***MISDIRECTION*** FOR SAKE OF SAVING TH WORLD WILL RESUM PROMPTLY IN THE

"WE HAVE MORE ORGANS TO RETRIEVE."
SAINT HADRIAN'S FINISHING SCHOOL FOR GIRLS.
A PRIVATE DORM AWAY FROM THE MAIN HALL.
10:48
MR. MALONE, THIS IS BIRD-WATCHER...
GETTING BETTER WITH THE HYPNOS, BUT STILL NO I.D. ON MISTER MINOS OR--
NOK NOK

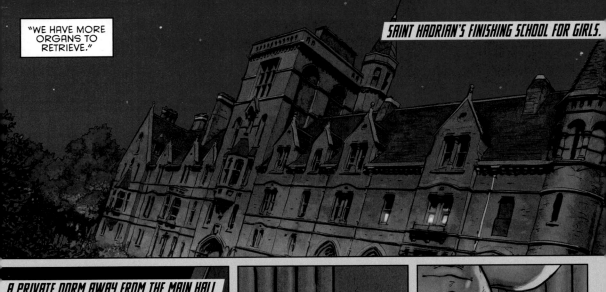

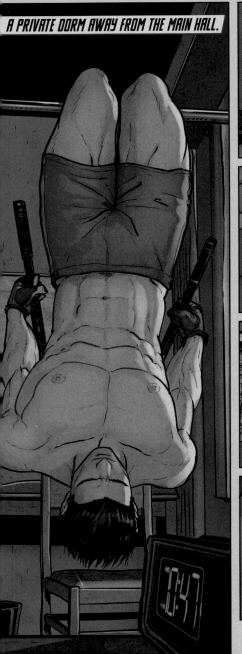

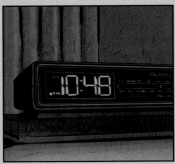

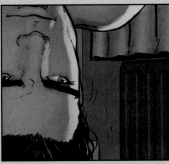

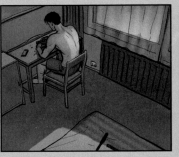

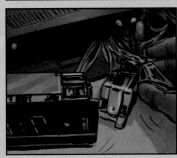

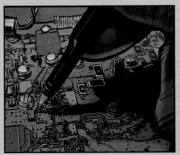

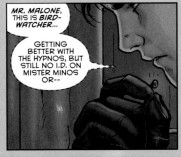

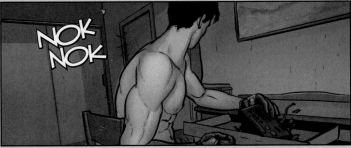

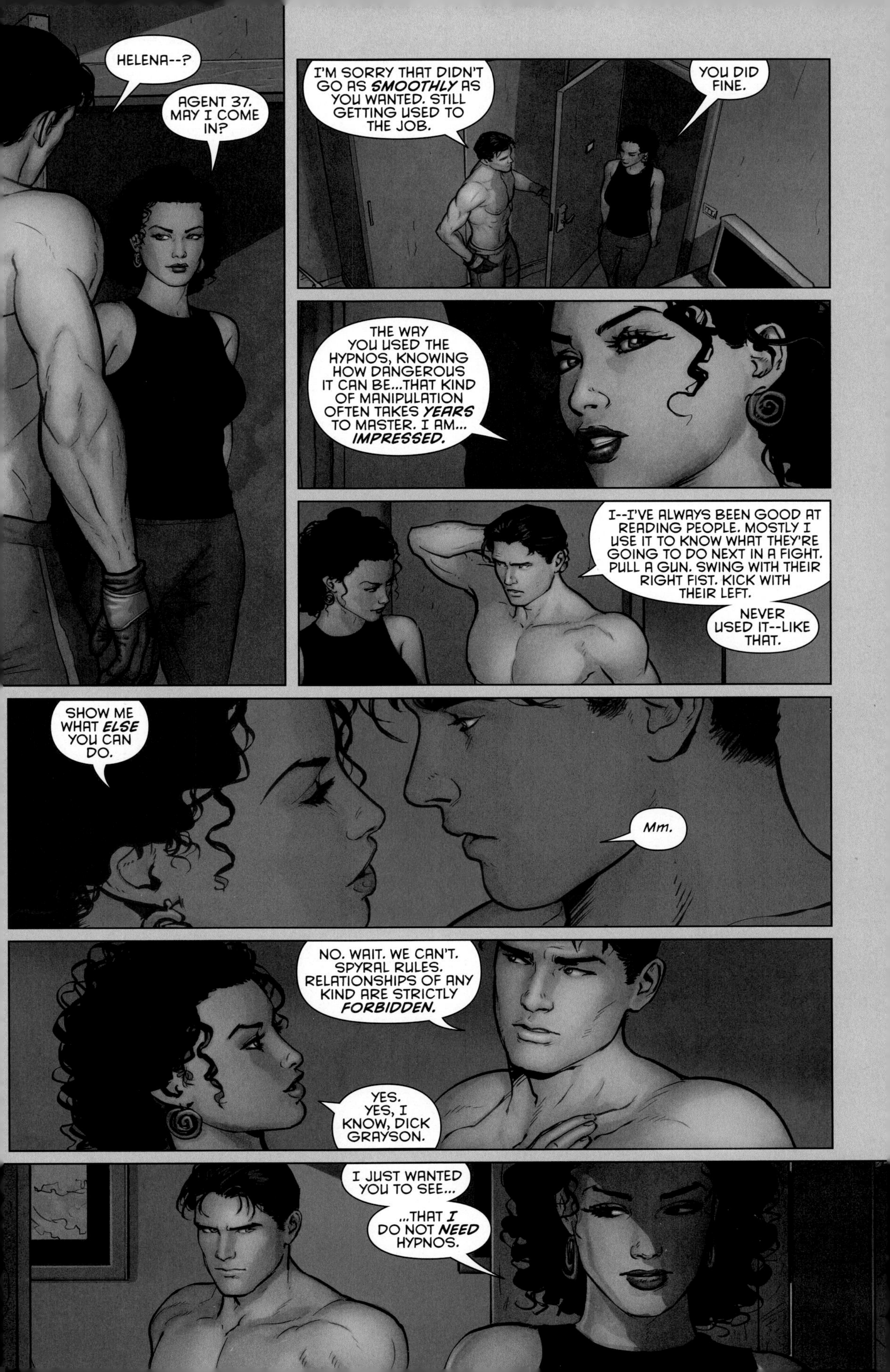
HELENA--?
AGENT 37. MAY I COME IN?
I'M SORRY THAT DIDN'T GO AS SMOOTHLY AS YOU WANTED. STILL GETTING USED TO THE JOB.
YOU DID FINE.
THE WAY YOU USED THE HYPNOS, KNOWING HOW DANGEROUS IT CAN BE...THAT KIND OF MANIPULATION OFTEN TAKES YEARS TO MASTER. I AM... IMPRESSED.
I--I'VE ALWAYS BEEN GOOD AT READING PEOPLE. MOSTLY I USE IT TO KNOW WHAT THEY'RE GOING TO DO NEXT IN A FIGHT. PULL A GUN. SWING WITH THEIR RIGHT FIST. KICK WITH THEIR LEFT.
NEVER USED IT--LIKE THAT.
SHOW ME WHAT ELSE YOU CAN DO.
Mm.
NO. WAIT. WE CAN'T. SPYRAL RULES. RELATIONSHIPS OF ANY KIND ARE STRICTLY FORBIDDEN.
YES. YES, I KNOW, DICK GRAYSON.
I JUST WANTED YOU TO SEE...
...THAT I DO NOT NEED HYPNOS.

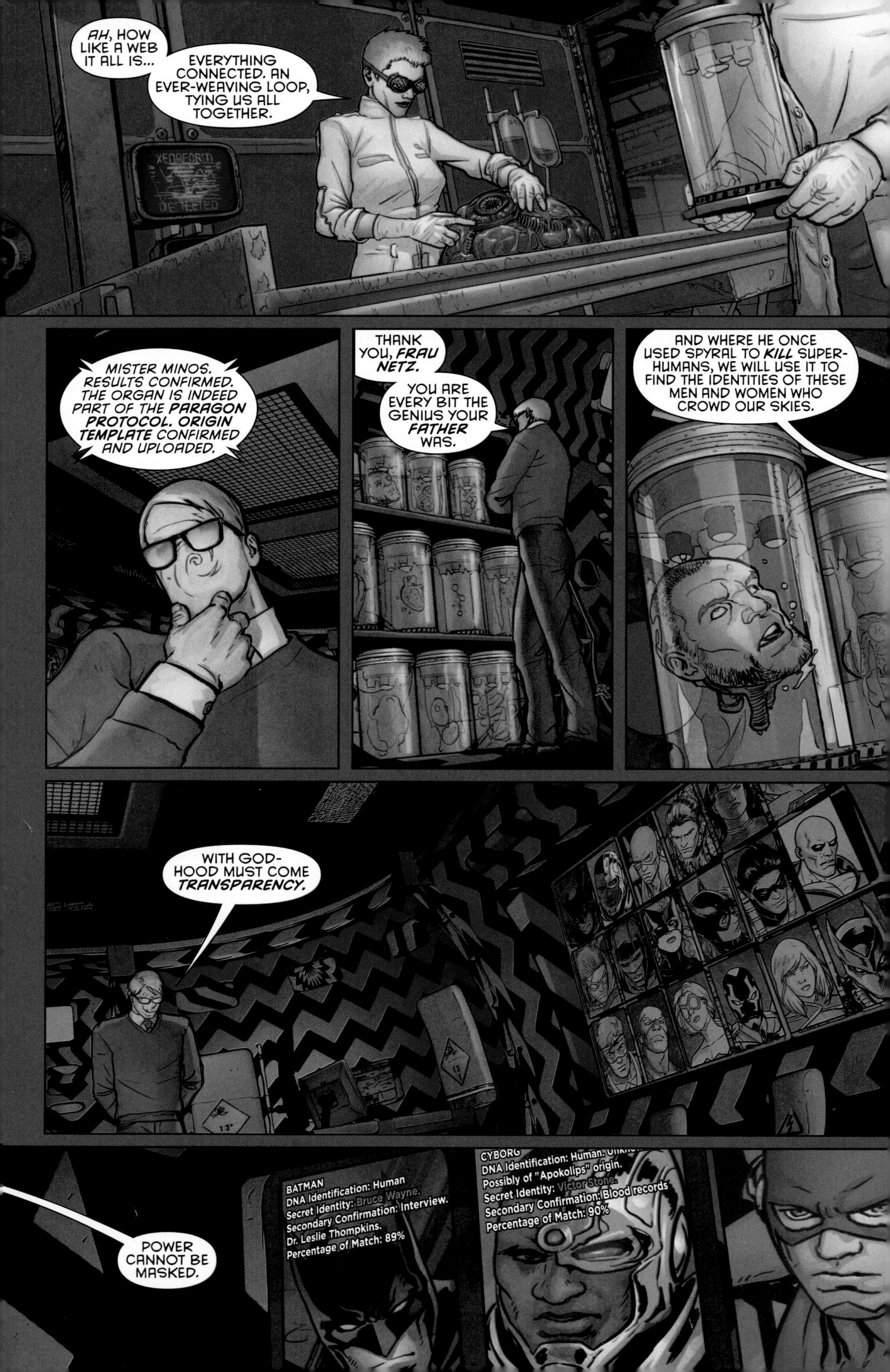
AH, HOW LIKE A WEB IT ALL IS...
EVERYTHING CONNECTED. AN EVER-WEAVING LOOP, TYING US ALL TOGETHER.
MISTER MINOS. RESULTS CONFIRMED. THE ORGAN IS INDEED PART OF THE PARAGON PROTOCOL. ORIGIN TEMPLATE CONFIRMED AND UPLOADED.
THANK YOU, FRAU NETZ.
YOU ARE EVERY BIT THE GENIUS YOUR FATHER WAS.
AND WHERE HE ONCE USED SPYRAL TO KILL SUPER-HUMANS, WE WILL USE IT TO FIND THE IDENTITIES OF THESE MEN AND WOMEN WHO CROWD OUR SKIES.
WITH GOD-HOOD MUST COME TRANSPARENCY.
POWER CANNOT BE MASKED.
BATMAN
DNA Identification: Human
Secret Identity: Bruce Wayne.
Secondary Confirmation: Interview.
Dr. Leslie Thompkins.
Percentage of Match: 89%
CYBORG
DNA Identification: Human.
Possibly of "Apokolips" origin.
Secret Identity: Victor Stone.
Secondary Confirmation: Blood records
Percentage of Match: 90%

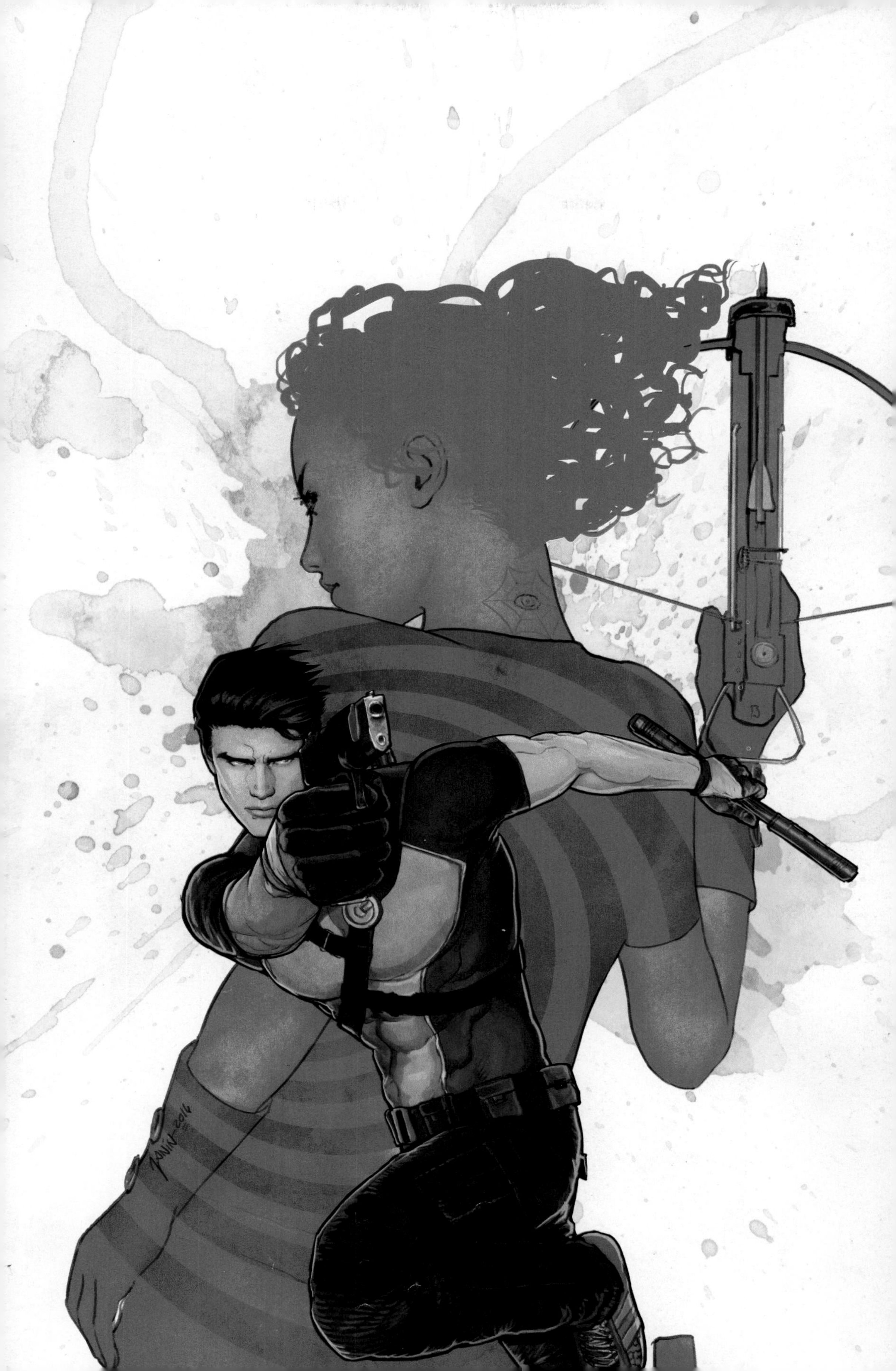

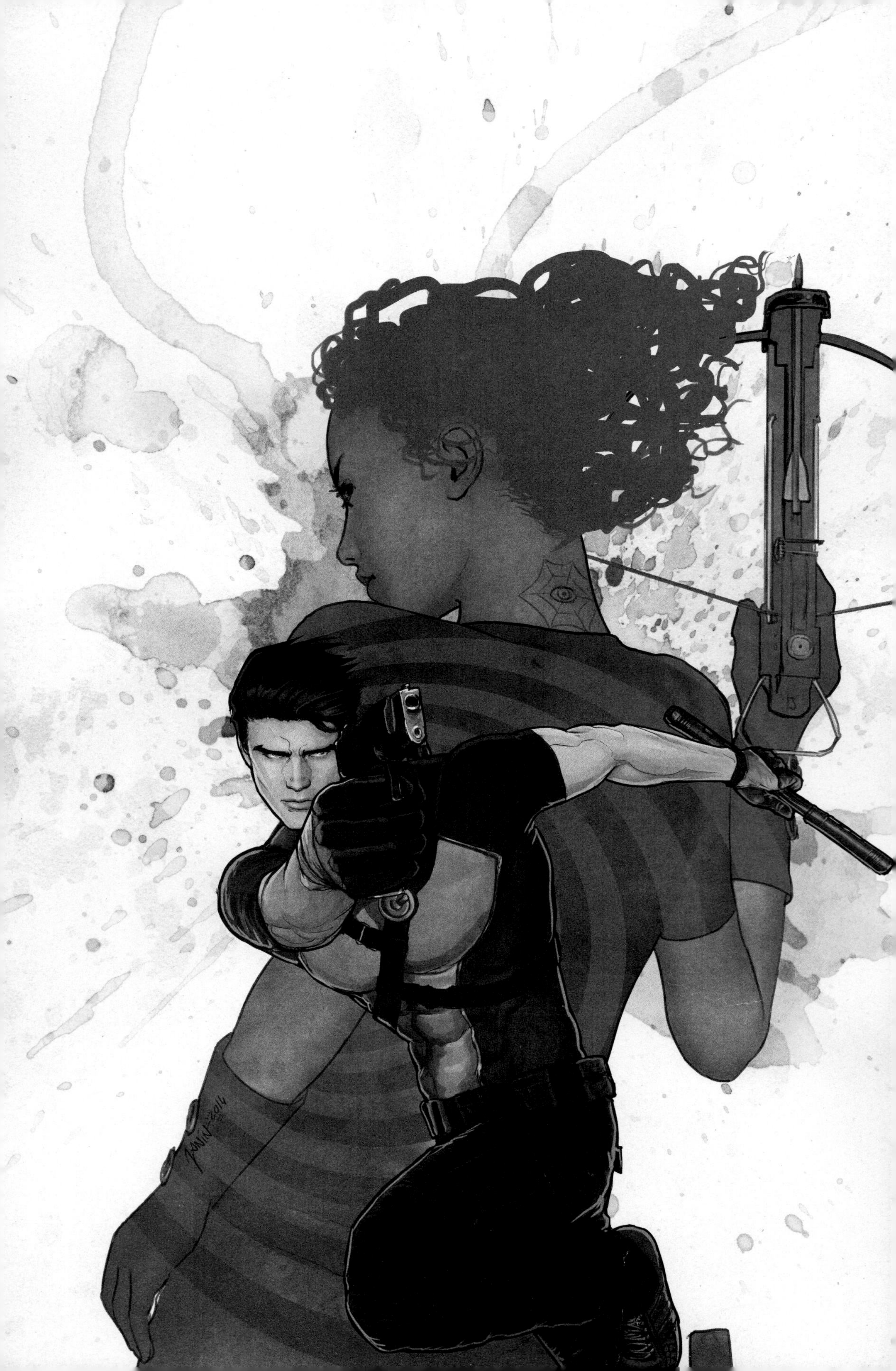

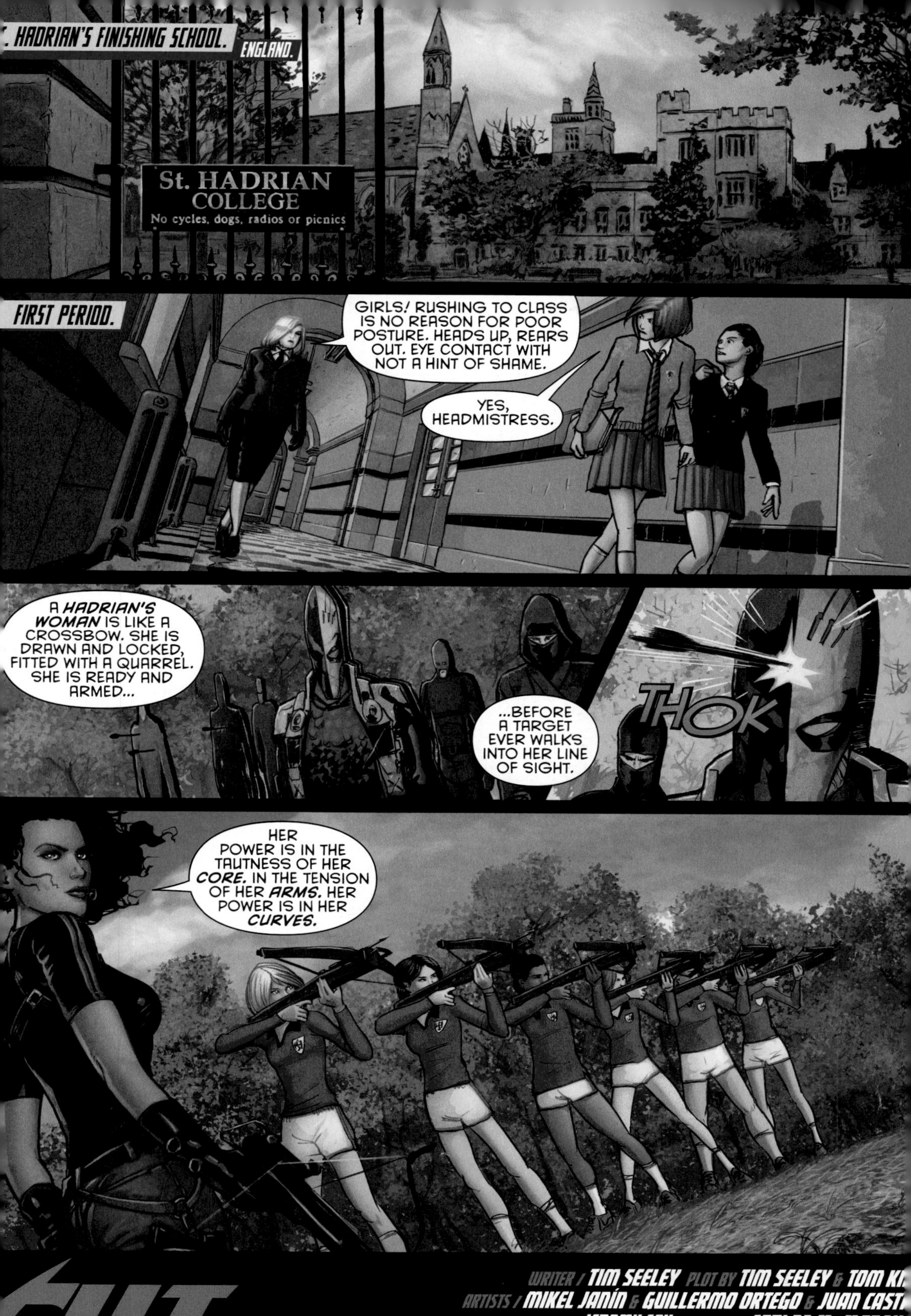

HADRIAN'S FINISHING SCHOOL.
ENGLAND.
St. HADRIAN COLLEGE
No cycles, dogs, radios or picnics
FIRST PERIOD.
GIRLS! RUSHING TO CLASS IS NO REASON FOR POOR POSTURE. HEADS UP, REARS OUT. EYE CONTACT WITH NOT A HINT OF SHAME.
YES, HEADMISTRESS.
A HADRIAN'S WOMAN IS LIKE A CROSSBOW. SHE IS DRAWN AND LOCKED, FITTED WITH A QUARREL. SHE IS READY AND ARMED...
...BEFORE A TARGET EVER WALKS INTO HER LINE OF SIGHT.
THOK
HER POWER IS IN THE TAUTNESS OF HER CORE. IN THE TENSION OF HER ARMS. HER POWER IS IN HER CURVES.

GUT FEELINGS

WRITER / TIM SEELEY PLOT BY TIM SEELEY & TOM KI
ARTISTS / MIKEL JANÍN & GUILLERMO ORTEGO & JUAN CAST
COLORIST / JEROMY COX LETTERER / CARLOS M MANGU
COVER / MIKEL JAN

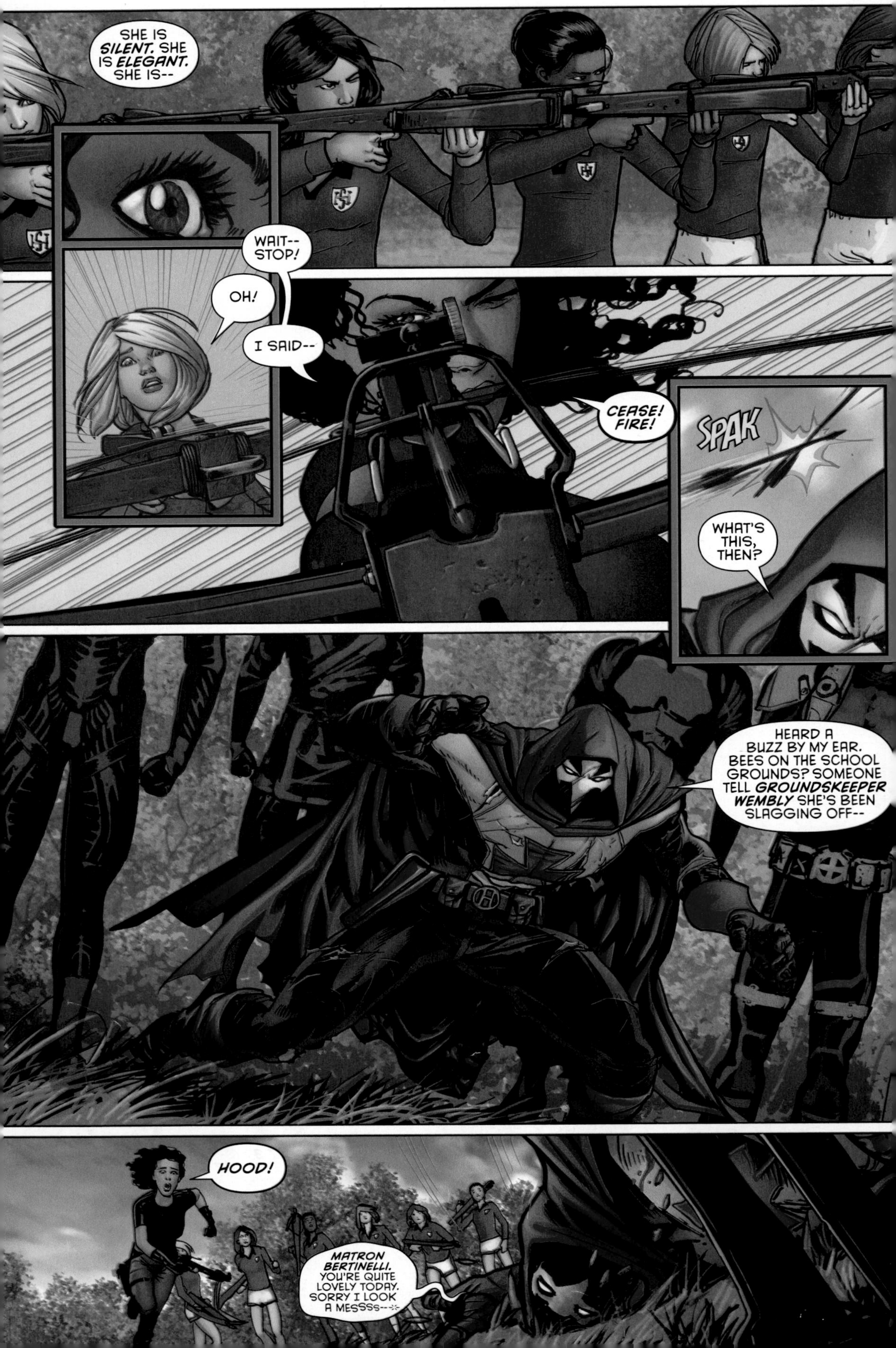
SHE IS SILENT. SHE IS ELEGANT. SHE IS--
WAIT-- STOP!
OH!
I SAID--
CEASE! FIRE!
SPAK
WHAT'S THIS, THEN?
HEARD A BUZZ BY MY EAR. BEES ON THE SCHOOL GROUNDS? SOMEONE TELL GROUNDSKEEPER WEMBLY SHE'S BEEN SLAGGING OFF--
HOOD!
MATRON BERTINELLI. YOU'RE QUITE LOVELY TODAY. SORRY I LOOK A MESSSS--

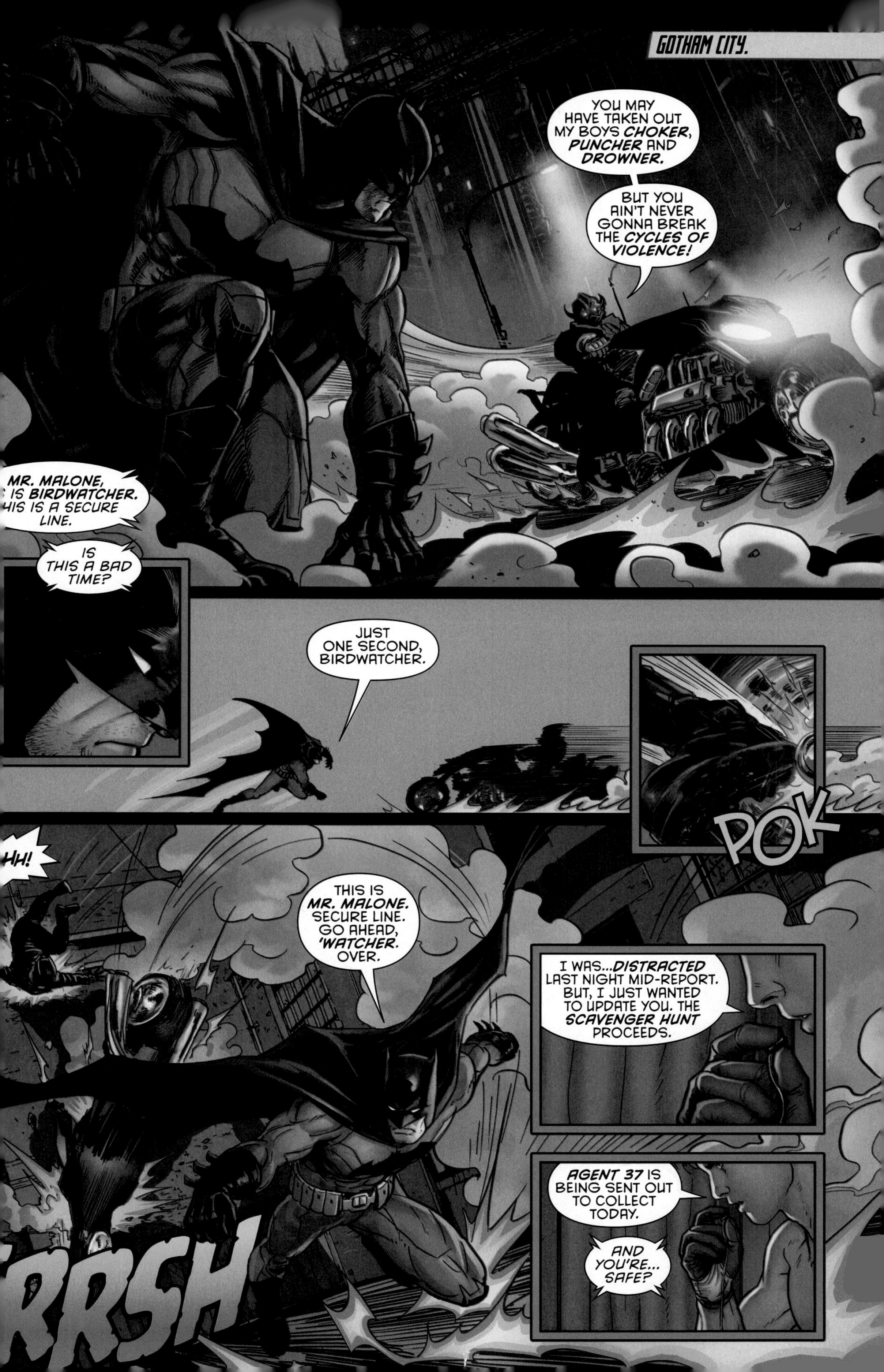
GOTHAM CITY.
YOU MAY HAVE TAKEN OUT MY BOYS CHOKER, PUNCHER AND DROWNER.
BUT YOU AIN'T NEVER GONNA BREAK THE CYCLES OF VIOLENCE!
MR. MALONE, IS BIRDWATCHER. HIS IS A SECURE LINE.
IS THIS A BAD TIME?
JUST ONE SECOND, BIRDWATCHER.
POK
HH!
THIS IS MR. MALONE. SECURE LINE. GO AHEAD, 'WATCHER. OVER.
I WAS...DISTRACTED LAST NIGHT MID-REPORT. BUT, I JUST WANTED TO UPDATE YOU. THE SCAVENGER HUNT PROCEEDS.
AGENT 37 IS BEING SENT OUT TO COLLECT TODAY.
AND YOU'RE... SAFE?
RRSH

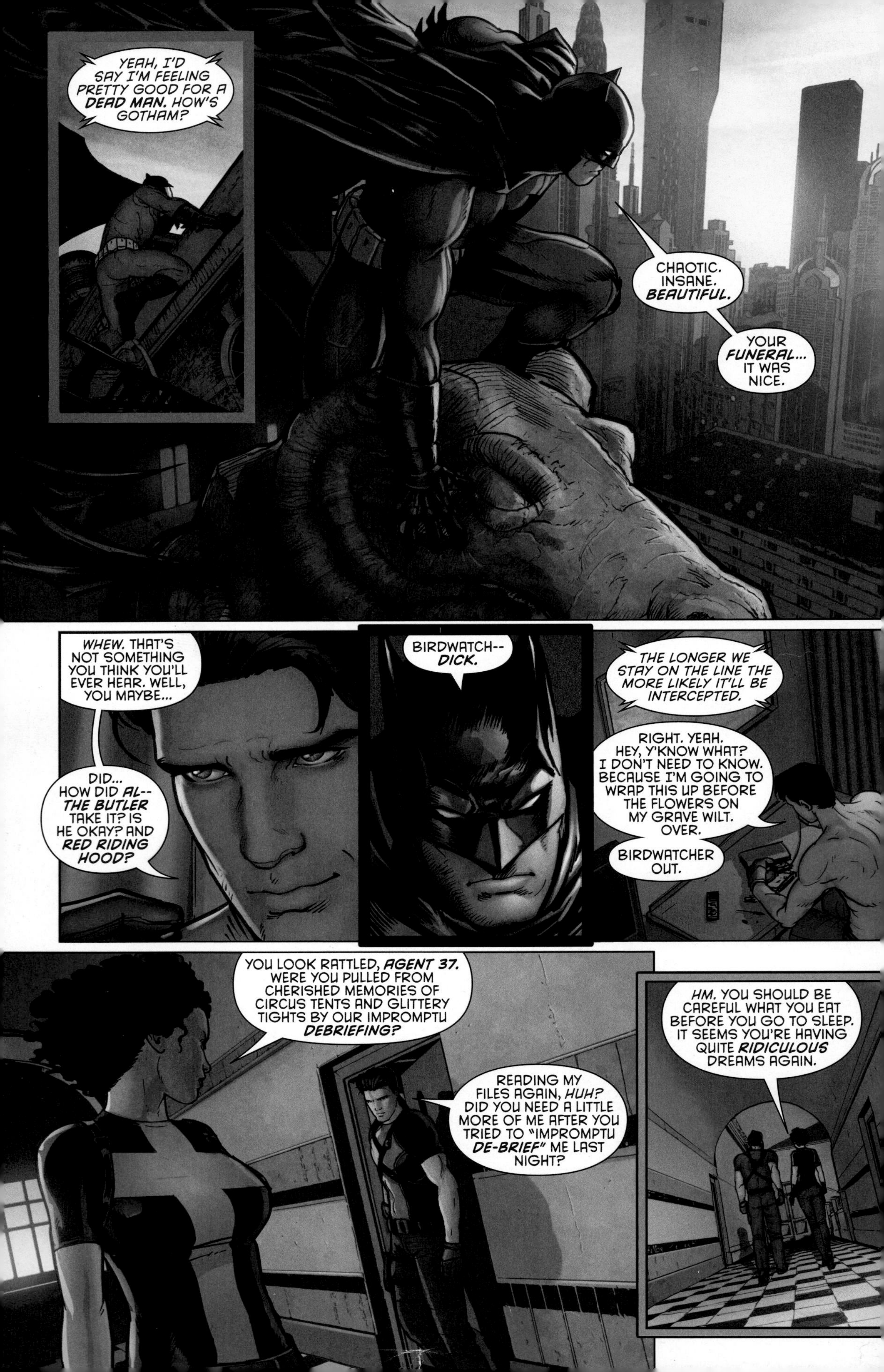
YEAH, I'D SAY I'M FEELING PRETTY GOOD FOR A DEAD MAN. HOW'S GOTHAM?
CHAOTIC. INSANE. BEAUTIFUL.
YOUR FUNERAL... IT WAS NICE.
WHEW. THAT'S NOT SOMETHING YOU THINK YOU'LL EVER HEAR. WELL, YOU MAYBE...
DID... HOW DID AL-- THE BUTLER TAKE IT? IS HE OKAY? AND RED RIDING HOOD?
BIRDWATCH-- DICK.
THE LONGER WE STAY ON THE LINE THE MORE LIKELY IT'LL BE INTERCEPTED.
RIGHT. YEAH. HEY, Y'KNOW WHAT? I DON'T NEED TO KNOW. BECAUSE I'M GOING TO WRAP THIS UP BEFORE THE FLOWERS ON MY GRAVE WILT. OVER.
BIRDWATCHER OUT.
YOU LOOK RATTLED, AGENT 37. WERE YOU PULLED FROM CHERISHED MEMORIES OF CIRCUS TENTS AND GLITTERY TIGHTS BY OUR IMPROMPTU DEBRIEFING?
READING MY FILES AGAIN, HUH? DID YOU NEED A LITTLE MORE OF ME AFTER YOU TRIED TO "IMPROMPTU DE-BRIEF" ME LAST NIGHT?
HM. YOU SHOULD BE CAREFUL WHAT YOU EAT BEFORE YOU GO TO SLEEP. IT SEEMS YOU'RE HAVING QUITE RIDICULOUS DREAMS AGAIN.

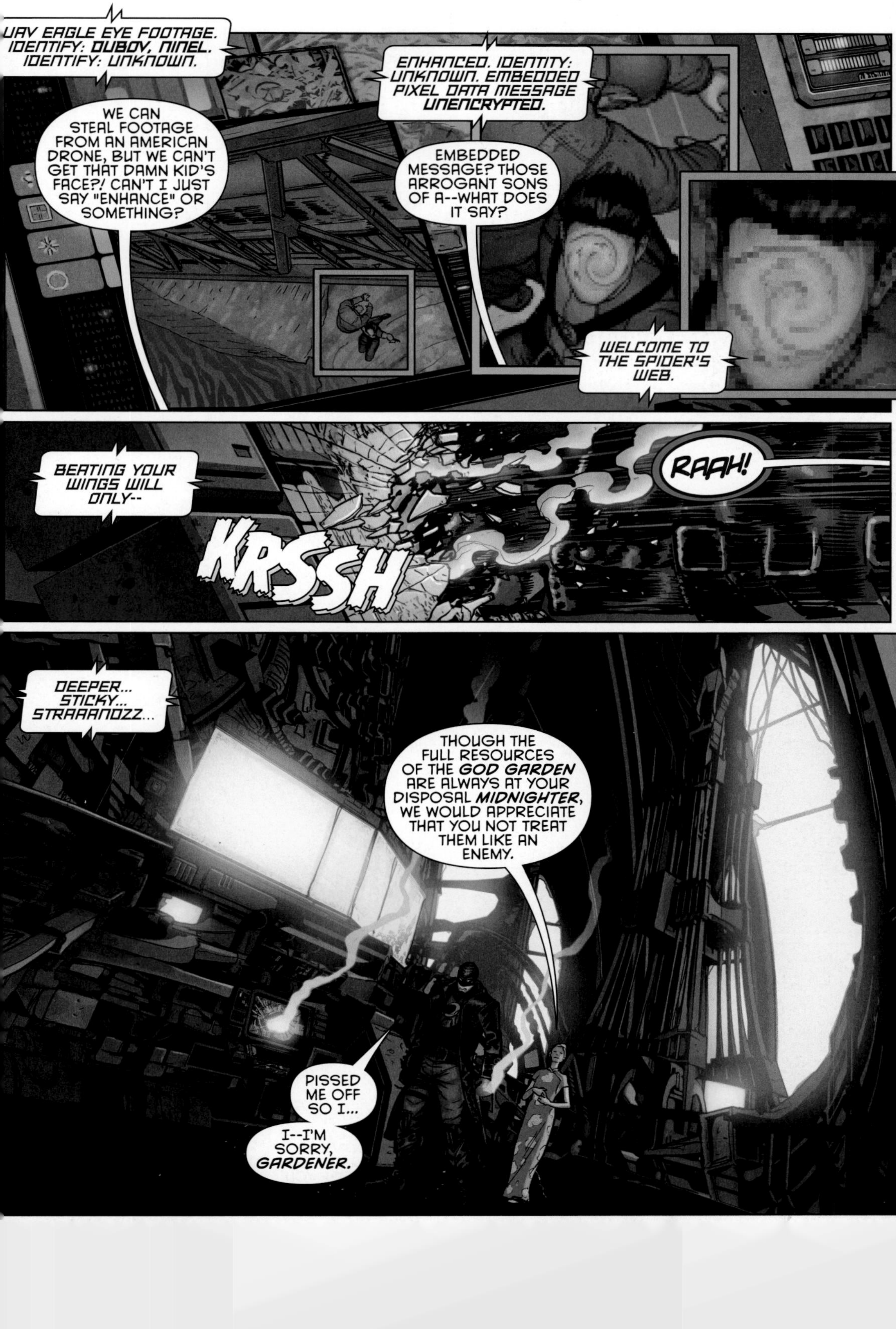
UAV EAGLE EYE FOOTAGE. IDENTIFY: DUBOV, NINEL. IDENTIFY: UNKNOWN.
WE CAN STEAL FOOTAGE FROM AN AMERICAN DRONE, BUT WE CAN'T GET THAT DAMN KID'S FACE?! CAN'T I JUST SAY "ENHANCE" OR SOMETHING?
ENHANCED. IDENTITY: UNKNOWN. EMBEDDED PIXEL DATA MESSAGE UNENCRYPTED.
EMBEDDED MESSAGE? THOSE ARROGANT SONS OF A--WHAT DOES IT SAY?
WELCOME TO THE SPIDER'S WEB.
BEATING YOUR WINGS WILL ONLY--
RAAH!
KRSSH
DEEPER... STICKY... STRAAANOZZ...
THOUGH THE FULL RESOURCES OF THE GOD GARDEN ARE ALWAYS AT YOUR DISPOSAL MIDNIGHTER, WE WOULD APPRECIATE THAT YOU NOT TREAT THEM LIKE AN ENEMY.
PISSED ME OFF SO I...
I--I'M SORRY, GARDENER.

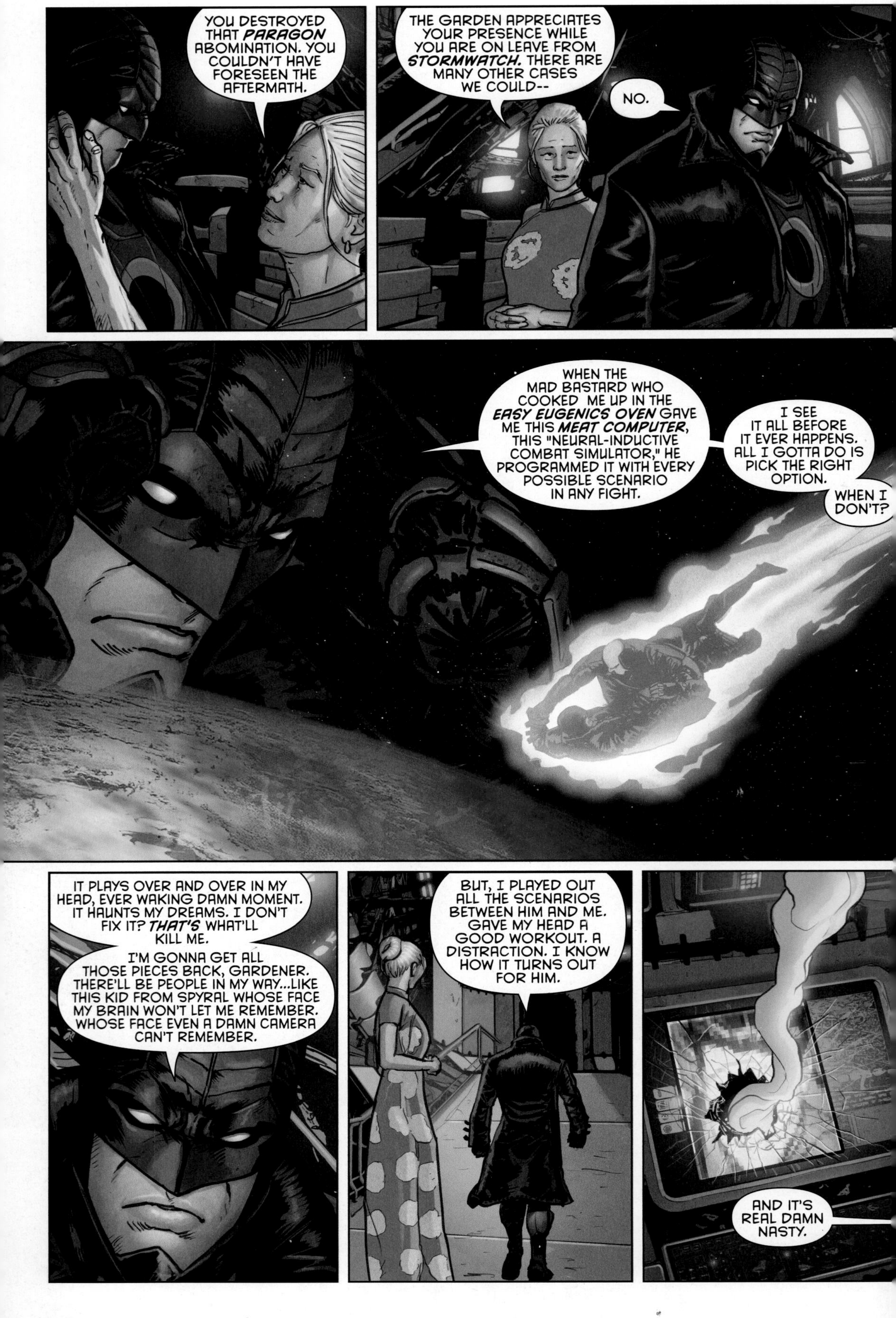
YOU DESTROYED THAT *PARAGON* ABOMINATION. YOU COULDN'T HAVE FORESEEN THE AFTERMATH.
THE GARDEN APPRECIATES YOUR PRESENCE WHILE YOU ARE ON LEAVE FROM *STORMWATCH.* THERE ARE MANY OTHER CASES WE COULD--
NO.
WHEN THE MAD BASTARD WHO COOKED ME UP IN THE *EASY EUGENICS OVEN* GAVE ME THIS *MEAT COMPUTER*, THIS "NEURAL-INDUCTIVE COMBAT SIMULATOR," HE PROGRAMMED IT WITH EVERY POSSIBLE SCENARIO IN ANY FIGHT.
I SEE IT ALL BEFORE IT EVER HAPPENS. ALL I GOTTA DO IS PICK THE RIGHT OPTION.
WHEN I DON'T?
IT PLAYS OVER AND OVER IN MY HEAD, EVER WAKING DAMN MOMENT. IT HAUNTS MY DREAMS. I DON'T FIX IT? *THAT'S* WHAT'LL KILL ME.
I'M GONNA GET ALL THOSE PIECES BACK, GARDENER. THERE'LL BE PEOPLE IN MY WAY...LIKE THIS KID FROM SPYRAL WHOSE FACE MY BRAIN WON'T LET ME REMEMBER. WHOSE FACE EVEN A DAMN CAMERA CAN'T REMEMBER.
BUT, I PLAYED OUT ALL THE SCENARIOS BETWEEN HIM AND ME. GAVE MY HEAD A GOOD WORKOUT. A DISTRACTION. I KNOW HOW IT TURNS OUT FOR HIM.
AND IT'S REAL DAMN NASTY.

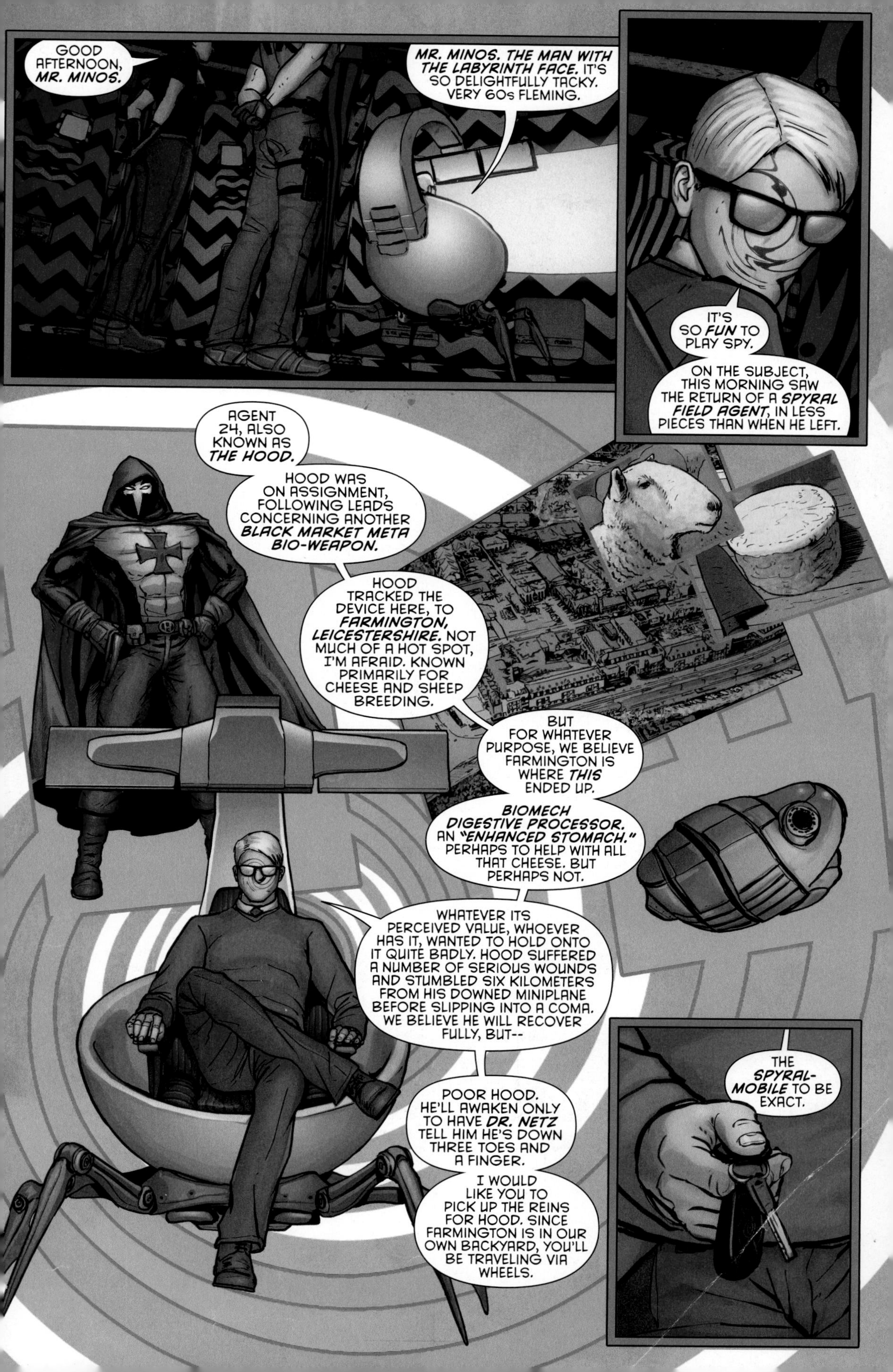
GOOD AFTERNOON, MR. MINOS.
MR. MINOS. THE MAN WITH THE LABYRINTH FACE. IT'S SO DELIGHTFULLY TACKY. VERY 60s FLEMING.
IT'S SO FUN TO PLAY SPY.
ON THE SUBJECT, THIS MORNING SAW THE RETURN OF A SPYRAL FIELD AGENT, IN LESS PIECES THAN WHEN HE LEFT.
AGENT 24, ALSO KNOWN AS THE HOOD.
HOOD WAS ON ASSIGNMENT, FOLLOWING LEADS CONCERNING ANOTHER BLACK MARKET META BIO-WEAPON.
HOOD TRACKED THE DEVICE HERE, TO FARMINGTON, LEICESTERSHIRE. NOT MUCH OF A HOT SPOT, I'M AFRAID. KNOWN PRIMARILY FOR CHEESE AND SHEEP BREEDING.
BUT FOR WHATEVER PURPOSE, WE BELIEVE FARMINGTON IS WHERE THIS ENDED UP.
BIOMECH DIGESTIVE PROCESSOR. AN "ENHANCED STOMACH." PERHAPS TO HELP WITH ALL THAT CHEESE. BUT PERHAPS NOT.
WHATEVER ITS PERCEIVED VALUE, WHOEVER HAS IT, WANTED TO HOLD ONTO IT QUITE BADLY. HOOD SUFFERED A NUMBER OF SERIOUS WOUNDS AND STUMBLED SIX KILOMETERS FROM HIS DOWNED MINIPLANE BEFORE SLIPPING INTO A COMA. WE BELIEVE HE WILL RECOVER FULLY, BUT--
POOR HOOD. HE'LL AWAKEN ONLY TO HAVE DR. NETZ TELL HIM HE'S DOWN THREE TOES AND A FINGER.
I WOULD LIKE YOU TO PICK UP THE REINS FOR HOOD. SINCE FARMINGTON IS IN OUR OWN BACKYARD, YOU'LL BE TRAVELING VIA WHEELS.
THE SPYRAL-MOBILE TO BE EXACT.

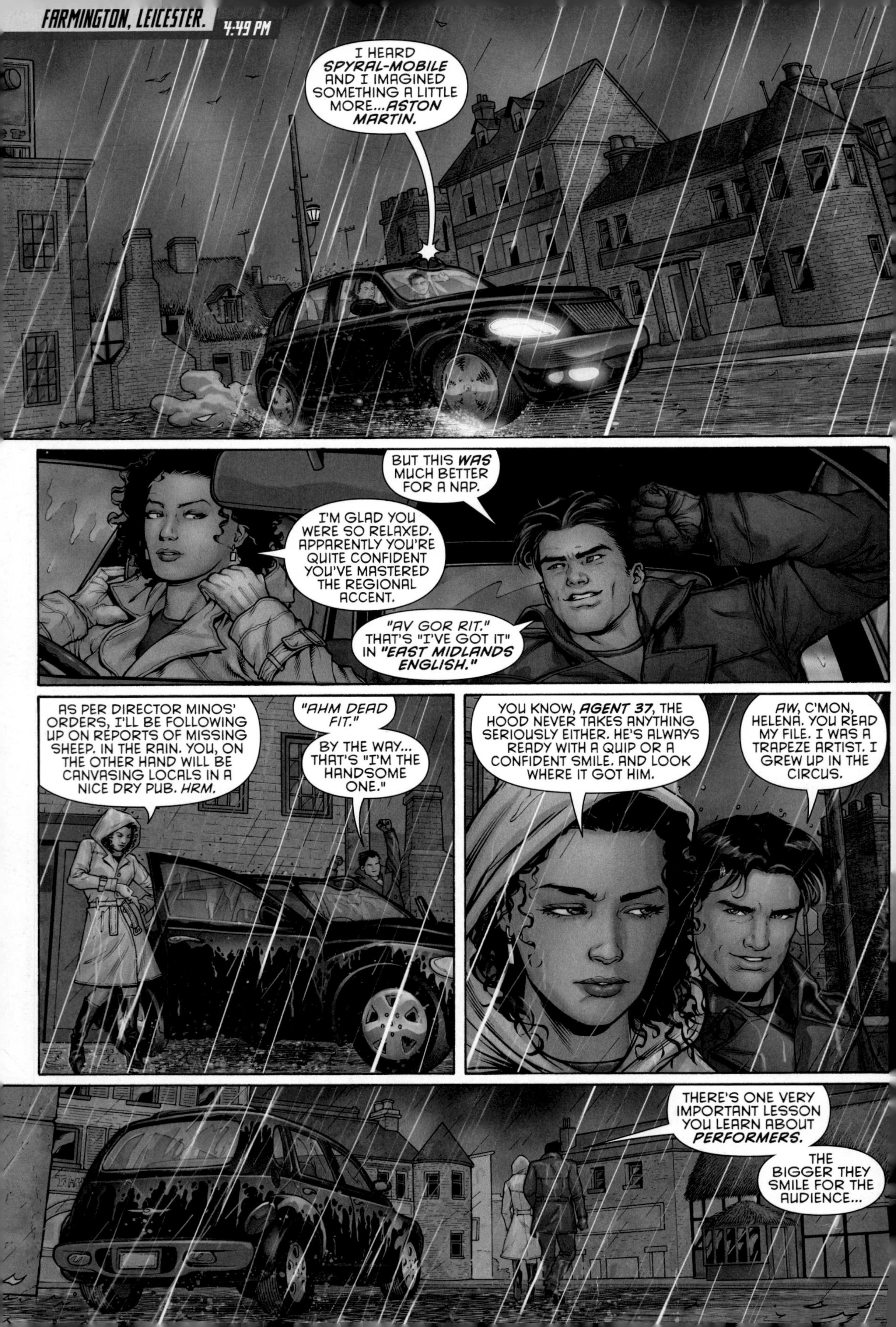
FARMINGTON, LEICESTER.
4:49 PM
I HEARD SPYRAL-MOBILE AND I IMAGINED SOMETHING A LITTLE MORE...ASTON MARTIN.
BUT THIS WAS MUCH BETTER FOR A NAP.
I'M GLAD YOU WERE SO RELAXED. APPARENTLY YOU'RE QUITE CONFIDENT YOU'VE MASTERED THE REGIONAL ACCENT.
"AV GOR RIT." THAT'S "I'VE GOT IT" IN "EAST MIDLANDS ENGLISH."
AS PER DIRECTOR MINOS' ORDERS, I'LL BE FOLLOWING UP ON REPORTS OF MISSING SHEEP. IN THE RAIN. YOU, ON THE OTHER HAND WILL BE CANVASING LOCALS IN A NICE DRY PUB. HRM.
"AHM DEAD FIT."
BY THE WAY... THAT'S "I'M THE HANDSOME ONE."
YOU KNOW, AGENT 37, THE HOOD NEVER TAKES ANYTHING SERIOUSLY EITHER. HE'S ALWAYS READY WITH A QUIP OR A CONFIDENT SMILE. AND LOOK WHERE IT GOT HIM.
AW, C'MON, HELENA. YOU READ MY FILE. I WAS A TRAPEZE ARTIST. I GREW UP IN THE CIRCUS.
THERE'S ONE VERY IMPORTANT LESSON YOU LEARN ABOUT PERFORMERS.
THE BIGGER THEY SMILE FOR THE AUDIENCE...

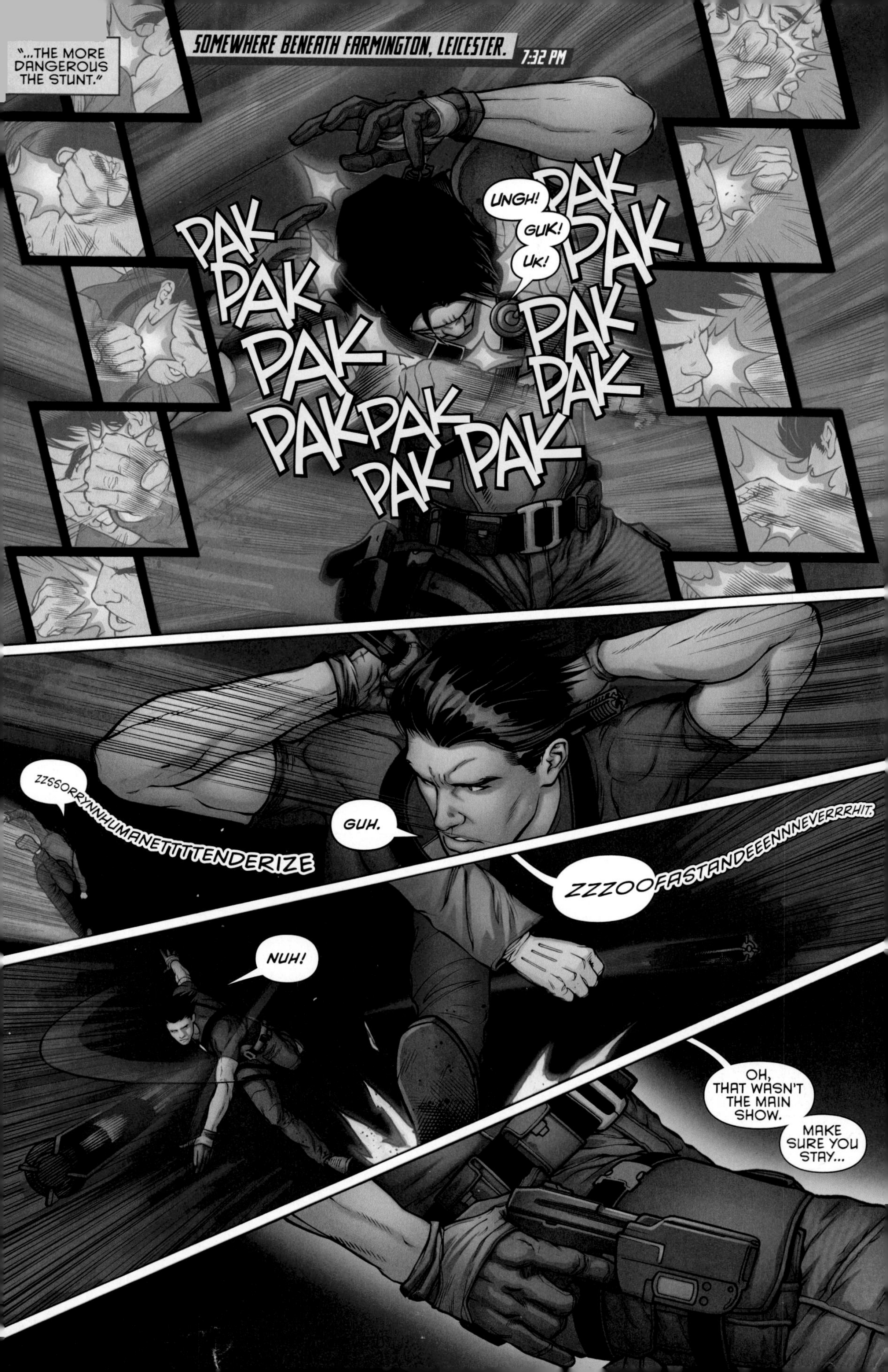
"...THE MORE DANGEROUS THE STUNT."
SOMEWHERE BENEATH FARMINGTON, LEICESTER. 7:32 PM
UNGH!
GUK!
UK!
PAK PAK PAK PAKPAK PAK PAK PAK PAK PAK PAK PAK
ZZSSORRYNNHUMANETTTTTENDERIZE
GUH.
ZZZOOFASTANDEEENNNEVERRRHIT.
NUH!
OH, THAT WASN'T THE MAIN SHOW.
MAKE SURE YOU STAY...

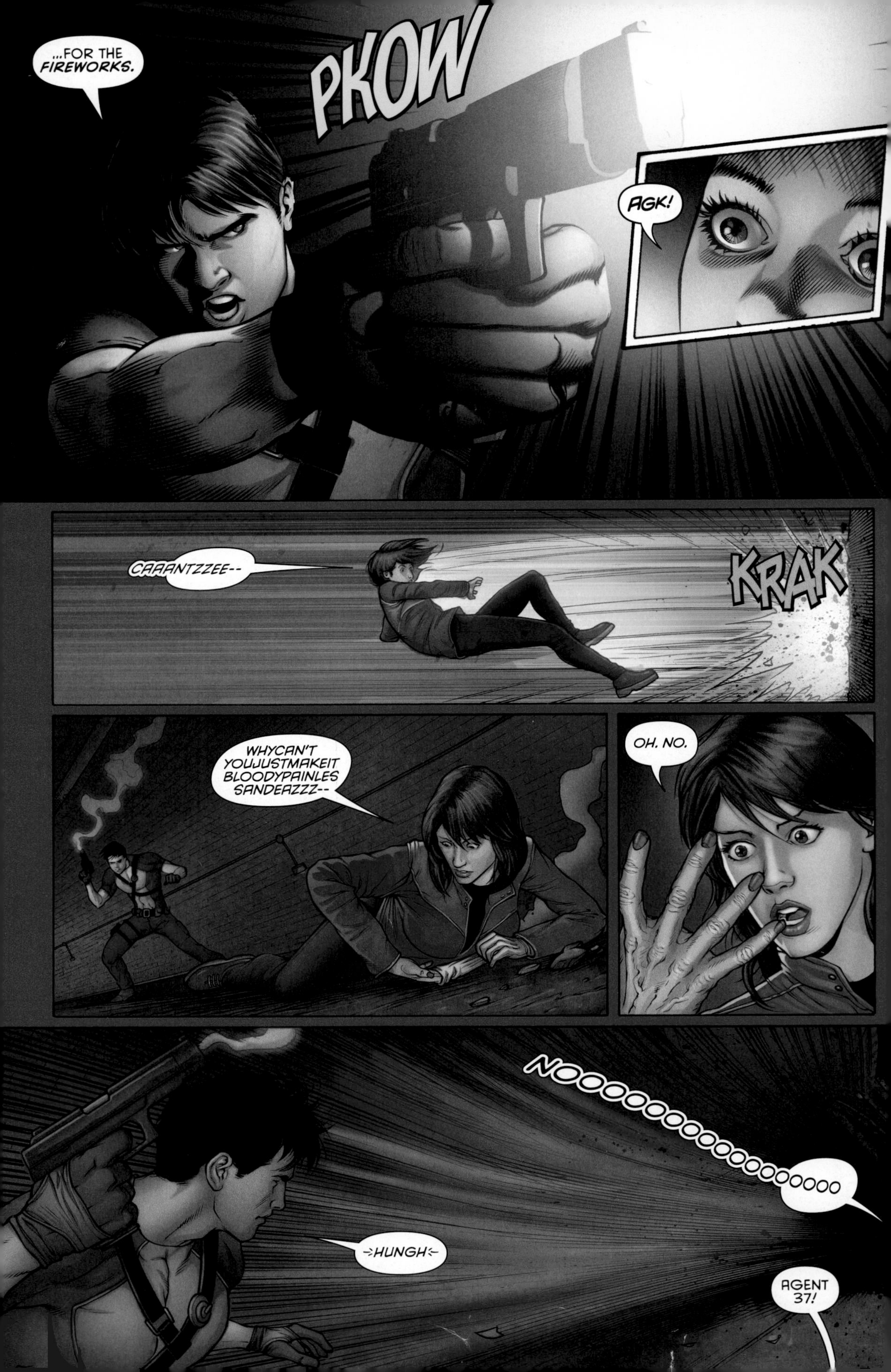
...FOR THE FIREWORKS.
PKOW
AGK!
CAAANTZZZEE--
KRAK
WHYCAN'T YOUJUSTMAKEIT BLOODYPAINLES SANDEAZZZ--
OH. NO.
NOOOOOOOOOOOOOOOOOOO
HUNGH
AGENT 37!

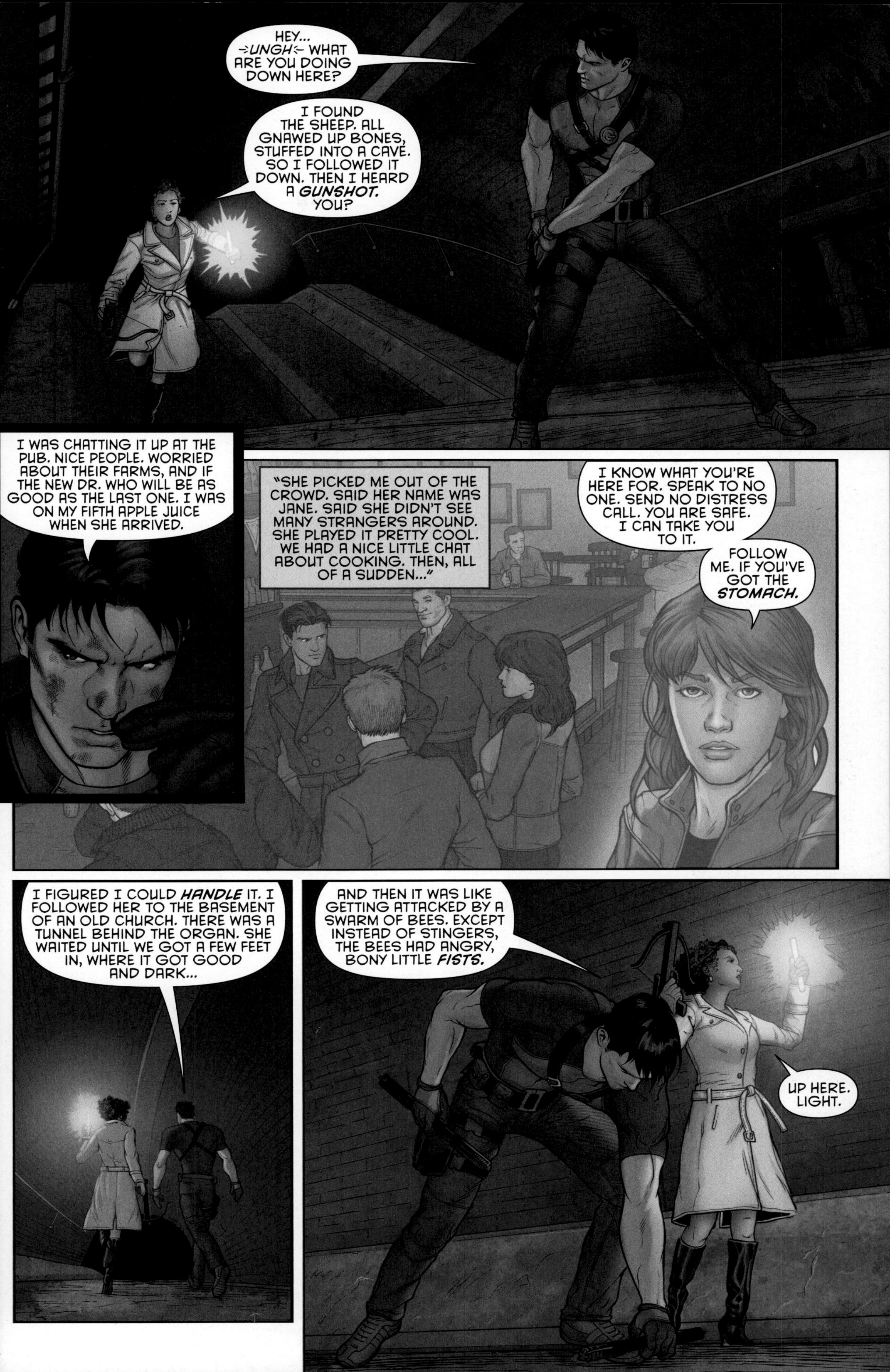

HEY... ⇒UNGH⇐ WHAT ARE YOU DOING DOWN HERE?
I FOUND THE SHEEP. ALL GNAWED UP BONES, STUFFED INTO A CAVE. SO I FOLLOWED IT DOWN. THEN I HEARD A *GUNSHOT.* YOU?
I WAS CHATTING IT UP AT THE PUB. NICE PEOPLE. WORRIED ABOUT THEIR FARMS, AND IF THE NEW DR. WHO WILL BE AS GOOD AS THE LAST ONE. I WAS ON MY FIFTH APPLE JUICE WHEN SHE ARRIVED.
"SHE PICKED ME OUT OF THE CROWD. SAID HER NAME WAS JANE. SAID SHE DIDN'T SEE MANY STRANGERS AROUND. SHE PLAYED IT PRETTY COOL. WE HAD A NICE LITTLE CHAT ABOUT COOKING. THEN, ALL OF A SUDDEN..."
I KNOW WHAT YOU'RE HERE FOR. SPEAK TO NO ONE. SEND NO DISTRESS CALL. YOU ARE SAFE. I CAN TAKE YOU TO IT.
FOLLOW ME. IF YOU'VE GOT THE *STOMACH.*
I FIGURED I COULD *HANDLE* IT. I FOLLOWED HER TO THE BASEMENT OF AN OLD CHURCH. THERE WAS A TUNNEL BEHIND THE ORGAN. SHE WAITED UNTIL WE GOT A FEW FEET IN, WHERE IT GOT GOOD AND DARK...
AND THEN IT WAS LIKE GETTING ATTACKED BY A SWARM OF BEES. EXCEPT INSTEAD OF STINGERS, THE BEES HAD ANGRY, BONY LITTLE *FISTS.*
UP HERE. LIGHT.

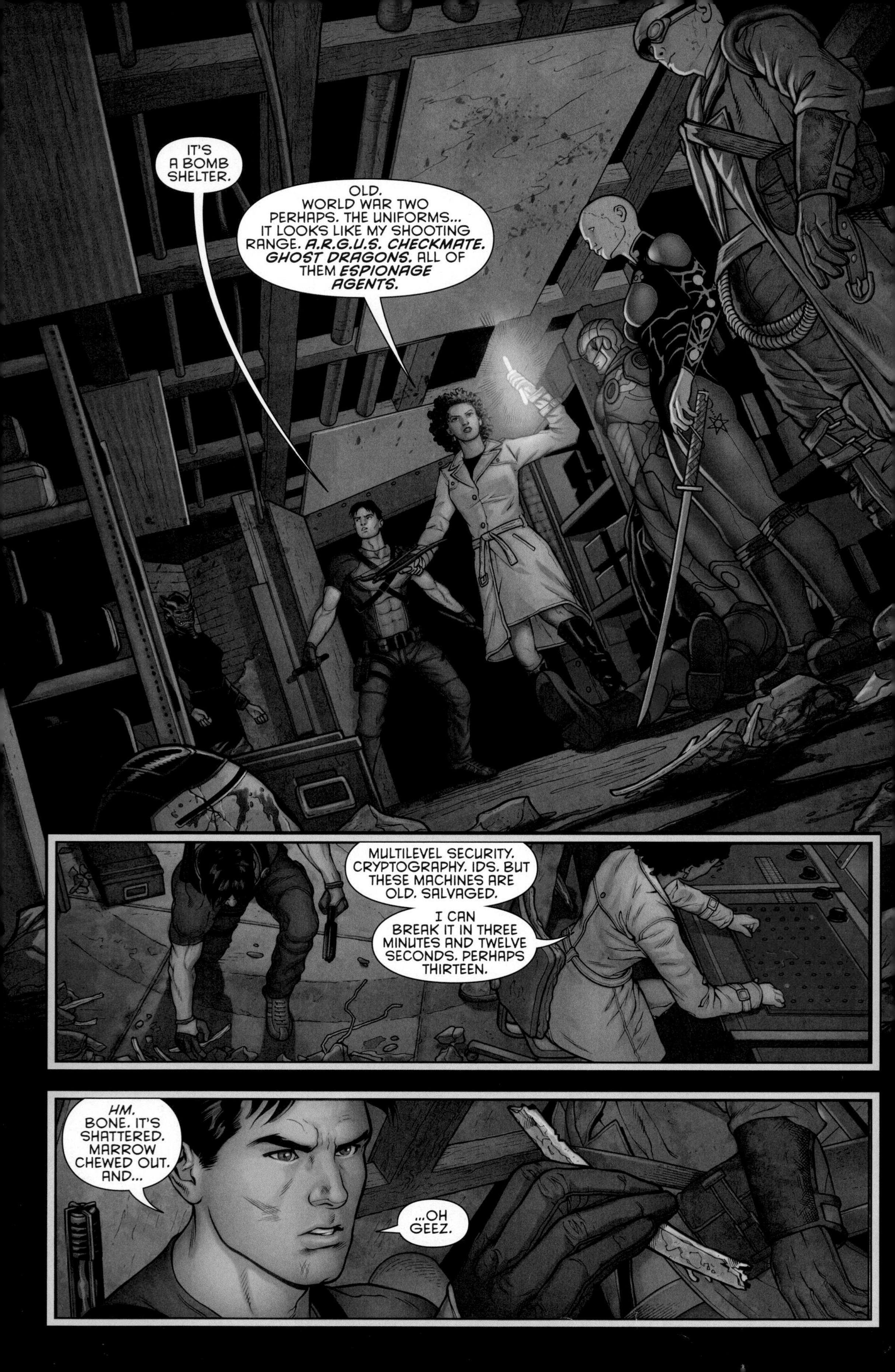
IT'S A BOMB SHELTER.
OLD. WORLD WAR TWO PERHAPS. THE UNIFORMS... IT LOOKS LIKE MY SHOOTING RANGE. *A.R.G.U.S. CHECKMATE. GHOST DRAGONS.* ALL OF THEM *ESPIONAGE AGENTS.*
MULTILEVEL SECURITY. CRYPTOGRAPHY. IDS. BUT THESE MACHINES ARE OLD. SALVAGED.
I CAN BREAK IT IN THREE MINUTES AND TWELVE SECONDS. PERHAPS THIRTEEN.
HM. BONE. IT'S SHATTERED. MARROW CHEWED OUT. AND...
...OH GEEZ.

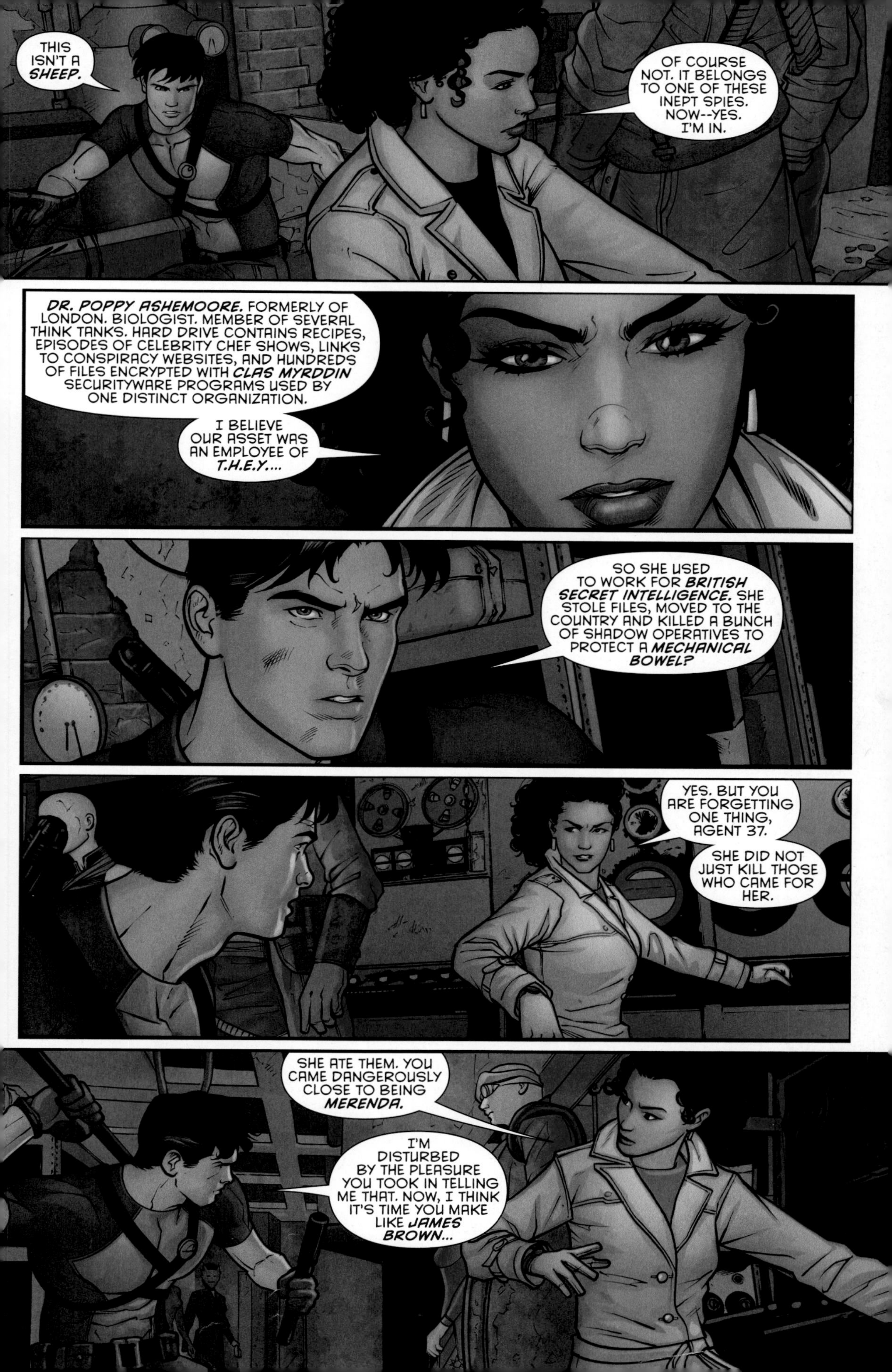
THIS ISN'T A *SHEEP.*
OF COURSE NOT. IT BELONGS TO ONE OF THESE INEPT SPIES. NOW--YES. I'M IN.
DR. POPPY ASHEMOORE. FORMERLY OF LONDON. BIOLOGIST. MEMBER OF SEVERAL THINK TANKS. HARD DRIVE CONTAINS RECIPES, EPISODES OF CELEBRITY CHEF SHOWS, LINKS TO CONSPIRACY WEBSITES, AND HUNDREDS OF FILES ENCRYPTED WITH *CLAS MYRDDIN* SECURITYWARE PROGRAMS USED BY ONE DISTINCT ORGANIZATION.
I BELIEVE OUR ASSET WAS AN EMPLOYEE OF *T.H.E.Y....*
SO SHE USED TO WORK FOR *BRITISH SECRET INTELLIGENCE.* SHE STOLE FILES, MOVED TO THE COUNTRY AND KILLED A BUNCH OF SHADOW OPERATIVES TO PROTECT A *MECHANICAL BOWEL?*
YES. BUT YOU ARE FORGETTING ONE THING, AGENT 37.
SHE DID NOT JUST KILL THOSE WHO CAME FOR HER.
SHE ATE THEM. YOU CAME DANGEROUSLY CLOSE TO BEING *MERENDA.*
I'M DISTURBED BY THE PLEASURE YOU TOOK IN TELLING ME THAT. NOW, I THINK IT'S TIME YOU MAKE LIKE *JAMES BROWN...*

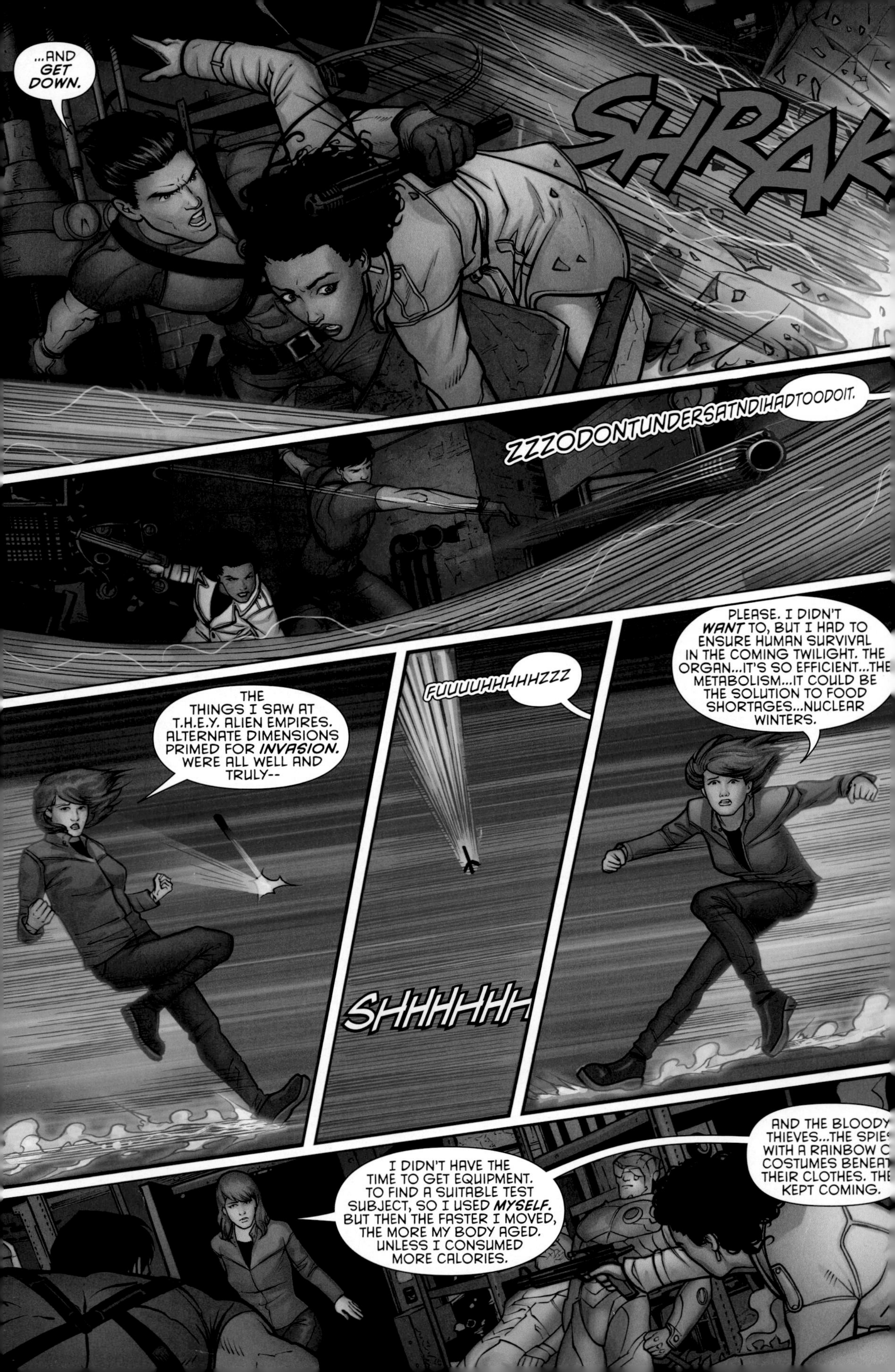

...AND GET DOWN.
SHRAK
ZZZODONTUNDERSATNDIHADTOODOIT.
THE THINGS I SAW AT T.H.E.Y. ALIEN EMPIRES. ALTERNATE DIMENSIONS PRIMED FOR INVASION. WERE ALL WELL AND TRULY--
FUUUUHHHHHZZZ
SHHHHHH
PLEASE. I DIDN'T WANT TO, BUT I HAD TO ENSURE HUMAN SURVIVAL IN THE COMING TWILIGHT. THE ORGAN...IT'S SO EFFICIENT...THE METABOLISM...IT COULD BE THE SOLUTION TO FOOD SHORTAGES...NUCLEAR WINTERS.
I DIDN'T HAVE THE TIME TO GET EQUIPMENT. TO FIND A SUITABLE TEST SUBJECT, SO I USED MYSELF. BUT THEN THE FASTER I MOVED, THE MORE MY BODY AGED. UNLESS I CONSUMED MORE CALORIES.
AND THE BLOODY THIEVES...THE SPIES WITH A RAINBOW OF COSTUMES BENEATH THEIR CLOTHES. THEY KEPT COMING.

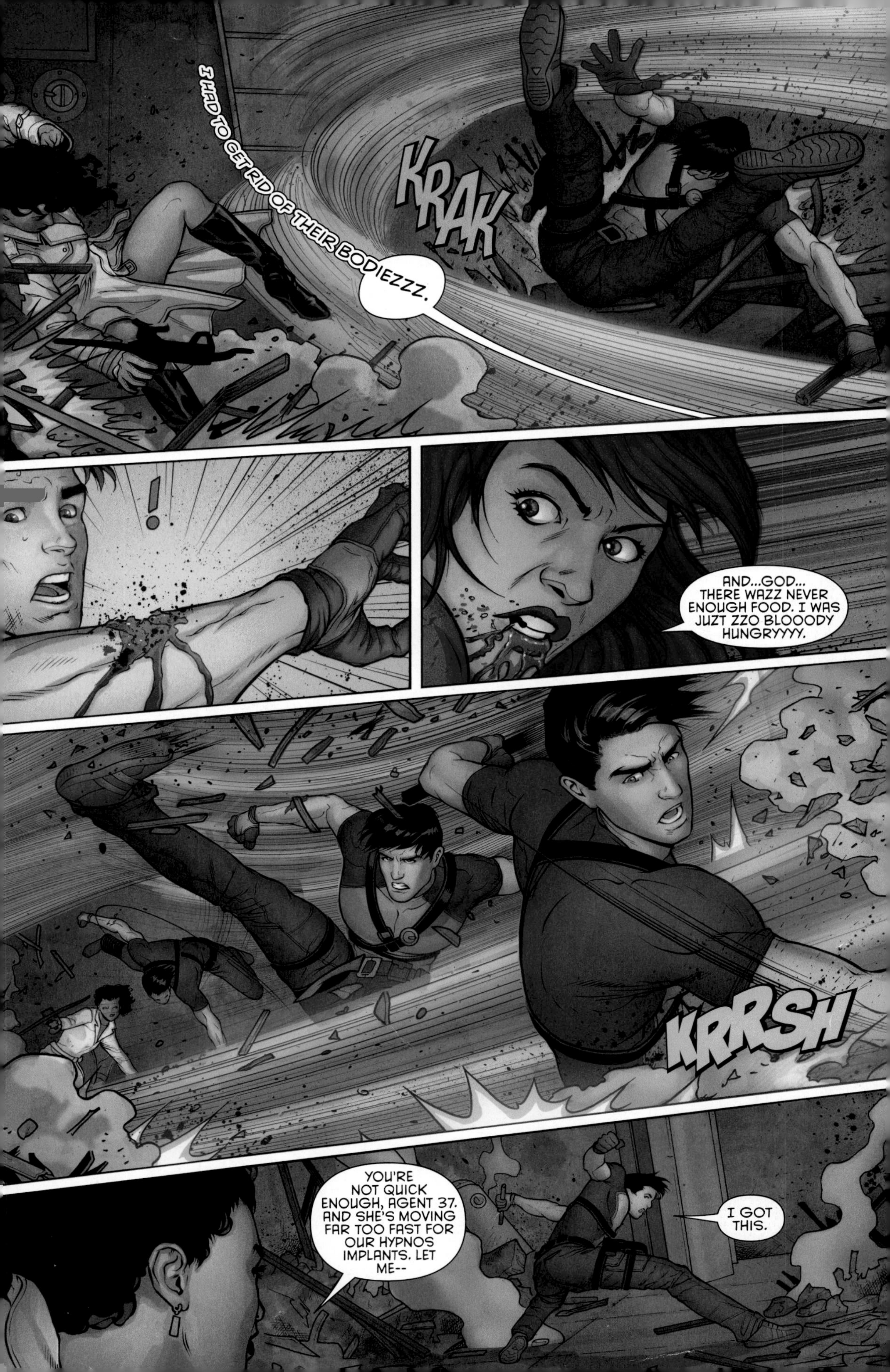
I HAD TO GET RID OF THEIR BODIEZZZ.
KRAK
!
AND...GOD... THERE WAZZ NEVER ENOUGH FOOD. I WAS JUZT ZZO BLOOODY HUNGRYYYY.
KRRSH
YOU'RE NOT QUICK ENOUGH, AGENT 37. AND SHE'S MOVING FAR TOO FAST FOR OUR HYPNOS IMPLANTS. LET ME--
I GOT THIS.

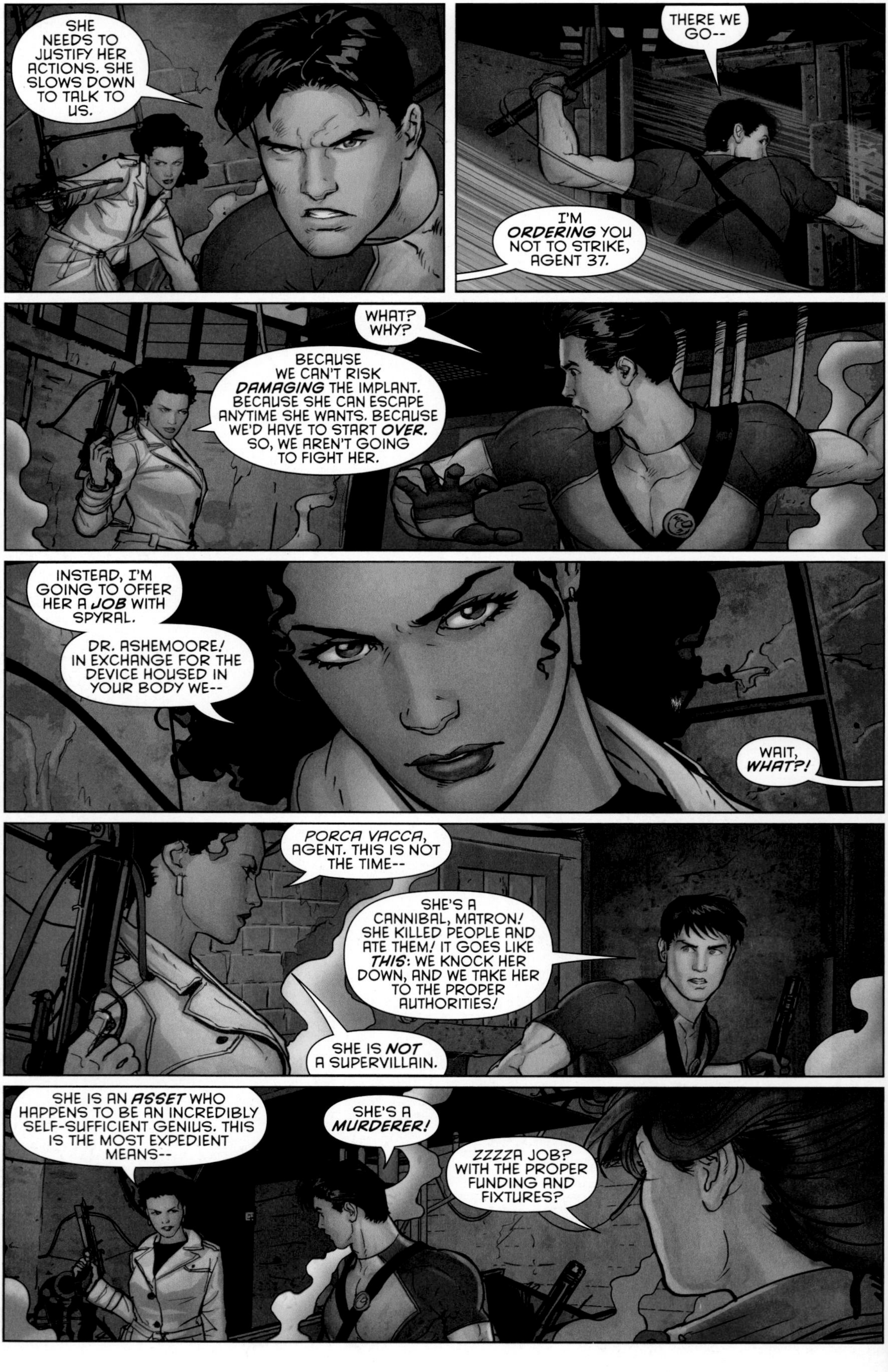
SHE NEEDS TO JUSTIFY HER ACTIONS. SHE SLOWS DOWN TO TALK TO US.
THERE WE GO--
I'M ***ORDERING*** YOU NOT TO STRIKE, AGENT 37.
WHAT? WHY?
BECAUSE WE CAN'T RISK ***DAMAGING*** THE IMPLANT. BECAUSE SHE CAN ESCAPE ANYTIME SHE WANTS. BECAUSE WE'D HAVE TO START ***OVER.*** SO, WE AREN'T GOING TO FIGHT HER.
INSTEAD, I'M GOING TO OFFER HER A ***JOB*** WITH SPYRAL.
DR. ASHEMOORE! IN EXCHANGE FOR THE DEVICE HOUSED IN YOUR BODY WE--
WAIT, ***WHAT?!***
PORCA VACCA, AGENT. THIS IS NOT THE TIME--
SHE'S A CANNIBAL, MATRON! SHE KILLED PEOPLE AND ATE THEM! IT GOES LIKE ***THIS***: WE KNOCK HER DOWN, AND WE TAKE HER TO THE PROPER AUTHORITIES!
SHE IS ***NOT*** A SUPERVILLAIN.
SHE IS AN ***ASSET*** WHO HAPPENS TO BE AN INCREDIBLY SELF-SUFFICIENT GENIUS. THIS IS THE MOST EXPEDIENT MEANS--
SHE'S A ***MURDERER!***
ZZZZA JOB? WITH THE PROPER FUNDING AND FIXTURES?

PAK

COME ON. YOU DIDN'T THINK I'D SEE THAT COMING? I CAN READ YOU.

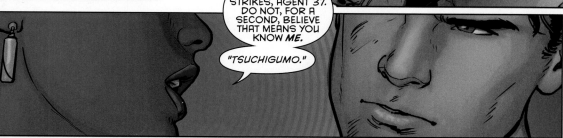

YOU CAN ANTICIPATE MY STRIKES, AGENT 37. DO NOT, FOR A SECOND, BELIEVE THAT MEANS YOU KNOW *ME.*

"TSUCHIGUMO."

SUBLIMINAL POST-HYPNOTIC *SUGGESTION.* CAUSES YOUR *HYPNOS IMPLANTS* TO EMIT A MILD SHOCK TO YOUR BRAIN.

GHK.

I WON'T TELL THE DIRECTOR ABOUT YOUR INDISCRETION THIS TIME.

NOW, DR. ASHEMOORE.

LET'S TALK ABOUT YOUR FUTURE. I ASSUME IT WON'T BE A PROBLEM TO MAKE IT *QUICK?*

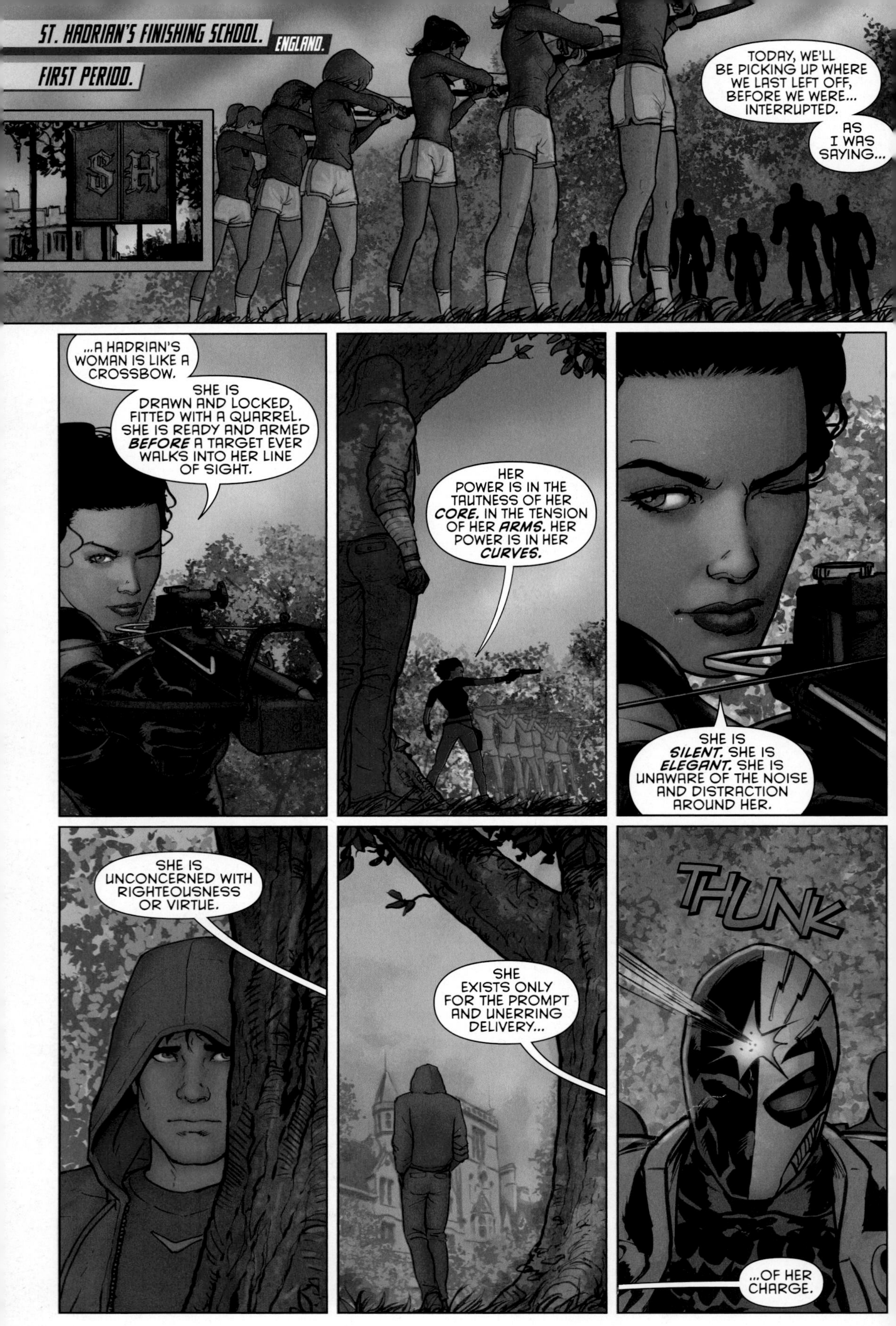
ST. HADRIAN'S FINISHING SCHOOL.
ENGLAND.
FIRST PERIOD.
TODAY, WE'LL BE PICKING UP WHERE WE LAST LEFT OFF, BEFORE WE WERE... INTERRUPTED.
AS I WAS SAYING...
...A HADRIAN'S WOMAN IS LIKE A CROSSBOW.
SHE IS DRAWN AND LOCKED, FITTED WITH A QUARREL. SHE IS READY AND ARMED BEFORE A TARGET EVER WALKS INTO HER LINE OF SIGHT.
HER POWER IS IN THE TAUTNESS OF HER CORE. IN THE TENSION OF HER ARMS. HER POWER IS IN HER CURVES.
SHE IS SILENT. SHE IS ELEGANT. SHE IS UNAWARE OF THE NOISE AND DISTRACTION AROUND HER.
SHE IS UNCONCERNED WITH RIGHTEOUSNESS OR VIRTUE.
SHE EXISTS ONLY FOR THE PROMPT AND UNERRING DELIVERY...
THUNK
...OF HER CHARGE.

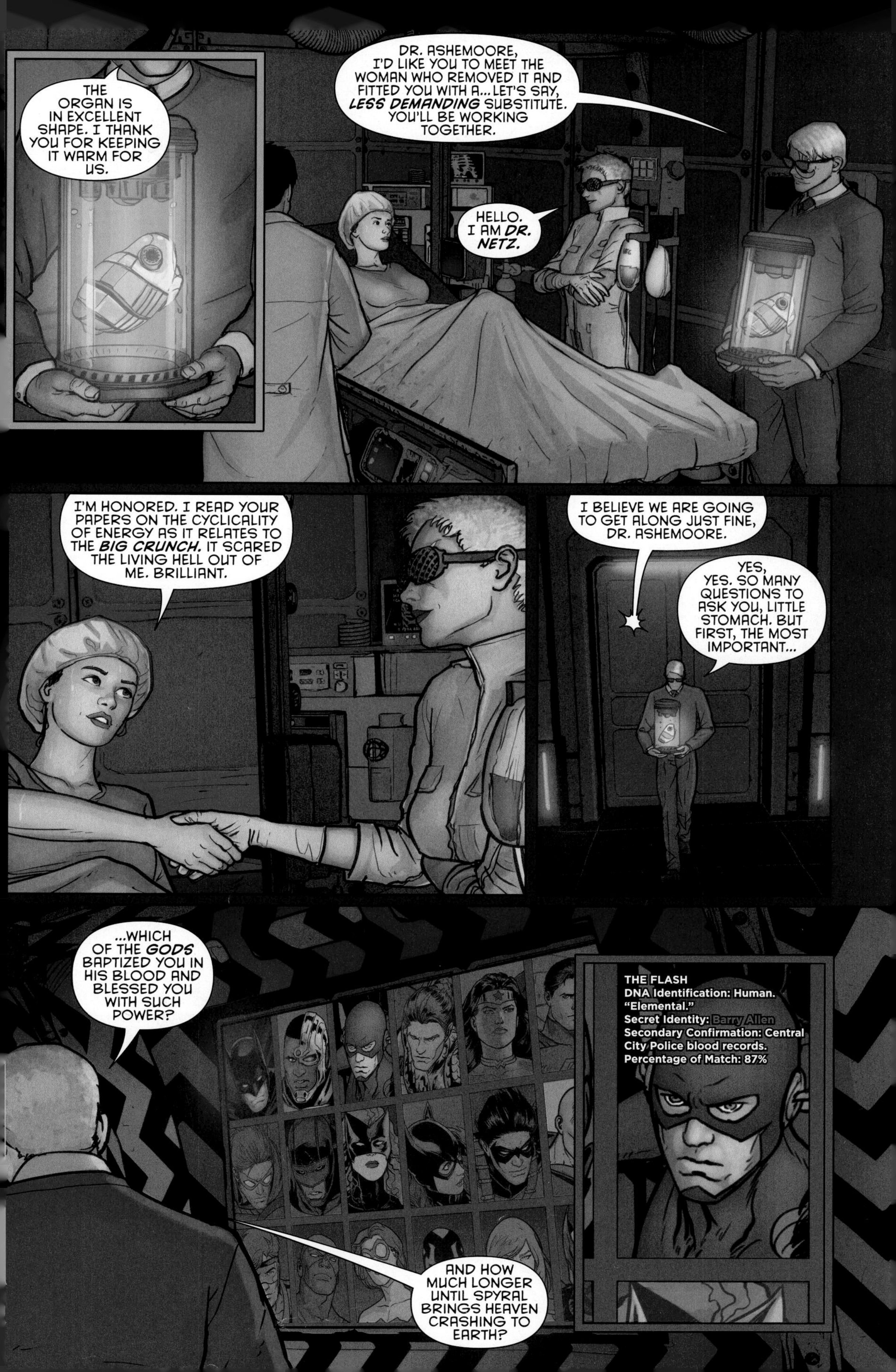
THE ORGAN IS IN EXCELLENT SHAPE. I THANK YOU FOR KEEPING IT WARM FOR US.
DR. ASHEMOORE, I'D LIKE YOU TO MEET THE WOMAN WHO REMOVED IT AND FITTED YOU WITH A...LET'S SAY, LESS DEMANDING SUBSTITUTE. YOU'LL BE WORKING TOGETHER.
HELLO. I AM DR. NETZ.
I'M HONORED. I READ YOUR PAPERS ON THE CYCLICALITY OF ENERGY AS IT RELATES TO THE BIG CRUNCH. IT SCARED THE LIVING HELL OUT OF ME. BRILLIANT.
I BELIEVE WE ARE GOING TO GET ALONG JUST FINE, DR. ASHEMOORE.
YES, YES. SO MANY QUESTIONS TO ASK YOU, LITTLE STOMACH. BUT FIRST, THE MOST IMPORTANT...
...WHICH OF THE GODS BAPTIZED YOU IN HIS BLOOD AND BLESSED YOU WITH SUCH POWER?
THE FLASH
DNA Identification: Human.
"Elemental."
Secret Identity: Barry Allen
Secondary Confirmation: Central City Police blood records.
Percentage of Match: 87%
AND HOW MUCH LONGER UNTIL SPYRAL BRINGS HEAVEN CRASHING TO EARTH?

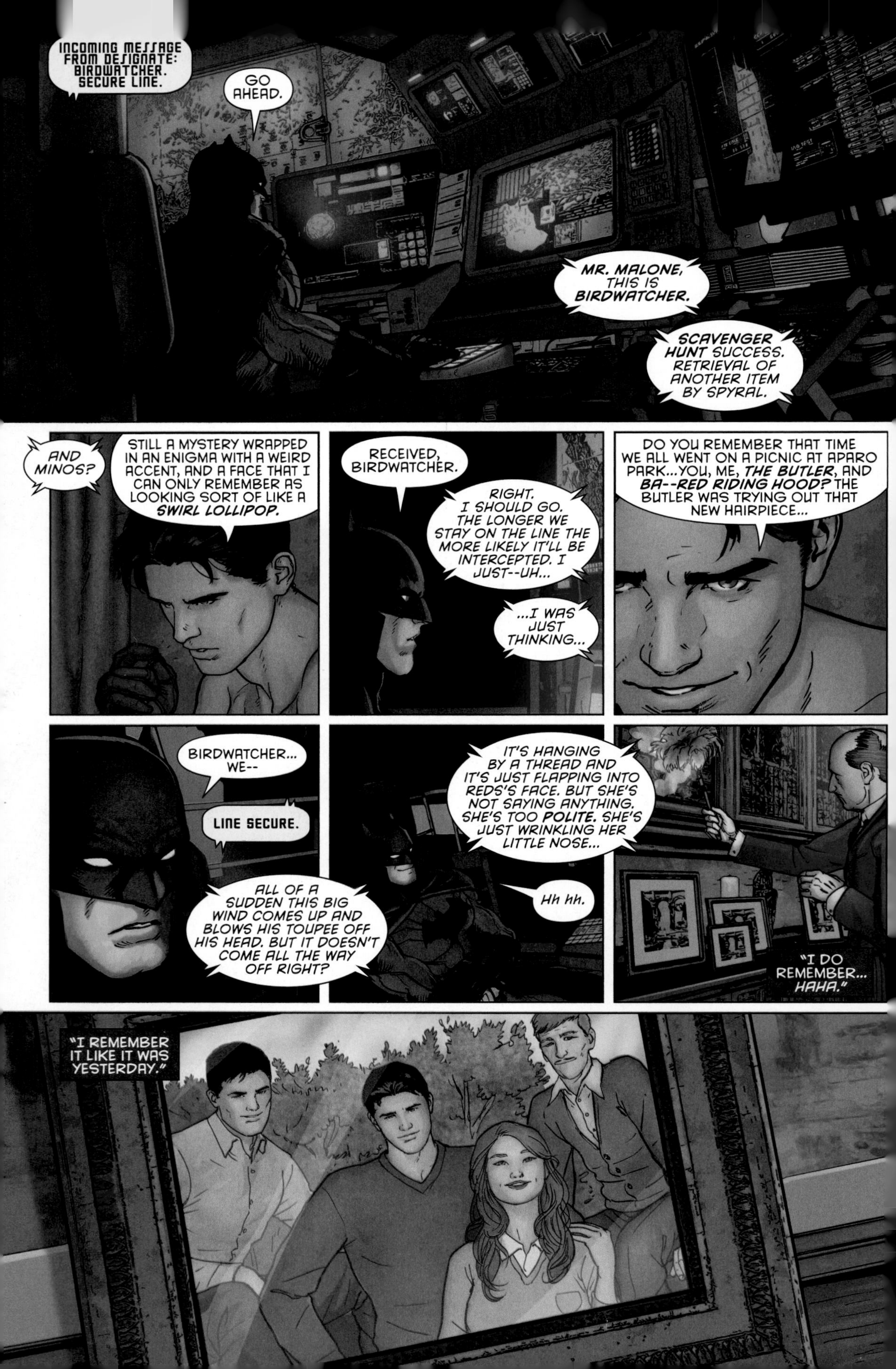
INCOMING MESSAGE FROM DESIGNATE: BIRDWATCHER. SECURE LINE.
GO AHEAD.
MR. MALONE, THIS IS BIRDWATCHER.
SCAVENGER HUNT SUCCESS. RETRIEVAL OF ANOTHER ITEM BY SPYRAL.
AND MINOS?
STILL A MYSTERY WRAPPED IN AN ENIGMA WITH A WEIRD ACCENT, AND A FACE THAT I CAN ONLY REMEMBER AS LOOKING SORT OF LIKE A SWIRL LOLLIPOP.
RECEIVED, BIRDWATCHER.
RIGHT. I SHOULD GO. THE LONGER WE STAY ON THE LINE THE MORE LIKELY IT'LL BE INTERCEPTED. I JUST--UH...
...I WAS JUST THINKING...
DO YOU REMEMBER THAT TIME WE ALL WENT ON A PICNIC AT APARO PARK...YOU, ME, THE BUTLER, AND BA--RED RIDING HOOD? THE BUTLER WAS TRYING OUT THAT NEW HAIRPIECE...
BIRDWATCHER... WE--
LINE SECURE.
ALL OF A SUDDEN THIS BIG WIND COMES UP AND BLOWS HIS TOUPEE OFF HIS HEAD. BUT IT DOESN'T COME ALL THE WAY OFF RIGHT?
IT'S HANGING BY A THREAD AND IT'S JUST FLAPPING INTO REDS'S FACE. BUT SHE'S NOT SAYING ANYTHING. SHE'S TOO POLITE. SHE'S JUST WRINKLING HER LITTLE NOSE...
Hh hh.
"I DO REMEMBER... HAHA."
"I REMEMBER IT LIKE IT WAS YESTERDAY."

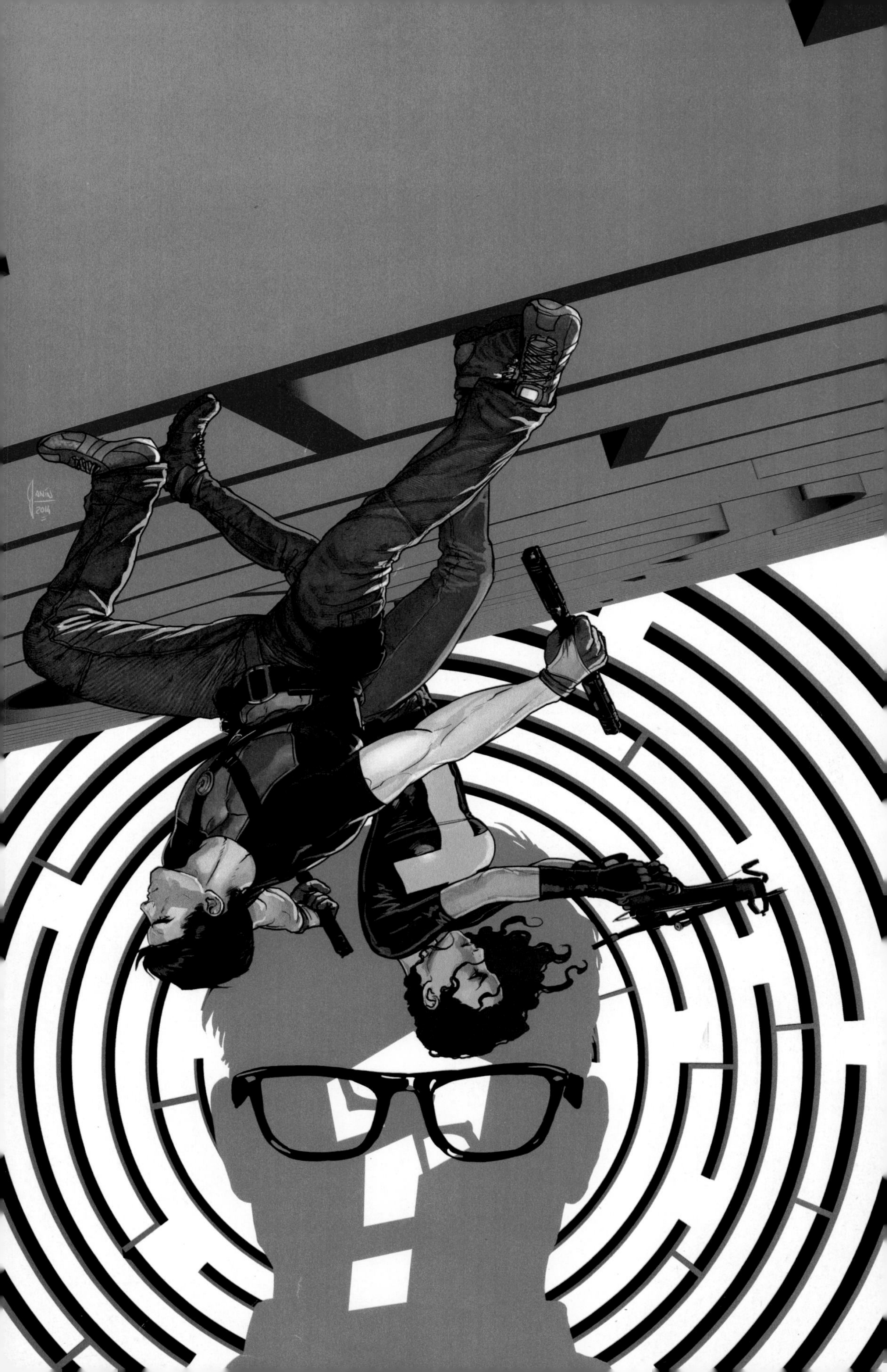

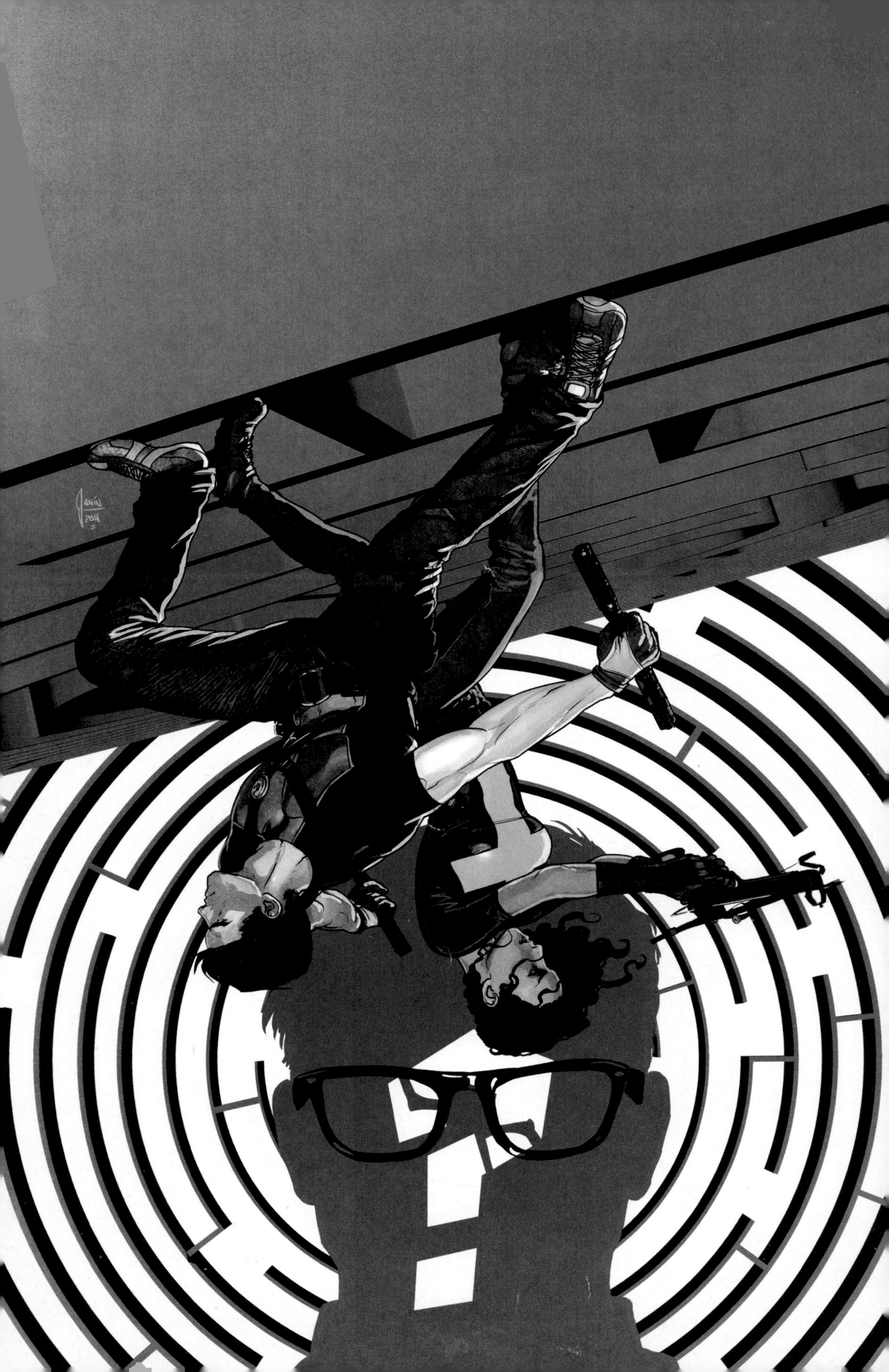

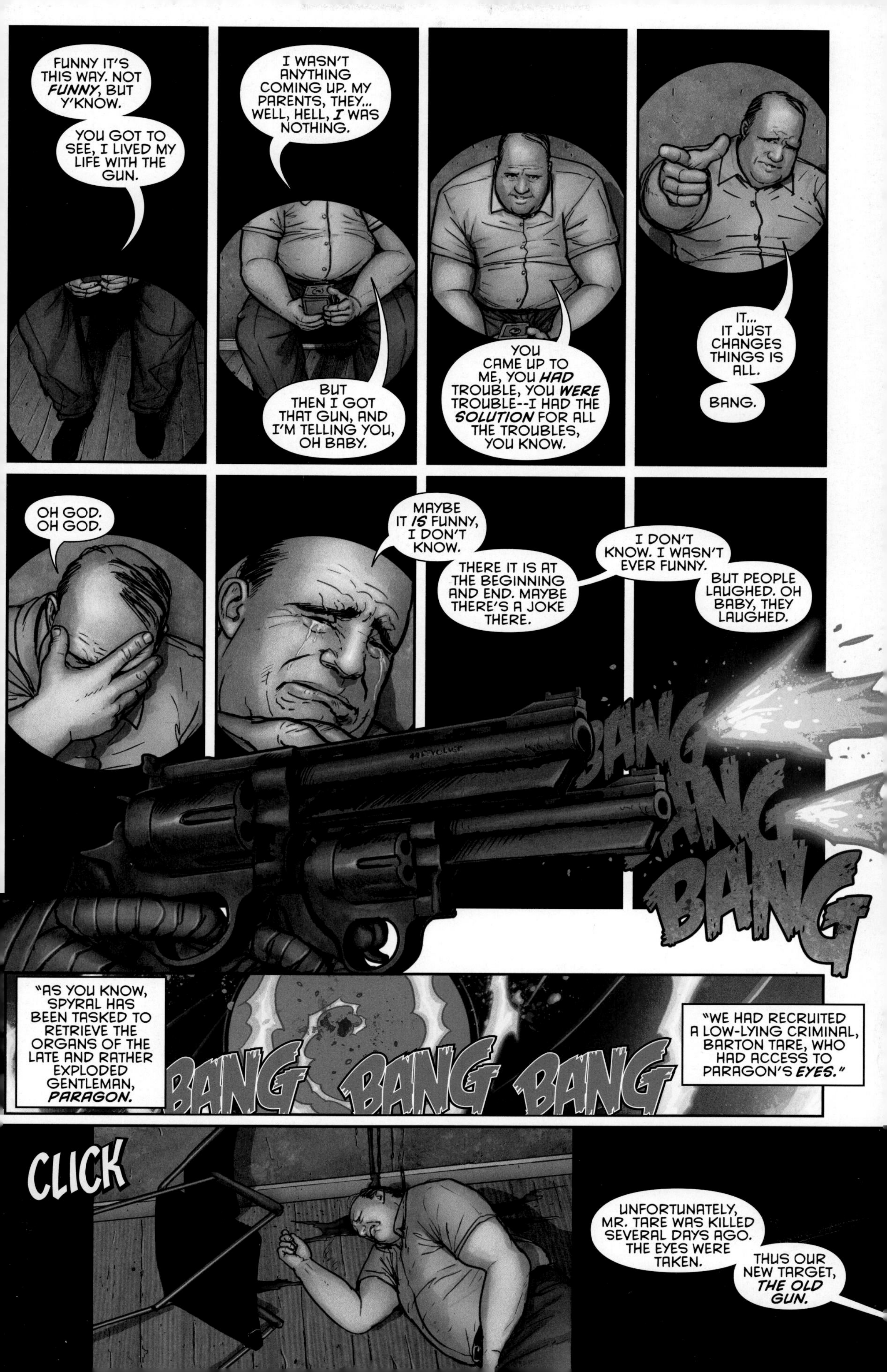
FUNNY IT'S THIS WAY. NOT *FUNNY*, BUT Y'KNOW.
YOU GOT TO SEE, I LIVED MY LIFE WITH THE GUN.
I WASN'T ANYTHING COMING UP. MY PARENTS, THEY... WELL, HELL, *I* WAS NOTHING.
BUT THEN I GOT THAT GUN, AND I'M TELLING YOU, OH BABY.
YOU CAME UP TO ME, YOU *HAD* TROUBLE, YOU *WERE* TROUBLE--I HAD THE *SOLUTION* FOR ALL THE TROUBLES, YOU KNOW.
IT... IT JUST CHANGES THINGS IS ALL.
BANG.
OH GOD. OH GOD.
MAYBE IT *IS* FUNNY, I DON'T KNOW.
THERE IT IS AT THE BEGINNING AND END. MAYBE THERE'S A JOKE THERE.
I DON'T KNOW. I WASN'T EVER FUNNY.
BUT PEOPLE LAUGHED. OH BABY, THEY LAUGHED.
BANG
BANG
BANG
"AS YOU KNOW, SPYRAL HAS BEEN TASKED TO RETRIEVE THE ORGANS OF THE LATE AND RATHER EXPLODED GENTLEMAN, *PARAGON*.
BANG BANG BANG
"WE HAD RECRUITED A LOW-LYING CRIMINAL, BARTON TARE, WHO HAD ACCESS TO PARAGON'S *EYES*."
CLICK
UNFORTUNATELY, MR. TARE WAS KILLED SEVERAL DAYS AGO. THE EYES WERE TAKEN.
THUS OUR NEW TARGET, *THE OLD GUN*.

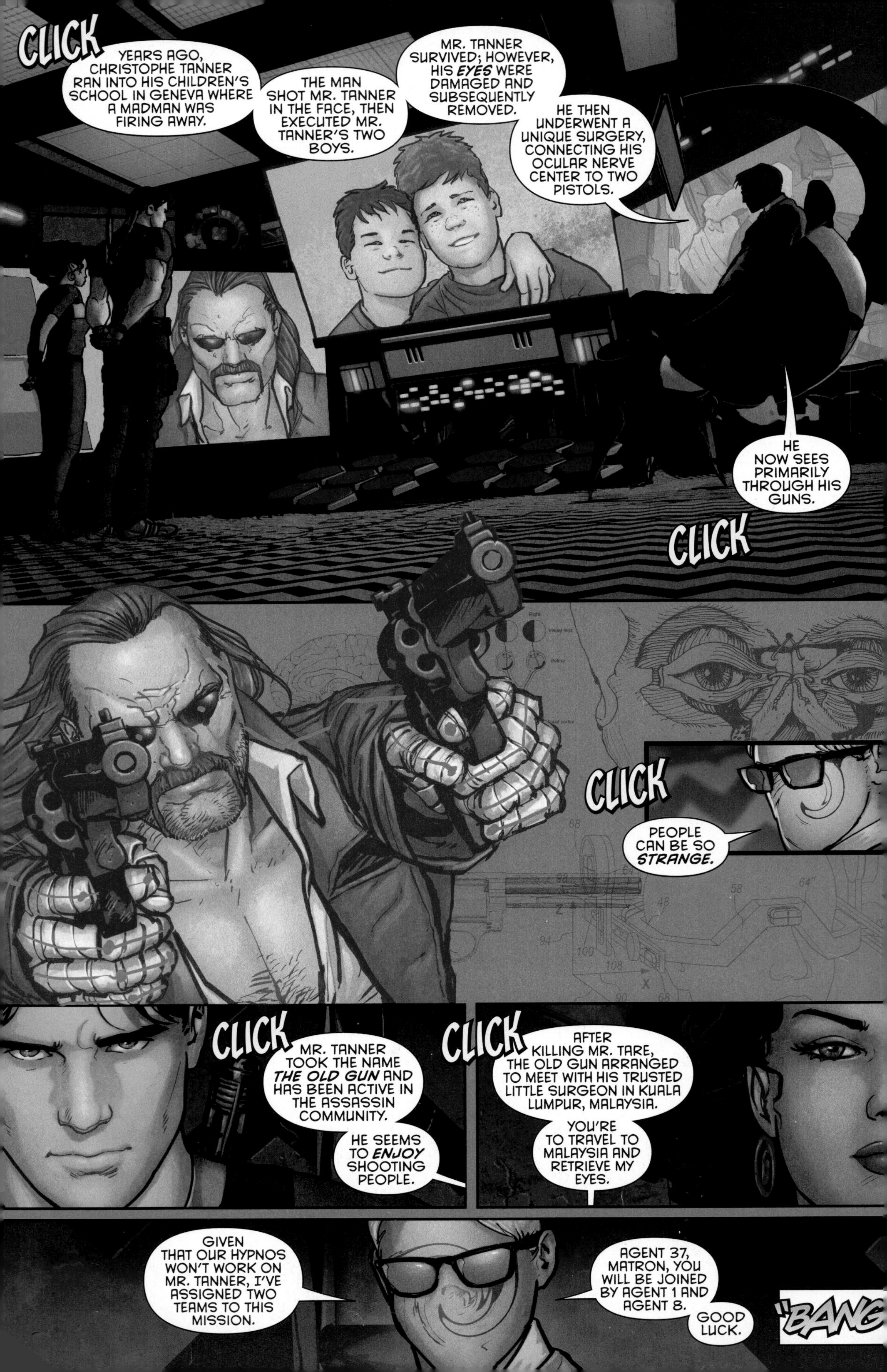
CLICK
YEARS AGO, CHRISTOPHE TANNER RAN INTO HIS CHILDREN'S SCHOOL IN GENEVA WHERE A MADMAN WAS FIRING AWAY.
THE MAN SHOT MR. TANNER IN THE FACE, THEN EXECUTED MR. TANNER'S TWO BOYS.
MR. TANNER SURVIVED; HOWEVER, HIS EYES WERE DAMAGED AND SUBSEQUENTLY REMOVED.
HE THEN UNDERWENT A UNIQUE SURGERY, CONNECTING HIS OCULAR NERVE CENTER TO TWO PISTOLS.
HE NOW SEES PRIMARILY THROUGH HIS GUNS.
CLICK
CLICK
PEOPLE CAN BE SO STRANGE.
CLICK
MR. TANNER TOOK THE NAME THE OLD GUN AND HAS BEEN ACTIVE IN THE ASSASSIN COMMUNITY.
HE SEEMS TO ENJOY SHOOTING PEOPLE.
CLICK
AFTER KILLING MR. TARE, THE OLD GUN ARRANGED TO MEET WITH HIS TRUSTED LITTLE SURGEON IN KUALA LUMPUR, MALAYSIA.
YOU'RE TO TRAVEL TO MALAYSIA AND RETRIEVE MY EYES.
GIVEN THAT OUR HYPNOS WON'T WORK ON MR. TANNER, I'VE ASSIGNED TWO TEAMS TO THIS MISSION.
AGENT 37, MATRON, YOU WILL BE JOINED BY AGENT 1 AND AGENT 8.
GOOD LUCK.
BANG

BANG

BANG BANG

REALLY? THIS IS HOW THE GREAT WING-KNIGHT SHOOTS?

I SEE WHY MR. MINOS HAS *AGENT 1* AND ME BAILING YOU OUT ON THIS MISSION.

NIGHTWING.

AND YOU SHOULD SEE ME WITH A SLINGSHOT, AGENT 8.

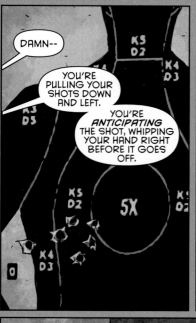

DAMN--

YOU'RE PULLING YOUR SHOTS DOWN AND LEFT.

YOU'RE *ANTICIPATING* THE SHOT, WHIPPING YOUR HAND RIGHT BEFORE IT GOES OFF.

5X

YOU JUST NEED SOME FINGER DISCIPLINE.

STOP THINKING ABOUT THE *GUN*.

START THINKING ABOUT THE *TARGET*.

FOCUS ON THE BACK SITES. THEN PUT YOUR FRONT SITE BETWEEN THEM.

GO SLOW. LINE IT UP. GLIDE IT IN.

NOW, YOU'RE READY. BUT REMEMBER, DON'T ANTICIPATE THE EXPLOSION. *CAUSE* THE EXPLOSION.

CAN YOU DO THAT, WING-KNIGHT? CAN YOU DO THAT FOR ME?

THAT'S NOT MY NAME.

MY NAME IS...

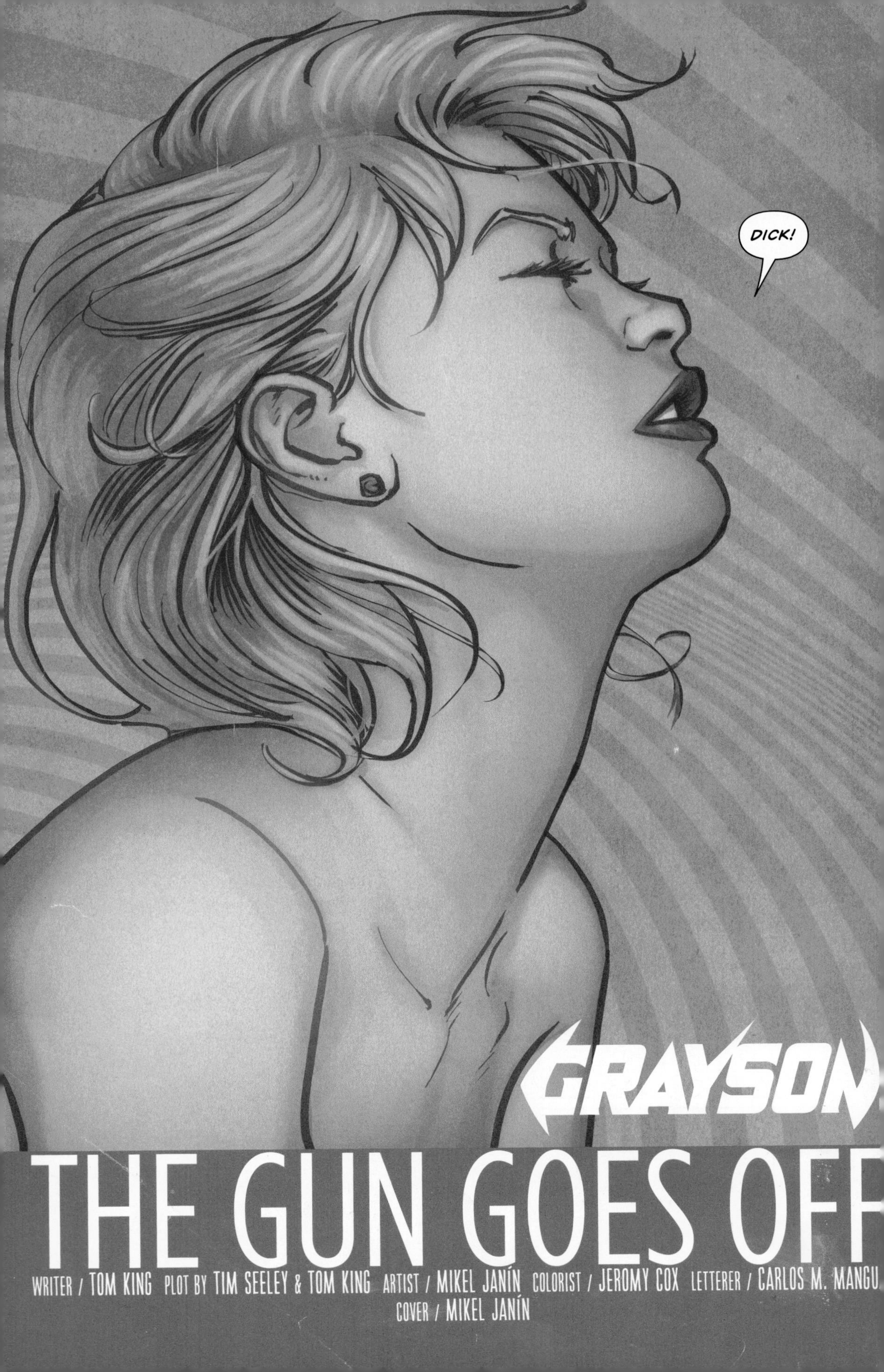
DICK!
GRAYSON
THE GUN GOES OFF
WRITER / TOM KING PLOT BY TIM SEELEY & TOM KING ARTIST / MIKEL JANÍN COLORIST / JEROMY COX LETTERER / CARLOS M. MANGU
COVER / MIKEL JANÍN

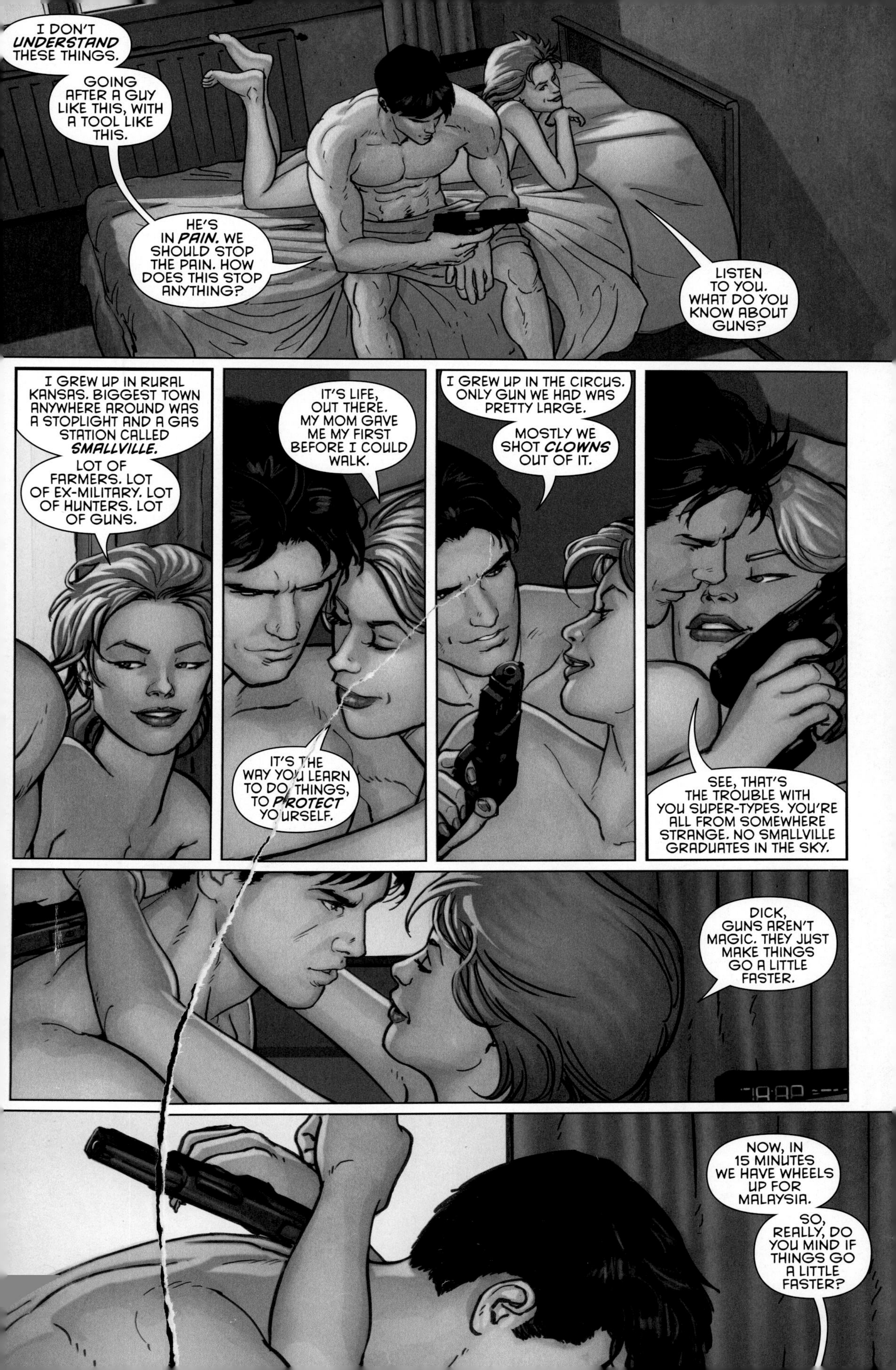
I DON'T *UNDERSTAND* THESE THINGS.
GOING AFTER A GUY LIKE THIS, WITH A TOOL LIKE THIS.
HE'S IN *PAIN.* WE SHOULD STOP THE PAIN. HOW DOES THIS STOP ANYTHING?
LISTEN TO YOU. WHAT DO YOU KNOW ABOUT GUNS?
I GREW UP IN RURAL KANSAS. BIGGEST TOWN ANYWHERE AROUND WAS A STOPLIGHT AND A GAS STATION CALLED *SMALLVILLE.*
LOT OF FARMERS. LOT OF EX-MILITARY. LOT OF HUNTERS. LOT OF GUNS.
IT'S LIFE, OUT THERE. MY MOM GAVE ME MY FIRST BEFORE I COULD WALK.
IT'S THE WAY YOU LEARN TO DO THINGS, TO *PROTECT* YOURSELF.
I GREW UP IN THE CIRCUS. ONLY GUN WE HAD WAS PRETTY LARGE.
MOSTLY WE SHOT *CLOWNS* OUT OF IT.
SEE, THAT'S THE TROUBLE WITH YOU SUPER-TYPES. YOU'RE ALL FROM SOMEWHERE STRANGE. NO SMALLVILLE GRADUATES IN THE SKY.
DICK, GUNS AREN'T MAGIC. THEY JUST MAKE THINGS GO A LITTLE FASTER.
NOW, IN 15 MINUTES WE HAVE WHEELS UP FOR MALAYSIA.
SO, REALLY, DO YOU MIND IF THINGS GO A LITTLE FASTER?

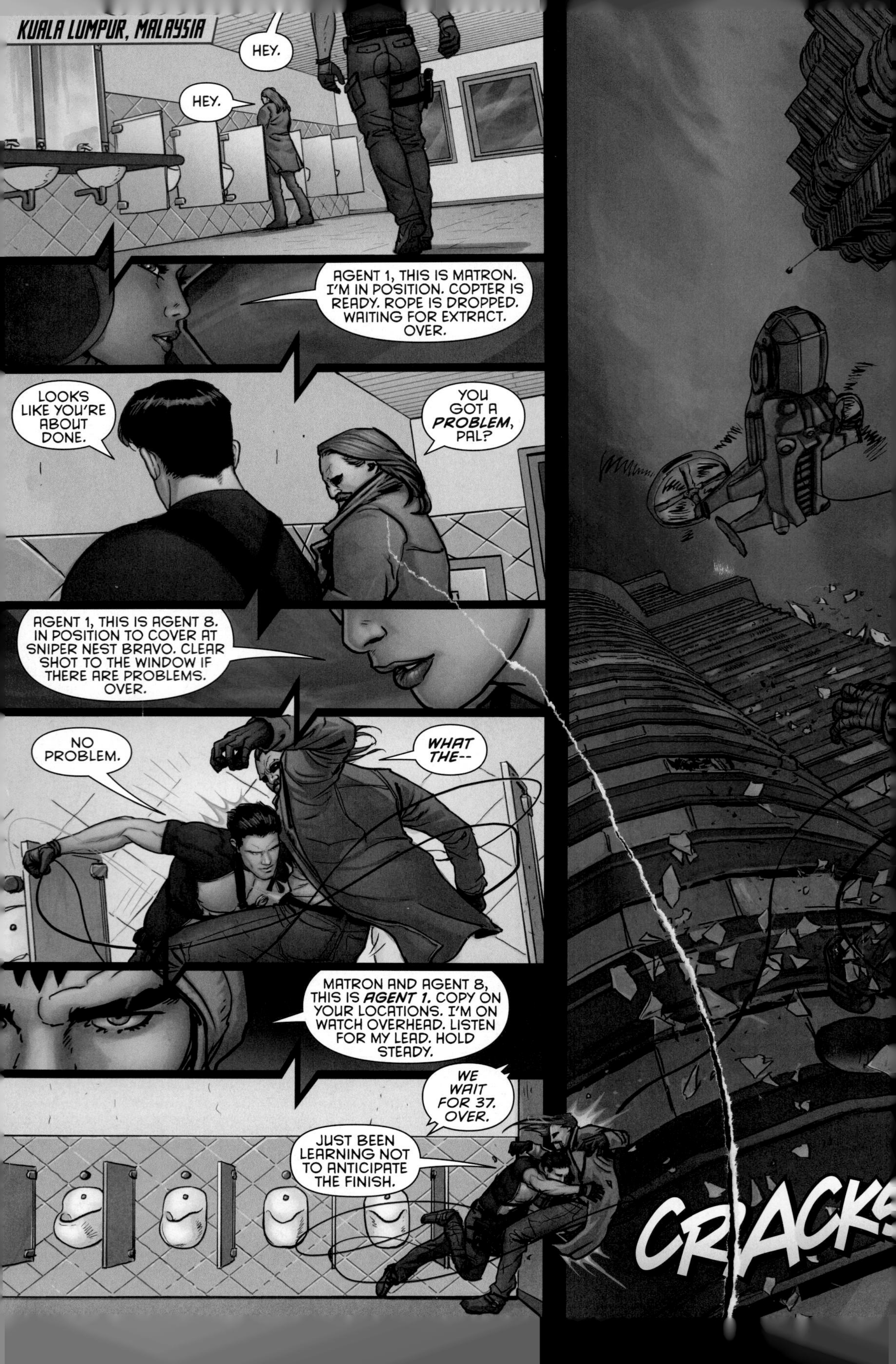
KUALA LUMPUR, MALAYSIA
HEY.
HEY.
AGENT 1, THIS IS MATRON. I'M IN POSITION. COPTER IS READY. ROPE IS DROPPED. WAITING FOR EXTRACT. OVER.
LOOKS LIKE YOU'RE ABOUT DONE.
YOU GOT A *PROBLEM*, PAL?
AGENT 1, THIS IS AGENT 8. IN POSITION TO COVER AT SNIPER NEST BRAVO. CLEAR SHOT TO THE WINDOW IF THERE ARE PROBLEMS. OVER.
NO PROBLEM.
WHAT THE--
MATRON AND AGENT 8, THIS IS *AGENT 1.* COPY ON YOUR LOCATIONS. I'M ON WATCH OVERHEAD. LISTEN FOR MY LEAD. HOLD STEADY.
WE WAIT FOR 37. OVER.
JUST BEEN LEARNING NOT TO ANTICIPATE THE FINISH.
CRACKS

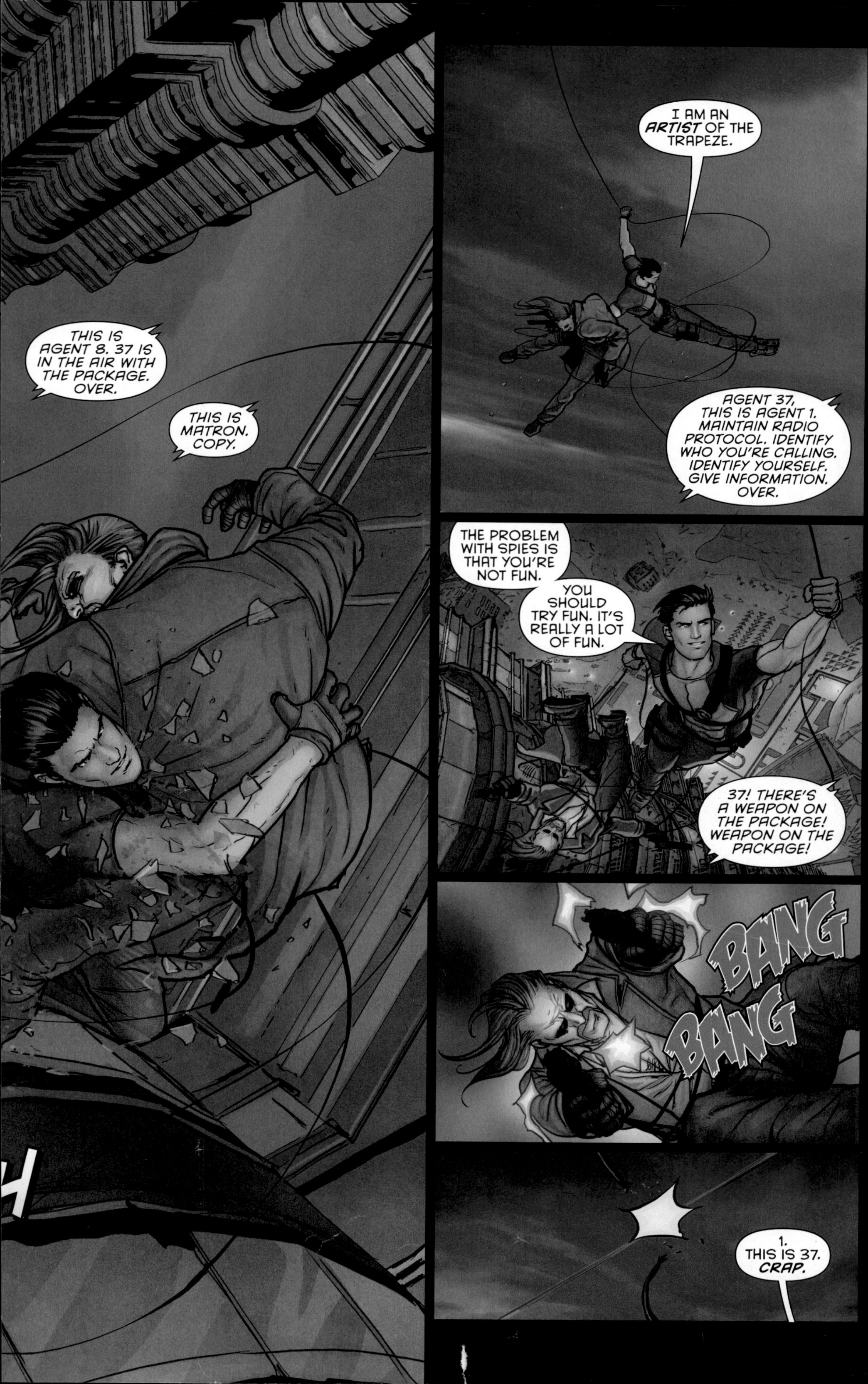
THIS IS AGENT 8. 37 IS IN THE AIR WITH THE PACKAGE. OVER.
THIS IS MATRON. COPY.
I AM AN *ARTIST* OF THE TRAPEZE.
AGENT 37, THIS IS AGENT 1. MAINTAIN RADIO PROTOCOL. IDENTIFY WHO YOU'RE CALLING. IDENTIFY YOURSELF. GIVE INFORMATION. OVER.
THE PROBLEM WITH SPIES IS THAT YOU'RE NOT FUN.
YOU SHOULD TRY FUN. IT'S REALLY A LOT OF FUN.
37! THERE'S A WEAPON ON THE PACKAGE! WEAPON ON THE PACKAGE!
BANG
BANG
1. THIS IS 37. *CRAP.*

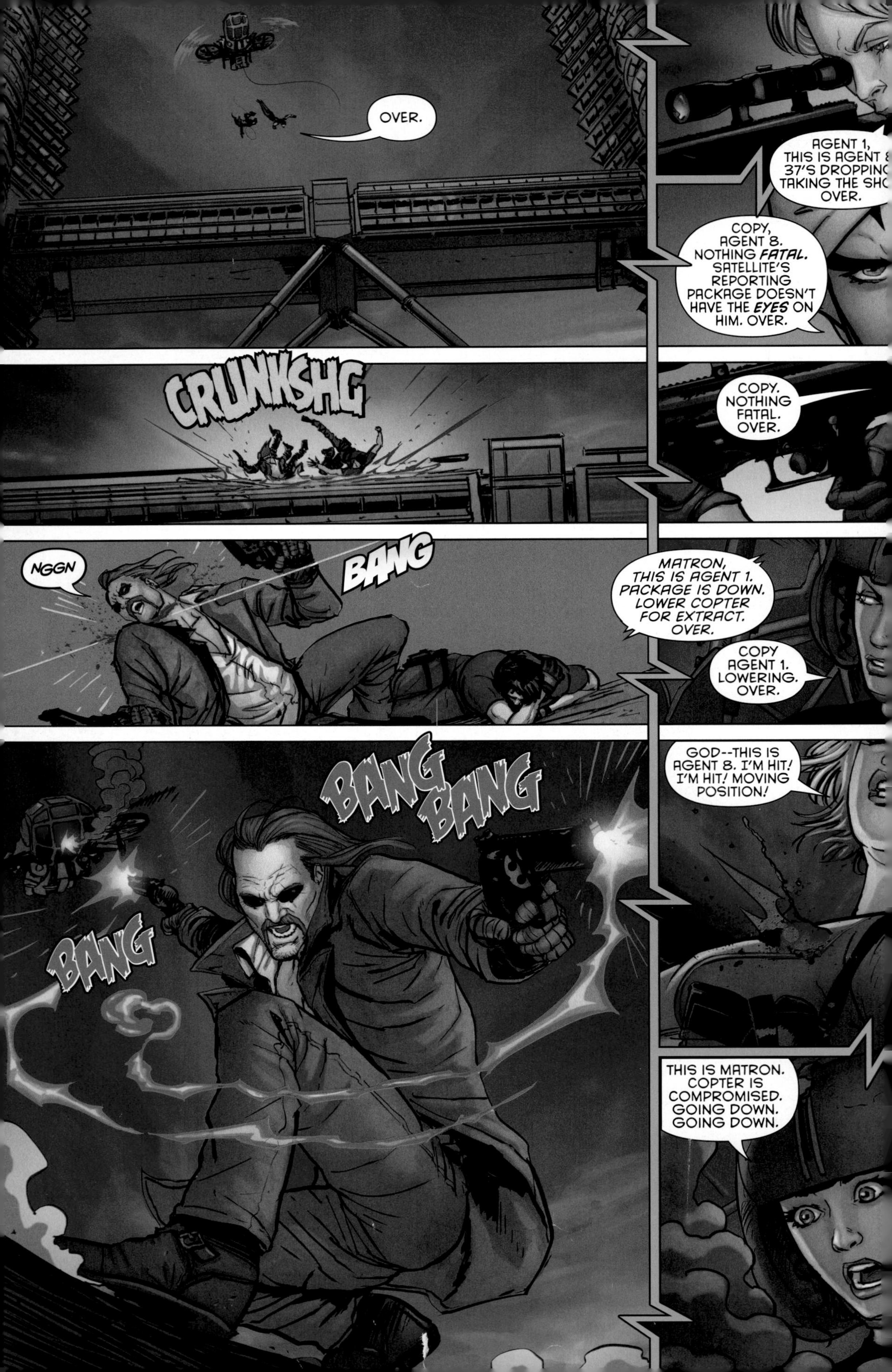
OVER.
AGENT 1, THIS IS AGENT 8 37'S DROPPING TAKING THE SHO OVER.
COPY, AGENT 8. NOTHING *FATAL.* SATELLITE'S REPORTING PACKAGE DOESN'T HAVE THE *EYES* ON HIM. OVER.
CRUNKSHG
COPY. NOTHING FATAL. OVER.
NGGN
BANG
MATRON, THIS IS AGENT 1. PACKAGE IS DOWN. LOWER COPTER FOR EXTRACT. OVER.
COPY AGENT 1. LOWERING. OVER.
BANG BANG
BANG
GOD--THIS IS AGENT 8. I'M HIT! I'M HIT! MOVING POSITION!
THIS IS MATRON. COPTER IS COMPROMISED. GOING DOWN. GOING DOWN.

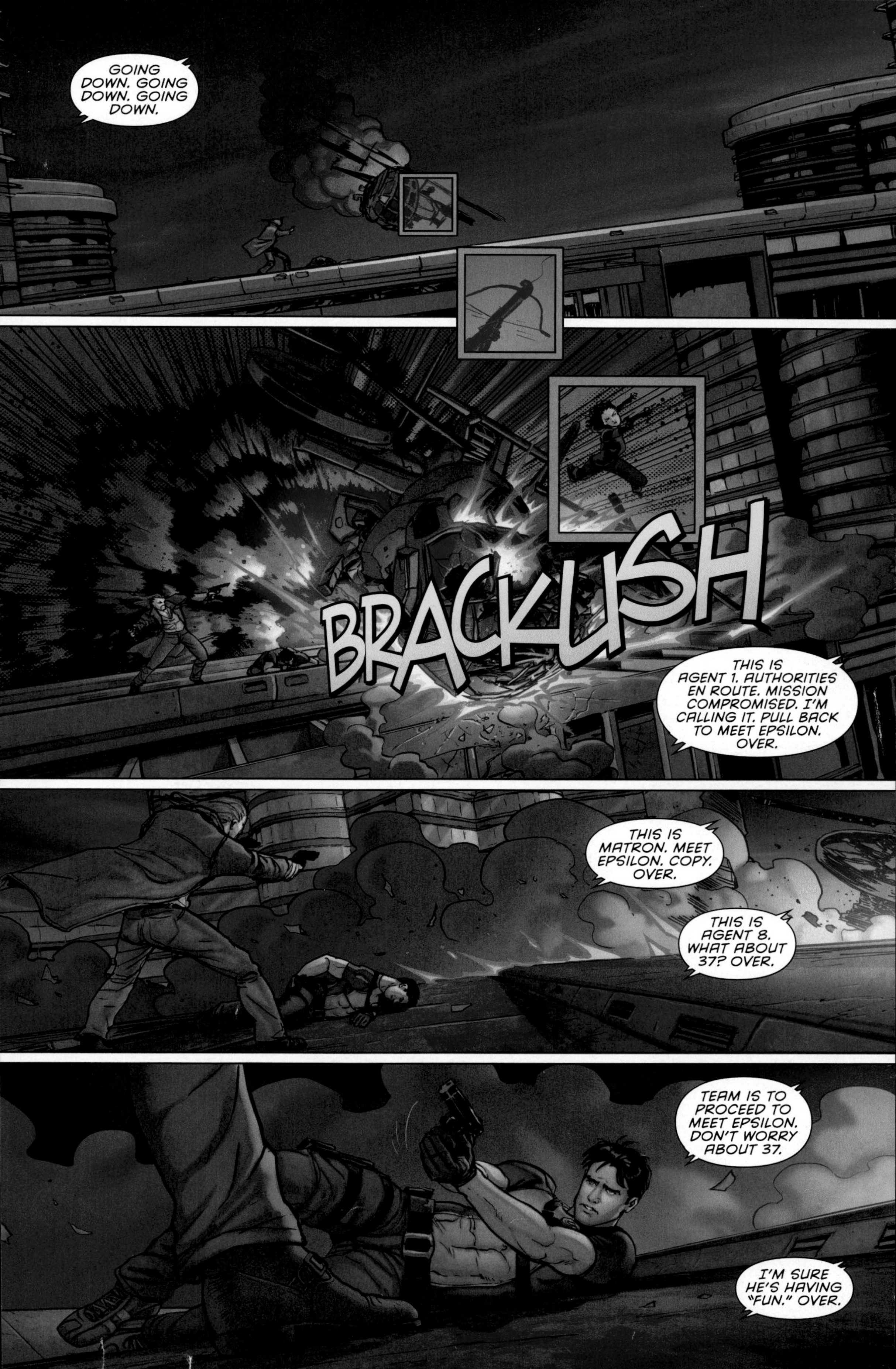
GOING DOWN. GOING DOWN. GOING DOWN.
BRACKUSH
THIS IS AGENT 1. AUTHORITIES EN ROUTE. MISSION COMPROMISED. I'M CALLING IT. PULL BACK TO MEET EPSILON. OVER.
THIS IS MATRON. MEET EPSILON. COPY. OVER.
THIS IS AGENT 8. WHAT ABOUT 37? OVER.
TEAM IS TO PROCEED TO MEET EPSILON. DON'T WORRY ABOUT 37.
I'M SURE HE'S HAVING "FUN." OVER.

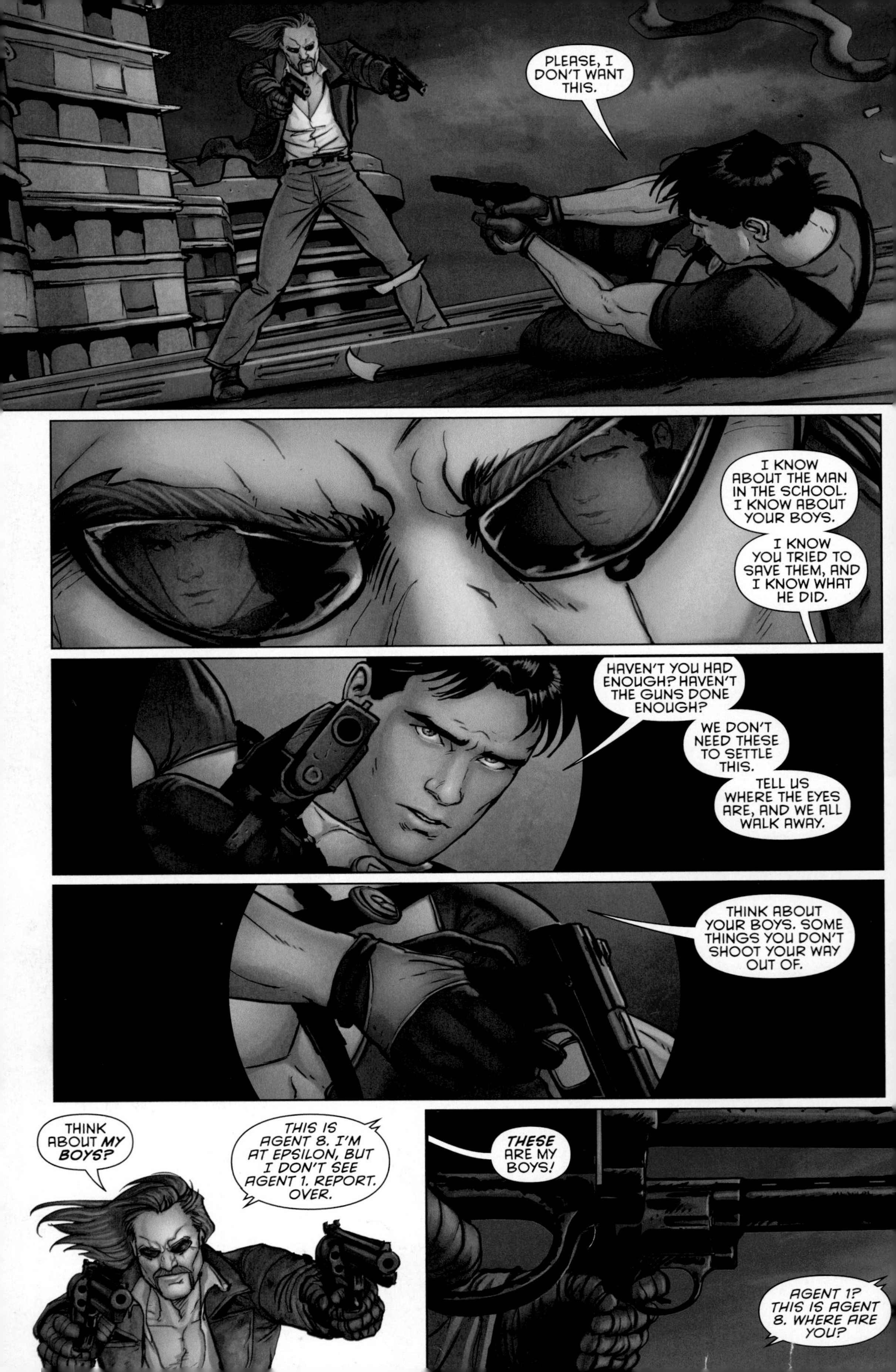
PLEASE, I DON'T WANT THIS.
I KNOW ABOUT THE MAN IN THE SCHOOL. I KNOW ABOUT YOUR BOYS.
I KNOW YOU TRIED TO SAVE THEM, AND I KNOW WHAT HE DID.
HAVEN'T YOU HAD ENOUGH? HAVEN'T THE GUNS DONE ENOUGH?
WE DON'T NEED THESE TO SETTLE THIS.
TELL US WHERE THE EYES ARE, AND WE ALL WALK AWAY.
THINK ABOUT YOUR BOYS. SOME THINGS YOU DON'T SHOOT YOUR WAY OUT OF.
THINK ABOUT *MY* BOYS?
THIS IS AGENT 8. I'M AT EPSILON, BUT I DON'T SEE AGENT 1. REPORT. OVER.
THESE ARE MY BOYS!
AGENT 1? THIS IS AGENT 8. WHERE ARE YOU?

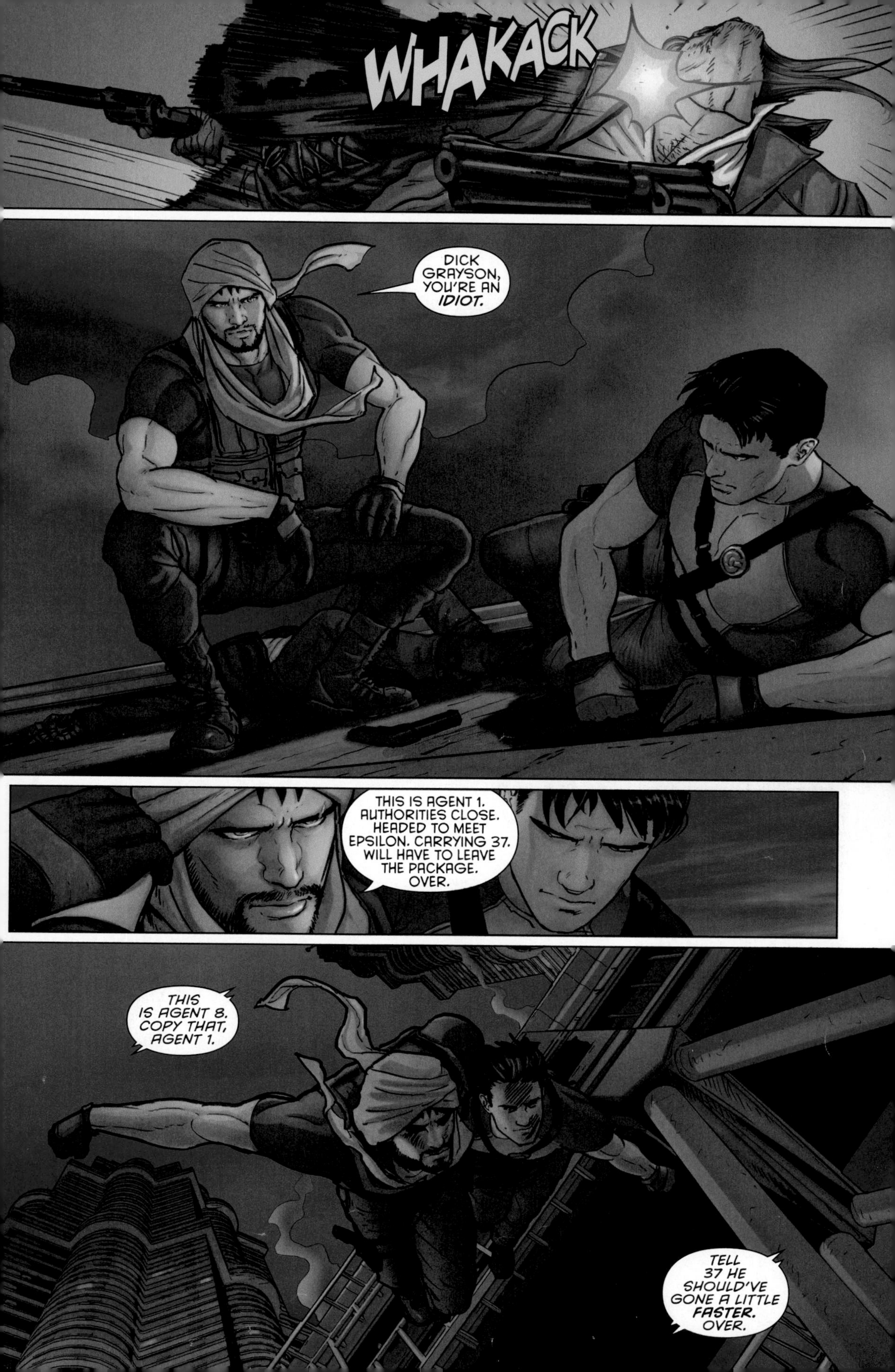
WHAKACK
DICK GRAYSON, YOU'RE AN IDIOT.
THIS IS AGENT 1. AUTHORITIES CLOSE. HEADED TO MEET EPSILON. CARRYING 37. WILL HAVE TO LEAVE THE PACKAGE. OVER.
THIS IS AGENT 8. COPY THAT, AGENT 1.
TELL 37 HE SHOULD'VE GONE A LITTLE FASTER. OVER.

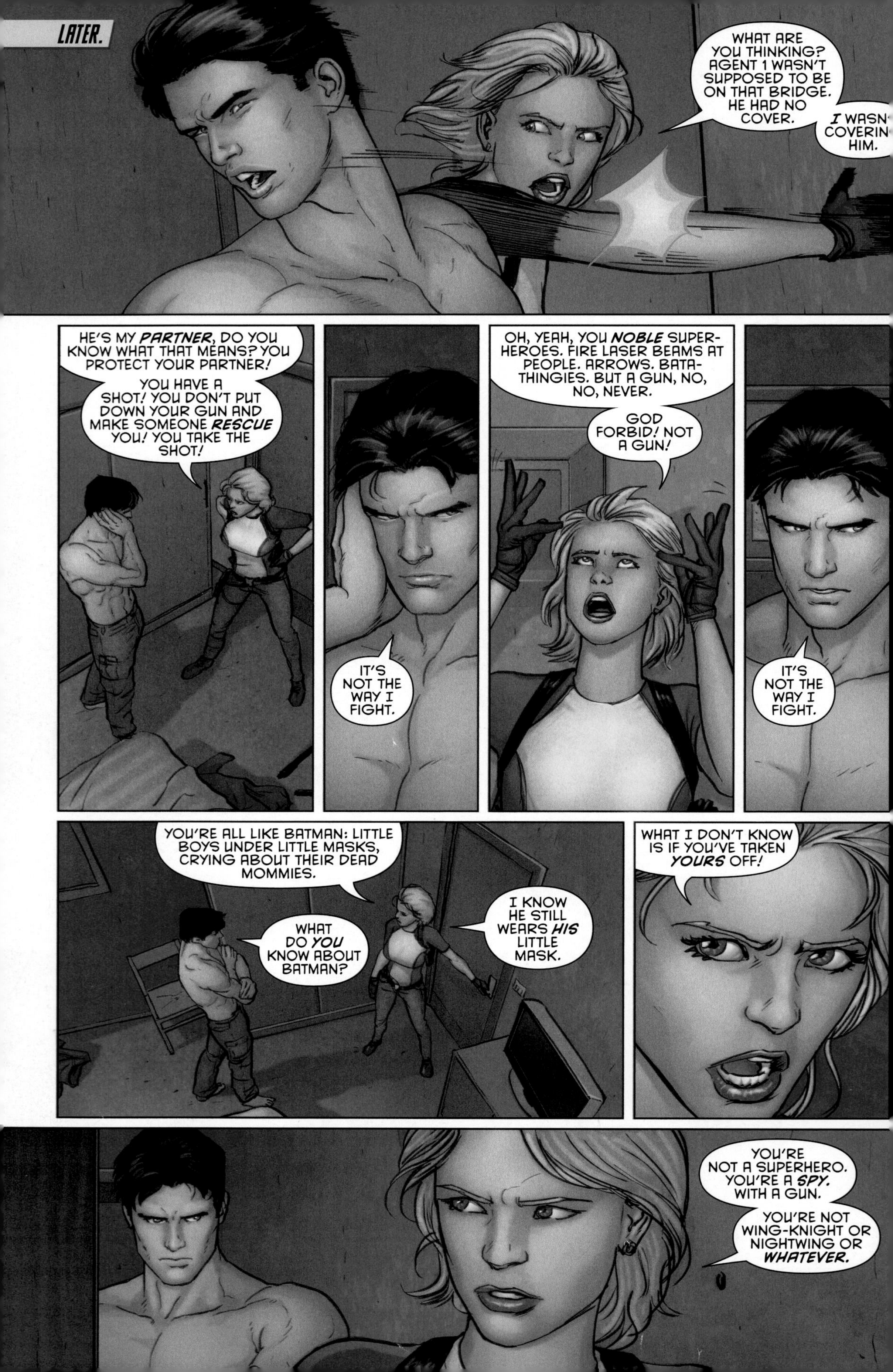
LATER.
WHAT ARE YOU THINKING? AGENT 1 WASN'T SUPPOSED TO BE ON THAT BRIDGE. HE HAD NO COVER.
I WASN' COVERIN HIM.
HE'S MY PARTNER, DO YOU KNOW WHAT THAT MEANS? YOU PROTECT YOUR PARTNER!
YOU HAVE A SHOT! YOU DON'T PUT DOWN YOUR GUN AND MAKE SOMEONE RESCUE YOU! YOU TAKE THE SHOT!
IT'S NOT THE WAY I FIGHT.
OH, YEAH, YOU NOBLE SUPER-HEROES. FIRE LASER BEAMS AT PEOPLE. ARROWS. BATA-THINGIES. BUT A GUN, NO, NO, NEVER.
GOD FORBID! NOT A GUN!
IT'S NOT THE WAY I FIGHT.
YOU'RE ALL LIKE BATMAN: LITTLE BOYS UNDER LITTLE MASKS, CRYING ABOUT THEIR DEAD MOMMIES.
WHAT DO YOU KNOW ABOUT BATMAN?
I KNOW HE STILL WEARS HIS LITTLE MASK.
WHAT I DON'T KNOW IS IF YOU'VE TAKEN YOURS OFF!
YOU'RE NOT A SUPERHERO. YOU'RE A SPY. WITH A GUN.
YOU'RE NOT WING-KNIGHT OR NIGHTWING OR WHATEVER.

"YOU'RE *AGENT 37*."

...WE CAN CONFIRM FROM THIS AGENT 8 THAT SPYRAL HAS THE BATMAN INFORMATION?

YEAH, SURE.

THAT'S GOOD WORK, BIRDWATCHER. YOU'RE DOING WELL.

YAY. GREAT FOR ME.

...

LOOK, I NEED A FAVOR.

ANYTHING.

THERE'S A GUY, CHRISTOPHE TANNER. HE WAS AT THAT SCHOOL SHOOTING IN GENEVA.

YOU HAVE ANYTHING ON HIM IN THE GOOD COMPUTER?

ONE SECOND...

...I SHOW A CHRISTOPHE TANNER ATTENDING THE GENEVA SCHOOL.

NO, THAT'S A MISTAKE. TRUST ME.

SORRY, YOU'RE CONFIRMED ON THAT, BIRDWATCHER. THAT'S A CHRISTOPHE TANNER, JUNIOR I HAD. ENROLLED THERE THIS FALL. STARTS PRE-SCHOOL THIS WEEK.

GETTING RECORDS NOW ON THE FATHER.

WAIT, *WHAT?*

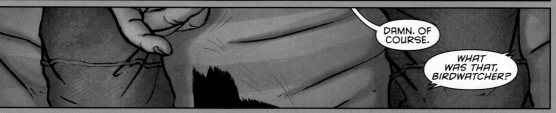

DAMN. OF COURSE.

WHAT WAS THAT, BIRDWATCHER?

A MAN DOESN'T NEED EYES, UNLESS HE'S GOT SOMETHING *WORTH* SEEING.

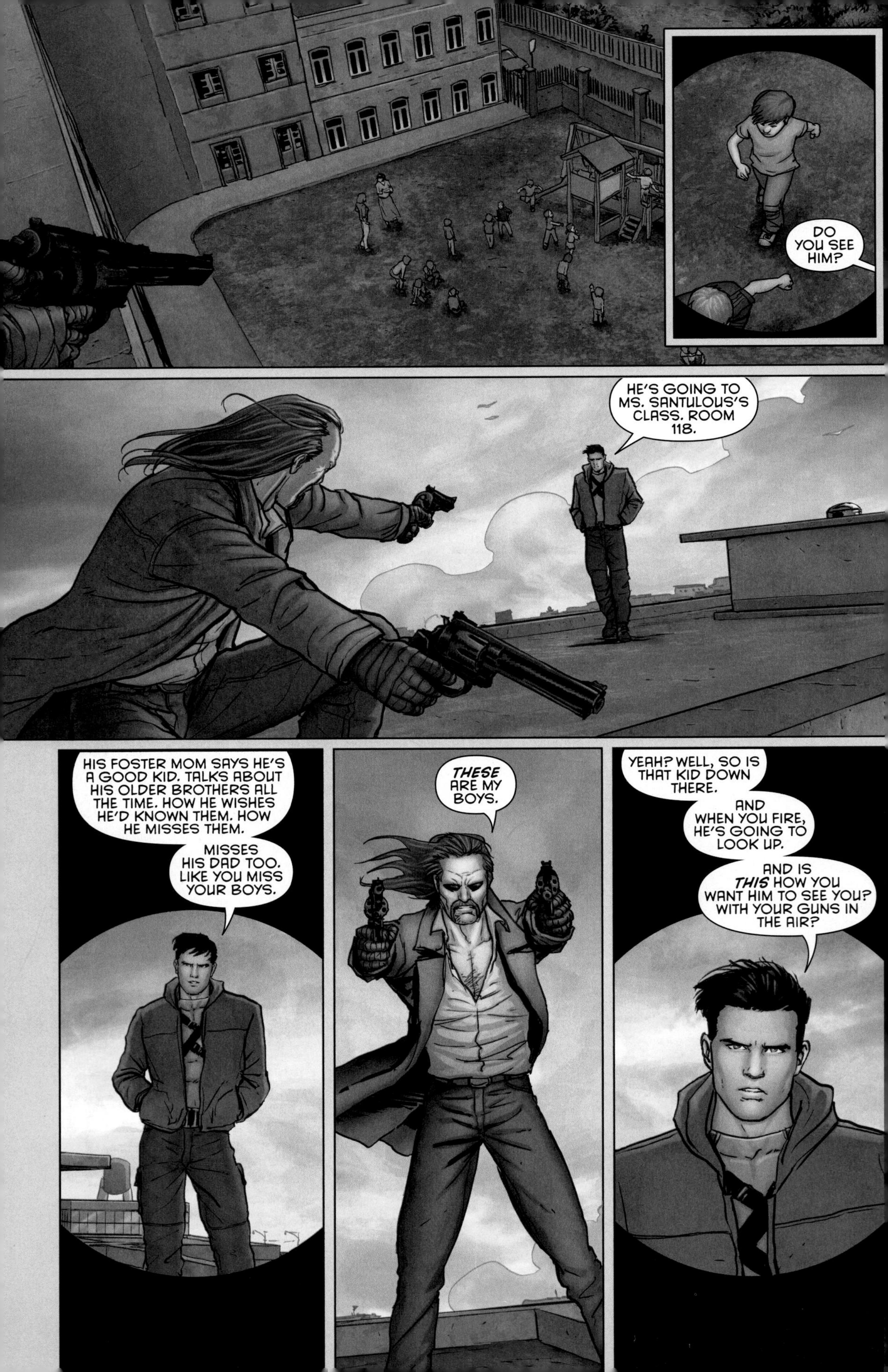
DO YOU SEE HIM?
HE'S GOING TO MS. SANTULOUS'S CLASS. ROOM 118.
HIS FOSTER MOM SAYS HE'S A GOOD KID. TALKS ABOUT HIS OLDER BROTHERS ALL THE TIME. HOW HE WISHES HE'D KNOWN THEM. HOW HE MISSES THEM.
MISSES HIS DAD TOO. LIKE YOU MISS YOUR BOYS.
THESE ARE MY BOYS.
YEAH? WELL, SO IS THAT KID DOWN THERE.
AND WHEN YOU FIRE, HE'S GOING TO LOOK UP.
AND IS THIS HOW YOU WANT HIM TO SEE YOU? WITH YOUR GUNS IN THE AIR?

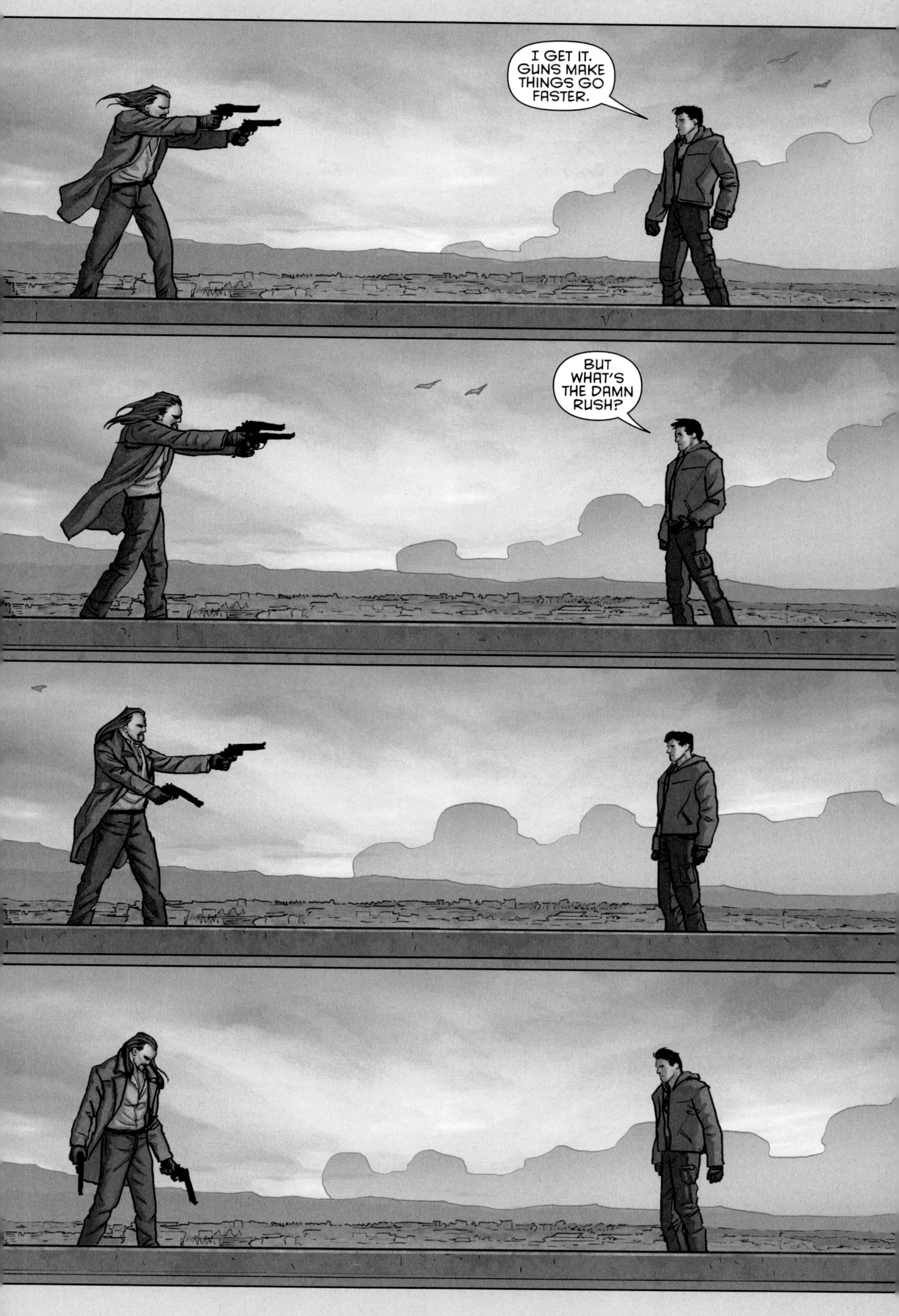
I GET IT. GUNS MAKE THINGS GO FASTER.
BUT WHAT'S THE DAMN RUSH?

I HAVE THE EYES.

DIDN'T WANT TO SEE THE BOY THROUGH THE GUN.

BUT DOC SAYS THEY'RE USELESS, WON'T WORK ON ME. ENHANCED OR NOT.

DON'T MATTER.

CAN'T UNPULL A TRIGGER, I GUESS.

YOU CAN HAVE YOUR EYES.

BEFORE WE DO WHAT WE GOT TO DO, I WANT TO MEET THE KID.

YOU THINK I LOOK ALL RIGHT FOR IT? DON'T WANT TO SCARE HIM.

YEAH...YEAH, MAN, YOU'RE GOOD.

I MEAN, IF YOU REALLY DON'T WANT TO SCARE HIM, YOU MIGHT CONSIDER BUTTONING THE SHIRT.

HAHAHA...

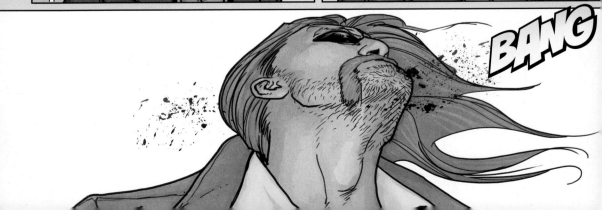

BANG

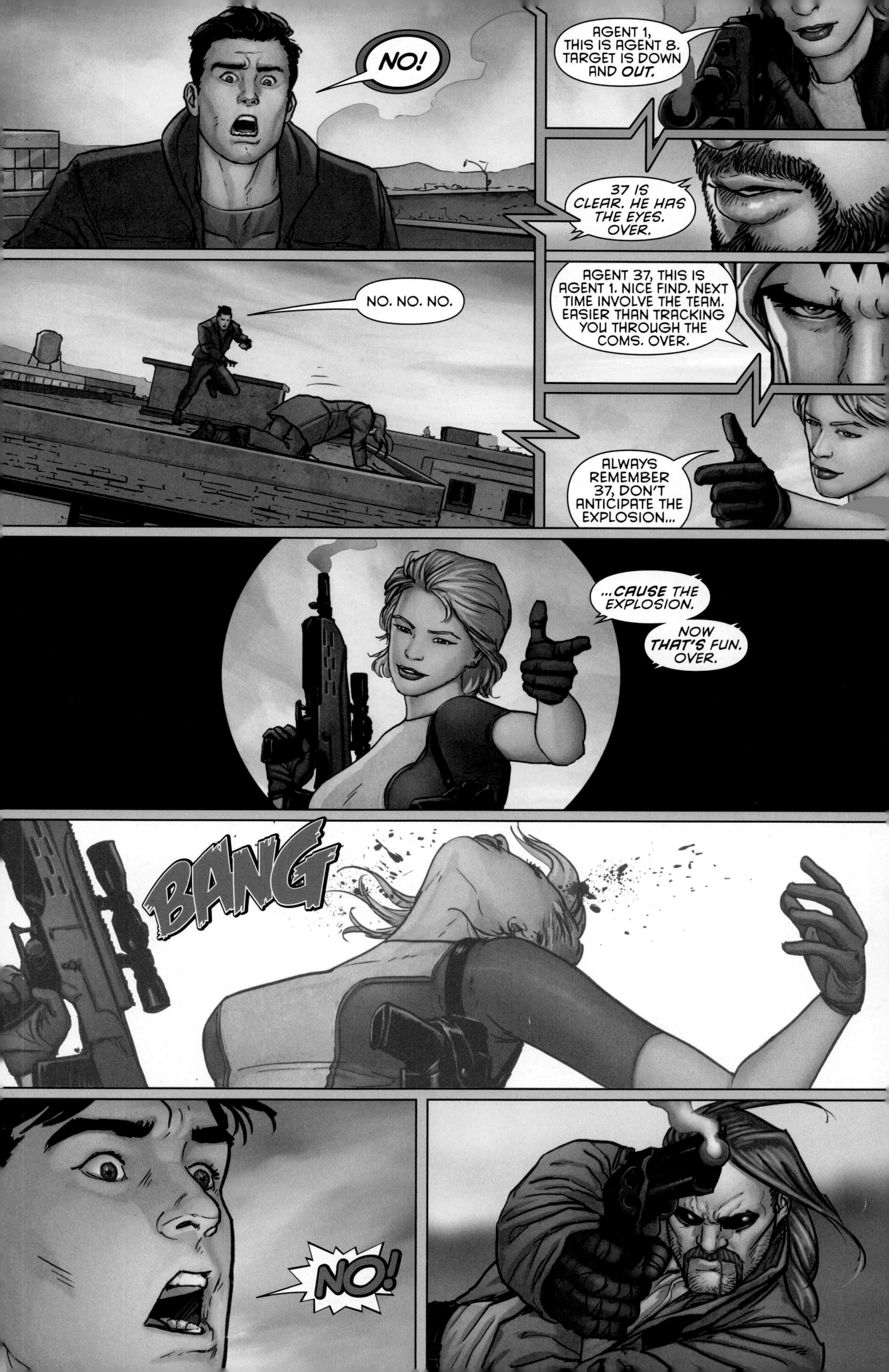
NO!
AGENT 1, THIS IS AGENT 8. TARGET IS DOWN AND OUT.
37 IS CLEAR. HE HAS THE EYES. OVER.
NO. NO. NO.
AGENT 37, THIS IS AGENT 1. NICE FIND. NEXT TIME INVOLVE THE TEAM. EASIER THAN TRACKING YOU THROUGH THE COMS. OVER.
ALWAYS REMEMBER 37, DON'T ANTICIPATE THE EXPLOSION...
...CAUSE THE EXPLOSION.
NOW THAT'S FUN. OVER.
BANG
NO!

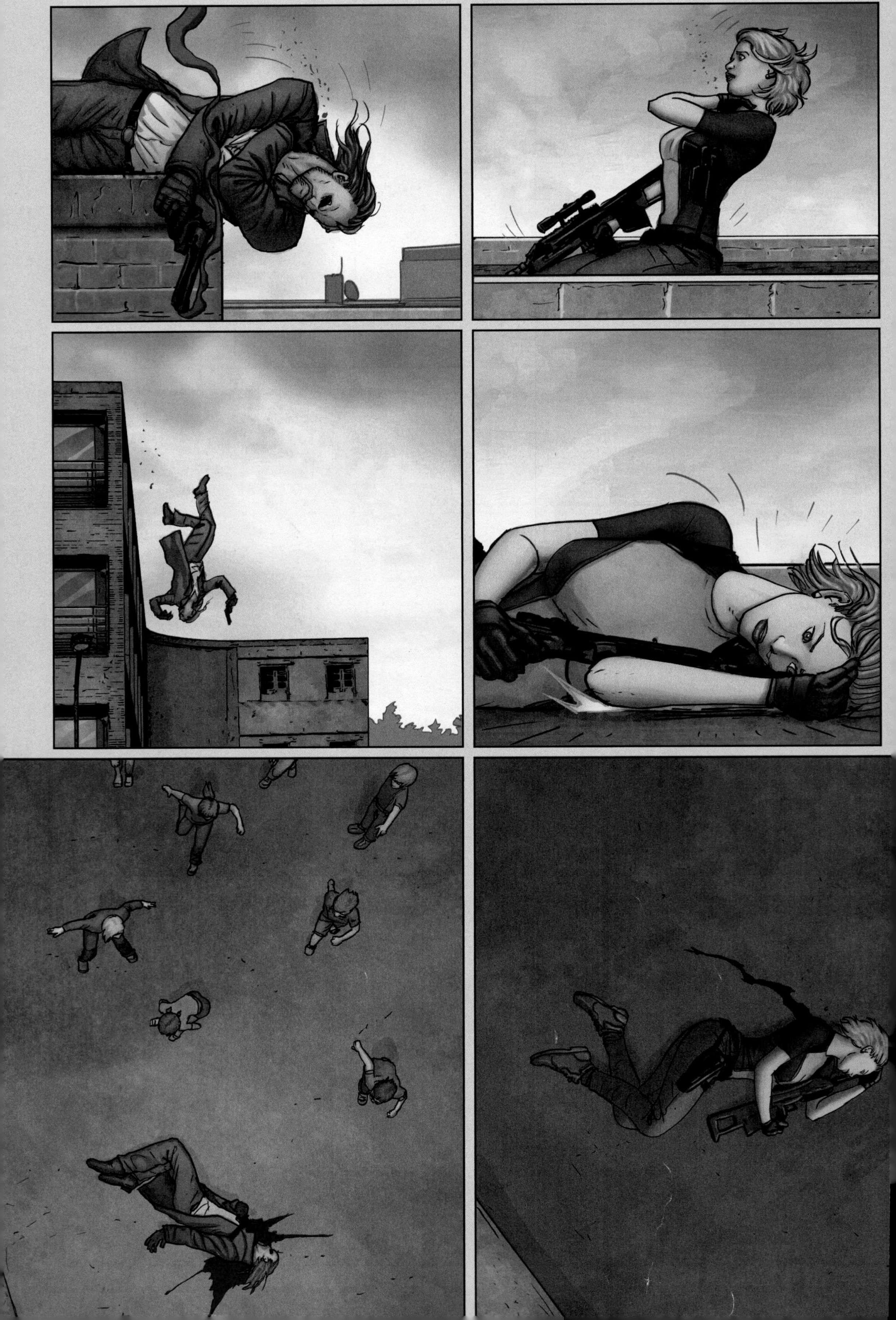

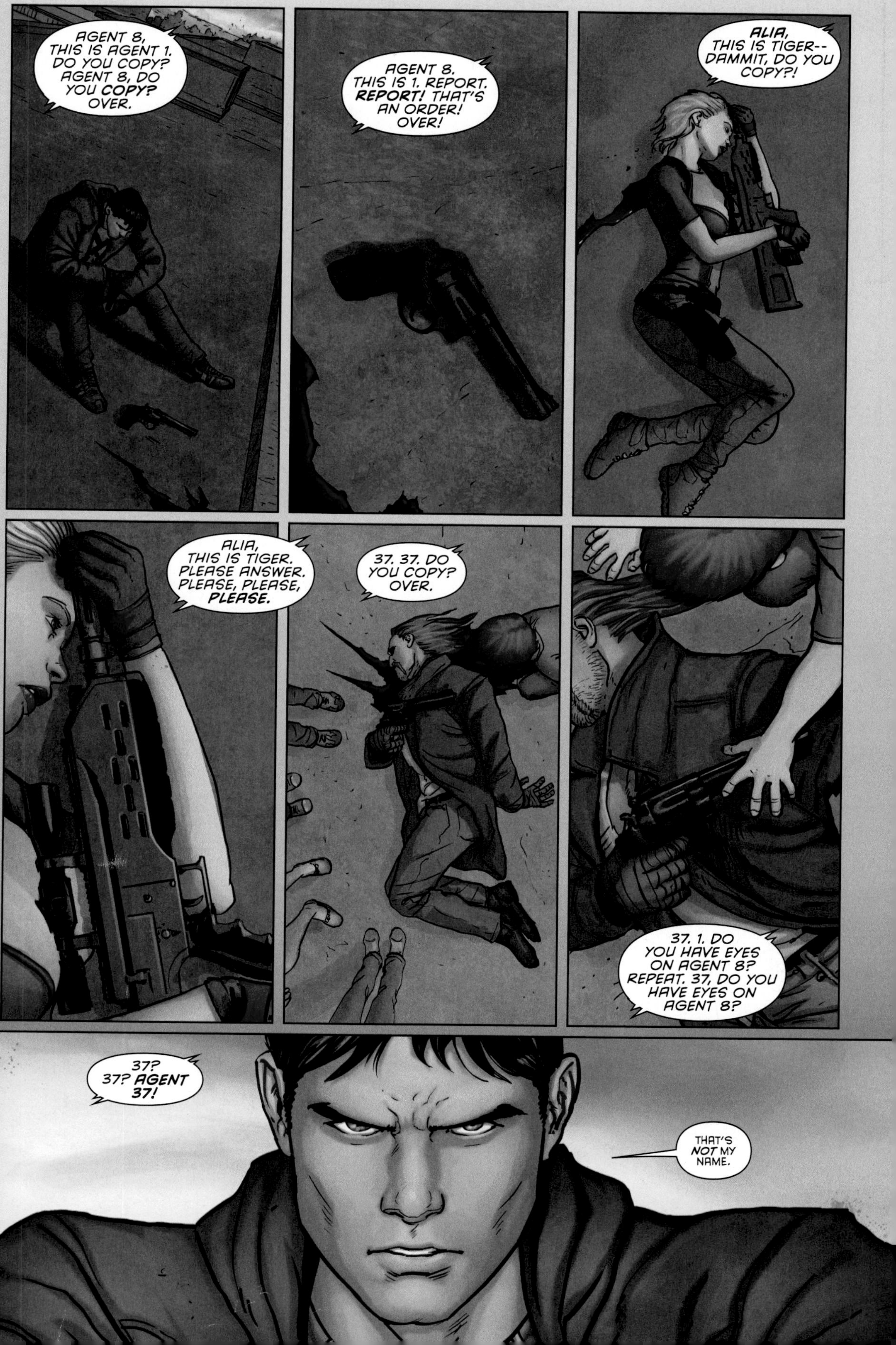
AGENT 8, THIS IS AGENT 1. DO YOU COPY? AGENT 8, DO YOU **COPY?** OVER.
AGENT 8. THIS IS 1. REPORT. **REPORT!** THAT'S AN ORDER! OVER!
ALIA, THIS IS TIGER-- DAMMIT, DO YOU COPY?!
ALIA, THIS IS TIGER. PLEASE ANSWER. PLEASE, PLEASE, ***PLEASE.***
37. 37. DO YOU COPY? OVER.
37. 1. DO YOU HAVE EYES ON AGENT 8? REPEAT. 37, DO YOU HAVE EYES ON AGENT 8?
37? 37? **AGENT 37!**
THAT'S ***NOT*** MY NAME.

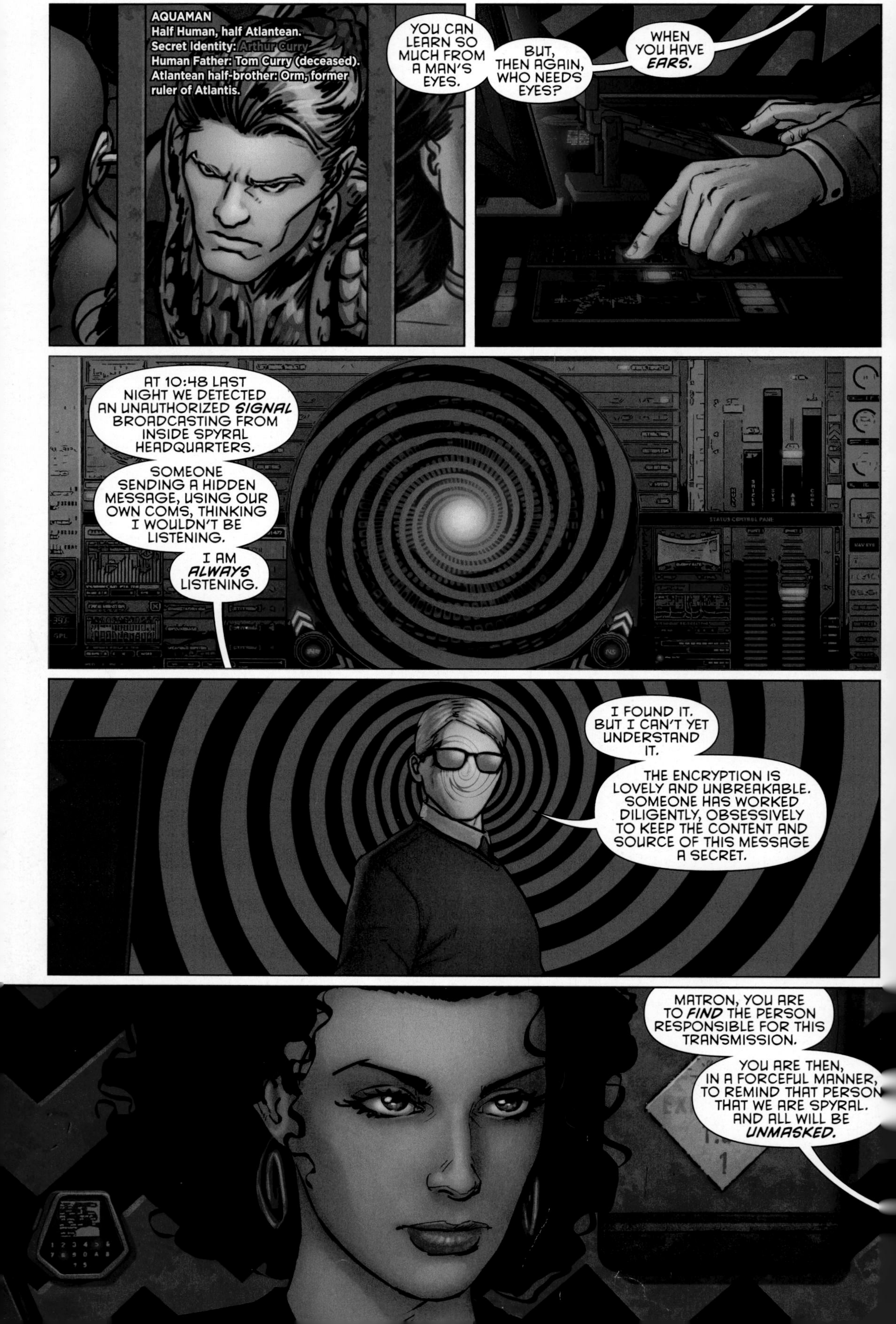
AQUAMAN
Half Human, half Atlantean.
Secret Identity: Arthur Curry
Human Father: Tom Curry (deceased).
Atlantean half-brother: Orm, former ruler of Atlantis.
YOU CAN LEARN SO MUCH FROM A MAN'S EYES.
BUT, THEN AGAIN, WHO NEEDS EYES?
WHEN YOU HAVE EARS.
AT 10:48 LAST NIGHT WE DETECTED AN UNAUTHORIZED SIGNAL BROADCASTING FROM INSIDE SPYRAL HEADQUARTERS.
SOMEONE SENDING A HIDDEN MESSAGE, USING OUR OWN COMS, THINKING I WOULDN'T BE LISTENING.
I AM ALWAYS LISTENING.
STATUS CONTROL PANE
I FOUND IT. BUT I CAN'T YET UNDERSTAND IT.
THE ENCRYPTION IS LOVELY AND UNBREAKABLE. SOMEONE HAS WORKED DILIGENTLY, OBSESSIVELY TO KEEP THE CONTENT AND SOURCE OF THIS MESSAGE A SECRET.
MATRON, YOU ARE TO FIND THE PERSON RESPONSIBLE FOR THIS TRANSMISSION.
YOU ARE THEN, IN A FORCEFUL MANNER, TO REMIND THAT PERSON THAT WE ARE SPYRAL. AND ALL WILL BE UNMASKED.

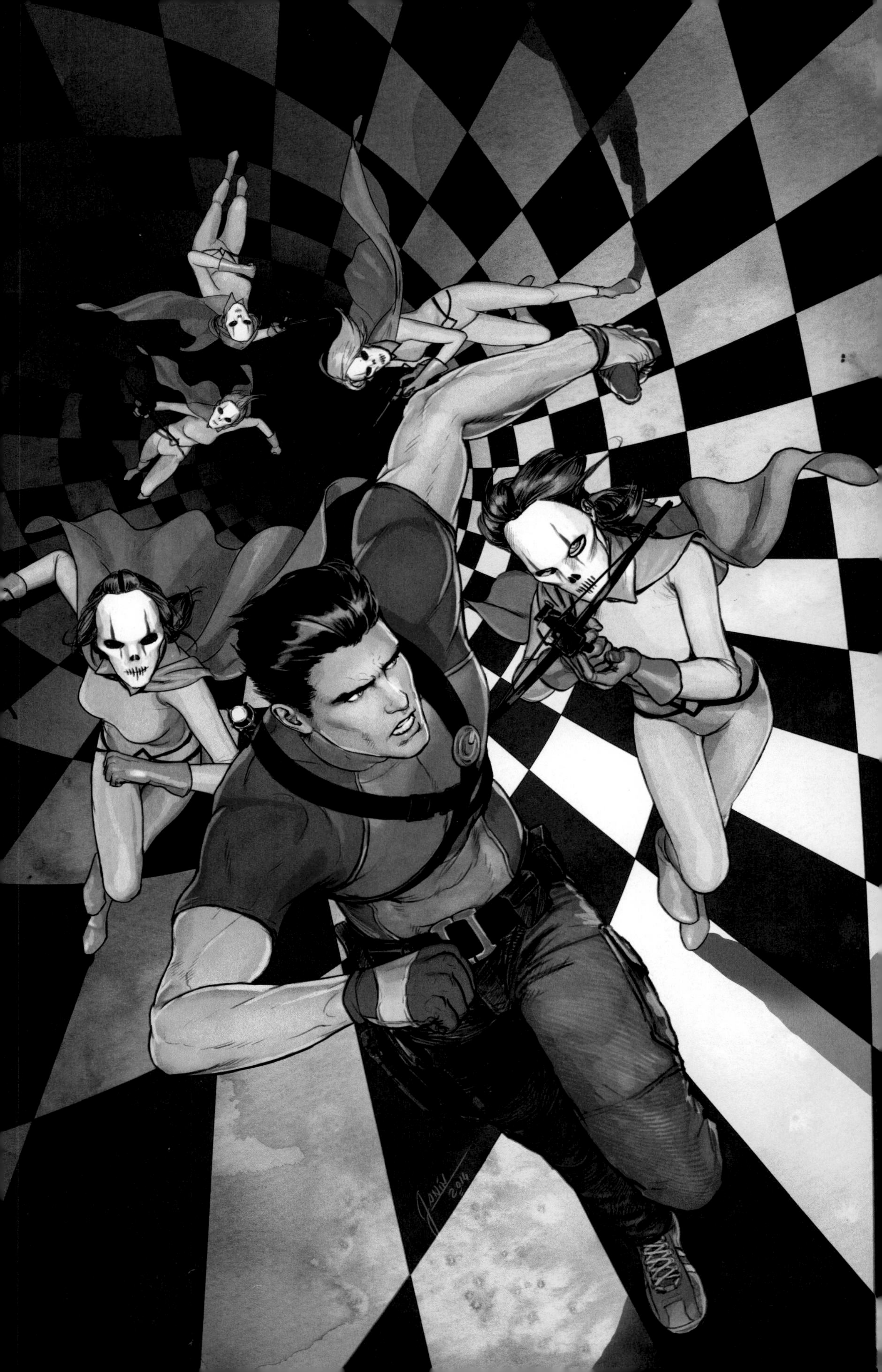

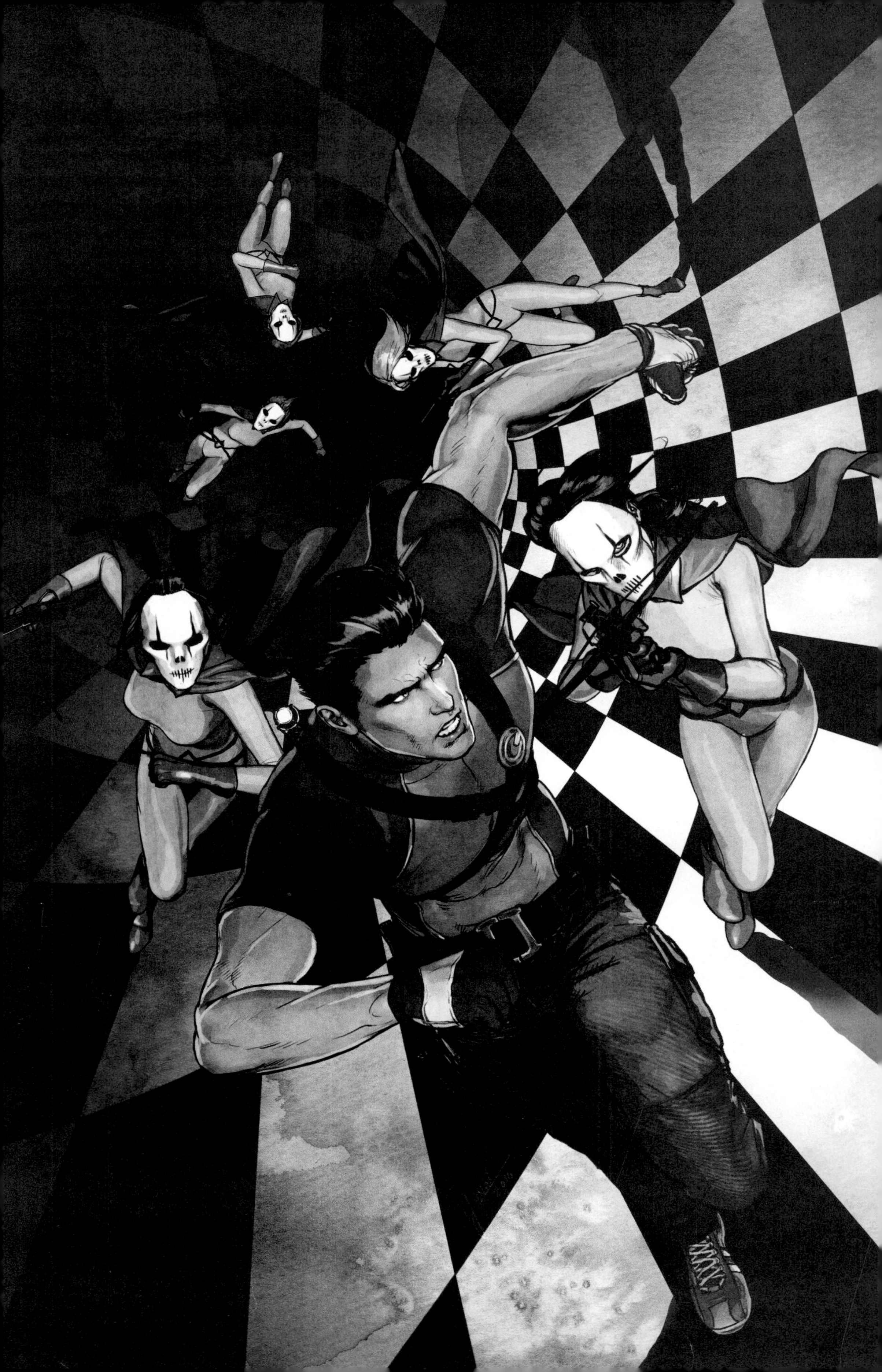

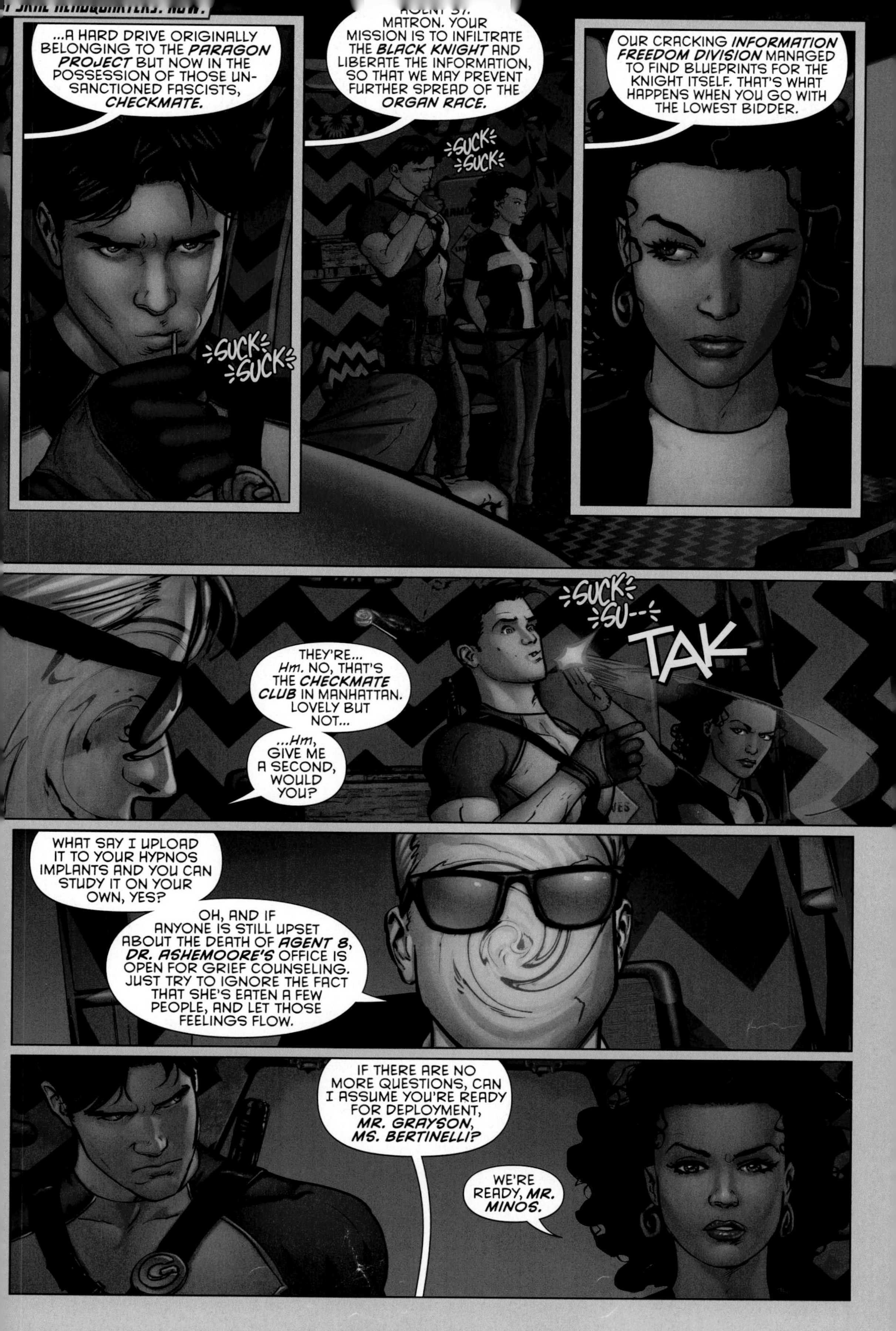

...A HARD DRIVE ORIGINALLY BELONGING TO THE PARAGON PROJECT BUT NOW IN THE POSSESSION OF THOSE UN-SANCTIONED FASCISTS, CHECKMATE.
SUCK SUCK
MATRON. YOUR MISSION IS TO INFILTRATE THE BLACK KNIGHT AND LIBERATE THE INFORMATION, SO THAT WE MAY PREVENT FURTHER SPREAD OF THE ORGAN RACE.
SUCK SUCK
OUR CRACKING INFORMATION FREEDOM DIVISION MANAGED TO FIND BLUEPRINTS FOR THE KNIGHT ITSELF. THAT'S WHAT HAPPENS WHEN YOU GO WITH THE LOWEST BIDDER.
THEY'RE... Hm. NO, THAT'S THE CHECKMATE CLUB IN MANHATTAN. LOVELY BUT NOT...
...Hm, GIVE ME A SECOND, WOULD YOU?
SUCK SU--
TAK
WHAT SAY I UPLOAD IT TO YOUR HYPNOS IMPLANTS AND YOU CAN STUDY IT ON YOUR OWN, YES?
OH, AND IF ANYONE IS STILL UPSET ABOUT THE DEATH OF AGENT 8, DR. ASHEMOORE'S OFFICE IS OPEN FOR GRIEF COUNSELING. JUST TRY TO IGNORE THE FACT THAT SHE'S EATEN A FEW PEOPLE, AND LET THOSE FEELINGS FLOW.
IF THERE ARE NO MORE QUESTIONS, CAN I ASSUME YOU'RE READY FOR DEPLOYMENT, MR. GRAYSON, MS. BERTINELLI?
WE'RE READY, MR. MINOS.

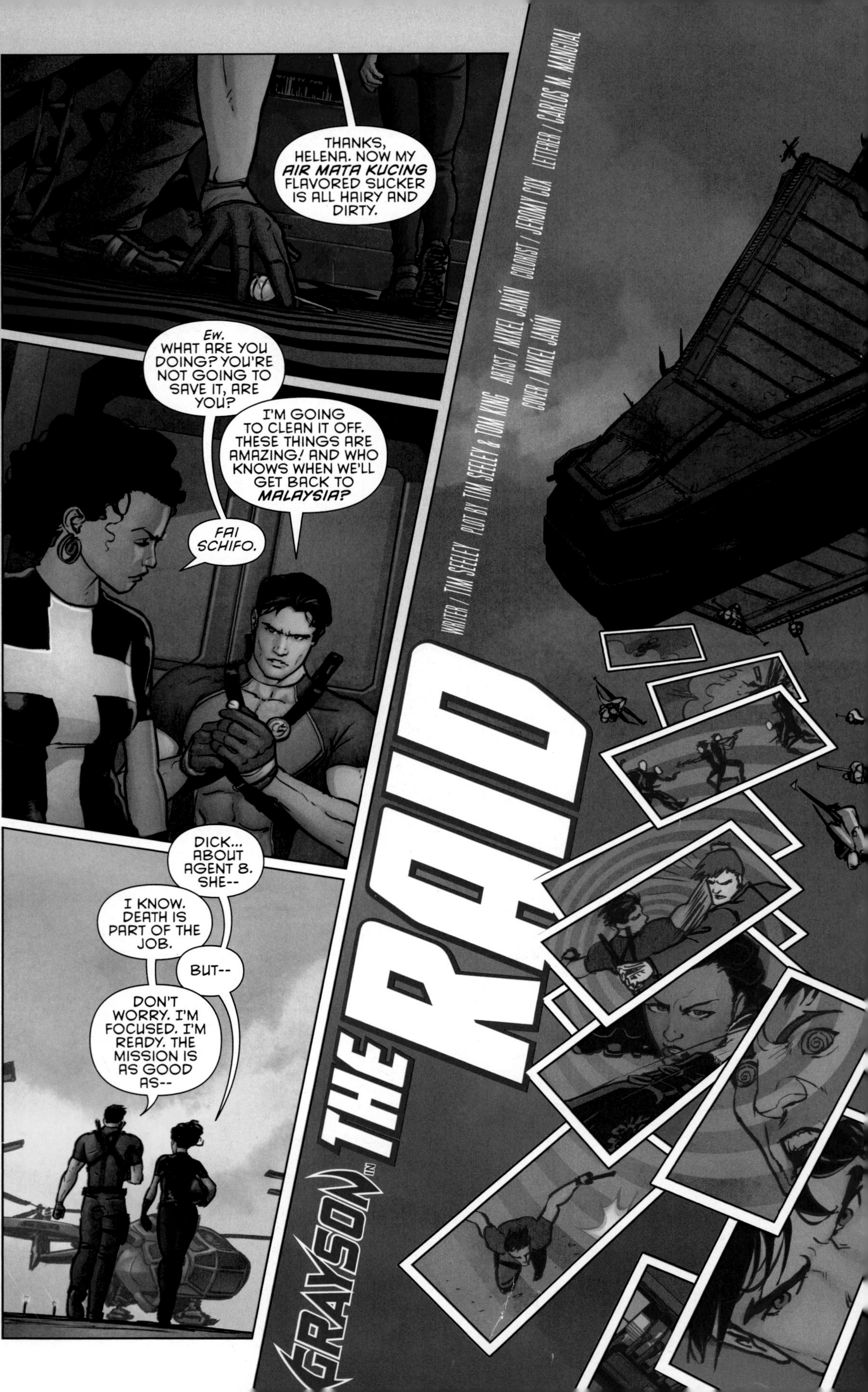

THANKS, HELENA. NOW MY *AIR MATA KUCING* FLAVORED SUCKER IS ALL HAIRY AND DIRTY.
EW. WHAT ARE YOU DOING? YOU'RE NOT GOING TO SAVE IT, ARE YOU?
I'M GOING TO CLEAN IT OFF. THESE THINGS ARE AMAZING! AND WHO KNOWS WHEN WE'LL GET BACK TO *MALAYSIA?*
FAI SCHIFO.
DICK... ABOUT AGENT 8. SHE--
I KNOW. DEATH IS PART OF THE JOB.
BUT--
DON'T WORRY. I'M FOCUSED. I'M READY. THE MISSION IS AS GOOD AS--
GRAYSON IN THE RAID
WRITER / TIM SEELEY PLOT BY TIM SEELEY & TOM KING ARTIST / MIKEL JANÍN COLORIST / JEREMY COX LETTERER / CARLOS M. MANGUAL
COVER / MIKEL JANÍN

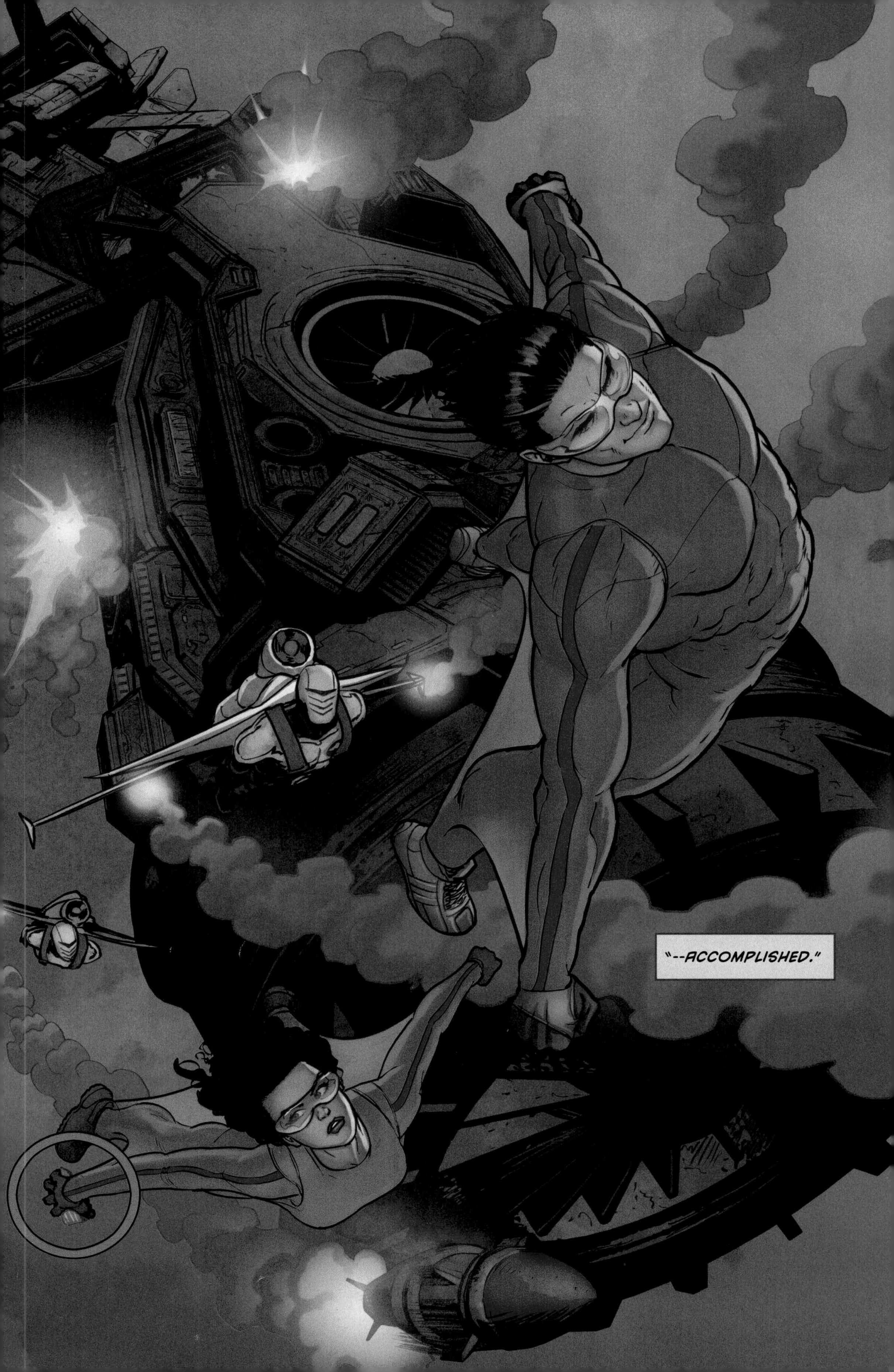
"--ACCOMPLISHED."

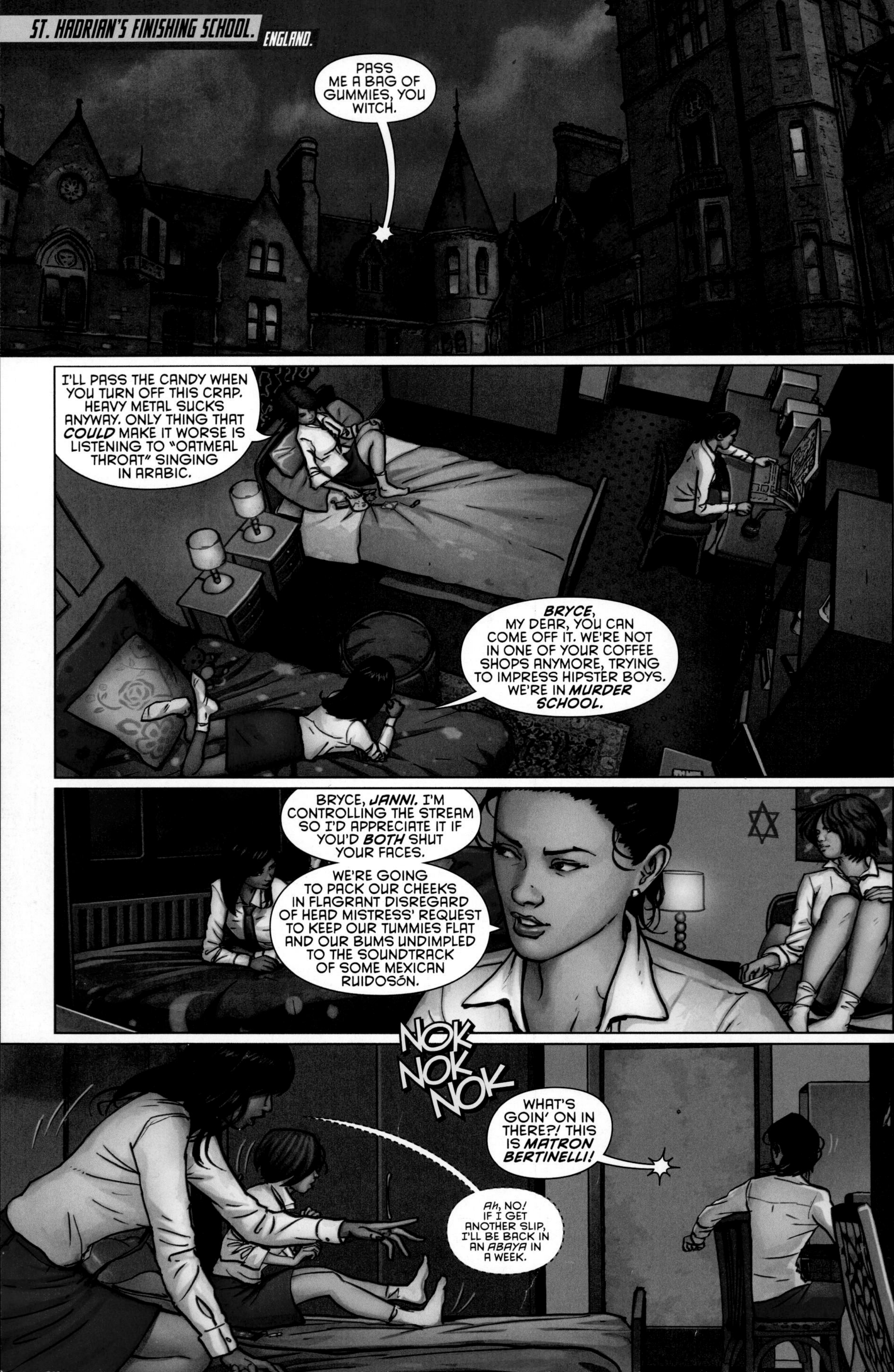
ST. HADRIAN'S FINISHING SCHOOL.
ENGLAND.
PASS ME A BAG OF GUMMIES, YOU WITCH.
I'LL PASS THE CANDY WHEN YOU TURN OFF THIS CRAP. HEAVY METAL SUCKS ANYWAY. ONLY THING THAT COULD MAKE IT WORSE IS LISTENING TO "OATMEAL THROAT" SINGING IN ARABIC.
BRYCE, MY DEAR, YOU CAN COME OFF IT. WE'RE NOT IN ONE OF YOUR COFFEE SHOPS ANYMORE, TRYING TO IMPRESS HIPSTER BOYS. WE'RE IN MURDER SCHOOL.
BRYCE, JANNI. I'M CONTROLLING THE STREAM SO I'D APPRECIATE IT IF YOU'D BOTH SHUT YOUR FACES.
WE'RE GOING TO PACK OUR CHEEKS IN FLAGRANT DISREGARD OF HEAD MISTRESS' REQUEST TO KEEP OUR TUMMIES FLAT AND OUR BUMS UNDIMPLED TO THE SOUNDTRACK OF SOME MEXICAN RUIDOSÓN.
NOK NOK NOK
WHAT'S GOIN' ON IN THERE?! THIS IS MATRON BERTINELLI!
AH, NO! IF I GET ANOTHER SLIP, I'LL BE BACK IN AN ABAYA IN A WEEK.

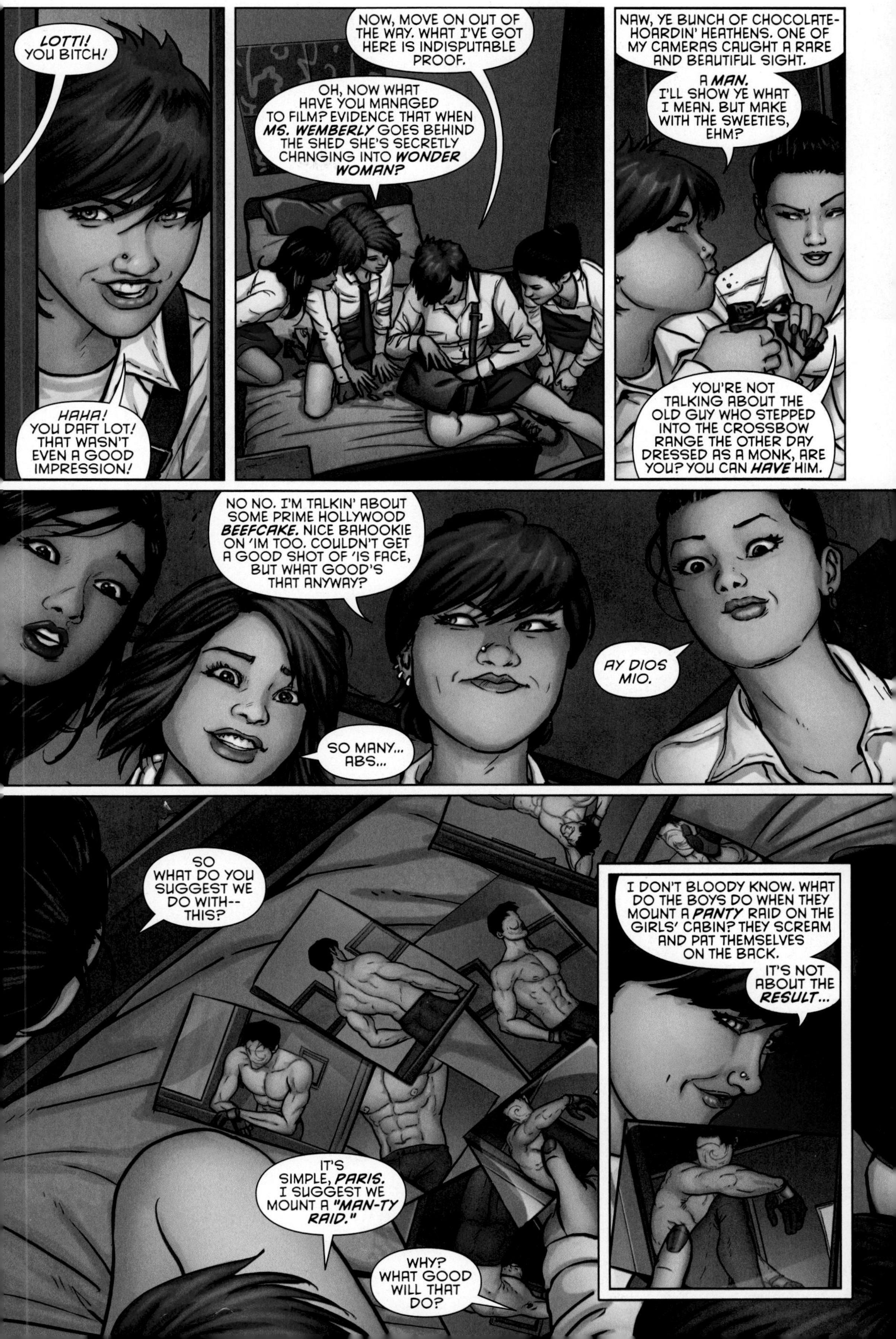
LOTTI! YOU BITCH!
HAHA! YOU DAFT LOT! THAT WASN'T EVEN A GOOD IMPRESSION!
NOW, MOVE ON OUT OF THE WAY. WHAT I'VE GOT HERE IS INDISPUTABLE PROOF.
OH, NOW WHAT HAVE YOU MANAGED TO FILM? EVIDENCE THAT WHEN MS. WEMBERLY GOES BEHIND THE SHED SHE'S SECRETLY CHANGING INTO WONDER WOMAN?
NAW, YE BUNCH OF CHOCOLATE-HOARDIN' HEATHENS. ONE OF MY CAMERAS CAUGHT A RARE AND BEAUTIFUL SIGHT.
A MAN. I'LL SHOW YE WHAT I MEAN. BUT MAKE WITH THE SWEETIES, EHM?
YOU'RE NOT TALKING ABOUT THE OLD GUY WHO STEPPED INTO THE CROSSBOW RANGE THE OTHER DAY DRESSED AS A MONK, ARE YOU? YOU CAN HAVE HIM.
NO NO. I'M TALKIN' ABOUT SOME PRIME HOLLYWOOD BEEFCAKE. NICE BAHOOKIE ON 'IM TOO. COULDN'T GET A GOOD SHOT OF 'IS FACE, BUT WHAT GOOD'S THAT ANYWAY?
AY DIOS MIO.
SO MANY... ABS...
SO WHAT DO YOU SUGGEST WE DO WITH-- THIS?
IT'S SIMPLE, PARIS. I SUGGEST WE MOUNT A "MAN-TY RAID."
WHY? WHAT GOOD WILL THAT DO?
I DON'T BLOODY KNOW. WHAT DO THE BOYS DO WHEN THEY MOUNT A PANTY RAID ON THE GIRLS' CABIN? THEY SCREAM AND PAT THEMSELVES ON THE BACK.
IT'S NOT ABOUT THE RESULT...

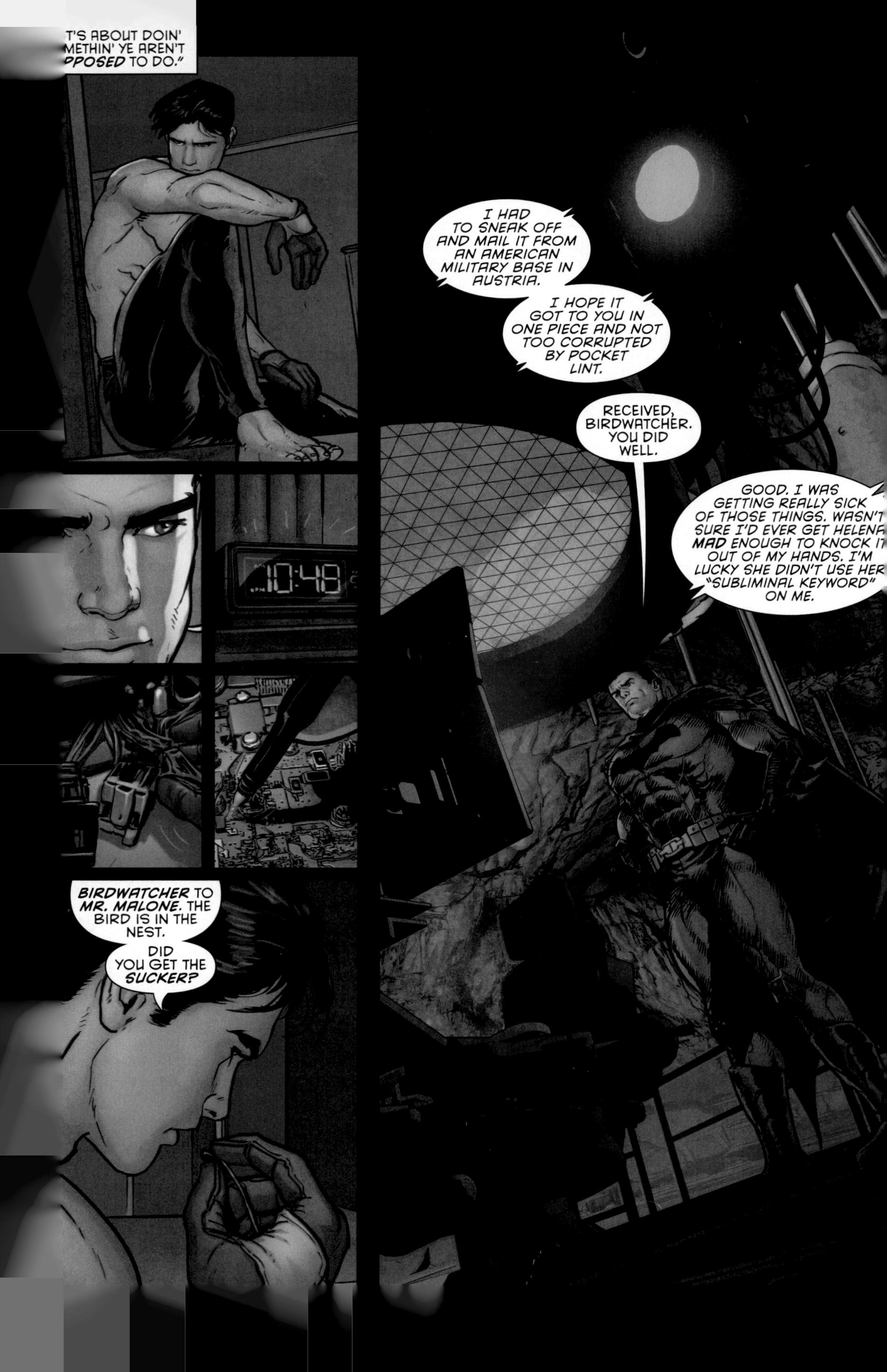

T'S ABOUT DOIN' METHIN' YE AREN'T PPOSED TO DO."
I HAD TO SNEAK OFF AND MAIL IT FROM AN AMERICAN MILITARY BASE IN AUSTRIA.
I HOPE IT GOT TO YOU IN ONE PIECE AND NOT TOO CORRUPTED BY POCKET LINT.
RECEIVED, BIRDWATCHER. YOU DID WELL.
GOOD. I WAS GETTING REALLY SICK OF THOSE THINGS. WASN'T SURE I'D EVER GET HELENA MAD ENOUGH TO KNOCK IT OUT OF MY HANDS. I'M LUCKY SHE DIDN'T USE HER "SUBLIMINAL KEYWORD" ON ME.
10:48
BIRDWATCHER TO MR. MALONE. THE BIRD IS IN THE NEST.
DID YOU GET THE SUCKER?

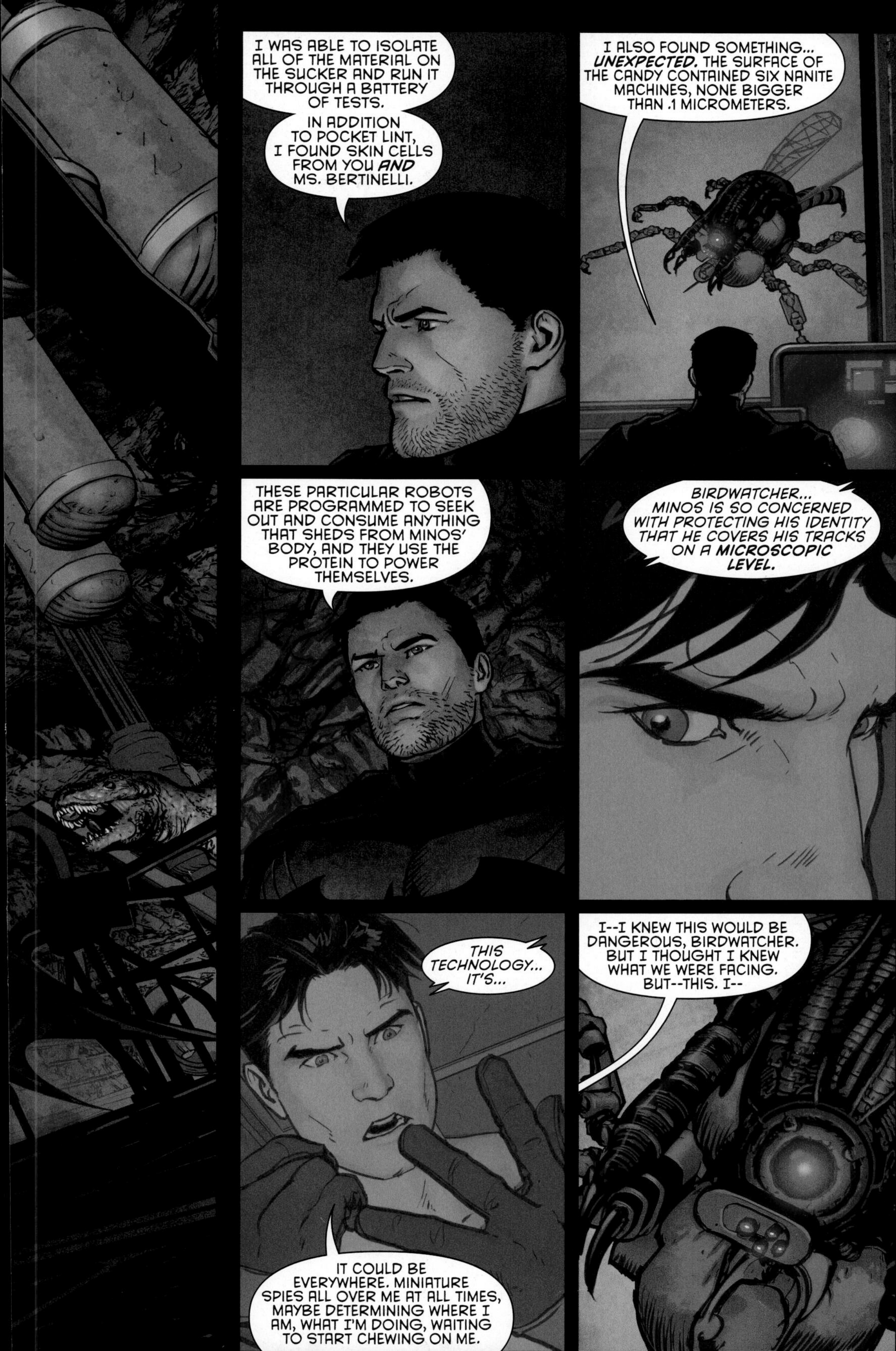

I WAS ABLE TO ISOLATE ALL OF THE MATERIAL ON THE SUCKER AND RUN IT THROUGH A BATTERY OF TESTS.
IN ADDITION TO POCKET LINT, I FOUND SKIN CELLS FROM YOU *AND* MS. BERTINELLI.
I ALSO FOUND SOMETHING... *UNEXPECTED.* THE SURFACE OF THE CANDY CONTAINED SIX NANITE MACHINES, NONE BIGGER THAN .1 MICROMETERS.
THESE PARTICULAR ROBOTS ARE PROGRAMMED TO SEEK OUT AND CONSUME ANYTHING THAT SHEDS FROM MINOS' BODY, AND THEY USE THE PROTEIN TO POWER THEMSELVES.
BIRDWATCHER... MINOS IS SO CONCERNED WITH PROTECTING HIS IDENTITY THAT HE COVERS HIS TRACKS ON A ***MICROSCOPIC LEVEL.***
THIS TECHNOLOGY... IT'S...
IT COULD BE EVERYWHERE. MINIATURE SPIES ALL OVER ME AT ALL TIMES, MAYBE DETERMINING WHERE I AM, WHAT I'M DOING, WAITING TO START CHEWING ON ME.
I--I KNEW THIS WOULD BE DANGEROUS, BIRDWATCHER. BUT I THOUGHT I KNEW WHAT WE WERE FACING. BUT--THIS. I--

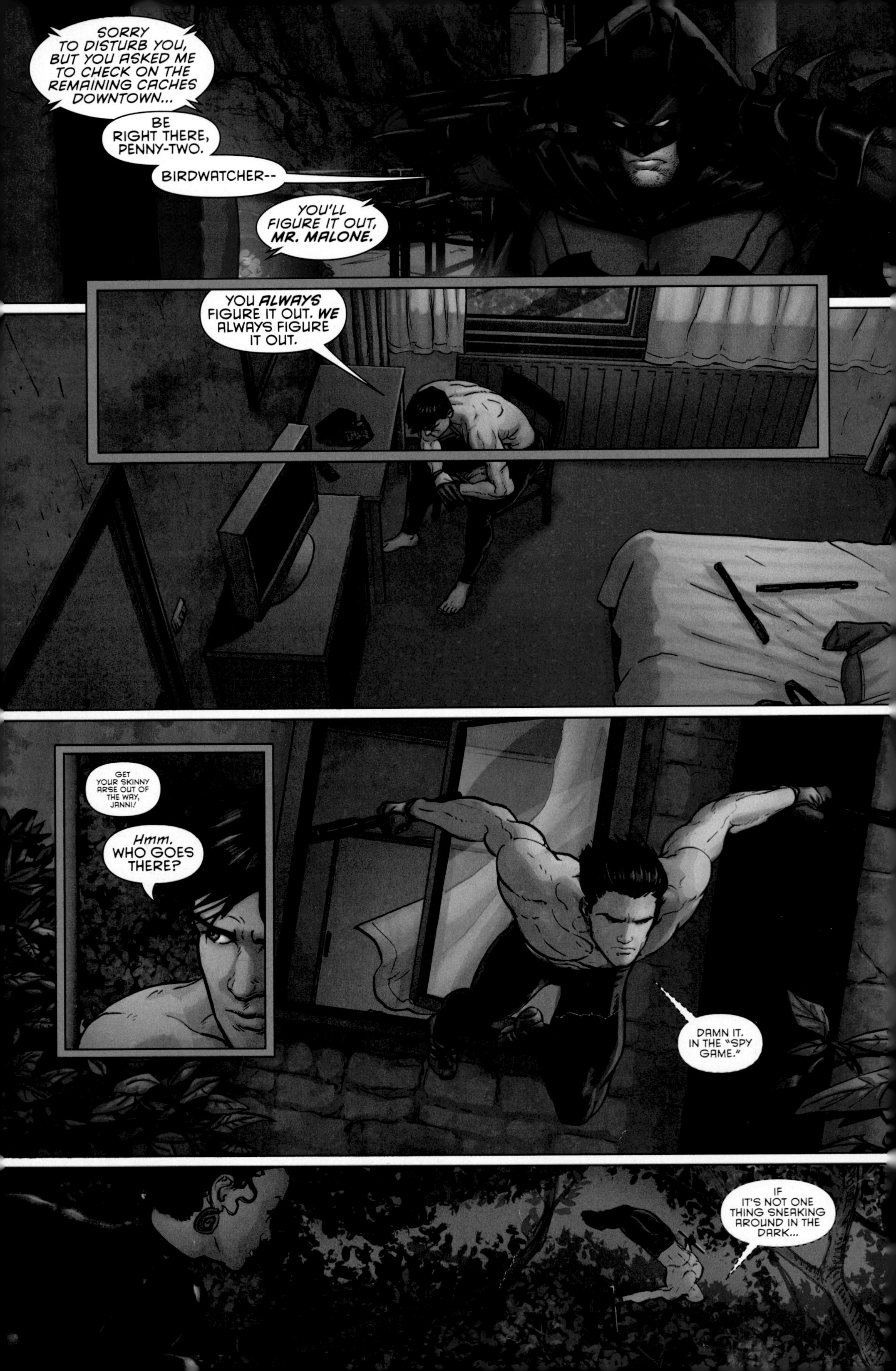
SORRY TO DISTURB YOU, BUT YOU ASKED ME TO CHECK ON THE REMAINING CACHES DOWNTOWN...
BE RIGHT THERE, PENNY-TWO.
BIRDWATCHER--
YOU'LL FIGURE IT OUT, MR. MALONE.
YOU ALWAYS FIGURE IT OUT. WE ALWAYS FIGURE IT OUT.
GET YOUR SKINNY ARSE OUT OF THE WAY, JANNI!
Hmm. WHO GOES THERE?
DAMN IT. IN THE "SPY GAME."
IF IT'S NOT ONE THING SNEAKING AROUND IN THE DARK...

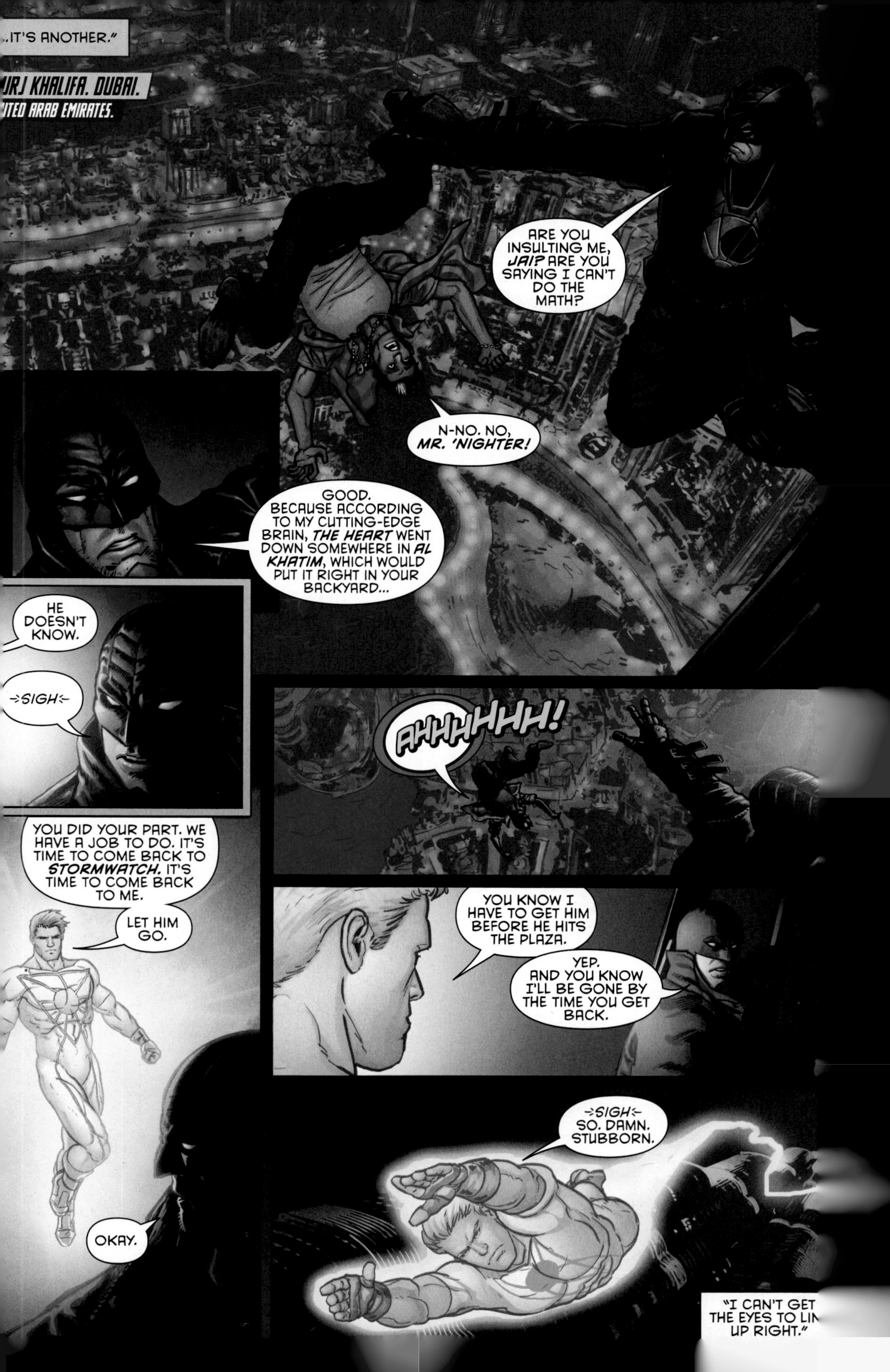
..IT'S ANOTHER."
URJ KHALIFA. DUBAI.
ITED ARAB EMIRATES.
ARE YOU INSULTING ME, JAI? ARE YOU SAYING I CAN'T DO THE MATH?
N-NO. NO, MR. 'NIGHTER!
GOOD. BECAUSE ACCORDING TO MY CUTTING-EDGE BRAIN, THE HEART WENT DOWN SOMEWHERE IN AL KHATIM, WHICH WOULD PUT IT RIGHT IN YOUR BACKYARD...
HE DOESN'T KNOW.
SIGH
AHHHHHH!
YOU DID YOUR PART. WE HAVE A JOB TO DO. IT'S TIME TO COME BACK TO STORMWATCH. IT'S TIME TO COME BACK TO ME.
LET HIM GO.
YOU KNOW I HAVE TO GET HIM BEFORE HE HITS THE PLAZA.
YEP. AND YOU KNOW I'LL BE GONE BY THE TIME YOU GET BACK.
OKAY.
SIGH SO. DAMN. STUBBORN.
"I CAN'T GET THE EYES TO LIN UP RIGHT."

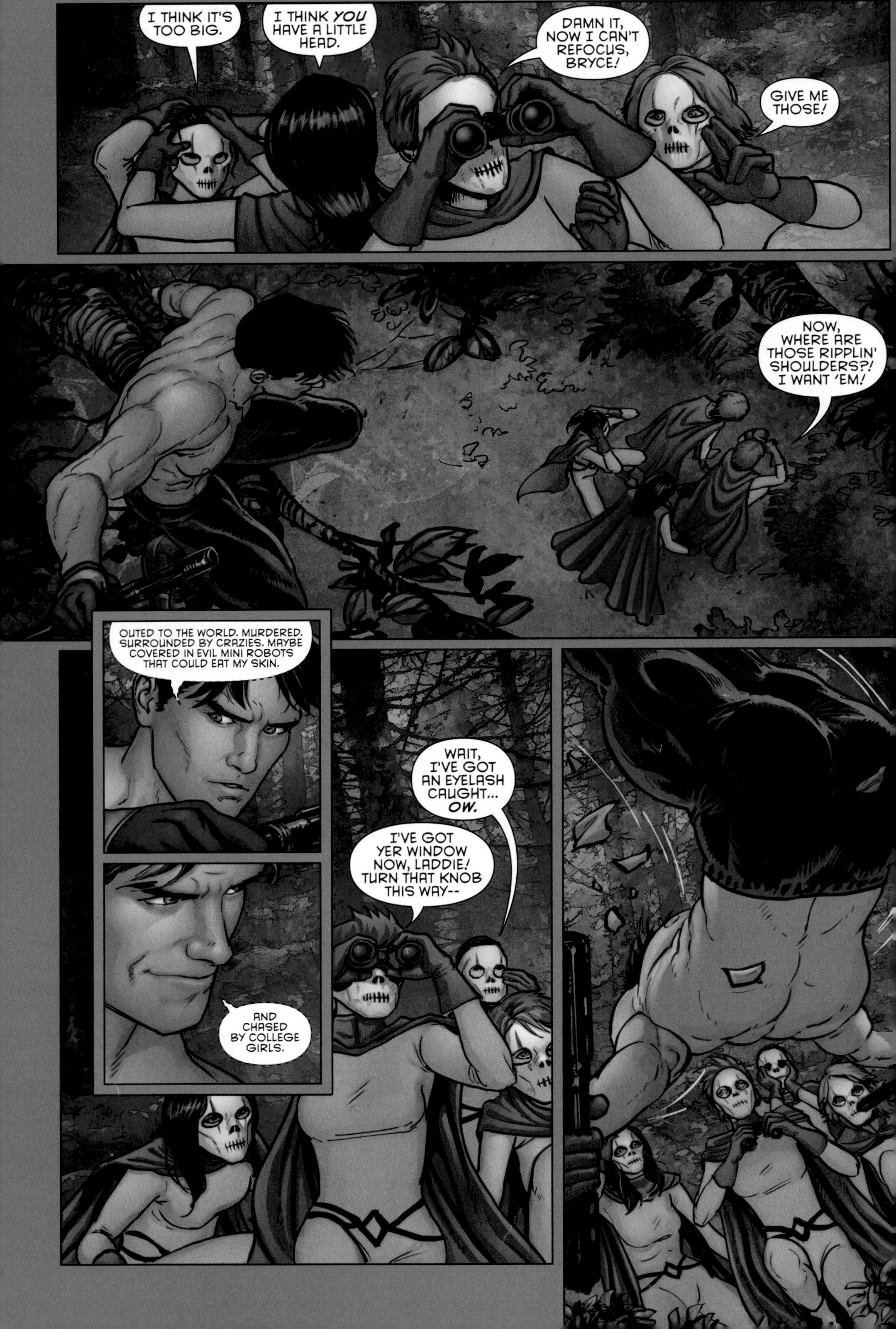
I THINK IT'S TOO BIG.
I THINK *YOU* HAVE A LITTLE HEAD.
DAMN IT, NOW I CAN'T REFOCUS, BRYCE!
GIVE ME THOSE!
NOW, WHERE ARE THOSE RIPPLIN' SHOULDERS?! I WANT 'EM!
OUTED TO THE WORLD. MURDERED. SURROUNDED BY CRAZIES. MAYBE COVERED IN EVIL MINI ROBOTS THAT COULD EAT MY SKIN.
AND CHASED BY COLLEGE GIRLS.
WAIT, I'VE GOT AN EYELASH CAUGHT... ***OW.***
I'VE GOT YER WINDOW NOW, LADDIE! TURN THAT KNOB THIS WAY--

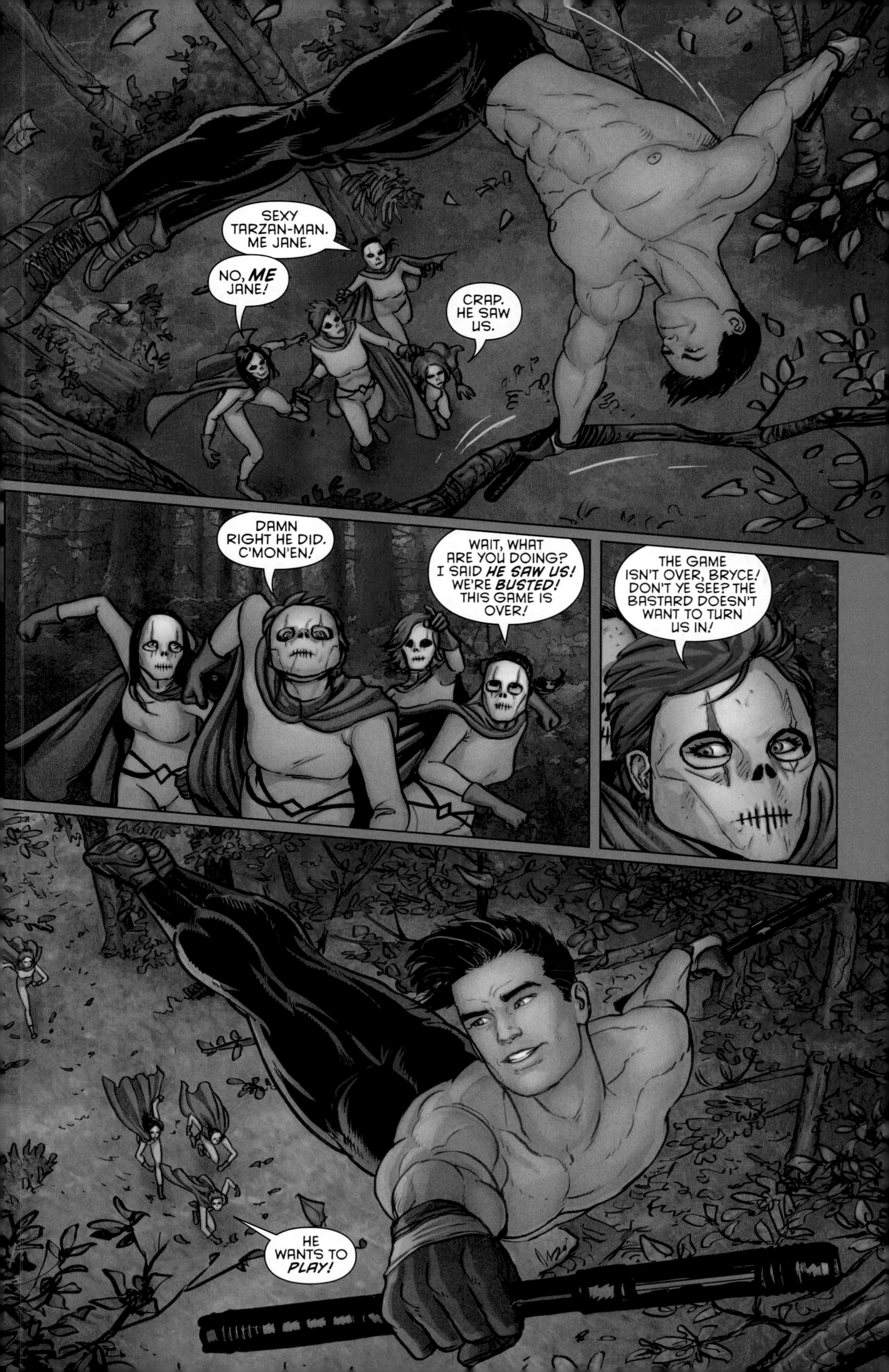
SEXY TARZAN-MAN. ME JANE.
NO, ME JANE!
CRAP. HE SAW US.
DAMN RIGHT HE DID. C'MON'EN!
WAIT, WHAT ARE YOU DOING? I SAID HE SAW US! WE'RE BUSTED! THIS GAME IS OVER!
THE GAME ISN'T OVER, BRYCE! DON'T YE SEE? THE BASTARD DOESN'T WANT TO TURN US IN!
HE WANTS TO PLAY!

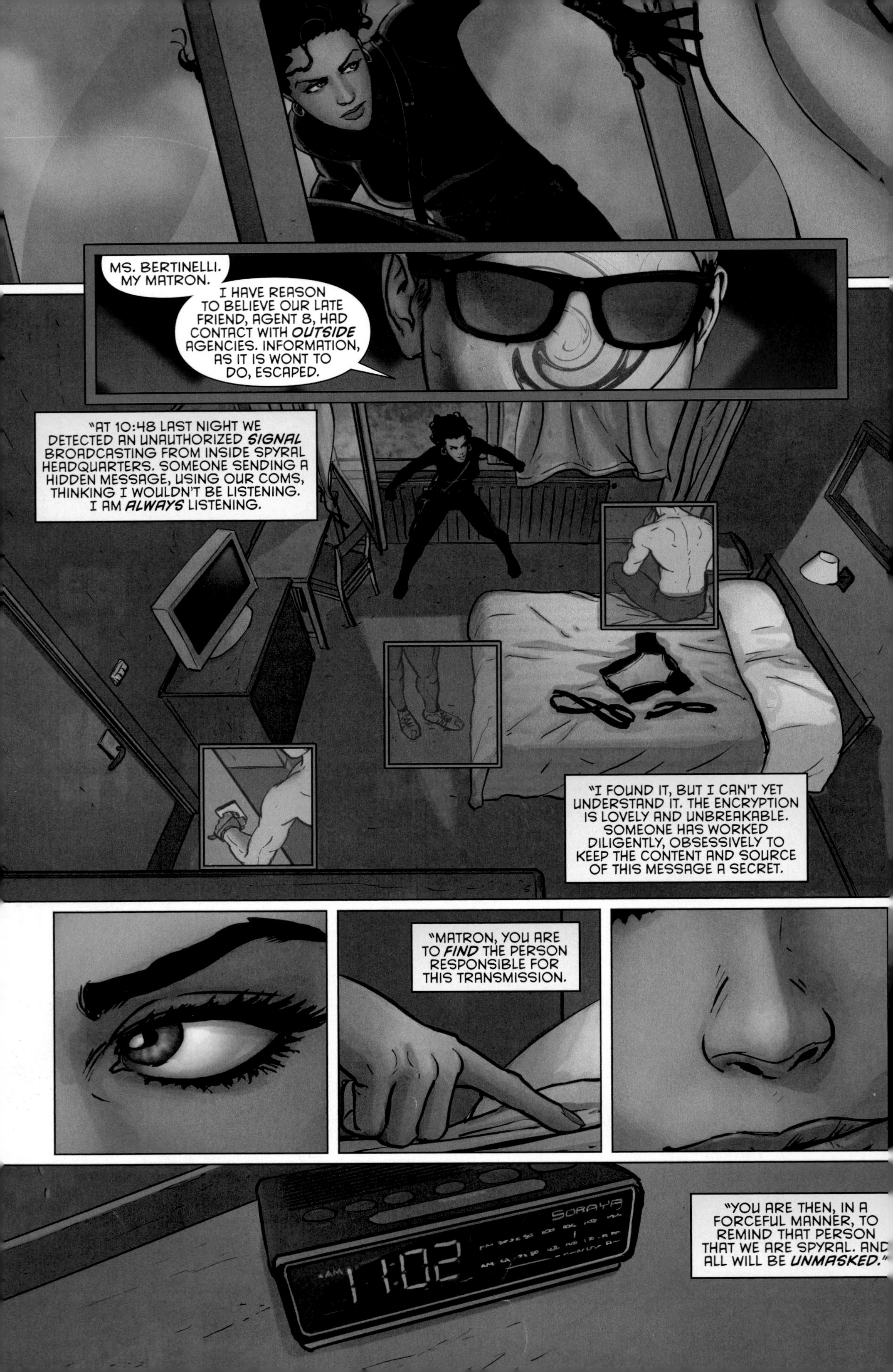

MS. BERTINELLI. MY MATRON.
I HAVE REASON TO BELIEVE OUR LATE FRIEND, AGENT 8, HAD CONTACT WITH OUTSIDE AGENCIES. INFORMATION, AS IT IS WONT TO DO, ESCAPED.
"AT 10:48 LAST NIGHT WE DETECTED AN UNAUTHORIZED SIGNAL BROADCASTING FROM INSIDE SPYRAL HEADQUARTERS. SOMEONE SENDING A HIDDEN MESSAGE, USING OUR COMS, THINKING I WOULDN'T BE LISTENING. I AM ALWAYS LISTENING.
"I FOUND IT, BUT I CAN'T YET UNDERSTAND IT. THE ENCRYPTION IS LOVELY AND UNBREAKABLE. SOMEONE HAS WORKED DILIGENTLY, OBSESSIVELY TO KEEP THE CONTENT AND SOURCE OF THIS MESSAGE A SECRET.
"MATRON, YOU ARE TO FIND THE PERSON RESPONSIBLE FOR THIS TRANSMISSION.
"YOU ARE THEN, IN A FORCEFUL MANNER, TO REMIND THAT PERSON THAT WE ARE SPYRAL. AND ALL WILL BE UNMASKED."

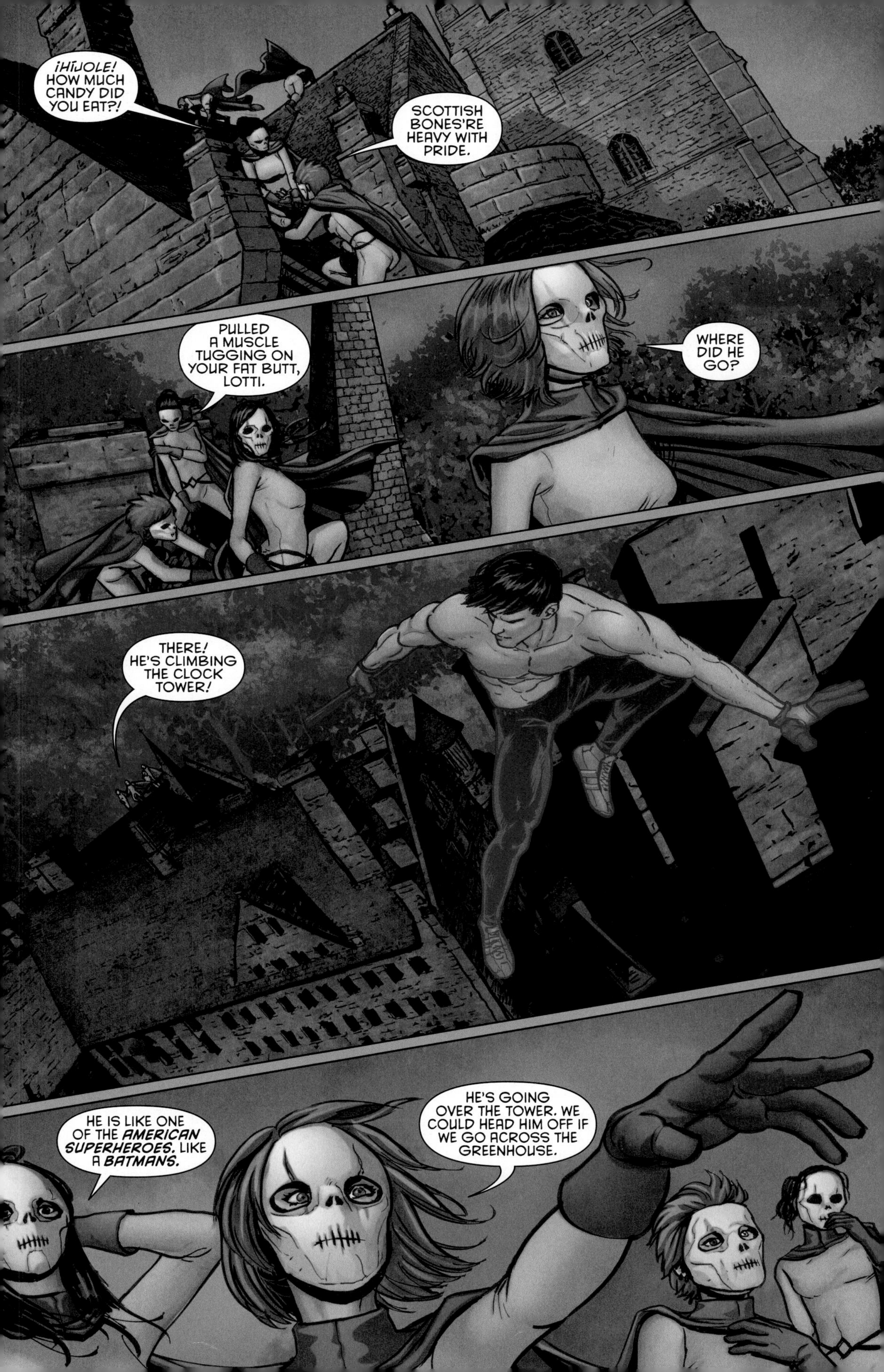
¡HÍJOLE! HOW MUCH CANDY DID YOU EAT?!
SCOTTISH BONES'RE HEAVY WITH PRIDE.
PULLED A MUSCLE TUGGING ON YOUR FAT BUTT, LOTTI.
WHERE DID HE GO?
THERE! HE'S CLIMBING THE CLOCK TOWER!
HE IS LIKE ONE OF THE *AMERICAN SUPERHEROES*. LIKE A *BATMANS*.
HE'S GOING OVER THE TOWER. WE COULD HEAD HIM OFF IF WE GO ACROSS THE GREENHOUSE.

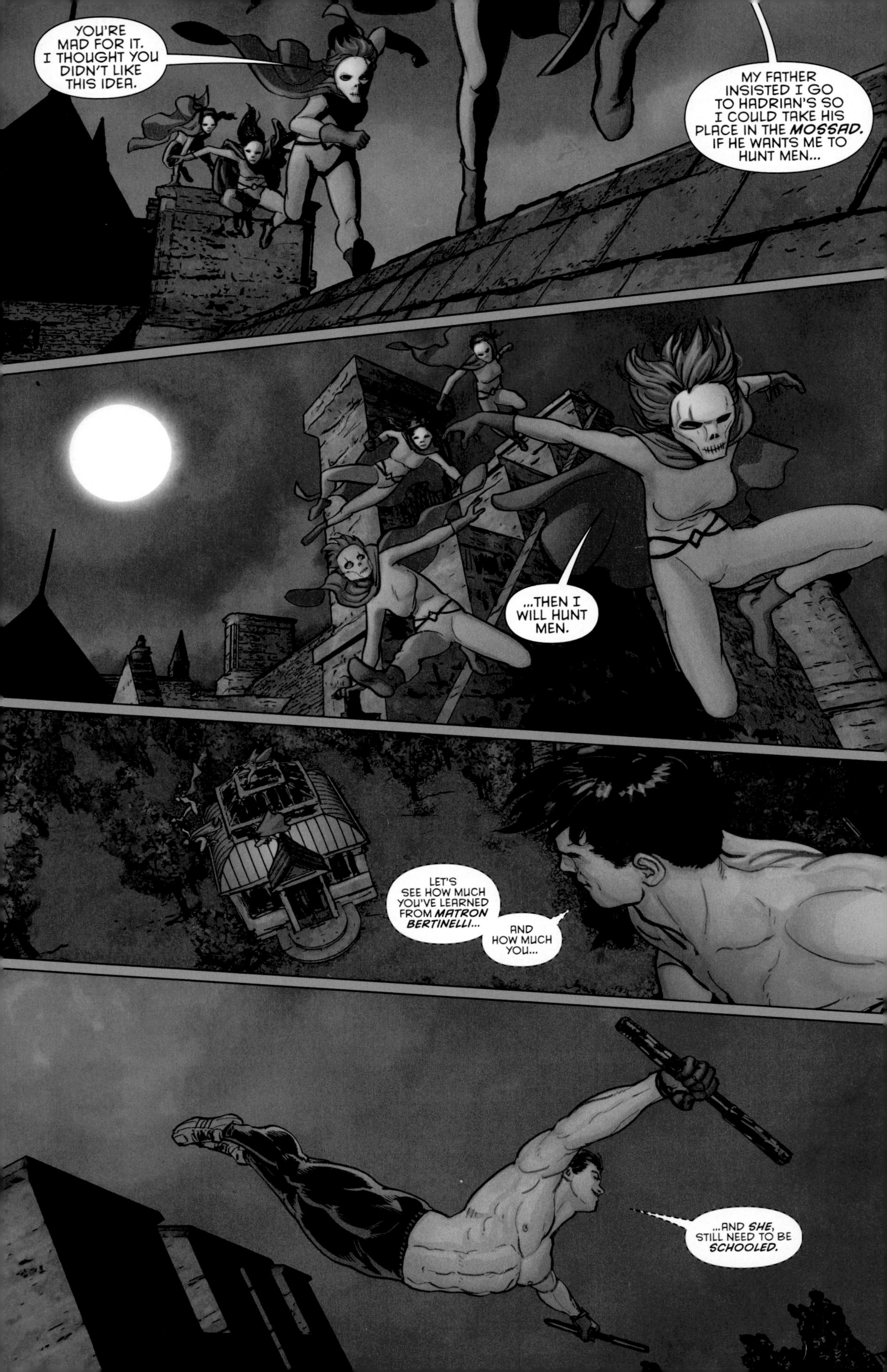
YOU'RE MAD FOR IT. I THOUGHT YOU DIDN'T LIKE THIS IDEA.
MY FATHER INSISTED I GO TO HADRIAN'S SO I COULD TAKE HIS PLACE IN THE MOSSAD. IF HE WANTS ME TO HUNT MEN...
...THEN I WILL HUNT MEN.
LET'S SEE HOW MUCH YOU'VE LEARNED FROM MATRON BERTINELLI...
AND HOW MUCH YOU...
...AND SHE, STILL NEED TO BE SCHOOLED.

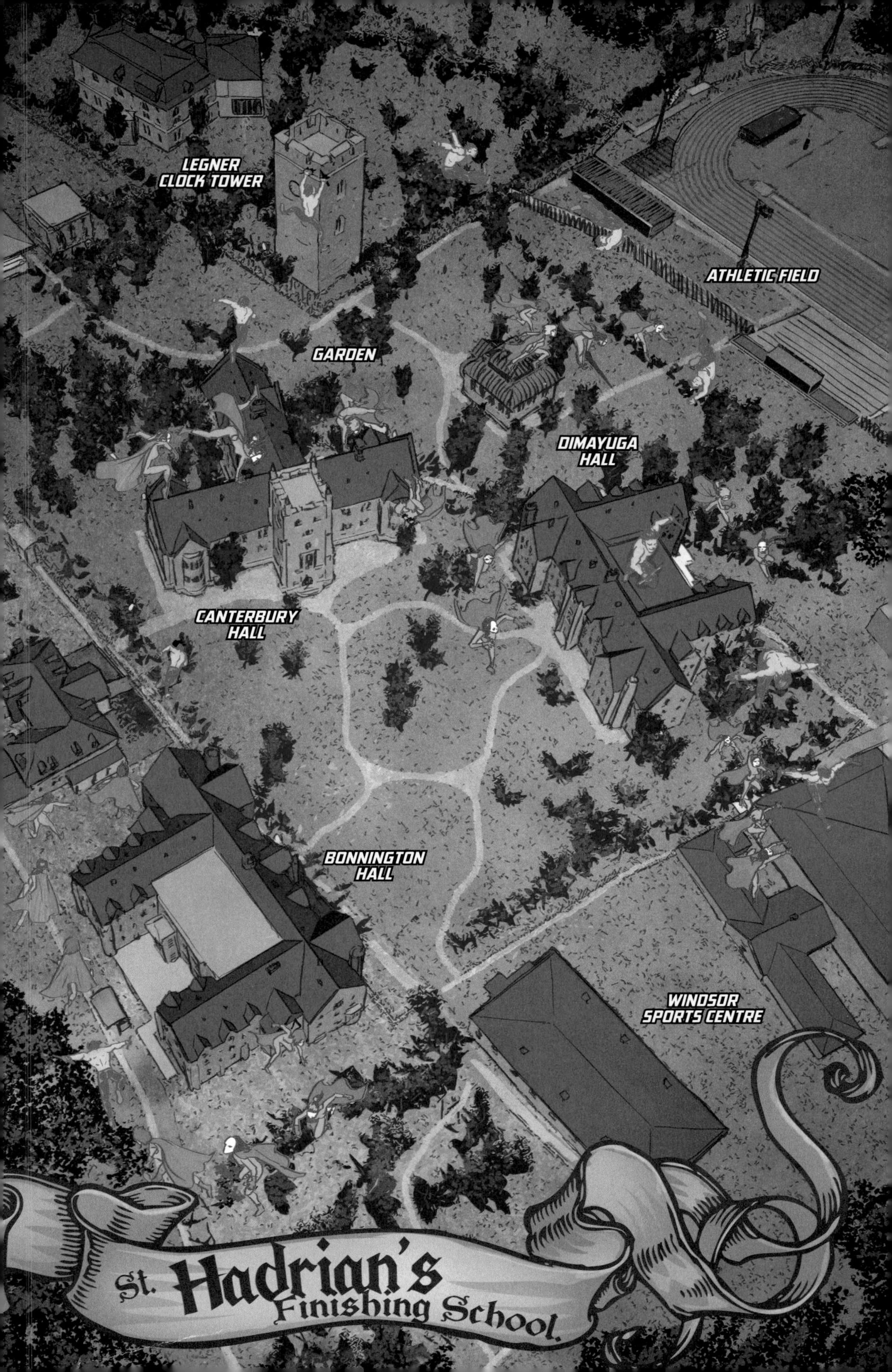
LEGNER CLOCK TOWER
ATHLETIC FIELD
GARDEN
DIMAYUGA HALL
CANTERBURY HALL
BONNINGTON HALL
WINDSOR SPORTS CENTRE
St. Hadrian's Finishing School.

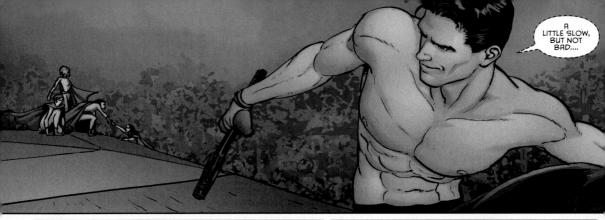

A LITTLE SLOW, BUT NOT BAD....

HE'S UP HERE!

NOWHERE TO GO BUT THE FOOTBALL FIELD NOW, AYE?

Ahhh, BAWS.

≥SIGH≤ "BAWS" IS RIGHT.

EVENIN', MATRON.

GIRLS. RETURN TO YOUR DORMS. IMMEDIATELY.

AND YOU, AGENT 37. FOLLOW ME. NOW.

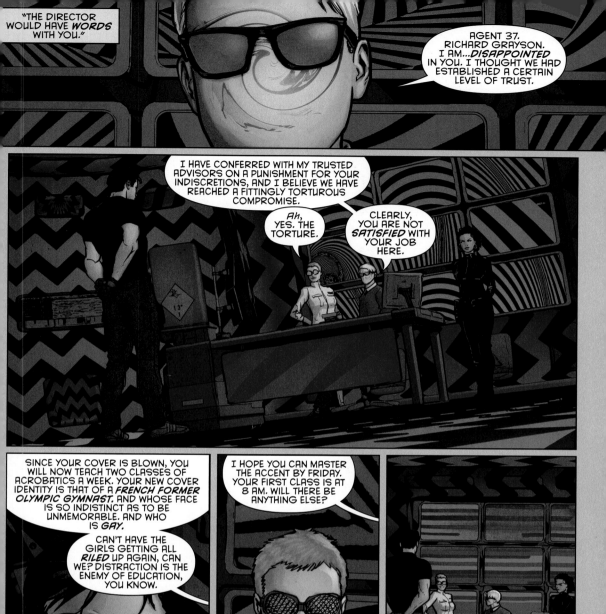

"THE DIRECTOR WOULD HAVE *WORDS* WITH YOU."

AGENT 37. RICHARD GRAYSON. I AM...*DISAPPOINTED* IN YOU. I THOUGHT WE HAD ESTABLISHED A CERTAIN LEVEL OF TRUST.

I HAVE CONFERRED WITH MY TRUSTED ADVISORS ON A PUNISHMENT FOR YOUR INDISCRETIONS, AND I BELIEVE WE HAVE REACHED A FITTINGLY TORTUROUS COMPROMISE.

Ah, YES. THE TORTURE.

CLEARLY, YOU ARE NOT *SATISFIED* WITH YOUR JOB HERE.

SINCE YOUR COVER IS BLOWN, YOU WILL NOW TEACH TWO CLASSES OF ACROBATICS A WEEK. YOUR NEW COVER IDENTITY IS THAT OF A *FRENCH FORMER OLYMPIC GYMNAST.* AND WHOSE FACE IS SO INDISTINCT AS TO BE UNMEMORABLE. AND WHO IS *GAY.*

CAN'T HAVE THE GIRLS GETTING ALL *RILED* UP AGAIN, CAN WE? DISTRACTION IS THE ENEMY OF EDUCATION, YOU KNOW.

I HOPE YOU CAN MASTER THE ACCENT BY FRIDAY. YOUR FIRST CLASS IS AT 8 AM. WILL THERE BE ANYTHING ELSE?

A GAY FRENCH GYMNAST? I'LL BE WRITING STORIES ABOUT YOU, AGENT 37. *SEXY STORIES.*

DO NOT DISAPPOINT ME AGAIN, AGENT 37. ARE WE COOL?

YEAH. THANK YOU, MR. MINOS.

YOU'RE RELIEVED.

MATRON, YOUR TURN.

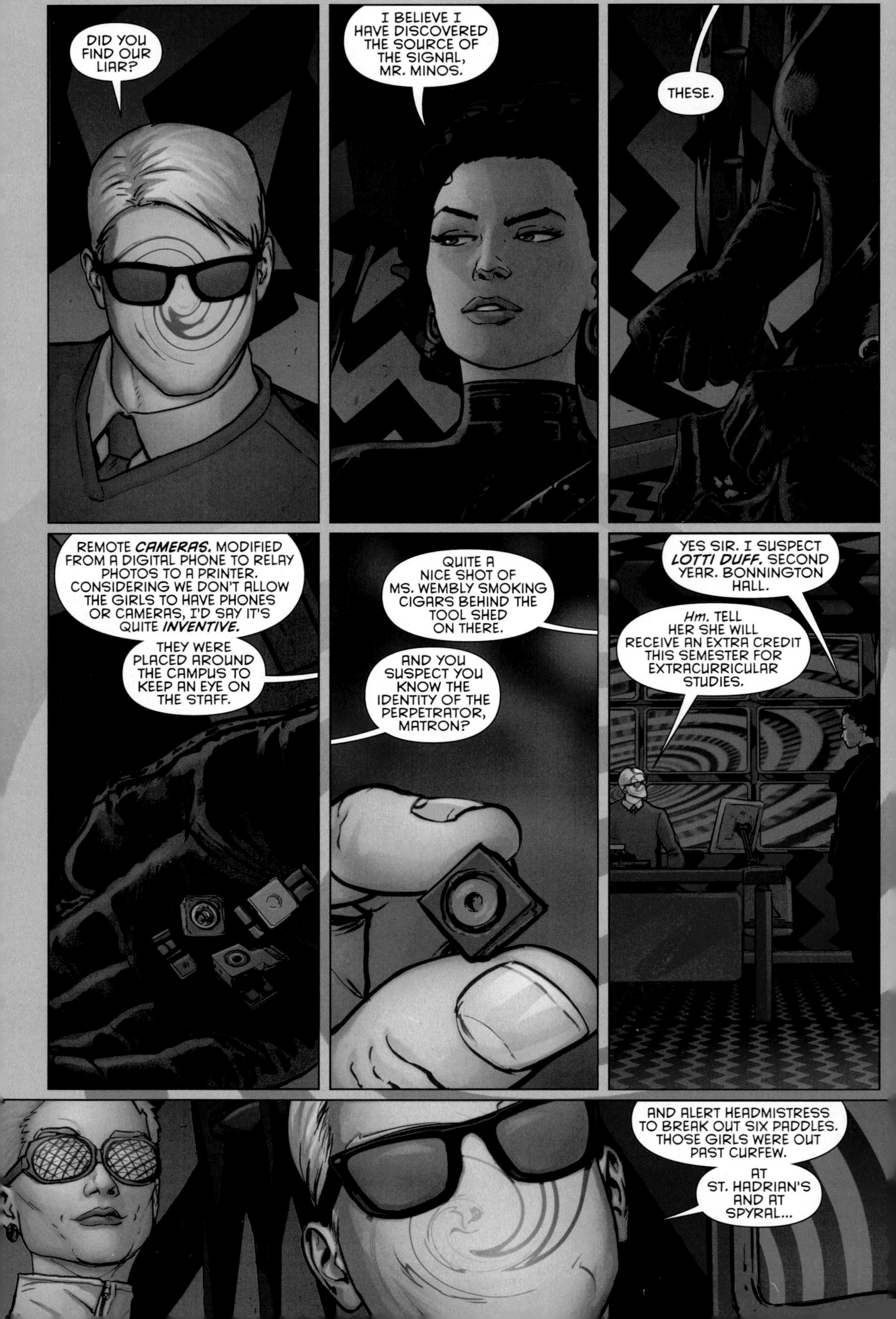
DID YOU FIND OUR LIAR?
I BELIEVE I HAVE DISCOVERED THE SOURCE OF THE SIGNAL, MR. MINOS.
THESE.
REMOTE CAMERAS. MODIFIED FROM A DIGITAL PHONE TO RELAY PHOTOS TO A PRINTER. CONSIDERING WE DON'T ALLOW THE GIRLS TO HAVE PHONES OR CAMERAS, I'D SAY IT'S QUITE INVENTIVE.
THEY WERE PLACED AROUND THE CAMPUS TO KEEP AN EYE ON THE STAFF.
QUITE A NICE SHOT OF MS. WEMBLY SMOKING CIGARS BEHIND THE TOOL SHED ON THERE.
AND YOU SUSPECT YOU KNOW THE IDENTITY OF THE PERPETRATOR, MATRON?
YES SIR. I SUSPECT LOTTI DUFF. SECOND YEAR. BONNINGTON HALL.
Hm. TELL HER SHE WILL RECEIVE AN EXTRA CREDIT THIS SEMESTER FOR EXTRACURRICULAR STUDIES.
AND ALERT HEADMISTRESS TO BREAK OUT SIX PADDLES. THOSE GIRLS WERE OUT PAST CURFEW.
AT ST. HADRIAN'S AND AT SPYRAL...

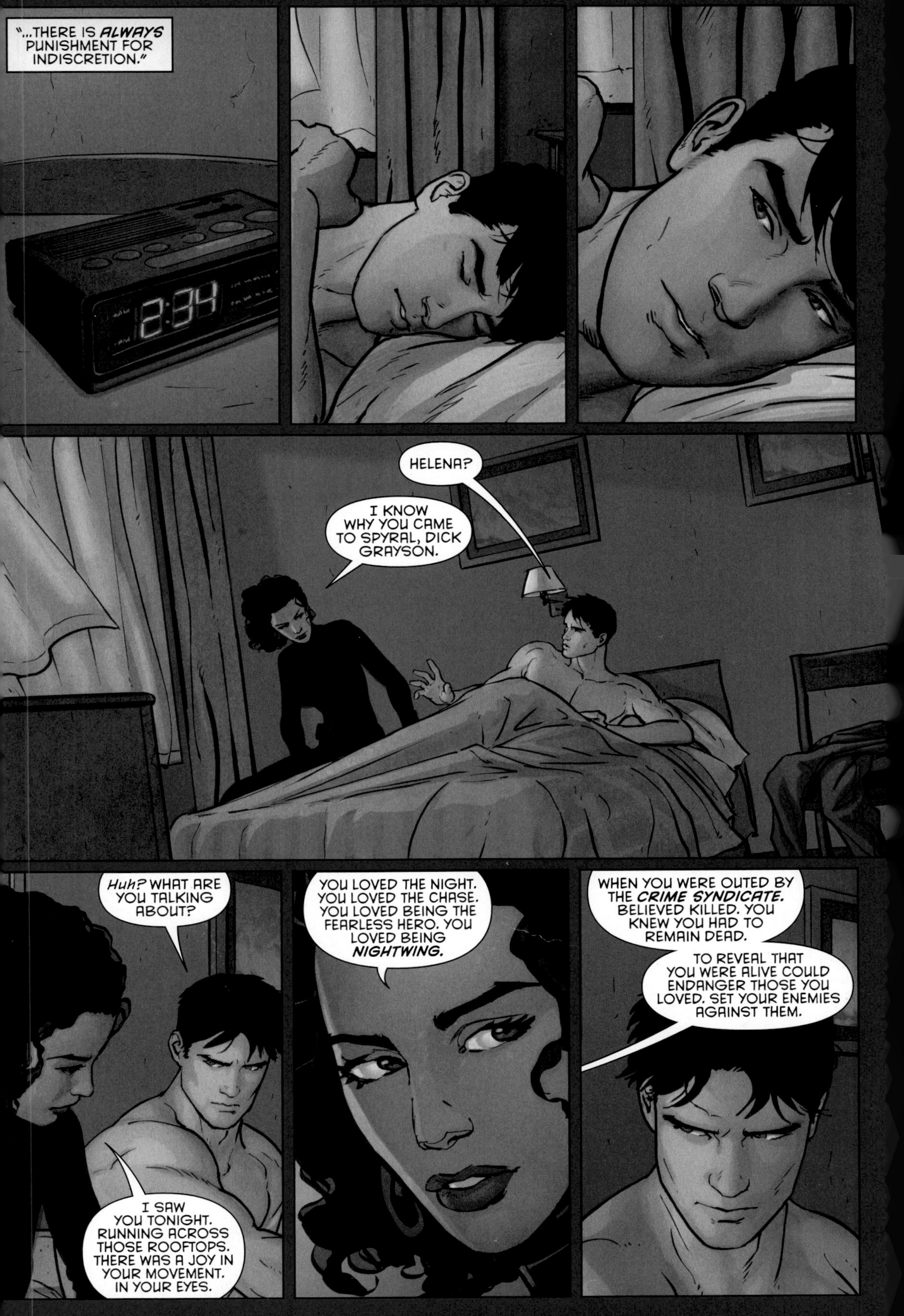
"...THERE IS *ALWAYS* PUNISHMENT FOR INDISCRETION."
2:34
HELENA?
I KNOW WHY YOU CAME TO SPYRAL, DICK GRAYSON.
Huh? WHAT ARE YOU TALKING ABOUT?
I SAW YOU TONIGHT. RUNNING ACROSS THOSE ROOFTOPS. THERE WAS A JOY IN YOUR MOVEMENT. IN YOUR EYES.
YOU LOVED THE NIGHT. YOU LOVED THE CHASE. YOU LOVED BEING THE FEARLESS HERO. YOU LOVED BEING *NIGHTWING.*
WHEN YOU WERE OUTED BY THE *CRIME SYNDICATE.* BELIEVED KILLED. YOU KNEW YOU HAD TO REMAIN DEAD.
TO REVEAL THAT YOU WERE ALIVE COULD ENDANGER THOSE YOU LOVED. SET YOUR ENEMIES AGAINST THEM.

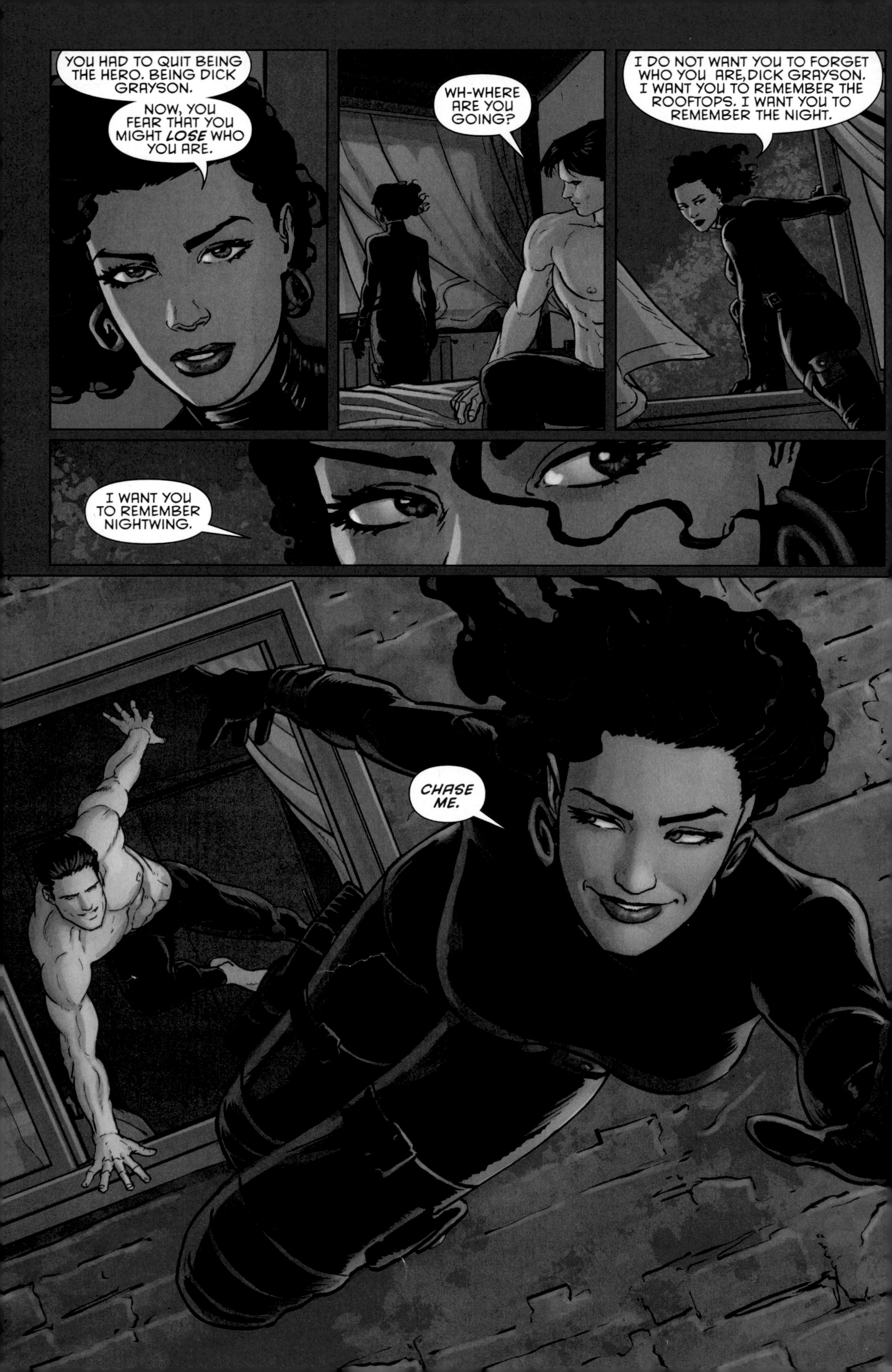
YOU HAD TO QUIT BEING THE HERO. BEING DICK GRAYSON.
NOW, YOU FEAR THAT YOU MIGHT *LOSE* WHO YOU ARE.
WH-WHERE ARE YOU GOING?
I DO NOT WANT YOU TO FORGET WHO YOU ARE, DICK GRAYSON. I WANT YOU TO REMEMBER THE ROOFTOPS. I WANT YOU TO REMEMBER THE NIGHT.
I WANT YOU TO REMEMBER NIGHTWING.
CHASE ME.

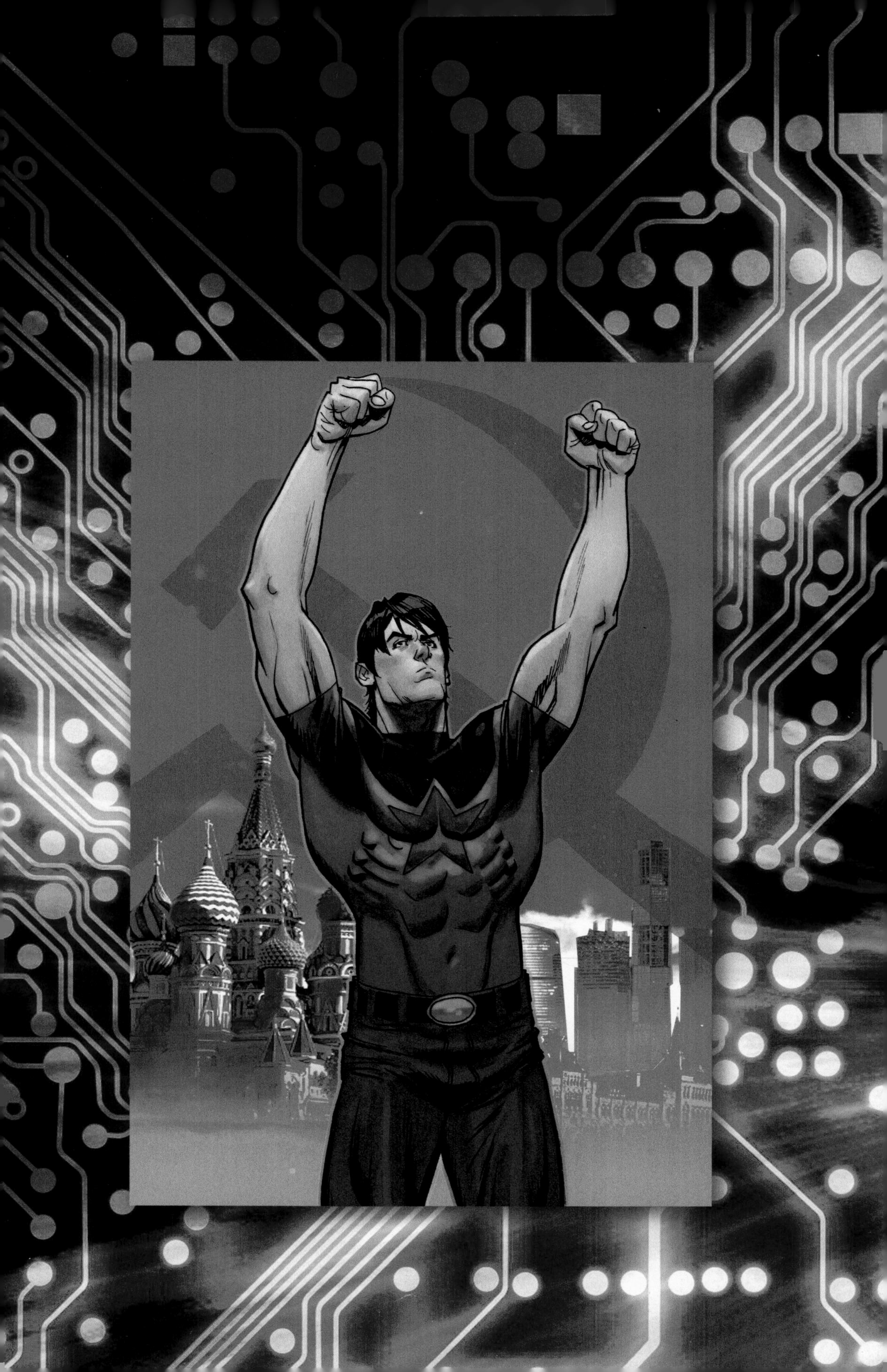

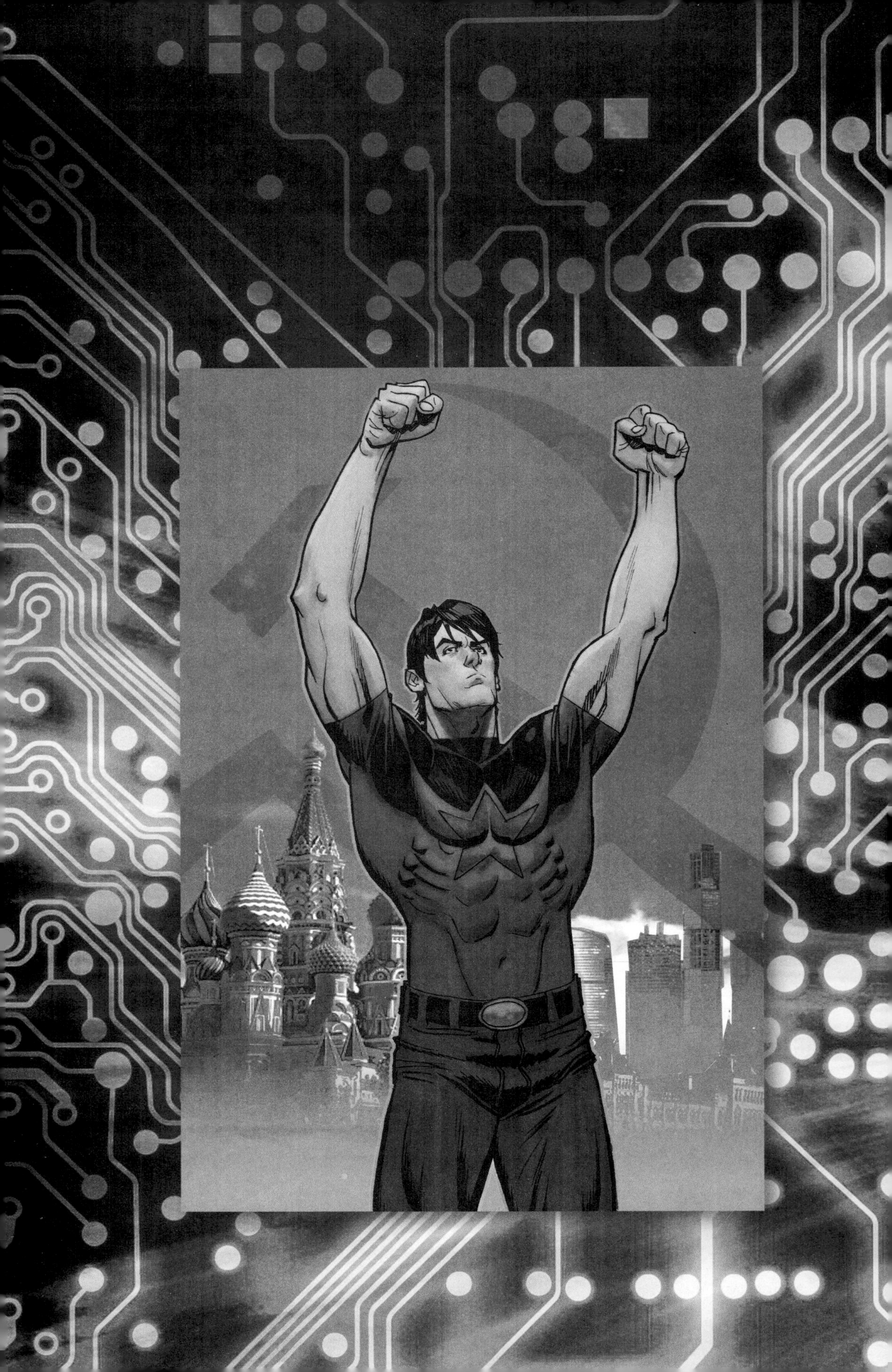

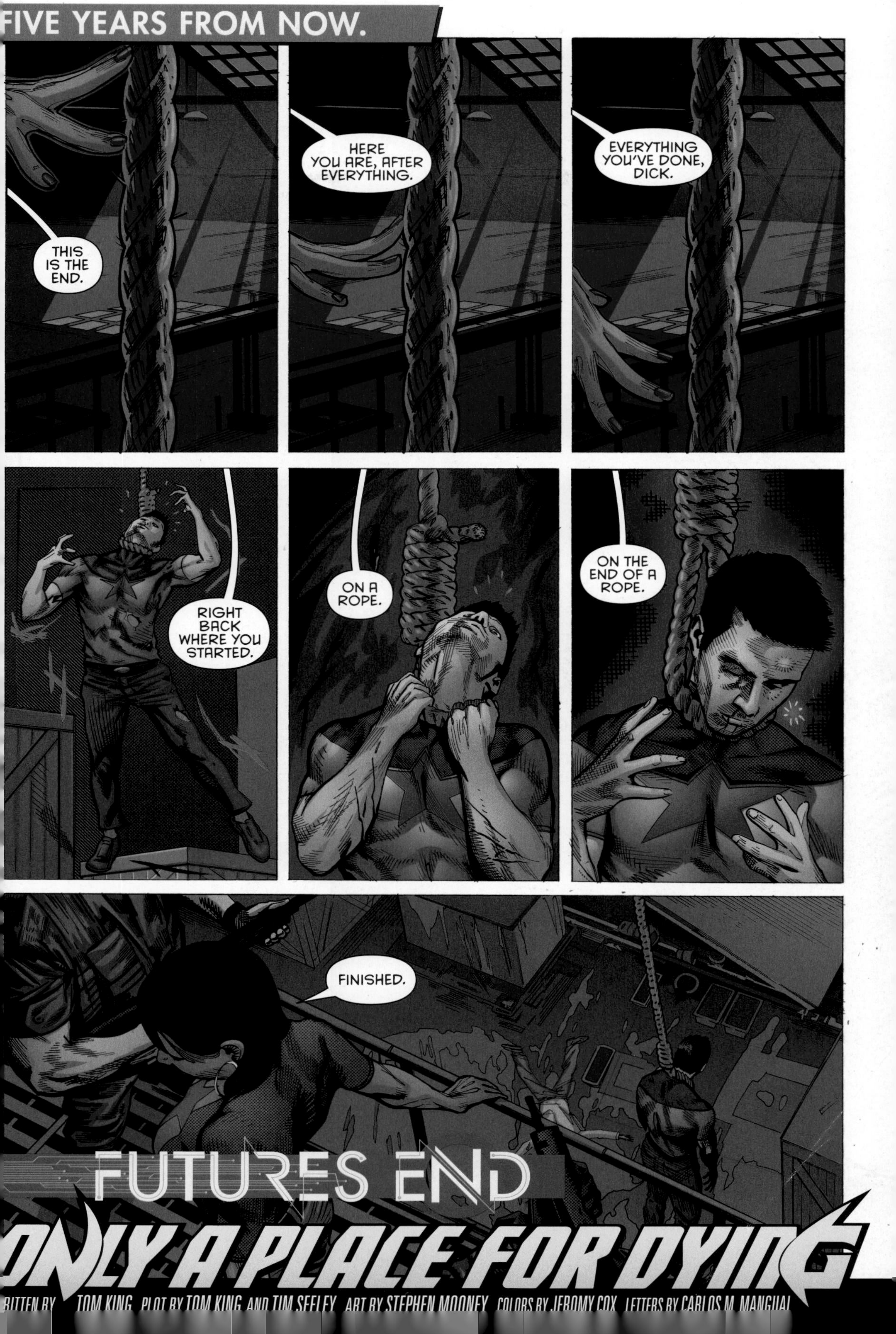
FIVE YEARS FROM NOW.
THIS IS THE END.
HERE YOU ARE, AFTER EVERYTHING.
EVERYTHING YOU'VE DONE, DICK.
RIGHT BACK WHERE YOU STARTED.
ON A ROPE.
ON THE END OF A ROPE.
FINISHED.
FUTURES END
ONLY A PLACE FOR DYING
RITTEN BY TOM KING PLOT BY TOM KING AND TIM SEELEY ART BY STEPHEN MOONEY COLORS BY JEROMY COX LETTERS BY CARLOS M. MANGUAL

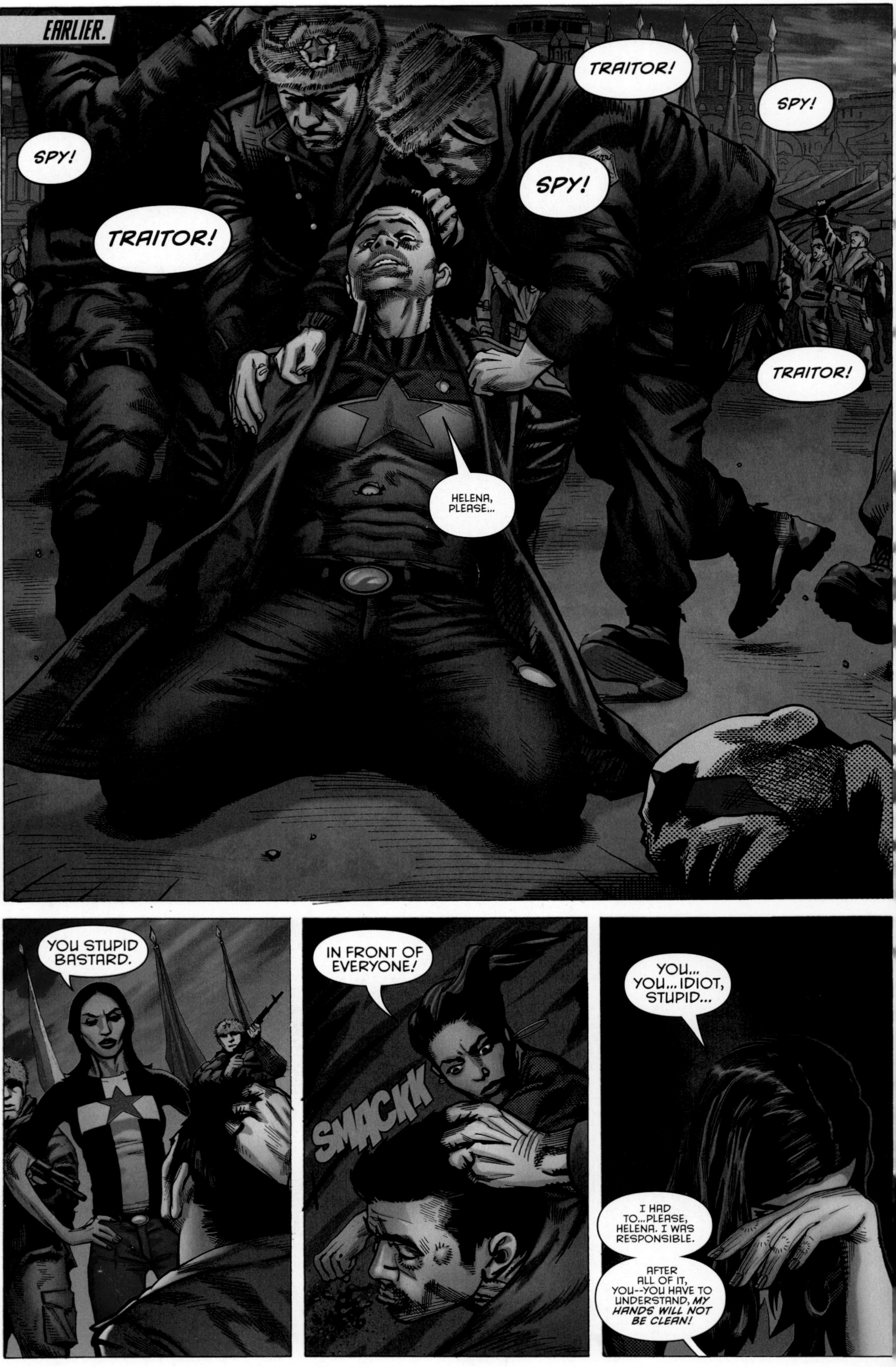
EARLIER.
TRAITOR!
SPY!
SPY!
TRAITOR!
SPY!
TRAITOR!
HELENA, PLEASE...
YOU STUPID BASTARD.
IN FRONT OF EVERYONE!
SMACKK
YOU... YOU... IDIOT, STUPID...
I HAD TO...PLEASE, HELENA. I WAS RESPONSIBLE.
AFTER ALL OF IT, YOU--YOU HAVE TO UNDERSTAND, MY HANDS WILL NOT BE CLEAN!

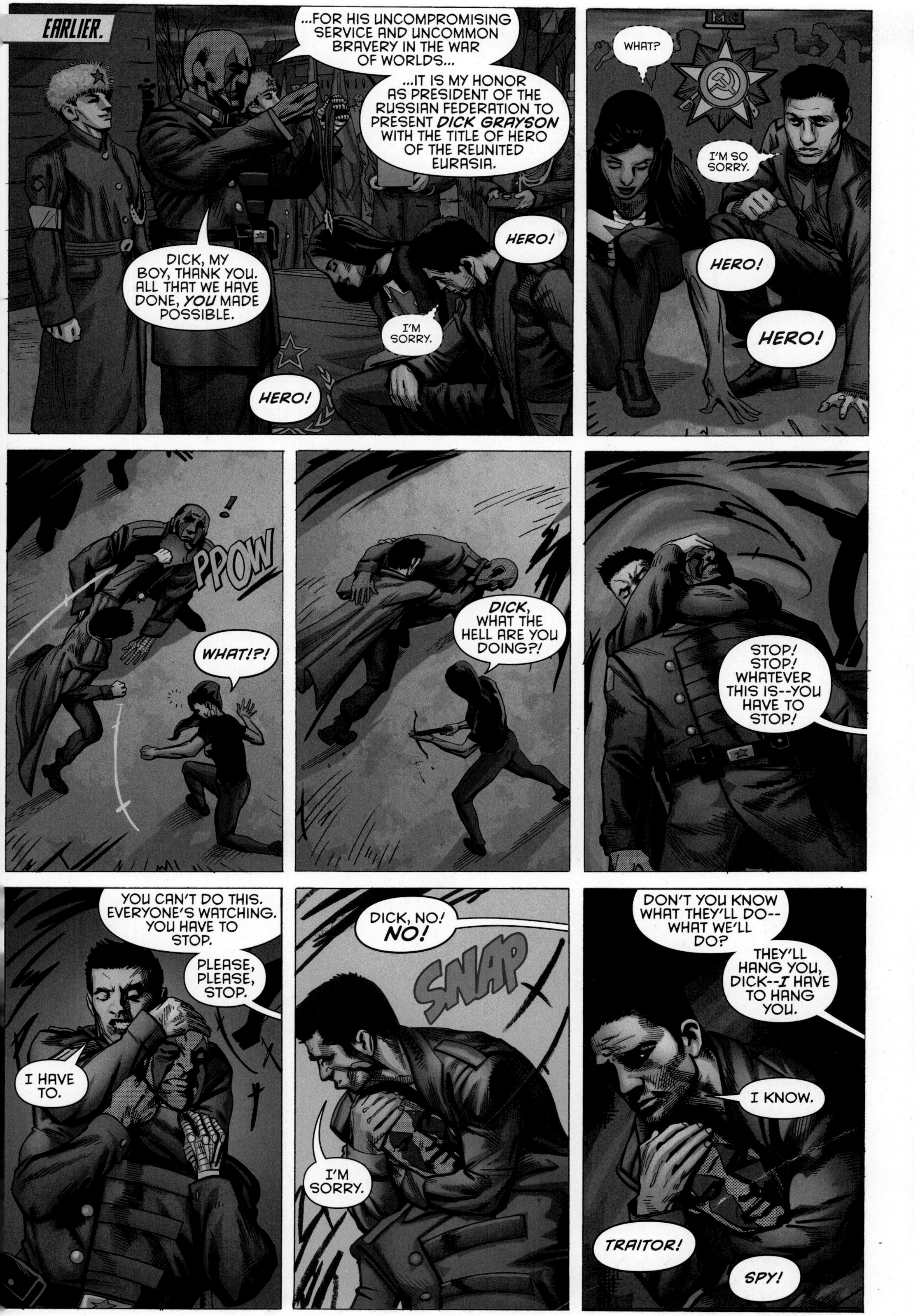
EARLIER.
...FOR HIS UNCOMPROMISING SERVICE AND UNCOMMON BRAVERY IN THE WAR OF WORLDS...
...IT IS MY HONOR AS PRESIDENT OF THE RUSSIAN FEDERATION TO PRESENT DICK GRAYSON WITH THE TITLE OF HERO OF THE REUNITED EURASIA.
DICK, MY BOY, THANK YOU. ALL THAT WE HAVE DONE, YOU MADE POSSIBLE.
HERO!
I'M SORRY.
HERO!
MC
WHAT?
I'M SO SORRY.
HERO!
HERO!
!
PPOW
WHAT!?!
DICK, WHAT THE HELL ARE YOU DOING?!
STOP! STOP! WHATEVER THIS IS--YOU HAVE TO STOP!
YOU CAN'T DO THIS. EVERYONE'S WATCHING. YOU HAVE TO STOP.
PLEASE, PLEASE, STOP.
I HAVE TO.
DICK, NO! NO!
SNAP
I'M SORRY.
DON'T YOU KNOW WHAT THEY'LL DO--WHAT WE'LL DO?
THEY'LL HANG YOU, DICK--I HAVE TO HANG YOU.
I KNOW.
TRAITOR!
SPY!

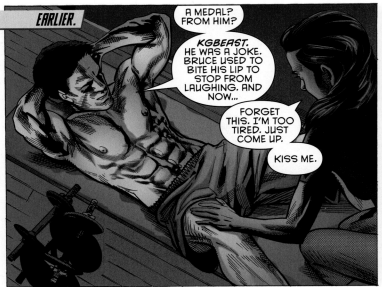

A MEDAL? FROM HIM?

KGBEAST. HE WAS A JOKE. BRUCE USED TO BITE HIS LIP TO STOP FROM LAUGHING. AND NOW...

FORGET THIS. I'M TOO TIRED. JUST COME UP.

KISS ME.

GOOD.

WE FOUGHT FOR HIM. SPYRAL FOUGHT FOR HIM.

WE HAD A COMMON ENEMY, AND WE *HELPED* HIM.

AND NOW. WHAT HE'S DOING. SINCE THE WAR, HE'S *CRUSHED* EUROPE. HE'S KILLING *THOUSANDS*, MORE. KIEV WAS THE BEGINNING.

AGAIN.

THE WAR IS OVER. WE GAVE EVERYTHING TO FIGHT IT. WE DESERVE THIS.

I HAVE TO *DO* SOMETHING. SOMEONE HAS TO BE RESPONSIBLE.

DICK, DARLING, STOP.

PLEASE, IT'S JUST A MEDAL...

...JUST SOMETHING ELSE TO HANG AROUND YOUR NECK.

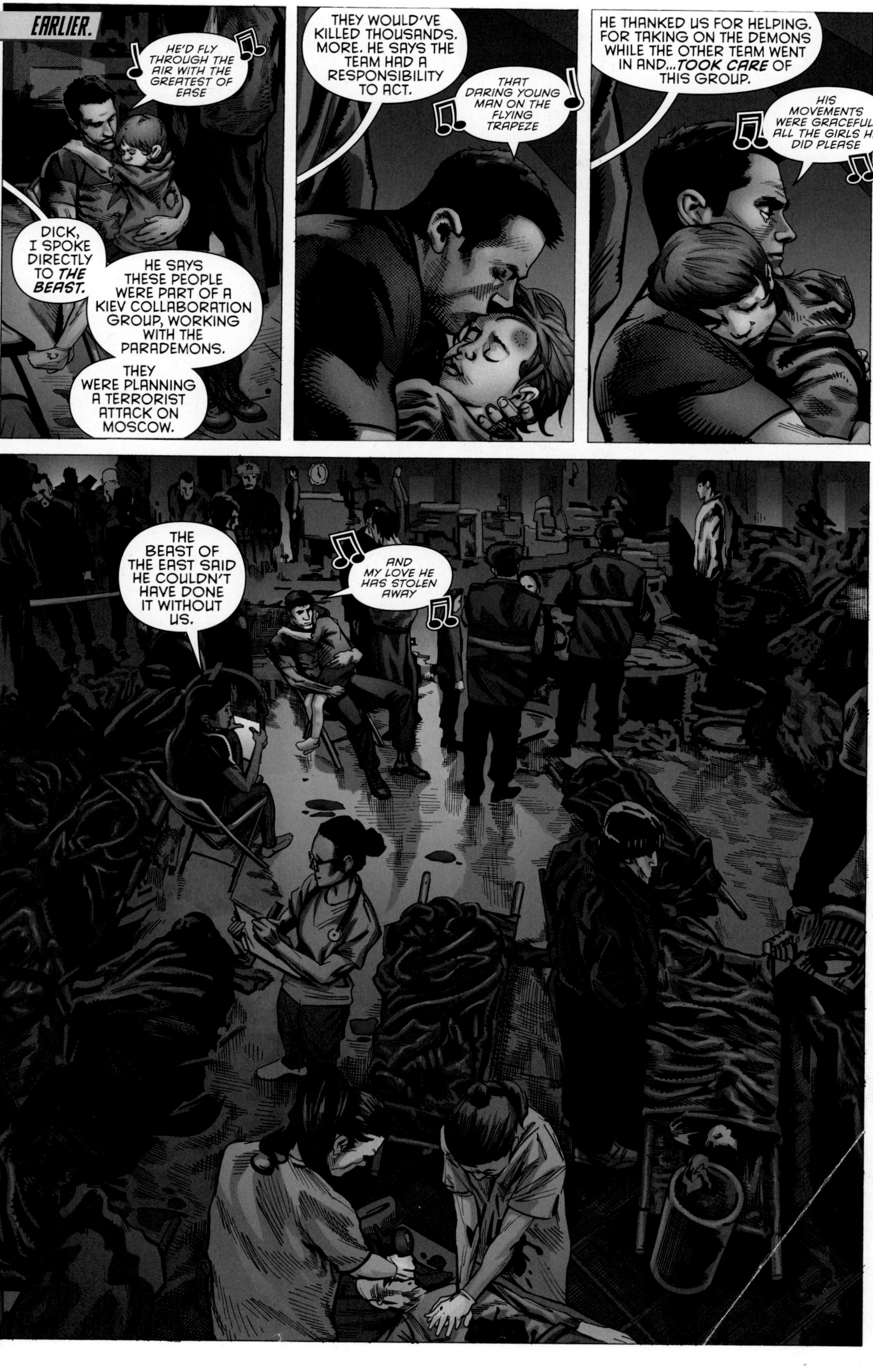
EARLIER.
HE'D FLY THROUGH THE AIR WITH THE GREATEST OF EASE
DICK, I SPOKE DIRECTLY TO THE BEAST.
HE SAYS THESE PEOPLE WERE PART OF A KIEV COLLABORATION GROUP, WORKING WITH THE PARADEMONS.
THEY WERE PLANNING A TERRORIST ATTACK ON MOSCOW.
THEY WOULD'VE KILLED THOUSANDS. MORE. HE SAYS THE TEAM HAD A RESPONSIBILITY TO ACT.
THAT DARING YOUNG MAN ON THE FLYING TRAPEZE
HE THANKED US FOR HELPING. FOR TAKING ON THE DEMONS WHILE THE OTHER TEAM WENT IN AND...TOOK CARE OF THIS GROUP.
HIS MOVEMENTS WERE GRACEFUL, ALL THE GIRLS HE DID PLEASE
THE BEAST OF THE EAST SAID HE COULDN'T HAVE DONE IT WITHOUT US.
AND MY LOVE HE HAS STOLEN AWAY

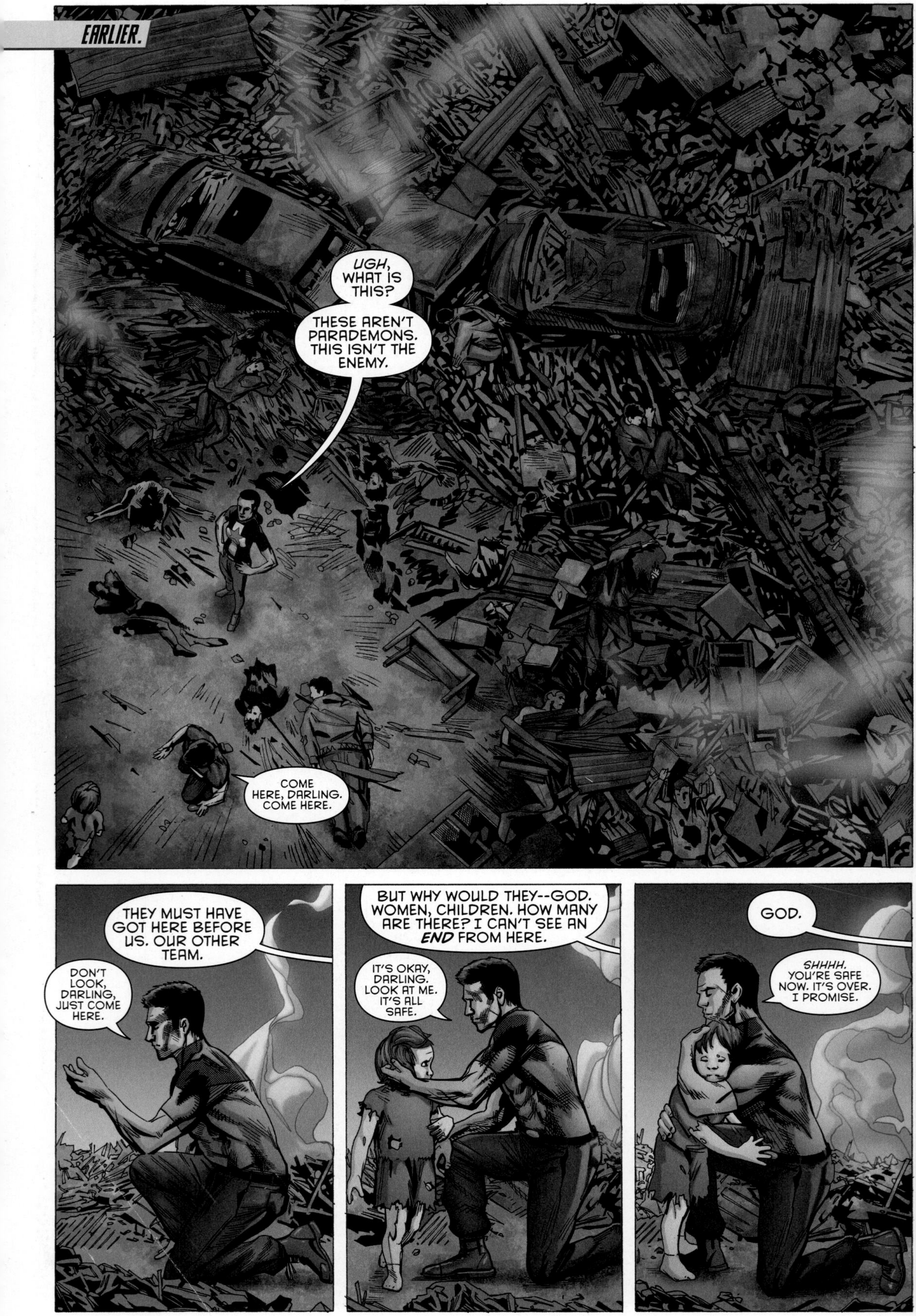
EARLIER.
UGH, WHAT IS THIS?
THESE AREN'T PARADEMONS. THIS ISN'T THE ENEMY.
COME HERE, DARLING. COME HERE.
THEY MUST HAVE GOT HERE BEFORE US. OUR OTHER TEAM.
DON'T LOOK, DARLING, JUST COME HERE.
BUT WHY WOULD THEY--GOD. WOMEN, CHILDREN. HOW MANY ARE THERE? I CAN'T SEE AN END FROM HERE.
IT'S OKAY, DARLING. LOOK AT ME. IT'S ALL SAFE.
GOD.
SHHHH. YOU'RE SAFE NOW. IT'S OVER. I PROMISE.

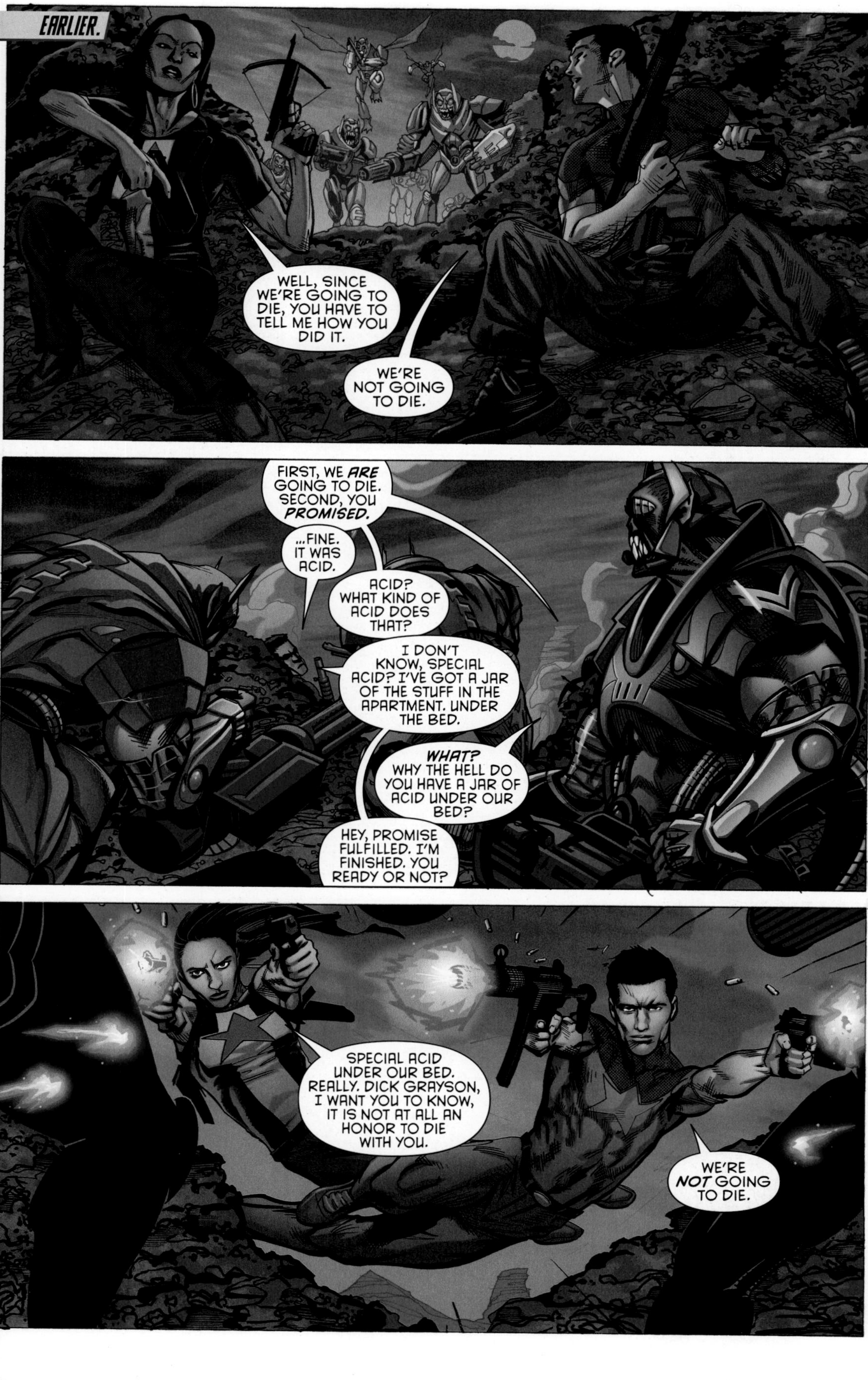
EARLIER.
WELL, SINCE WE'RE GOING TO DIE, YOU HAVE TO TELL ME HOW YOU DID IT.
WE'RE NOT GOING TO DIE.
FIRST, WE ***ARE*** GOING TO DIE. SECOND, YOU ***PROMISED.***
...FINE. IT WAS ACID.
ACID? WHAT KIND OF ACID DOES THAT?
I DON'T KNOW, SPECIAL ACID? I'VE GOT A JAR OF THE STUFF IN THE APARTMENT. UNDER THE BED.
WHAT? WHY THE HELL DO YOU HAVE A JAR OF ACID UNDER OUR BED?
HEY, PROMISE FULFILLED. I'M FINISHED. YOU READY OR NOT?
SPECIAL ACID UNDER OUR BED. REALLY. DICK GRAYSON, I WANT YOU TO KNOW, IT IS NOT AT ALL AN HONOR TO DIE WITH YOU.
WE'RE ***NOT*** GOING TO DIE.

THE RUSSIAN FEDERATION CANNOT PROPERLY THANK YOU AND SPYRAL FOR JOINING OUR EFFORTS AGAINST THIS EARTH-2 MENACE.

TOGETHER WE WILL FIND VICTORY!

WHEN DO WE MEET *THE BEAST?*

NO, NO, NO, PLEASE, I AM AFRAID YOU ARE MISINFORMED. YOU WILL NOT MEET OUR DEAR LEADER. HE MAKES VERY FEW PERSONAL APPEARANCES.

FOR *SECURITY,* YOU UNDERSTAND.

SEE, WHAT'D I TELL YOU? YOU DON'T MEET THE BEAST.

FOR *SECURITY,* YOU UNDERSTAND.

AND...AND WE DO NOT REFER TO OUR *DEAR LEADER* AS THE BEAST. HE NO LONGER USES THIS...TITLE.

HE IS NOW *PRESIDENT ANATOLI KNYAZEV.*

WHAT ABOUT THE RUMORS THAT THE BEAST IS KILLING CIVILIANS WHO DON'T COOPER--

PLEASE EXCUSE MY RATHER RUDE PARTNER.

WHAT HE MEANS IS, WHAT ABOUT THE RUMORS THAT *PRESIDENT ANATOLI KNYAZEV* IS KILLING CIVILIANS WHO DON'T COOPERATE?

NO, NO, NO, THIS IS VERY MUCH NONSENSE.

I HAVE HEARD SUCH RUMORS AS WELL.

THE BEAS-- THE *PRESIDENT* WOULD NOT TOLERATE SUCH HORRORS. SAVAGERY IS FOR THE DEMONS.

WE RUSSIANS ALWAYS FIGHT WITH COMPASSION.

AND AFTER IT'S OVER, WILL THE BEAST GIVE BACK THE TERRITORY HE'S TAKEN TO FIGHT THIS WAR? EUROPE, ASIA--WILL THEY BE FREE?

WHEN THIS WAR'S DONE, IS IT DONE?

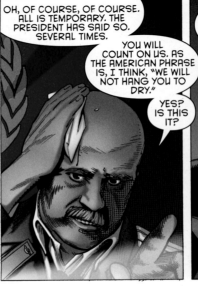

OH, OF COURSE, OF COURSE. ALL IS TEMPORARY. THE PRESIDENT HAS SAID SO. SEVERAL TIMES.

YOU WILL COUNT ON US. AS THE AMERICAN PHRASE IS, I THINK, "WE WILL NOT HANG YOU TO DRY."

YES? IS THIS IT?

CLOSE ENOUGH FOR GOVERNMENT WORK.

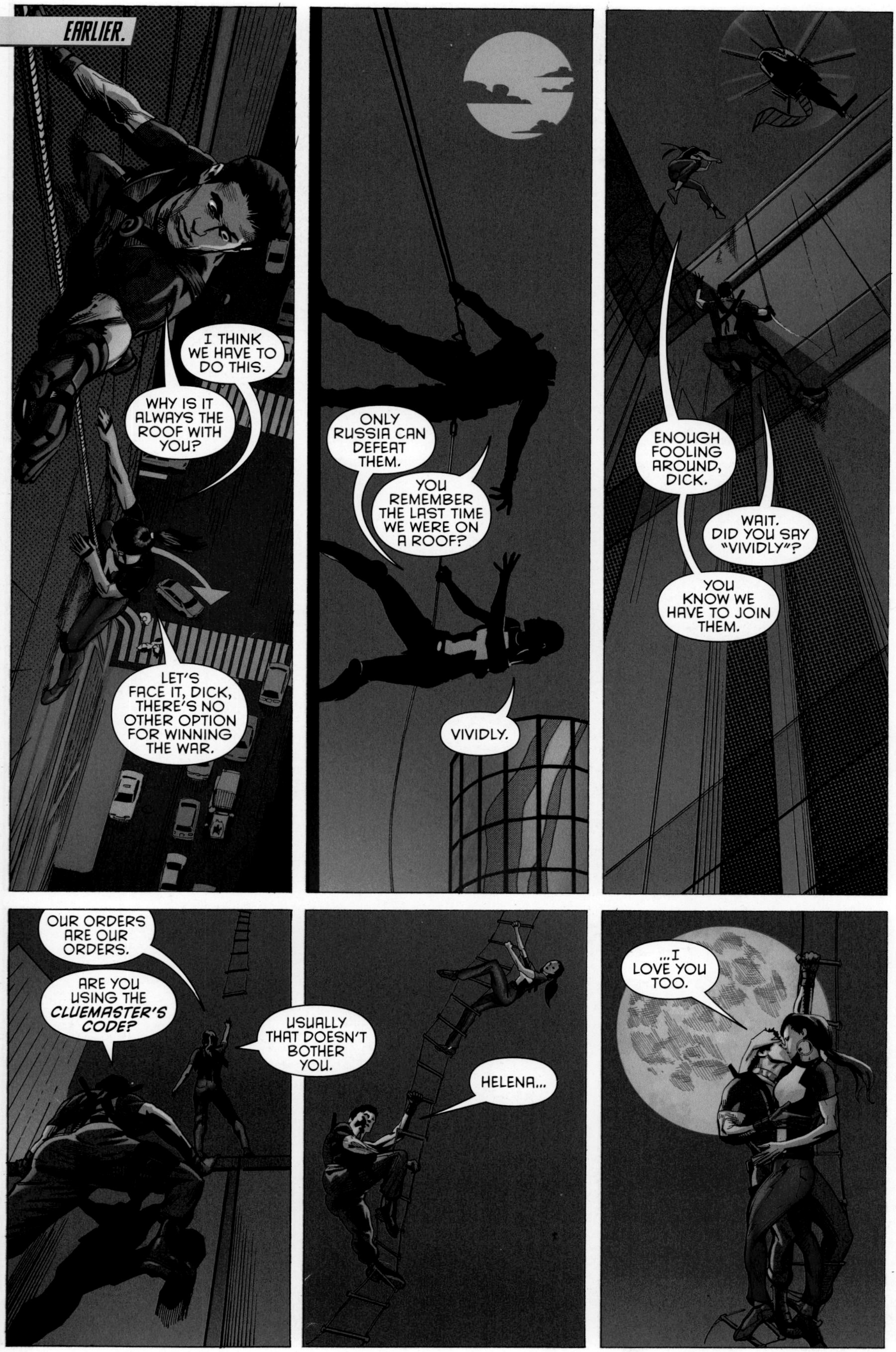
EARLIER.
I THINK WE HAVE TO DO THIS.
WHY IS IT ALWAYS THE ROOF WITH YOU?
LET'S FACE IT, DICK, THERE'S NO OTHER OPTION FOR WINNING THE WAR.
ONLY RUSSIA CAN DEFEAT THEM.
YOU REMEMBER THE LAST TIME WE WERE ON A ROOF?
VIVIDLY.
ENOUGH FOOLING AROUND, DICK.
WAIT. DID YOU SAY "VIVIDLY"?
YOU KNOW WE HAVE TO JOIN THEM.
OUR ORDERS ARE OUR ORDERS.
ARE YOU USING THE *CLUEMASTER'S CODE?*
USUALLY THAT DOESN'T BOTHER YOU.
HELENA...
...I LOVE YOU TOO.

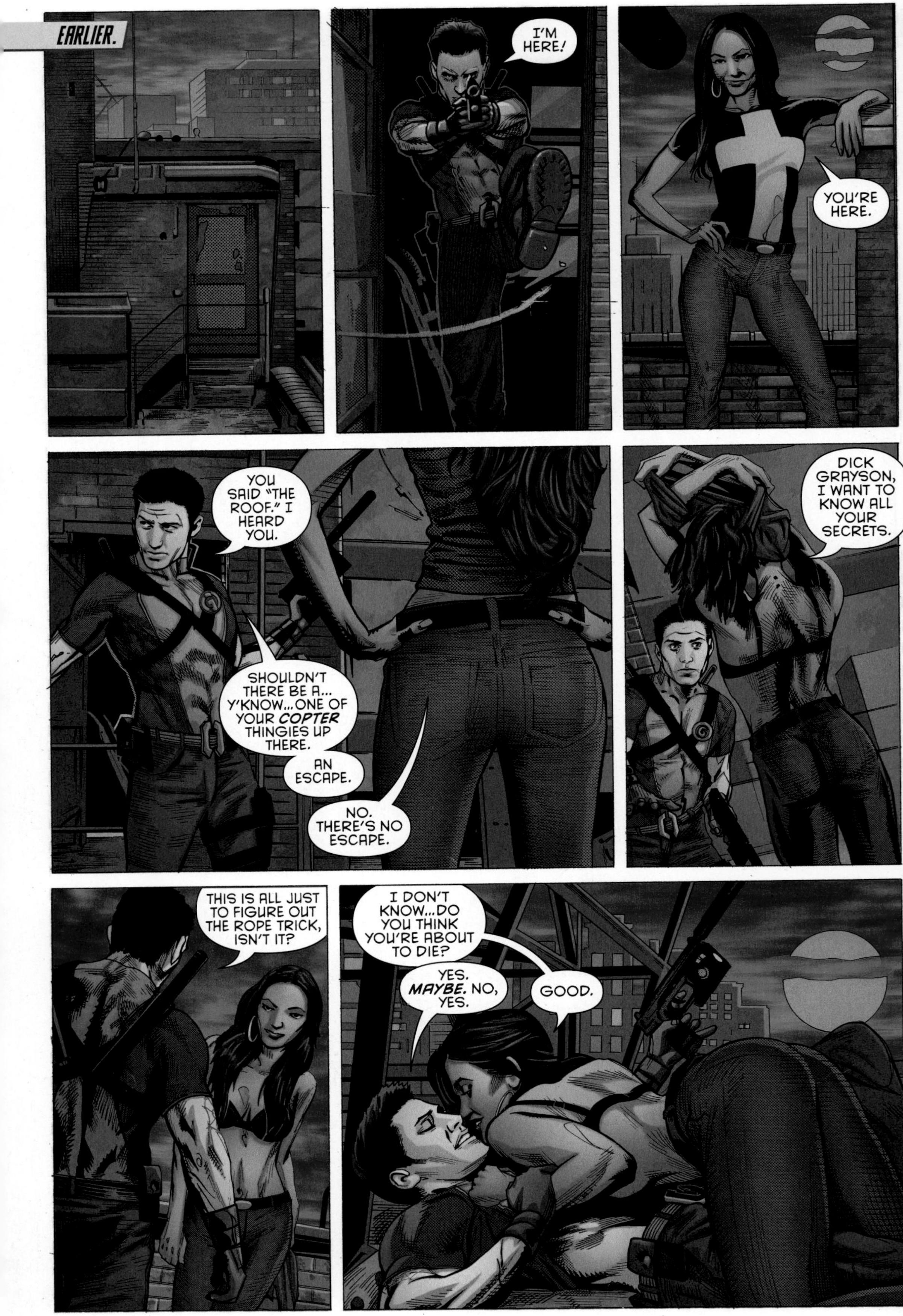
EARLIER.
I'M HERE!
YOU'RE HERE.
YOU SAID "THE ROOF." I HEARD YOU.
SHOULDN'T THERE BE A... Y'KNOW...ONE OF YOUR COPTER THINGIES UP THERE.
AN ESCAPE.
NO. THERE'S NO ESCAPE.
DICK GRAYSON, I WANT TO KNOW ALL YOUR SECRETS.
THIS IS ALL JUST TO FIGURE OUT THE ROPE TRICK, ISN'T IT?
I DON'T KNOW...DO YOU THINK YOU'RE ABOUT TO DIE?
YES. MAYBE. NO, YES.
GOOD.

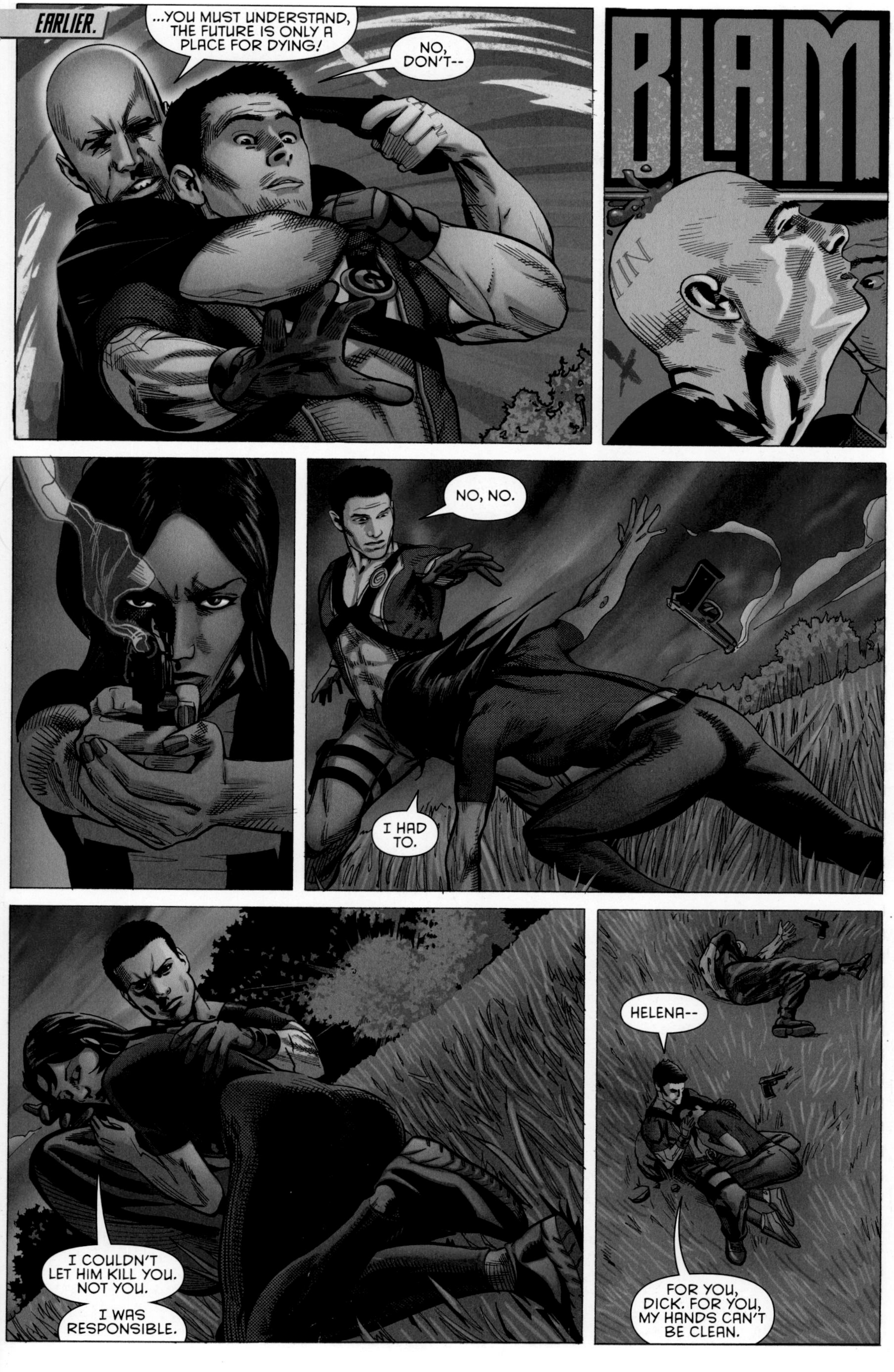
EARLIER.
...YOU MUST UNDERSTAND, THE FUTURE IS ONLY A PLACE FOR DYING!
NO, DON'T--
BLAM
NO, NO.
I HAD TO.
I COULDN'T LET HIM KILL YOU. NOT YOU.
I WAS RESPONSIBLE.
HELENA--
FOR YOU, DICK. FOR YOU, MY HANDS CAN'T BE CLEAN.

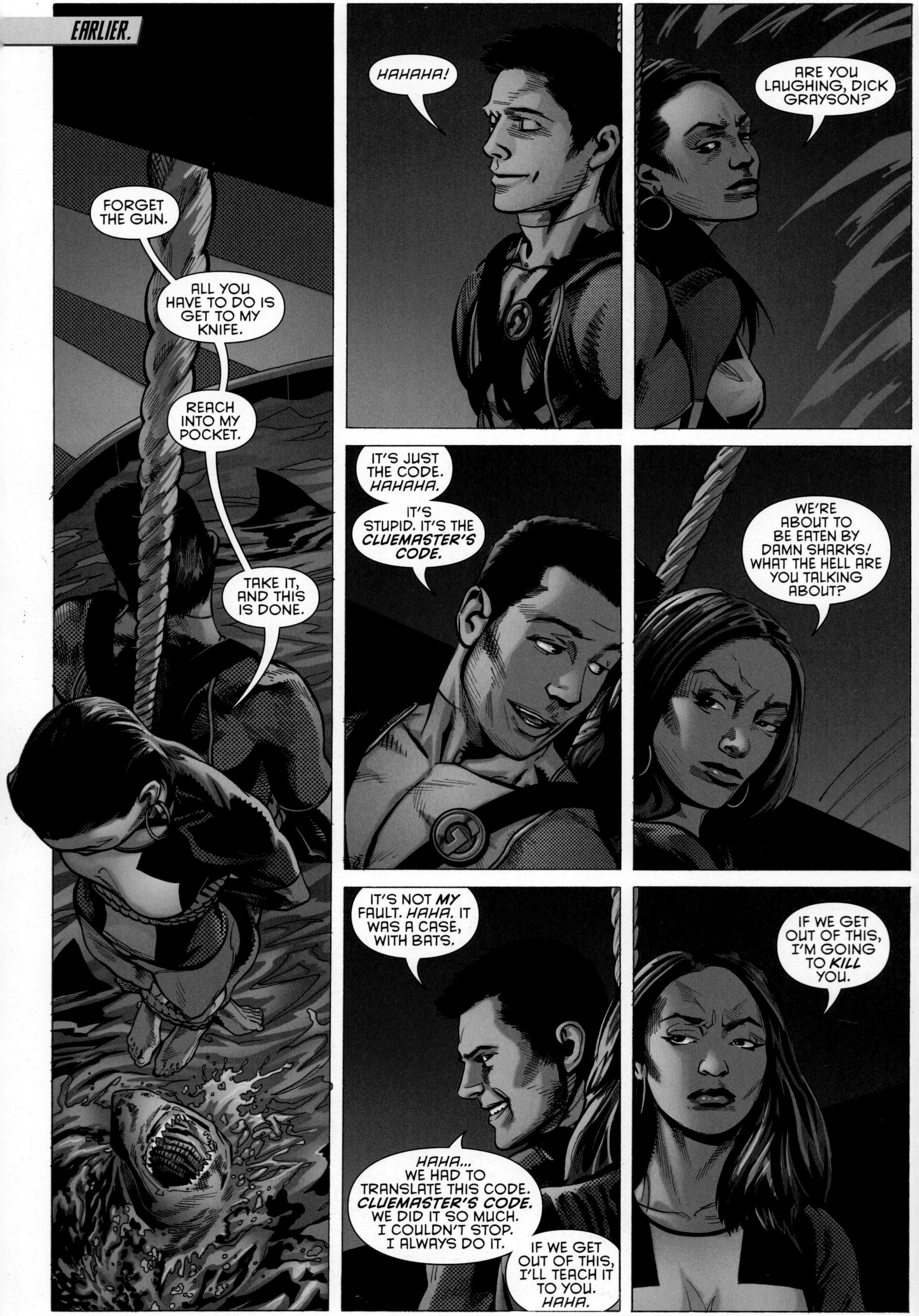
EARLIER.
FORGET THE GUN.
ALL YOU HAVE TO DO IS GET TO MY KNIFE.
REACH INTO MY POCKET.
TAKE IT, AND THIS IS DONE.
HAHAHA!
ARE YOU LAUGHING, DICK GRAYSON?
IT'S JUST THE CODE. HAHAHA.
IT'S STUPID. IT'S THE CLUEMASTER'S CODE.
WE'RE ABOUT TO BE EATEN BY DAMN SHARKS! WHAT THE HELL ARE YOU TALKING ABOUT?
IT'S NOT MY FAULT. HAHA. IT WAS A CASE, WITH BATS.
HAHA... WE HAD TO TRANSLATE THIS CODE. CLUEMASTER'S CODE. WE DID IT SO MUCH. I COULDN'T STOP. I ALWAYS DO IT.
IF WE GET OUT OF THIS, I'LL TEACH IT TO YOU. HAHA.
IF WE GET OUT OF THIS, I'M GOING TO KILL YOU.

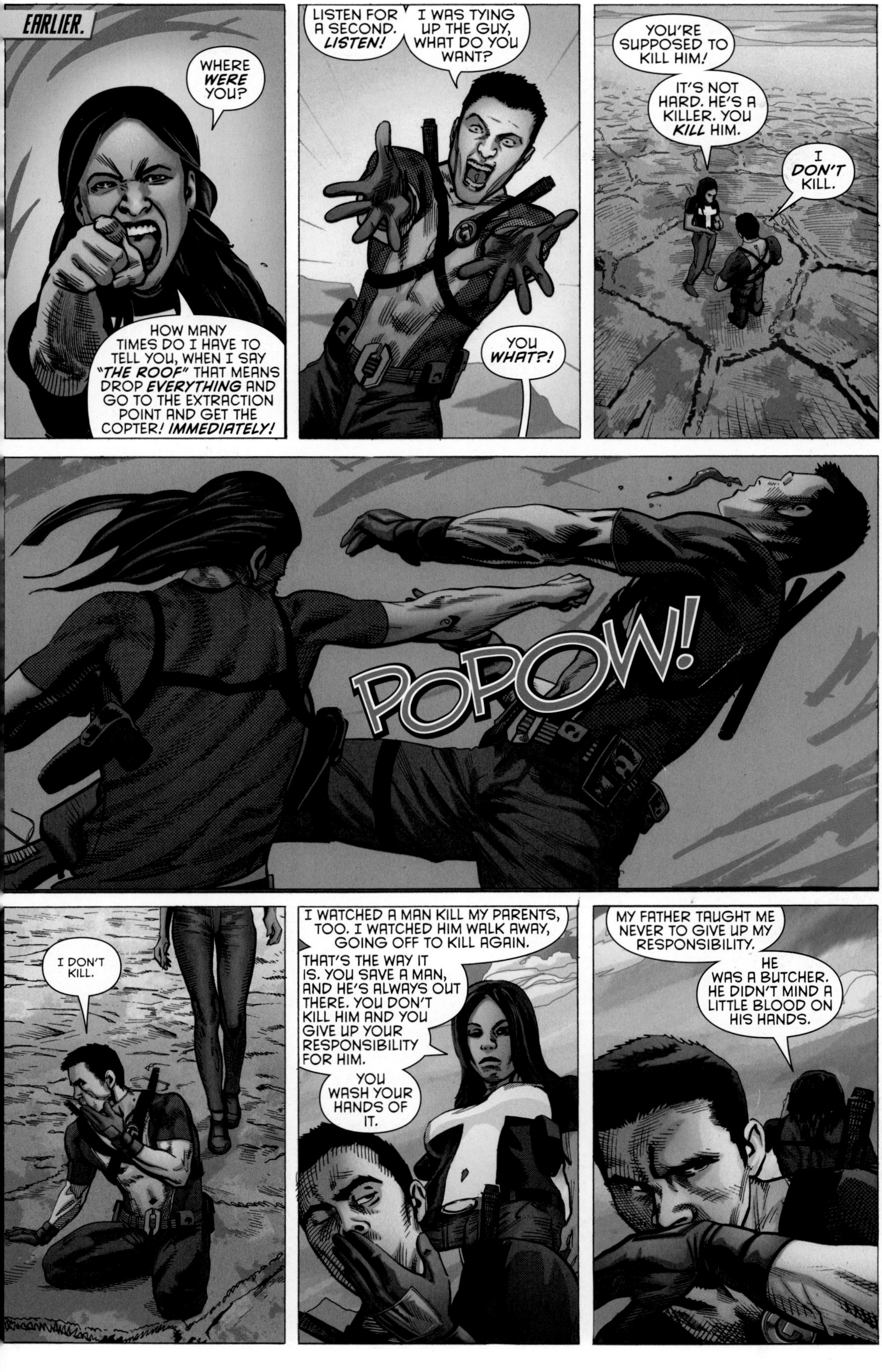

EARLIER.
WHERE WERE YOU?
HOW MANY TIMES DO I HAVE TO TELL YOU, WHEN I SAY "THE ROOF" THAT MEANS DROP EVERYTHING AND GO TO THE EXTRACTION POINT AND GET THE COPTER! IMMEDIATELY!
LISTEN FOR A SECOND. LISTEN!
I WAS TYING UP THE GUY, WHAT DO YOU WANT?
YOU WHAT?!
YOU'RE SUPPOSED TO KILL HIM!
IT'S NOT HARD. HE'S A KILLER. YOU KILL HIM.
I DON'T KILL.
POPOW!
I DON'T KILL.
I WATCHED A MAN KILL MY PARENTS, TOO. I WATCHED HIM WALK AWAY, GOING OFF TO KILL AGAIN.
THAT'S THE WAY IT IS. YOU SAVE A MAN, AND HE'S ALWAYS OUT THERE. YOU DON'T KILL HIM AND YOU GIVE UP YOUR RESPONSIBILITY FOR HIM.
YOU WASH YOUR HANDS OF IT.
MY FATHER TAUGHT ME NEVER TO GIVE UP MY RESPONSIBILITY.
HE WAS A BUTCHER. HE DIDN'T MIND A LITTLE BLOOD ON HIS HANDS.

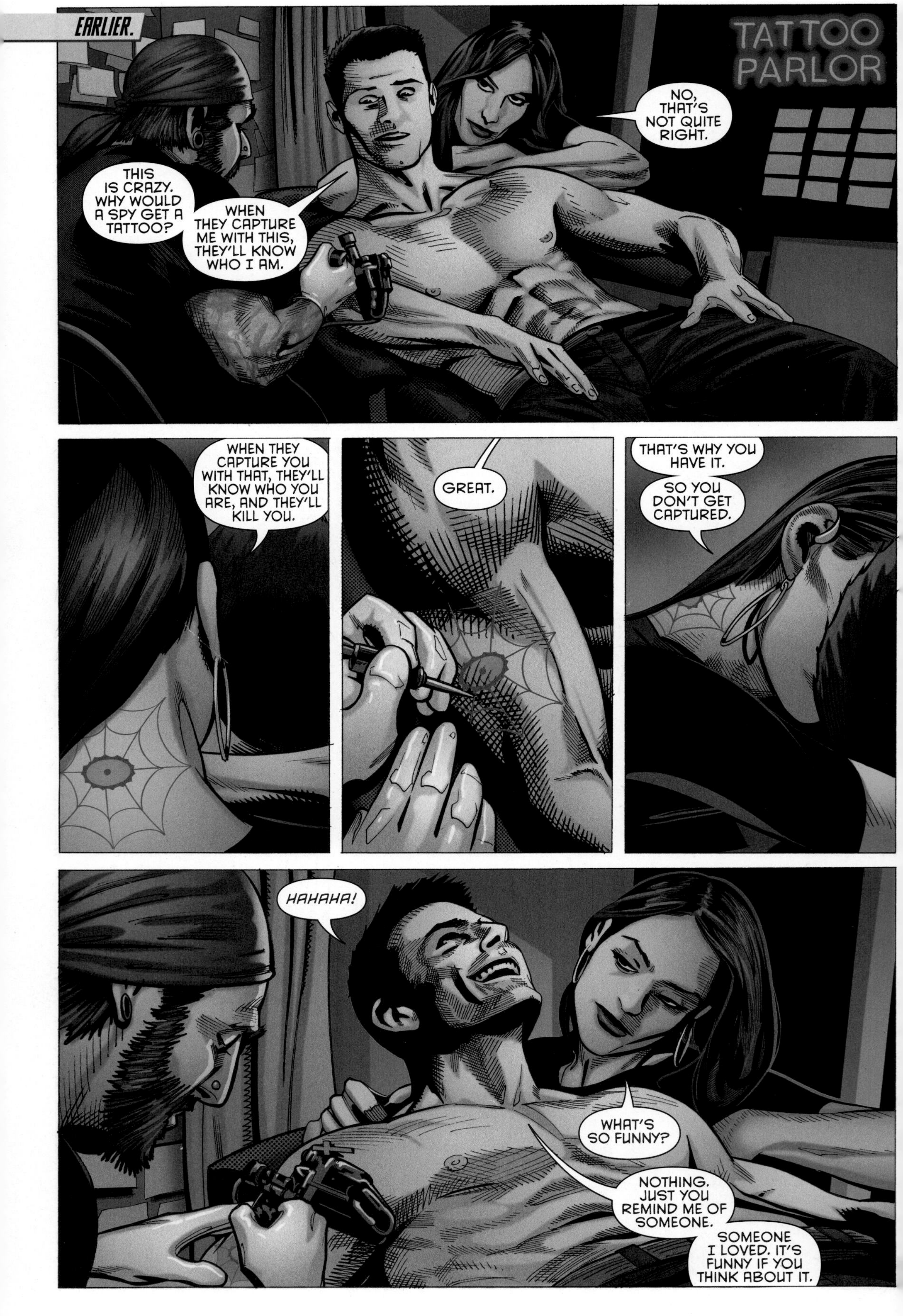
EARLIER.
TATTOO PARLOR
THIS IS CRAZY. WHY WOULD A SPY GET A TATTOO?
WHEN THEY CAPTURE ME WITH THIS, THEY'LL KNOW WHO I AM.
NO, THAT'S NOT QUITE RIGHT.
WHEN THEY CAPTURE YOU WITH THAT, THEY'LL KNOW WHO YOU ARE, AND THEY'LL KILL YOU.
GREAT.
THAT'S WHY YOU HAVE IT.
SO YOU DON'T GET CAPTURED.
HAHAHA!
WHAT'S SO FUNNY?
NOTHING. JUST YOU REMIND ME OF SOMEONE.
SOMEONE I LOVED. IT'S FUNNY IF YOU THINK ABOUT IT.

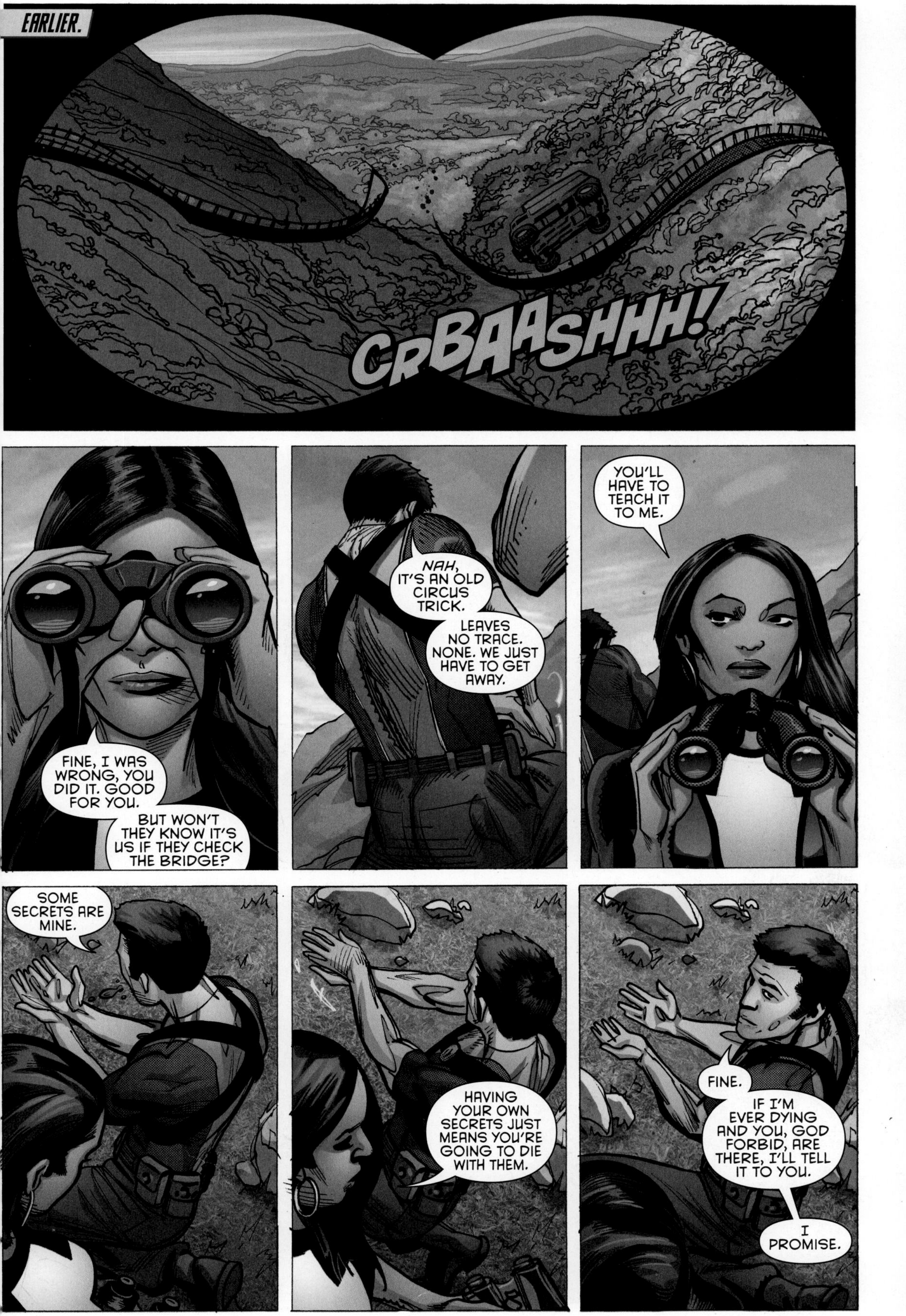
EARLIER.
CRBAASHHH!
FINE, I WAS WRONG, YOU DID IT. GOOD FOR YOU.
BUT WON'T THEY KNOW IT'S US IF THEY CHECK THE BRIDGE?
NAH, IT'S AN OLD CIRCUS TRICK.
LEAVES NO TRACE. NONE. WE JUST HAVE TO GET AWAY.
YOU'LL HAVE TO TEACH IT TO ME.
SOME SECRETS ARE MINE.
HAVING YOUR OWN SECRETS JUST MEANS YOU'RE GOING TO DIE WITH THEM.
FINE.
IF I'M EVER DYING AND YOU, GOD FORBID, ARE THERE, I'LL TELL IT TO YOU.
I PROMISE.

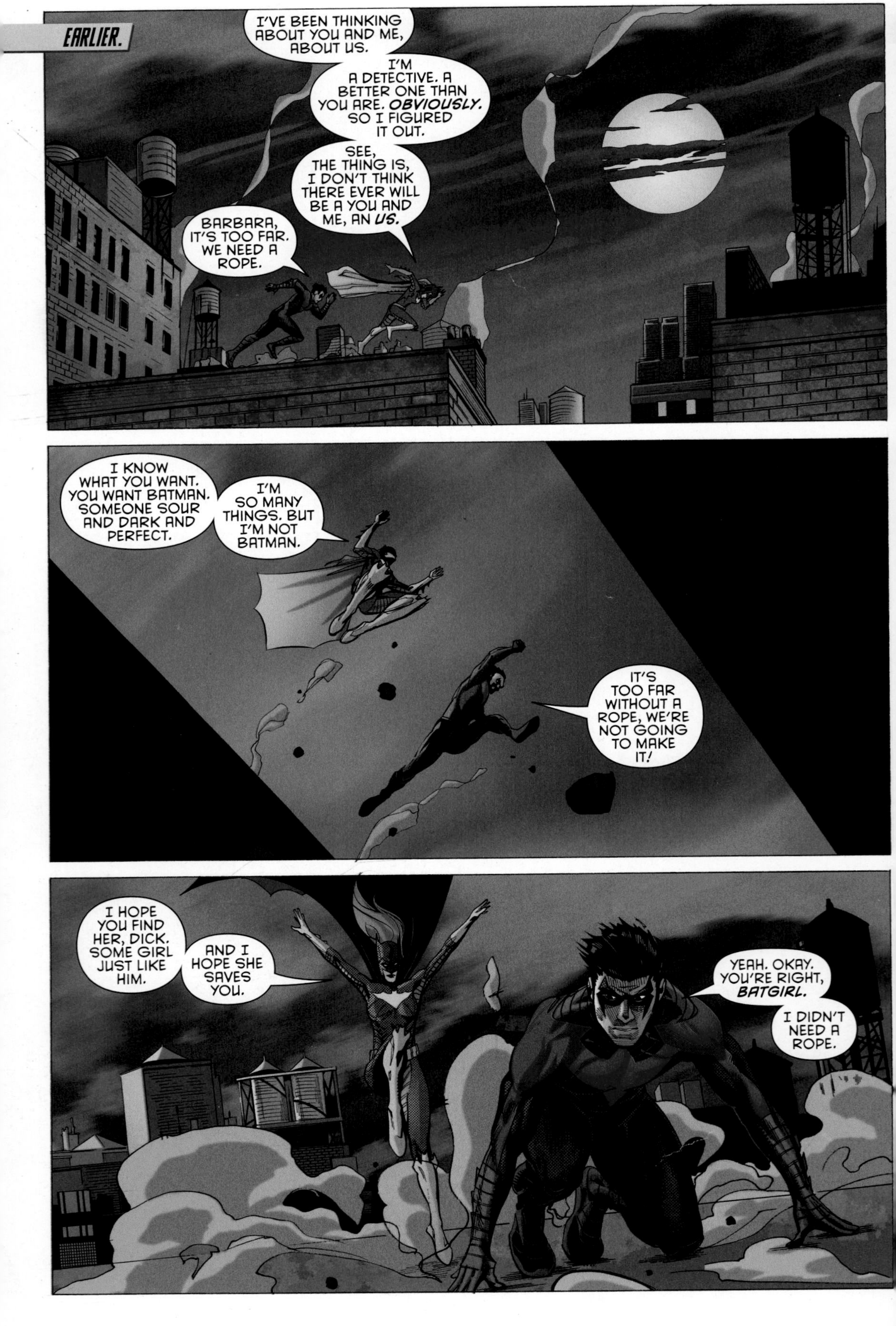
EARLIER.
I'VE BEEN THINKING ABOUT YOU AND ME, ABOUT US.
I'M A DETECTIVE. A BETTER ONE THAN YOU ARE. OBVIOUSLY. SO I FIGURED IT OUT.
SEE, THE THING IS, I DON'T THINK THERE EVER WILL BE A YOU AND ME, AN US.
BARBARA, IT'S TOO FAR. WE NEED A ROPE.
I KNOW WHAT YOU WANT. YOU WANT BATMAN. SOMEONE SOUR AND DARK AND PERFECT.
I'M SO MANY THINGS. BUT I'M NOT BATMAN.
IT'S TOO FAR WITHOUT A ROPE, WE'RE NOT GOING TO MAKE IT!
I HOPE YOU FIND HER, DICK. SOME GIRL JUST LIKE HIM.
AND I HOPE SHE SAVES YOU.
YEAH. OKAY. YOU'RE RIGHT, BATGIRL.
I DIDN'T NEED A ROPE.

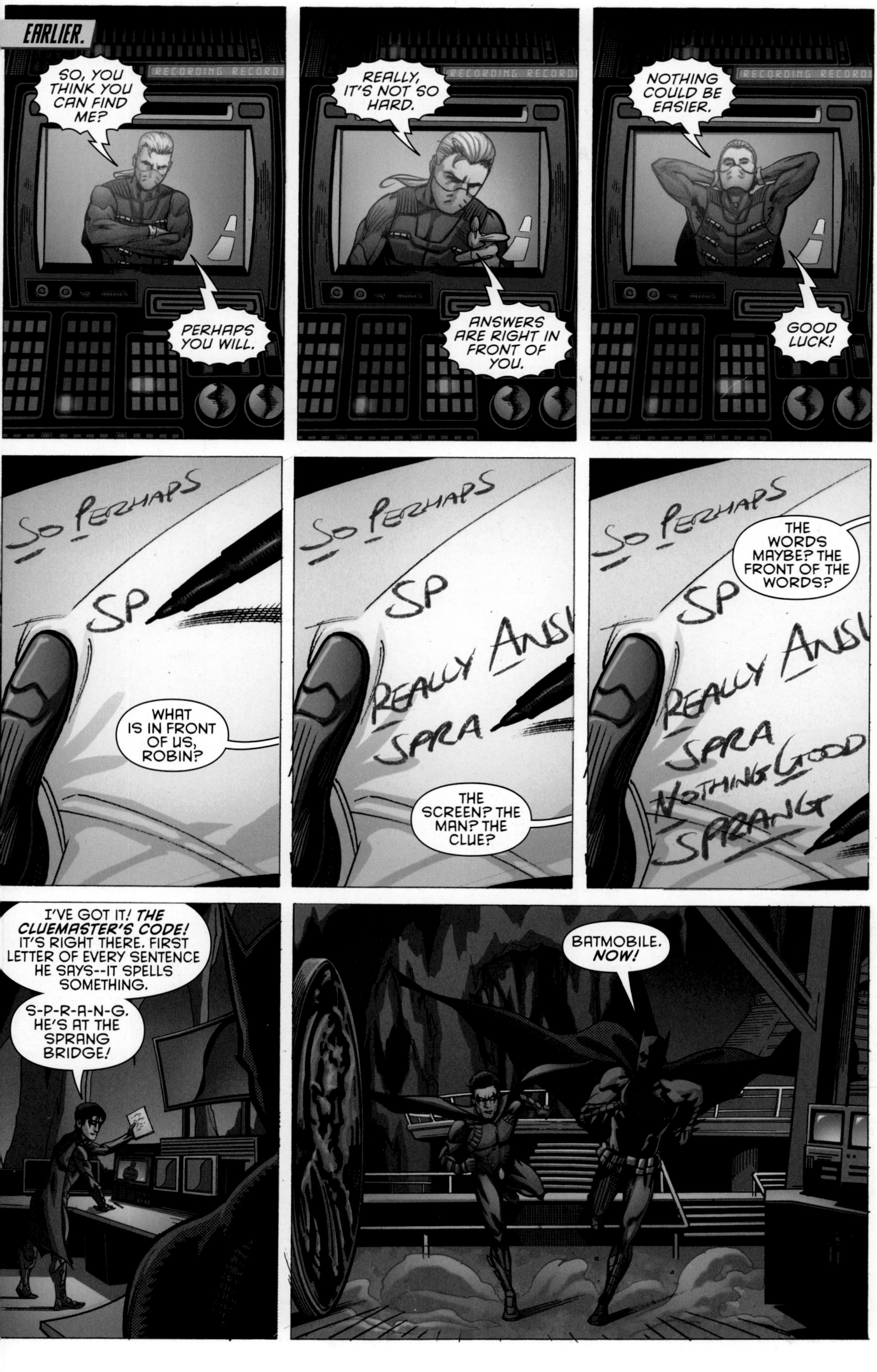
EARLIER.
RECORDING RECORDI
SO, YOU THINK YOU CAN FIND ME?
PERHAPS YOU WILL.
REALLY, IT'S NOT SO HARD.
ANSWERS ARE RIGHT IN FRONT OF YOU.
NOTHING COULD BE EASIER.
GOOD LUCK!
So Perhaps
SP
WHAT IS IN FRONT OF US, ROBIN?
Really Ans
SPRA
THE SCREEN? THE MAN? THE CLUE?
THE WORDS MAYBE? THE FRONT OF THE WORDS?
Nothing Good
SPRANG
I'VE GOT IT! THE CLUEMASTER'S CODE! IT'S RIGHT THERE. FIRST LETTER OF EVERY SENTENCE HE SAYS--IT SPELLS SOMETHING.
S-P-R-A-N-G. HE'S AT THE SPRANG BRIDGE!
BATMOBILE. NOW!

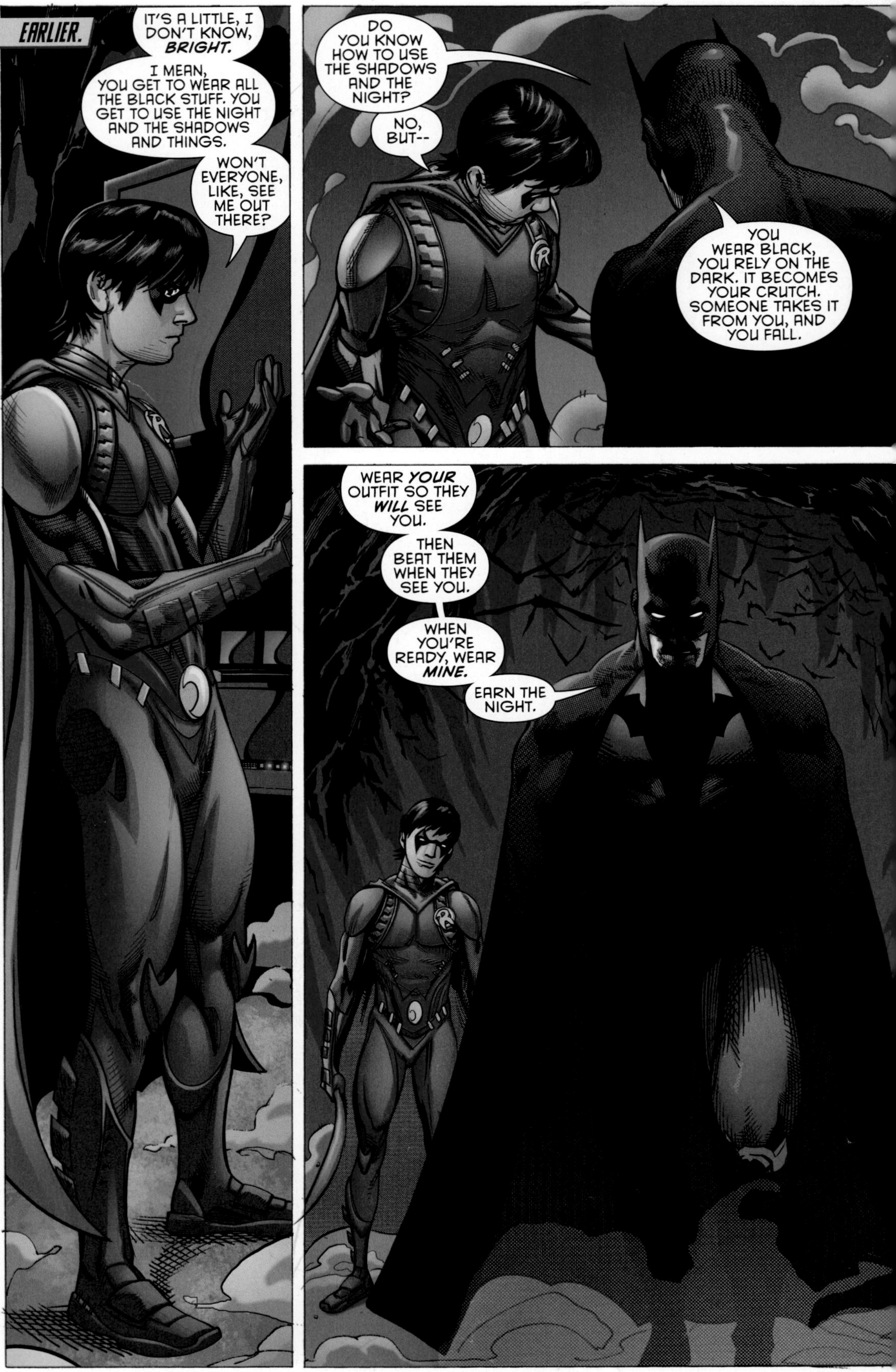
EARLIER.
IT'S A LITTLE, I DON'T KNOW, BRIGHT.
I MEAN, YOU GET TO WEAR ALL THE BLACK STUFF. YOU GET TO USE THE NIGHT AND THE SHADOWS AND THINGS.
WON'T EVERYONE, LIKE, SEE ME OUT THERE?
DO YOU KNOW HOW TO USE THE SHADOWS AND THE NIGHT?
NO, BUT--
YOU WEAR BLACK, YOU RELY ON THE DARK. IT BECOMES YOUR CRUTCH. SOMEONE TAKES IT FROM YOU, AND YOU FALL.
WEAR YOUR OUTFIT SO THEY WILL SEE YOU.
THEN BEAT THEM WHEN THEY SEE YOU.
WHEN YOU'RE READY, WEAR MINE.
EARN THE NIGHT.

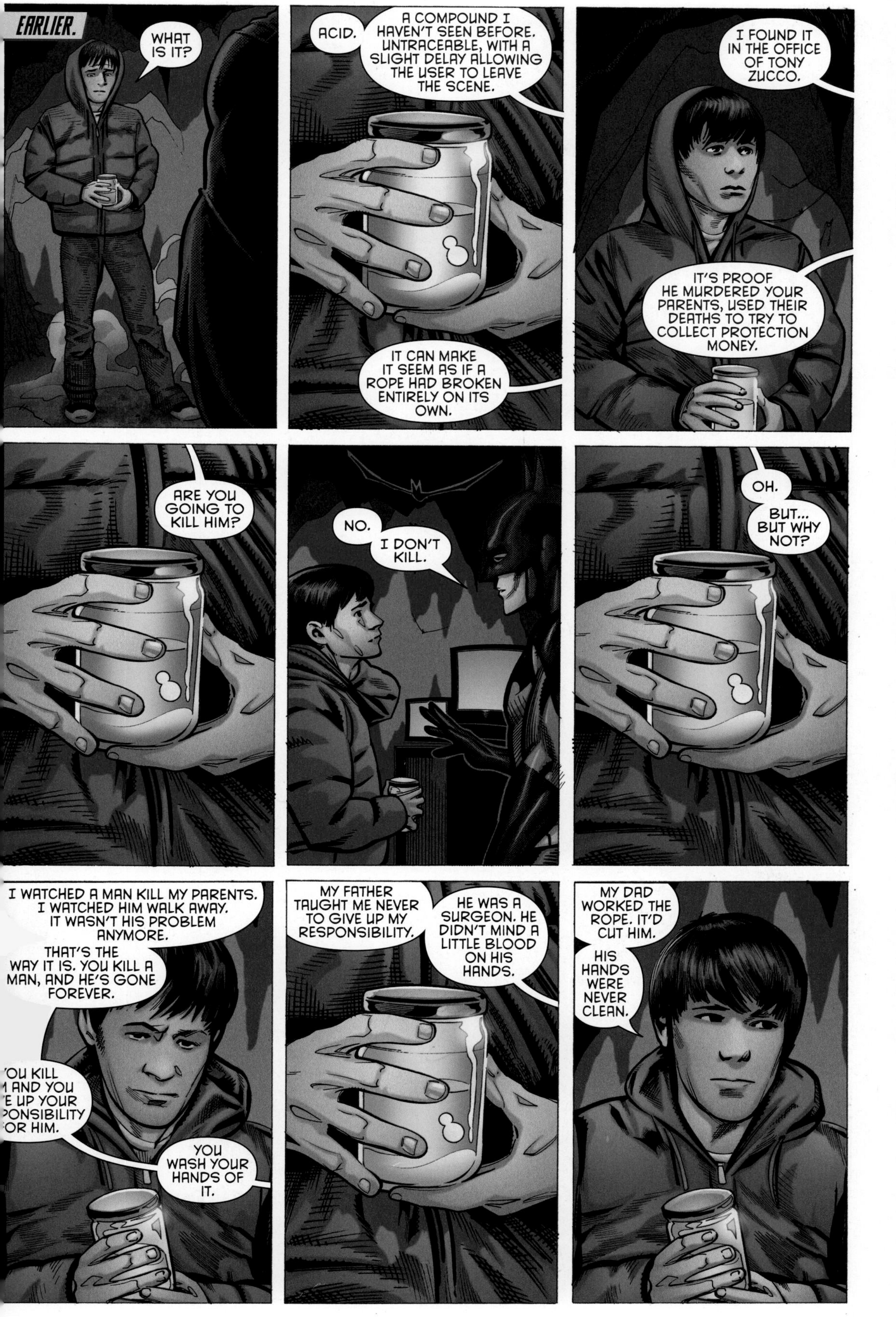
EARLIER.
WHAT IS IT?
ACID.
A COMPOUND I HAVEN'T SEEN BEFORE. UNTRACEABLE, WITH A SLIGHT DELAY ALLOWING THE USER TO LEAVE THE SCENE.
IT CAN MAKE IT SEEM AS IF A ROPE HAD BROKEN ENTIRELY ON ITS OWN.
I FOUND IT IN THE OFFICE OF TONY ZUCCO.
IT'S PROOF HE MURDERED YOUR PARENTS, USED THEIR DEATHS TO TRY TO COLLECT PROTECTION MONEY.
ARE YOU GOING TO KILL HIM?
NO.
I DON'T KILL.
OH.
BUT... BUT WHY NOT?
I WATCHED A MAN KILL MY PARENTS. I WATCHED HIM WALK AWAY. IT WASN'T HIS PROBLEM ANYMORE.
THAT'S THE WAY IT IS. YOU KILL A MAN, AND HE'S GONE FOREVER.
YOU KILL M AND YOU E UP YOUR PONSIBILITY OR HIM.
YOU WASH YOUR HANDS OF IT.
MY FATHER TAUGHT ME NEVER TO GIVE UP MY RESPONSIBILITY.
HE WAS A SURGEON. HE DIDN'T MIND A LITTLE BLOOD ON HIS HANDS.
MY DAD WORKED THE ROPE. IT'D CUT HIM.
HIS HANDS WERE NEVER CLEAN.

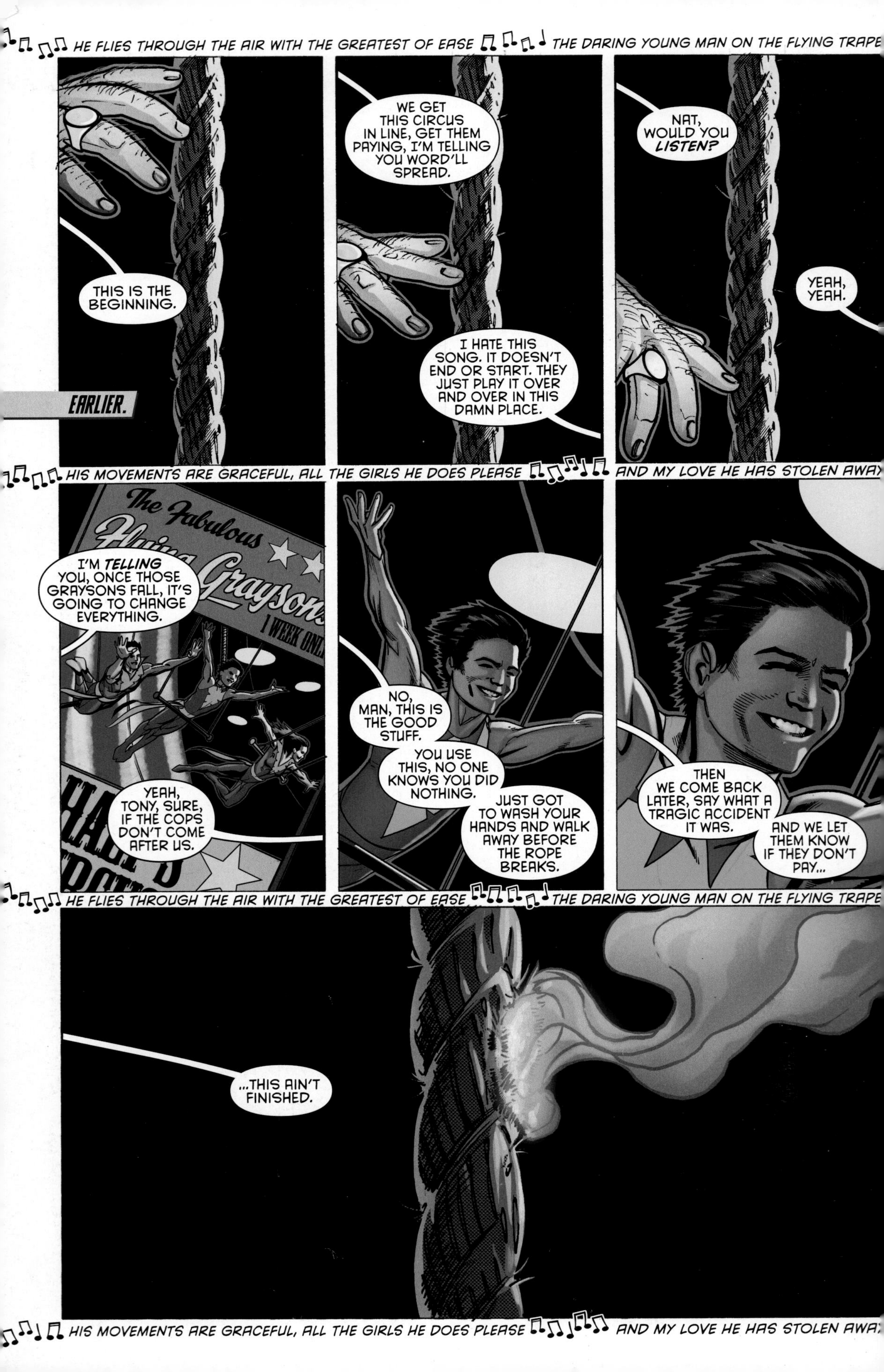
HE FLIES THROUGH THE AIR WITH THE GREATEST OF EASE
THE DARING YOUNG MAN ON THE FLYING TRAPE
THIS IS THE BEGINNING.
EARLIER.
WE GET THIS CIRCUS IN LINE, GET THEM PAYING, I'M TELLING YOU WORD'LL SPREAD.
I HATE THIS SONG. IT DOESN'T END OR START. THEY JUST PLAY IT OVER AND OVER IN THIS DAMN PLACE.
NAT, WOULD YOU LISTEN?
YEAH, YEAH.
HIS MOVEMENTS ARE GRACEFUL, ALL THE GIRLS HE DOES PLEASE
AND MY LOVE HE HAS STOLEN AWAY
The Fabulous
Graysons
1 WEEK ONL
I'M TELLING YOU, ONCE THOSE GRAYSONS FALL, IT'S GOING TO CHANGE EVERYTHING.
YEAH, TONY, SURE, IF THE COPS DON'T COME AFTER US.
NO, MAN, THIS IS THE GOOD STUFF.
YOU USE THIS, NO ONE KNOWS YOU DID NOTHING.
JUST GOT TO WASH YOUR HANDS AND WALK AWAY BEFORE THE ROPE BREAKS.
THEN WE COME BACK LATER, SAY WHAT A TRAGIC ACCIDENT IT WAS.
AND WE LET THEM KNOW IF THEY DON'T PAY...
HE FLIES THROUGH THE AIR WITH THE GREATEST OF EASE
THE DARING YOUNG MAN ON THE FLYING TRAPE
...THIS AIN'T FINISHED.
HIS MOVEMENTS ARE GRACEFUL, ALL THE GIRLS HE DOES PLEASE
AND MY LOVE HE HAS STOLEN AWA

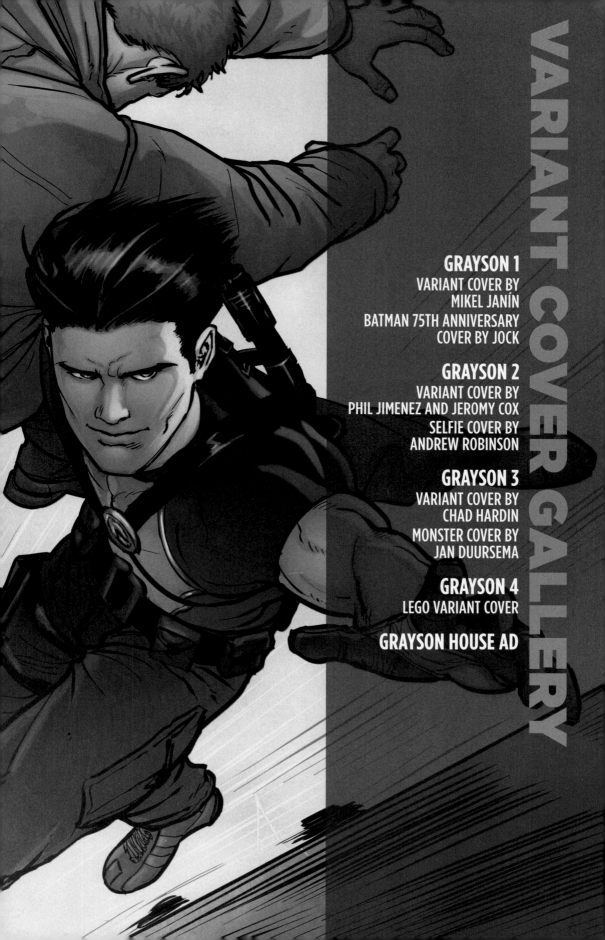

GRAYSON 1
VARIANT COVER BY
MIKEL JANÍN
BATMAN 75TH ANNIVERSARY
COVER BY JOCK

GRAYSON 2
VARIANT COVER BY
PHIL JIMENEZ AND JEROMY COX
SELFIE COVER BY
ANDREW ROBINSON

GRAYSON 3
VARIANT COVER BY
CHAD HARDIN
MONSTER COVER BY
JAN DUURSEMA

GRAYSON 4
LEGO VARIANT COVER

GRAYSON HOUSE AD

VARIANT COVER GALLERY

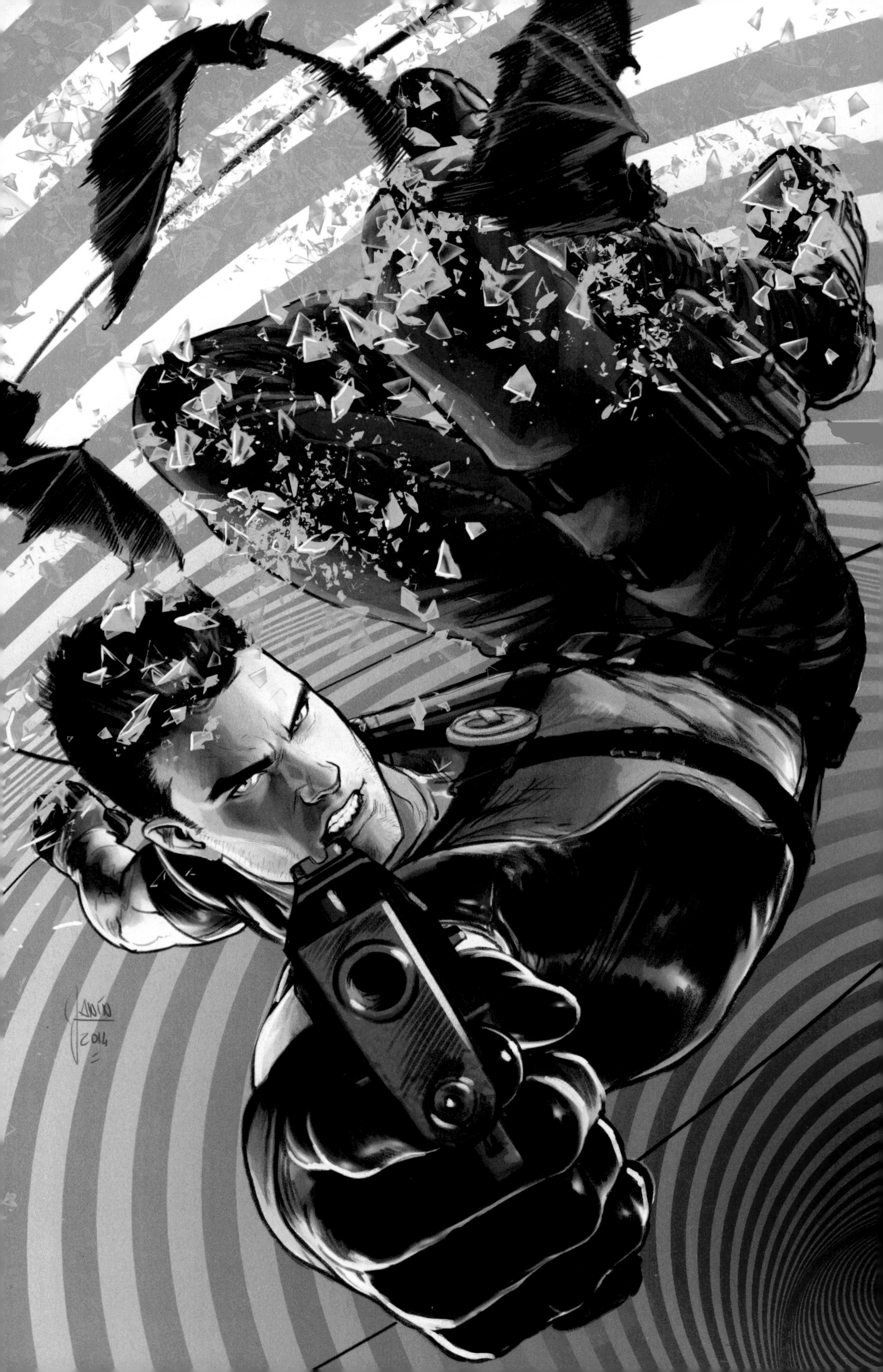

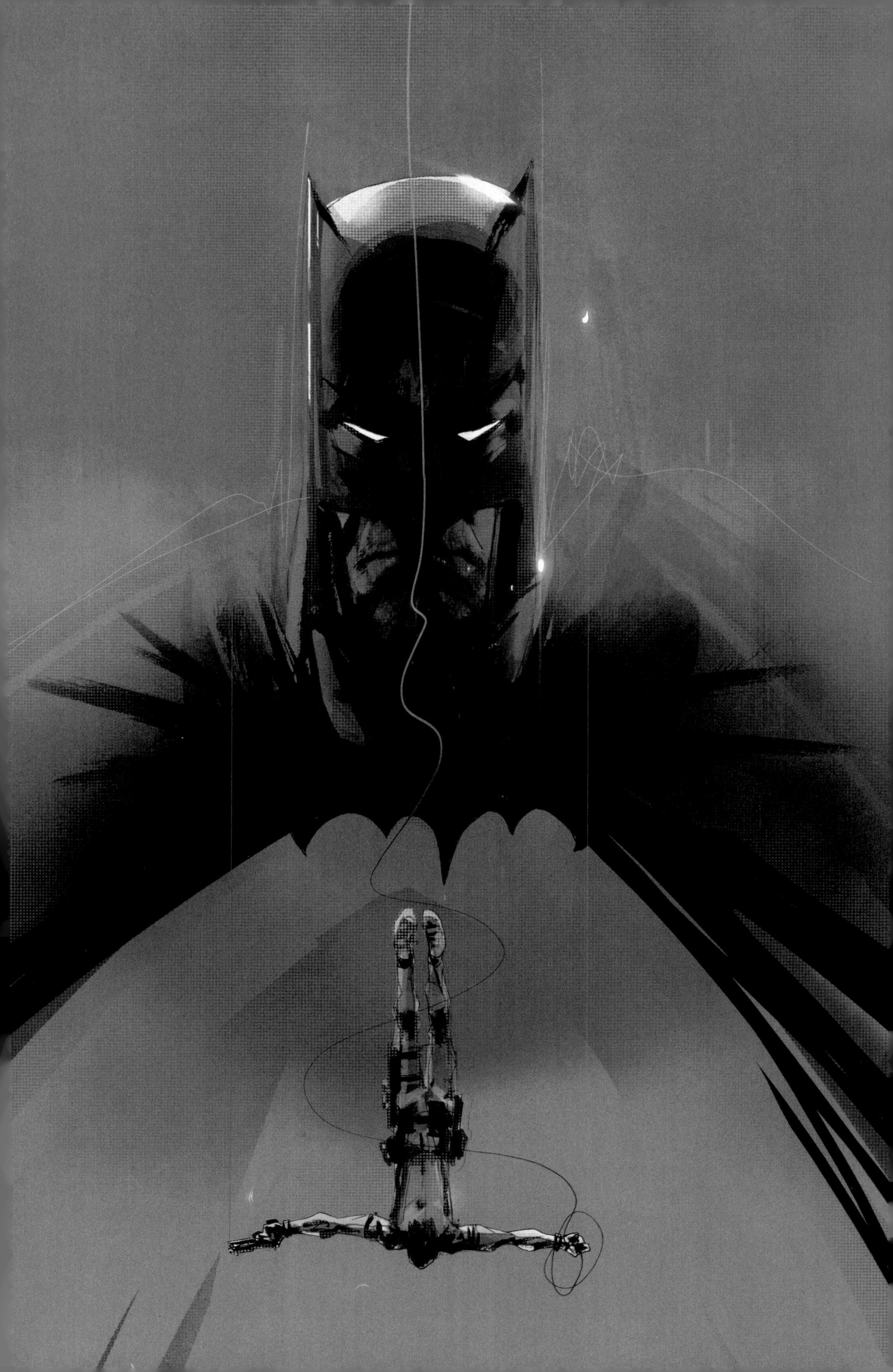

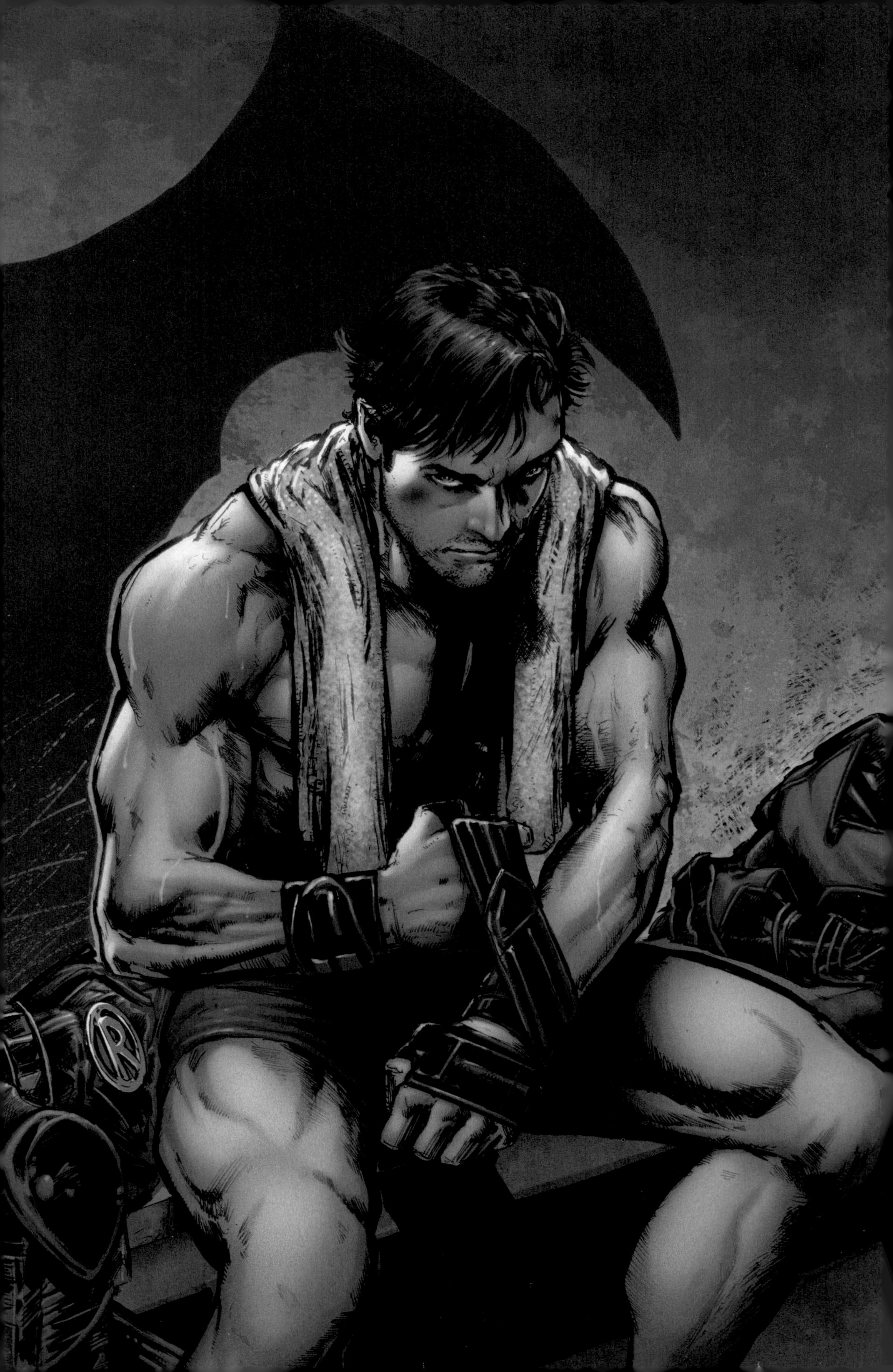

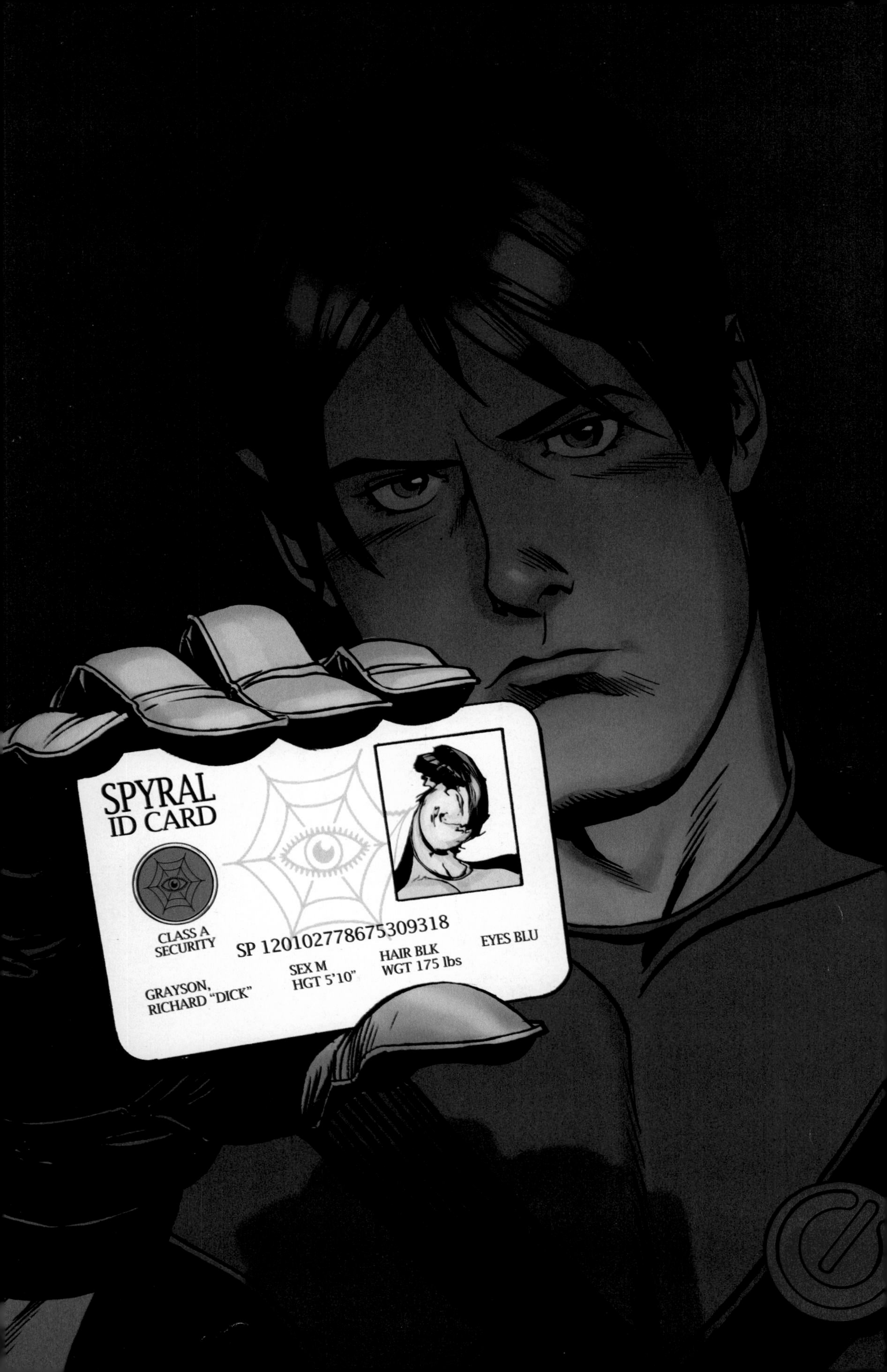
SPYRAL
ID CARD
CLASS A
SECURITY
SP 120102778675309318
EYES BLU
SEX M
HGT 5'10"
HAIR BLK
WGT 175 lbs
GRAYSON,
RICHARD "DICK"

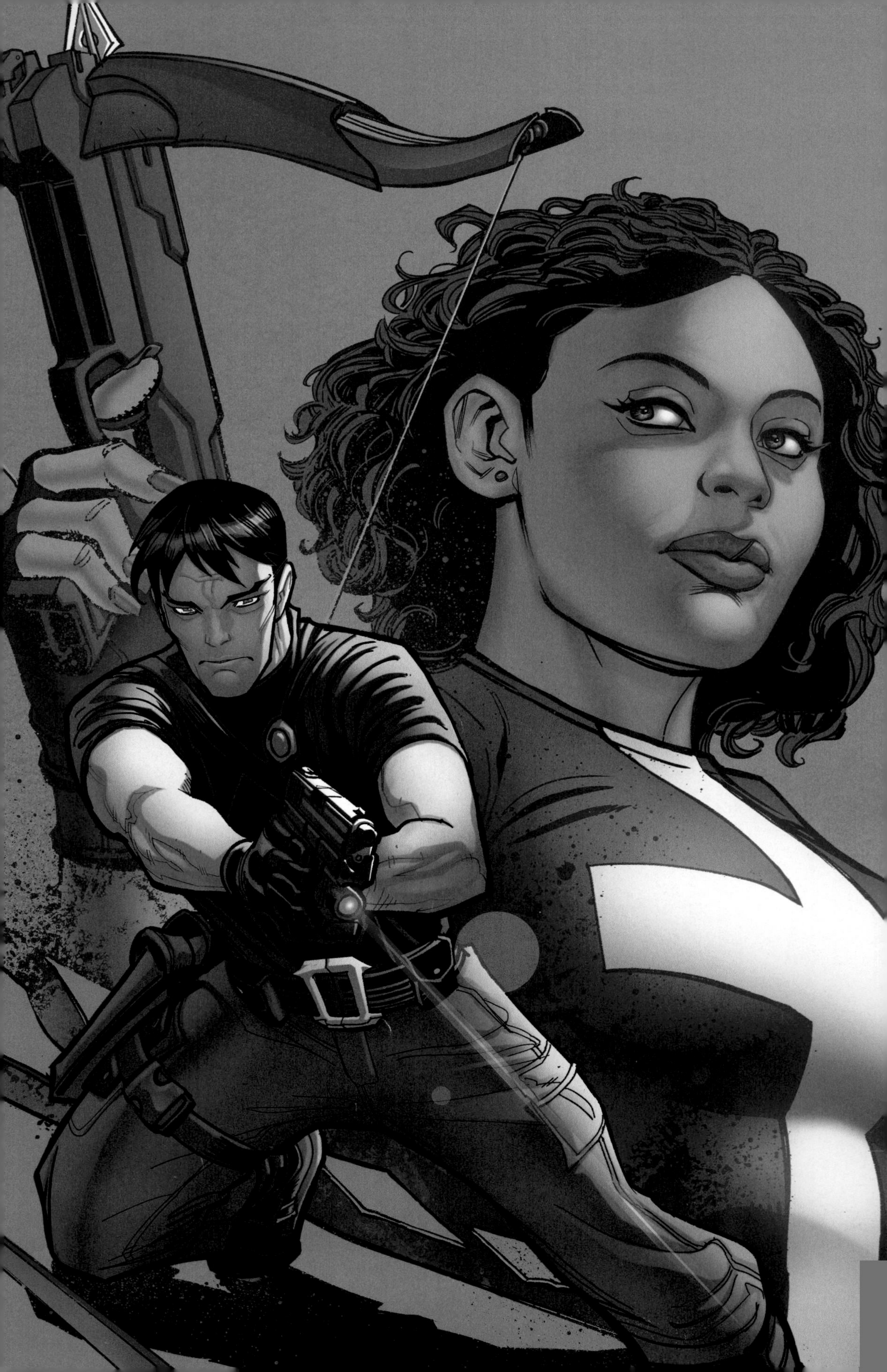

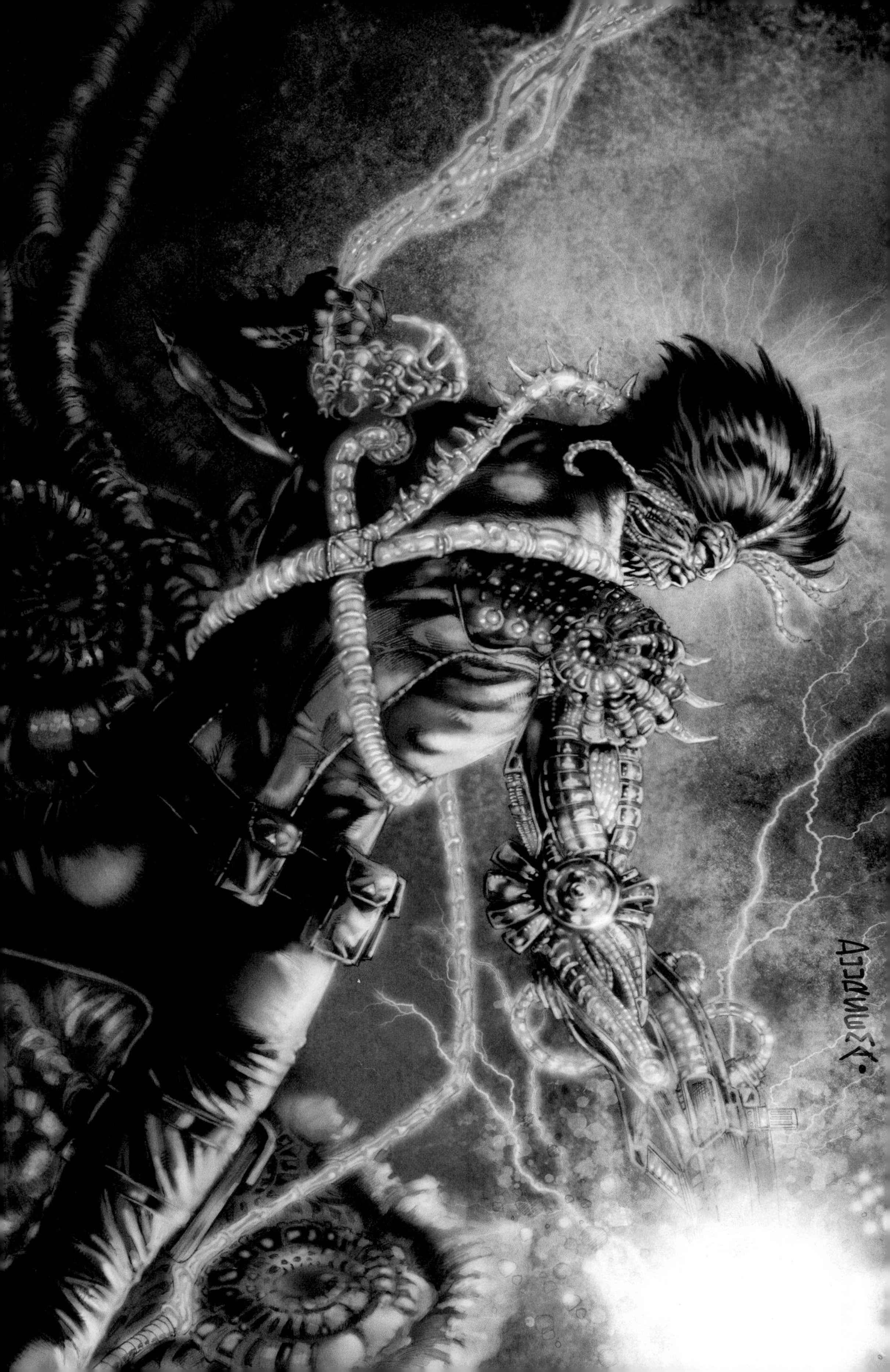

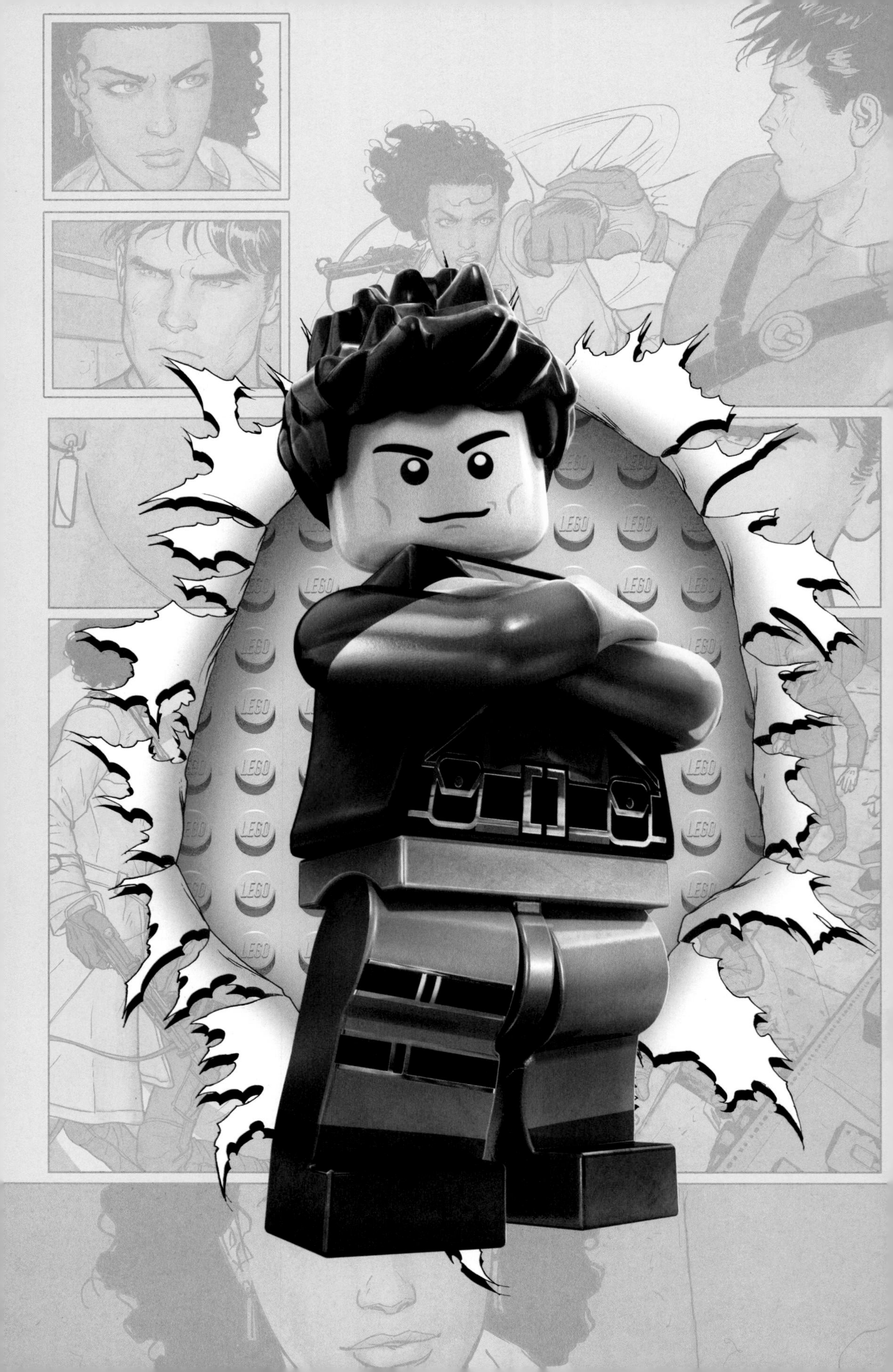

YOU THINK YOU KNOW NIGHTWING...
YOU DON'T KNOW DICK

A New Monthly Series

Tim Seeley
Tom King
Mikel Janin

July 2014

THIS IS **GRAYSON**

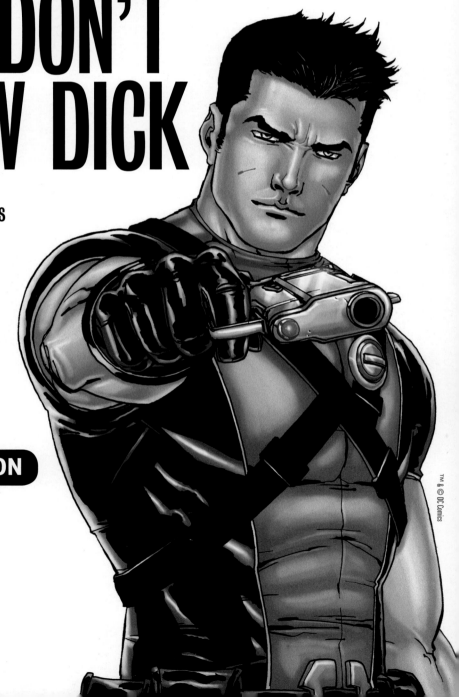

DC
COMICS™

THE NEW **52!**

GRAYSON
series pitch
by Tim Seeley
2-14-2014

DICK GRAYSON. Former sidekick. Former superhero.
His identity revealed to the world. Believed dead by
everyone, save his mentor, Batman, Dick is man who
does not exist.

SPYRAL. An international spy organization run
by Kathy Kane. Specializes in mind erosion,
brainwashing and misdirection. Tasked with keeping
an unblinking eye on all emerging superhumans,
and trapping those that cross the line in their
sticky threads. Kathy Kane has given Batman clear
instructions that he should never try to find Spyral.
They do not exist.

Batman has never listened particularly well to
instructions.

Now, clandestinely funded and backed by Batman,
Dick Grayson will infiltrate SPYRAL, a spy for them,
and a spy on them. He will navigate the shadowy,
morally grey world of international superhuman
espionage. He will battle great evils, and be asked
to commit them.

And with every decision he makes, Dick will ask
himself if it came of his own freewill or because
the insidious mind tricks employed by his beautiful
and seductive boss, Kathy Kane. Is Dick the hero
he spent his young life training to be? Or is he
someone new? When Dick Grayson no longer exists,
who is Dick Grayson?

DICK GRAYSON AGENT OF SPYRAL

"SPYRAL SPECIALIZES IN MIND EROSION, BRAINWASHING, AND MISDIRECTION..."

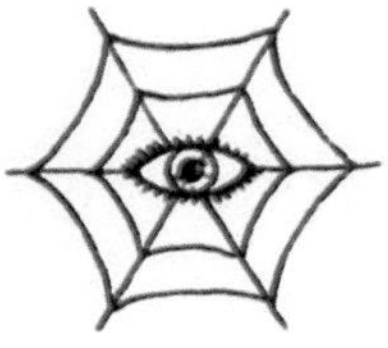

DICK GRAYSON
AGENT 37

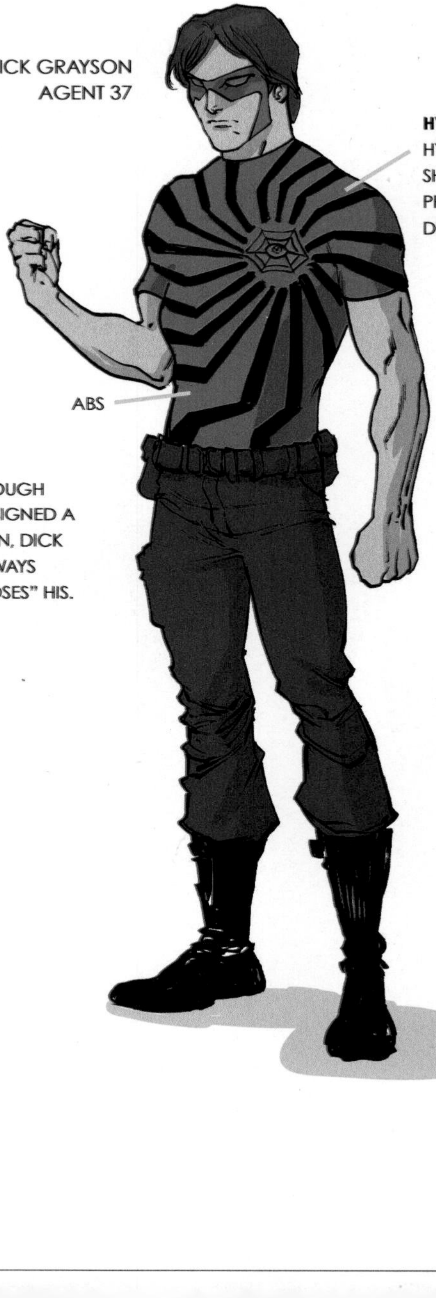

HYPNOS SUIT
HYPNOTIC SUGGESTION SHIRT, APPEARS AS PREPROGRAMMED DISGUISE

ABS

THOUGH ASSIGNED A GUN, DICK ALWAYS "LOSES" HIS.

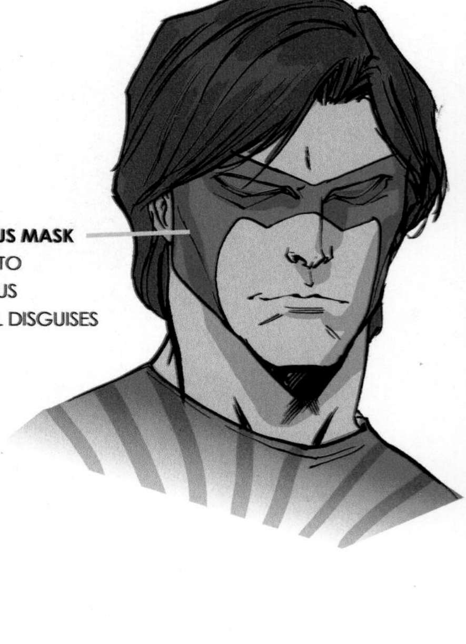

PROTEUS MASK
SHIFTS TO VARIOUS FACIAL DISGUISES

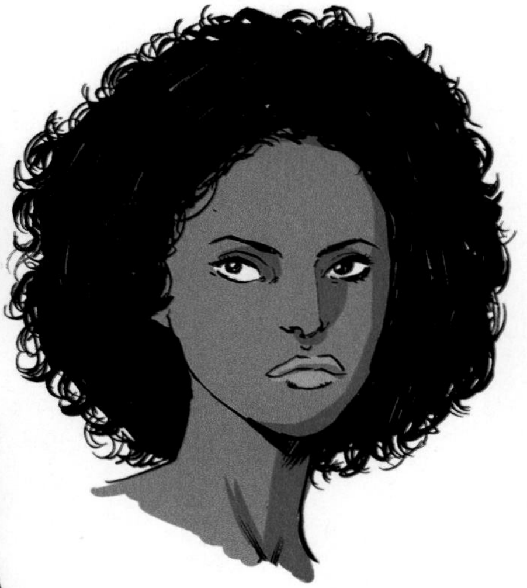

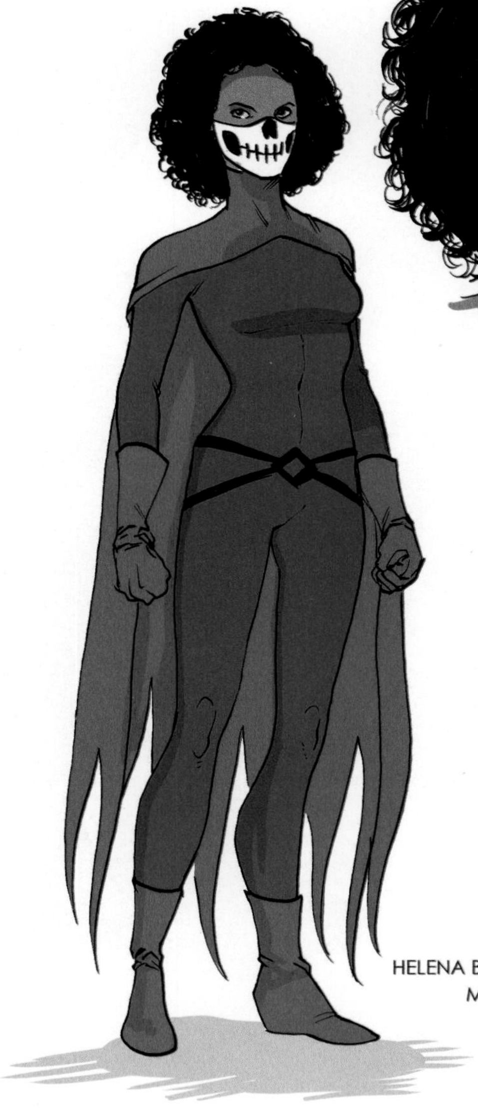

DERIVED
FROM
SPYRAL
AGENTS FROM
“FINISHING
SCHOOL.”

COLOR
INDICATES
RANK.

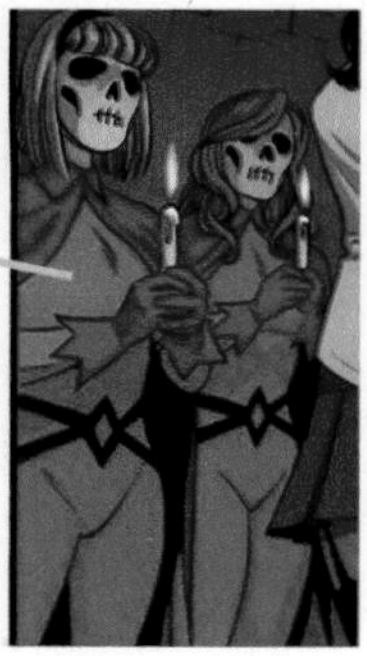

HELENA BERTINELLI
MATRON 1

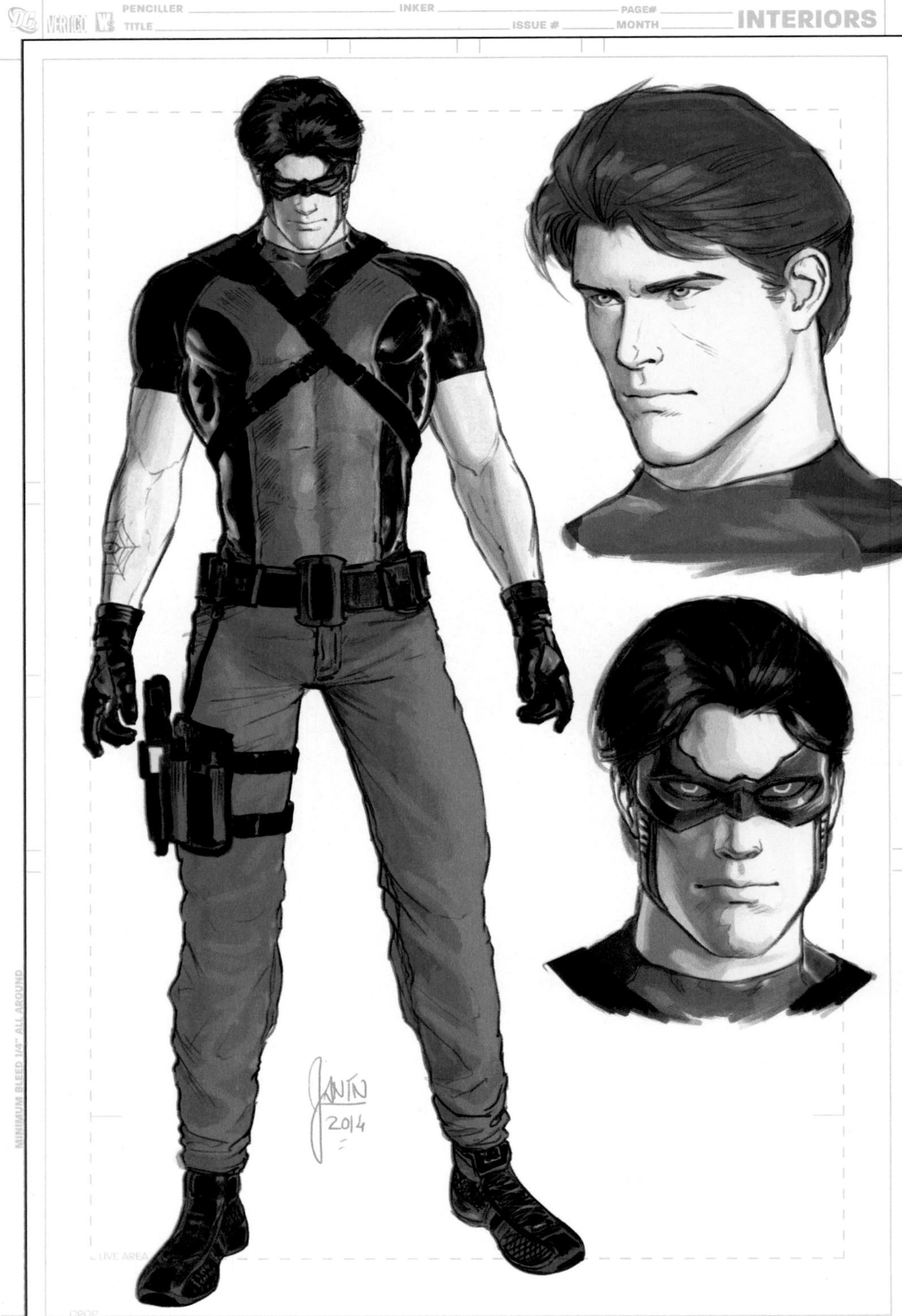
PENCILLER
INKER
PAGE#
TITLE
ISSUE #
MONTH
INTERIORS
MINIMUM BLEED 1/4" ALL AROUND
LIVE AREA
CROP
BLEED
JANIN
2014
CUT RIGHT-HAND PAGE AT THIS LINE
DOUBLE PAGE SPREAD: CUT AS SHOWN, ABUT PAGE EDGES, TAPE ON BACK, DO NOT OVERLAP
CUT LEFT HAND PAGE AT THIS LINE

PENCILLER _____
TITLE _____
INKER _____
ISSUE # _____
PAGE# _____
MONTH _____
INTERIORS

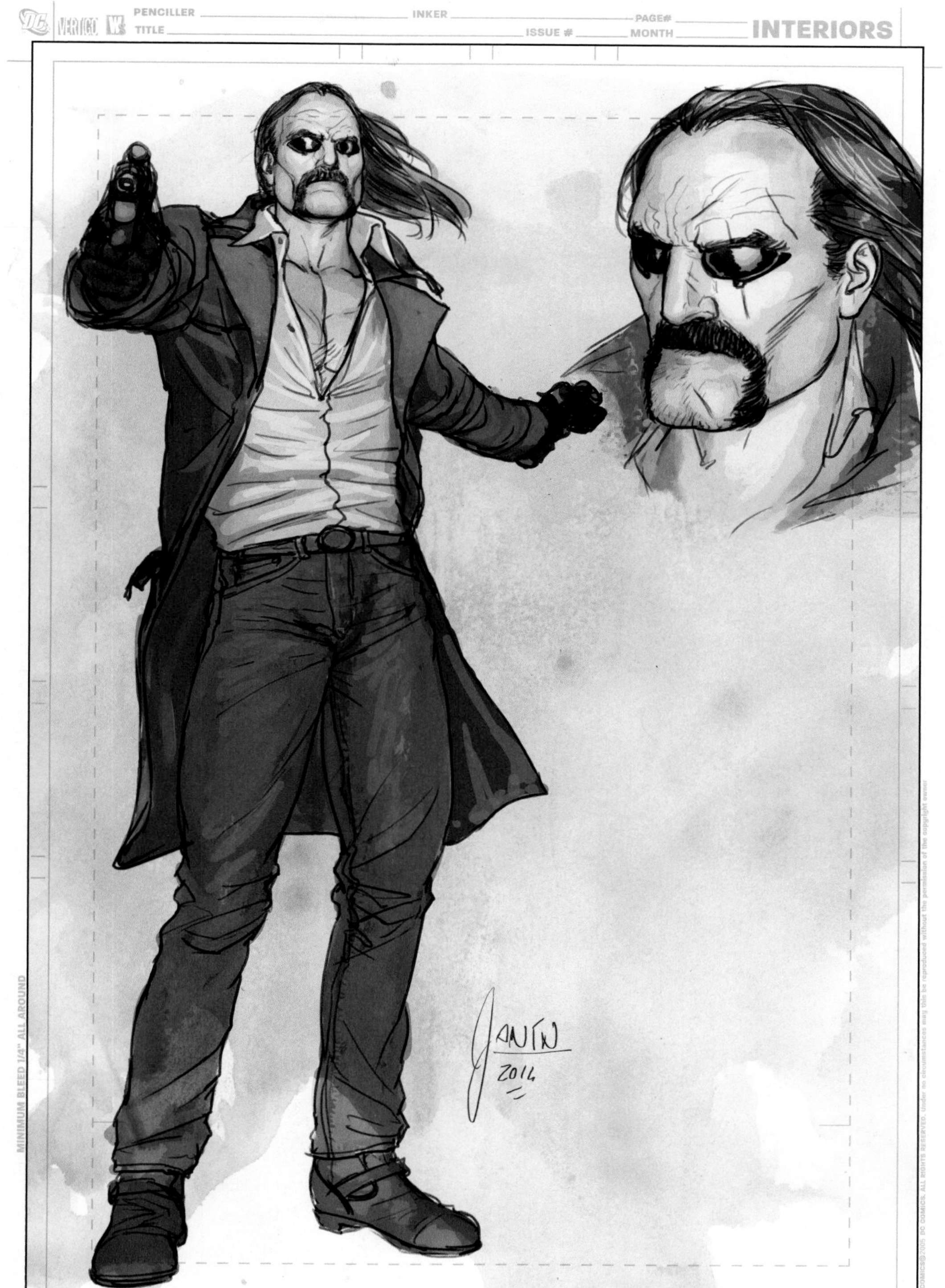
PENCILLER
INKER
PAGE#
TITLE
ISSUE #
MONTH
INTERIORS
MINIMUM BLEED 1/4" ALL AROUND
CROP
BLEED
CUT RIGHT-HAND PAGE AT THIS LINE
DOUBLE PAGE SPREAD: CUT AS SHOWN, ABUT PAGE EDGES, TAPE ON BACK, DO NOT OVERLAP
CUT LEFT HAND PAGE AT THIS LINE

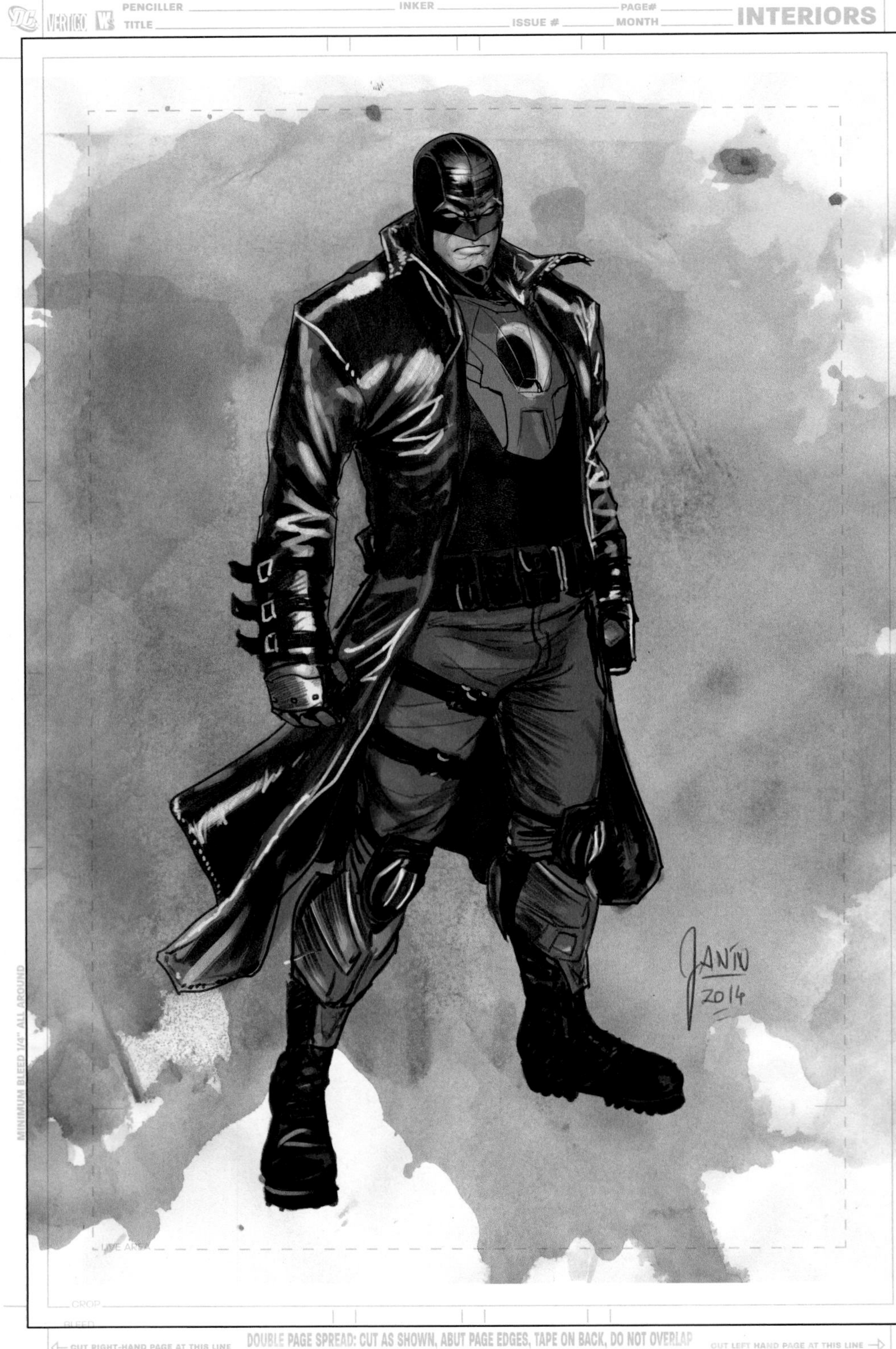
PENCILLER
INKER
PAGE#
INTERIORS
TITLE
ISSUE #
MONTH
JANÍN
2014
MINIMUM BLEED 1/4" ALL AROUND
CUT RIGHT-HAND PAGE AT THIS LINE
DOUBLE PAGE SPREAD: CUT AS SHOWN, ABUT PAGE EDGES, TAPE ON BACK, DO NOT OVERLAP
CUT LEFT HAND PAGE AT THIS LINE

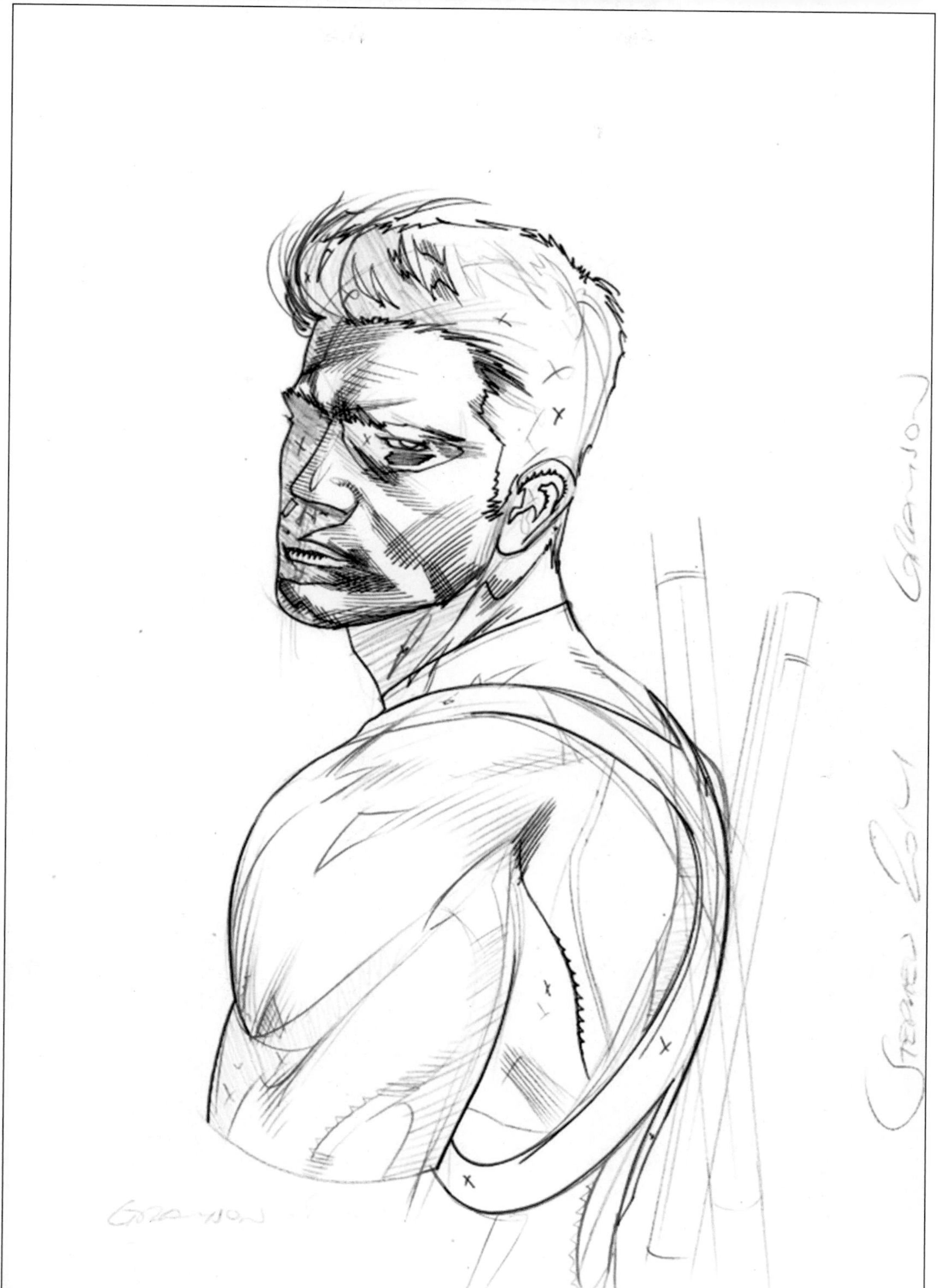

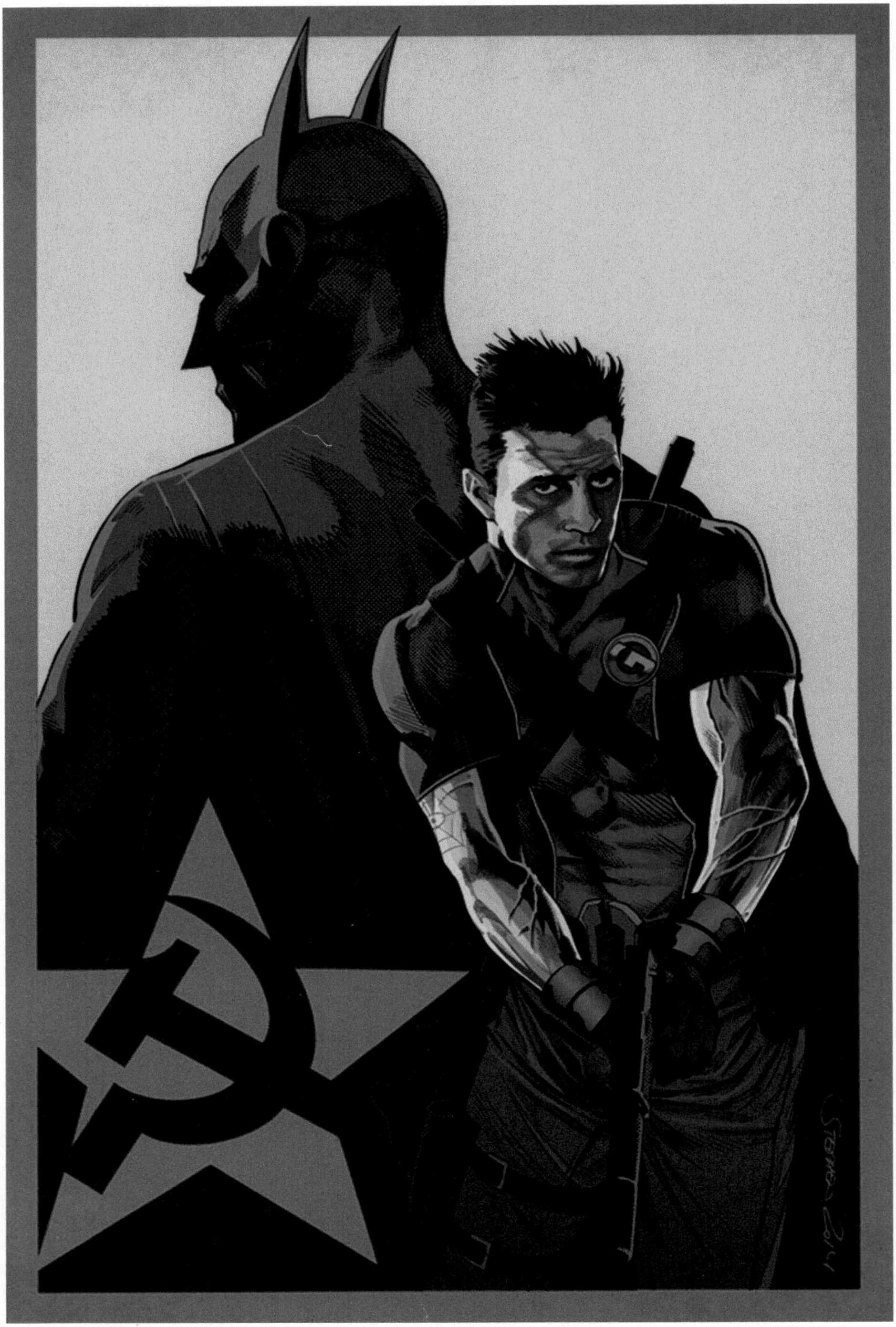

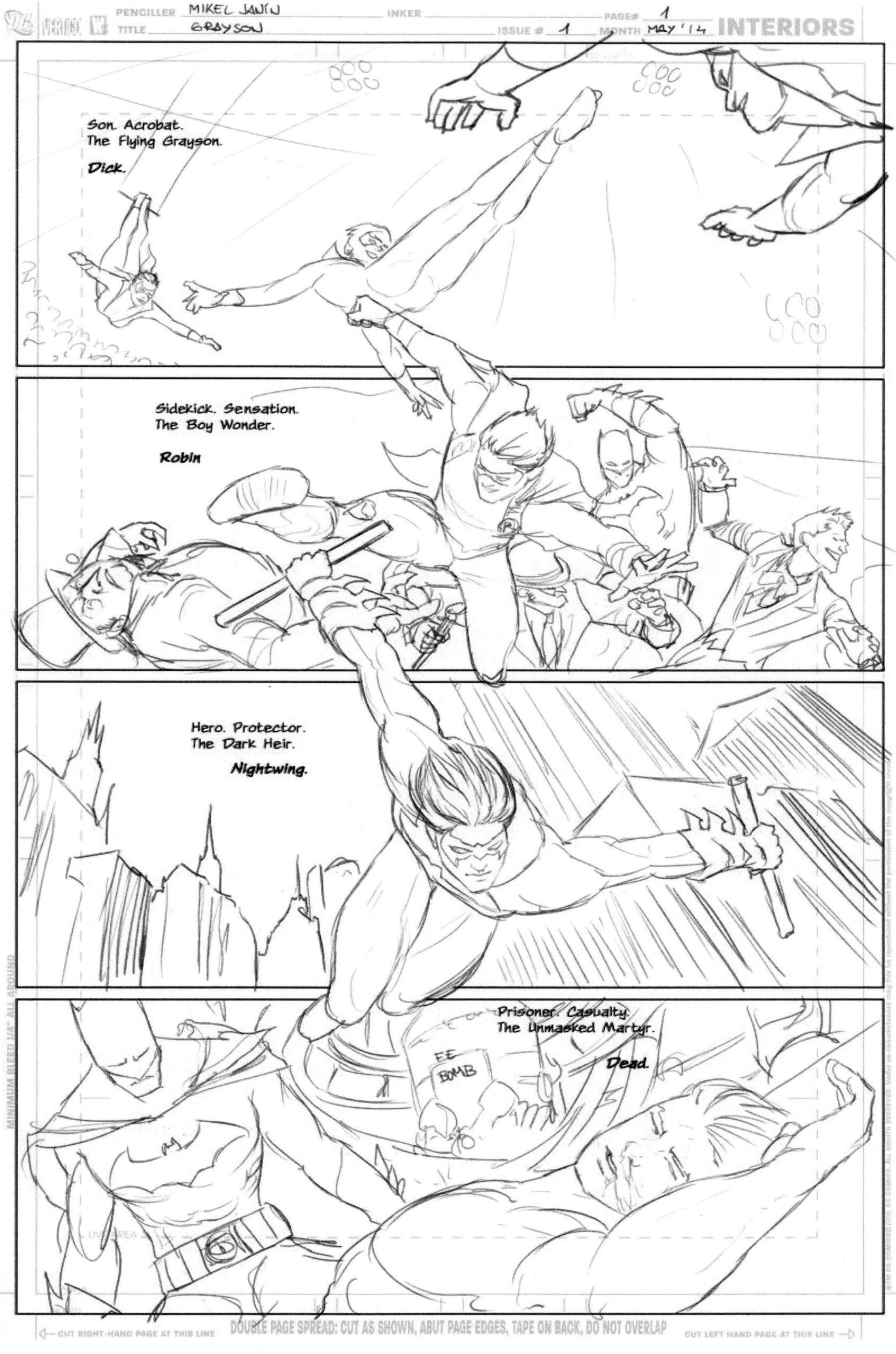
PENCILLER MIKEL JANIN
INKER
PAGE# 1
TITLE GRAYSON
ISSUE # 1
MONTH MAY '14
INTERIORS
Son. Acrobat.
The Flying Grayson.
Dick.
Sidekick. Sensation.
The Boy Wonder.
Robin
Hero. Protector.
The Dark Heir.
Nightwing.
Prisoner. Casualty.
The Unmasked Martyr.
Dead.
EE
BOMB
MINIMUM BLEED 1/4" ALL AROUND
CUT RIGHT-HAND PAGE AT THIS LINE
DOUBLE PAGE SPREAD: CUT AS SHOWN, ABUT PAGE EDGES, TAPE ON BACK, DO NOT OVERLAP
CUT LEFT HAND PAGE AT THIS LINE

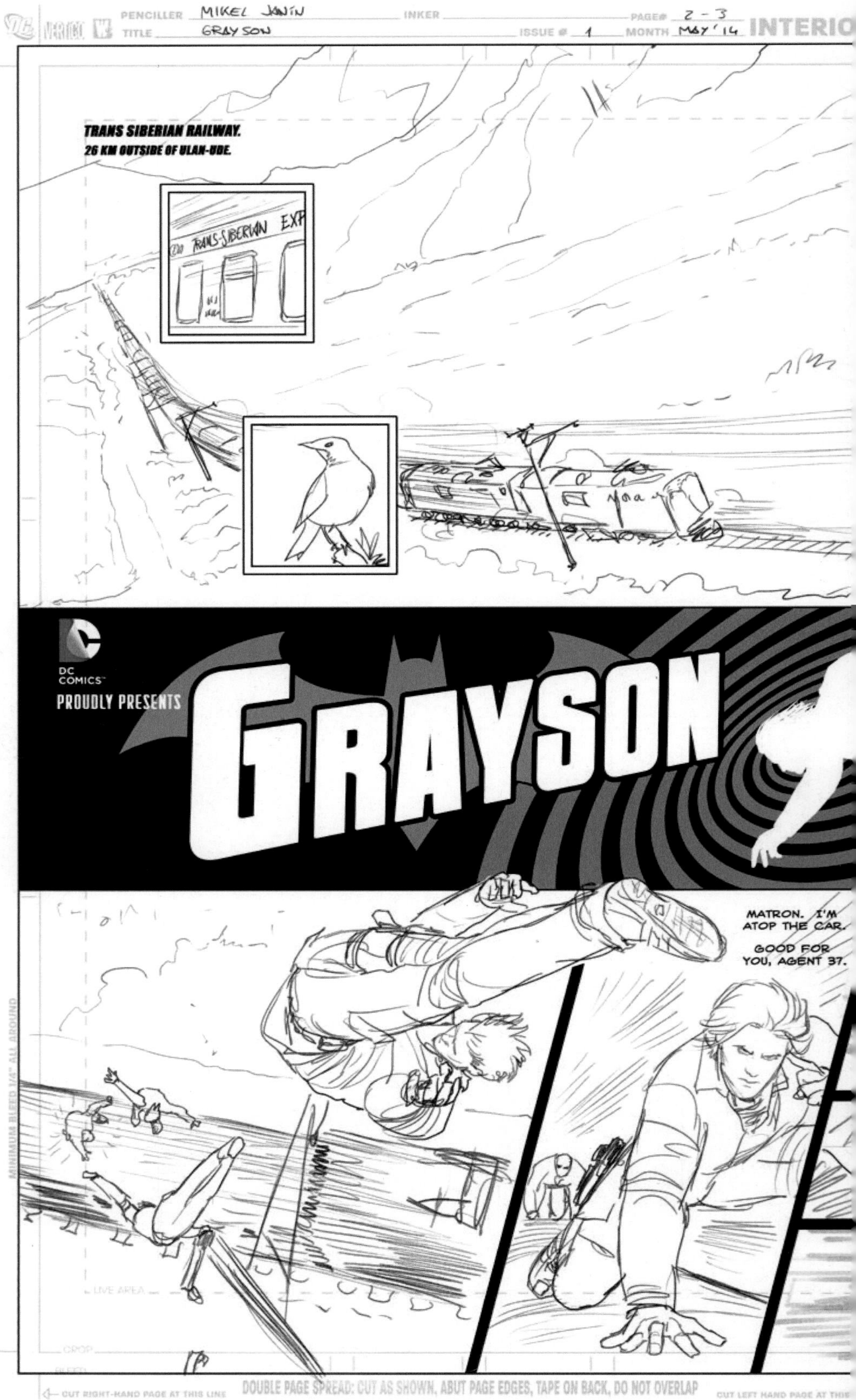
PENCILLER MIKEL JANIN
INKER
PAGE# 2 - 3
TITLE GRAYSON
ISSUE # 1
MONTH MAY '14
INTERIO
TRANS SIBERIAN RAILWAY.
26 KM OUTSIDE OF ULAN-UDE.
TRANS-SIBERIAN EXP
DC COMICS
PROUDLY PRESENTS
GRAYSON
MATRON. I'M ATOP THE CAR.
GOOD FOR YOU, AGENT 37.
MINIMUM BLEED 1/4" ALL AROUND
LIVE AREA
CROP
BLEED
CUT RIGHT-HAND PAGE AT THIS LINE
DOUBLE PAGE SPREAD: CUT AS SHOWN, ABUT PAGE EDGES, TAPE ON BACK, DO NOT OVERLAP
CUT LEFT HAND PAGE AT THIS

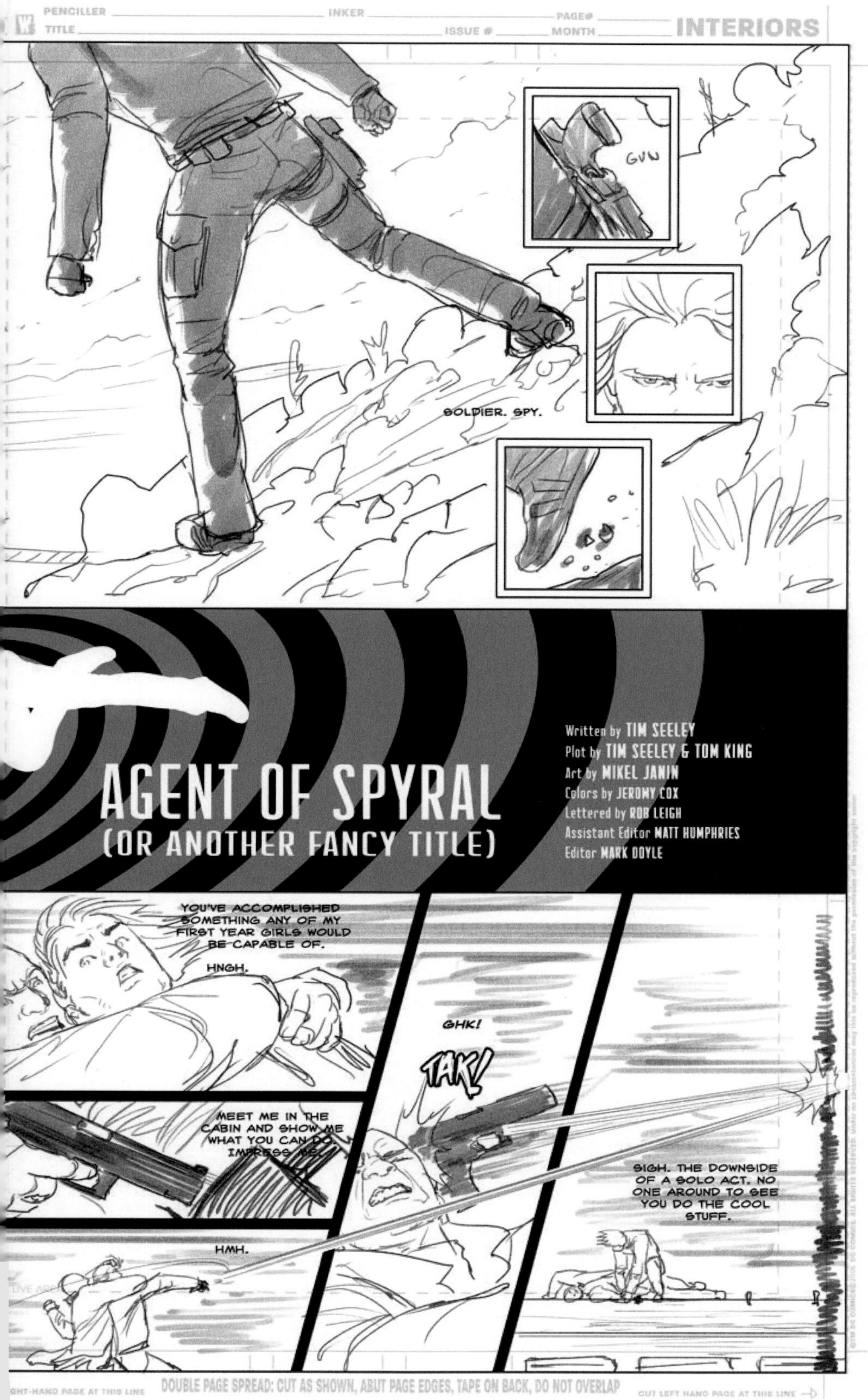
PENCILLER
INKER
PAGE#
TITLE
ISSUE #
MONTH
INTERIORS
GUN
SOLDIER. SPY.
AGENT OF SPYRAL
(OR ANOTHER FANCY TITLE)
Written by TIM SEELEY
Plot by TIM SEELEY & TOM KING
Art by MIKEL JANIN
Colors by JEROMY COX
Lettered by ROB LEIGH
Assistant Editor MATT HUMPHRIES
Editor MARK DOYLE
YOU'VE ACCOMPLISHED SOMETHING ANY OF MY FIRST YEAR GIRLS WOULD BE CAPABLE OF.
HNGH.
GHK!
TAK!
MEET ME IN THE CABIN AND SHOW ME WHAT YOU CAN DO. IMPRESS ME.
SIGH. THE DOWNSIDE OF A SOLO ACT. NO ONE AROUND TO SEE YOU DO THE COOL STUFF.
HMH.
DOUBLE PAGE SPREAD: CUT AS SHOWN, ABUT PAGE EDGES, TAPE ON BACK, DO NOT OVERLAP
CUT LEFT HAND PAGE AT THIS LINE

DAMN. THAT WAS PRETTY COOL.

METEOROLOGIST, THIS IS RAINMAKER. RUSSIAN FOREIGN INTELLIGENCE AND UNKNOWN PLAYER EN ROUTE TO ASSET. LOOKS LIKE WE'VE GOT A HOT ONE.

<TICKETS. NEED YOUR TICKETS>

<EXCUSE ME SIR. TICKET?>

BUT OF COURSE, KRASEEVAYA DEVOCHKA.

OH. HA. WELCOME TO THE TRANS MONGOLIAN LINE, SIR. ENJOY YOUR TRIP.

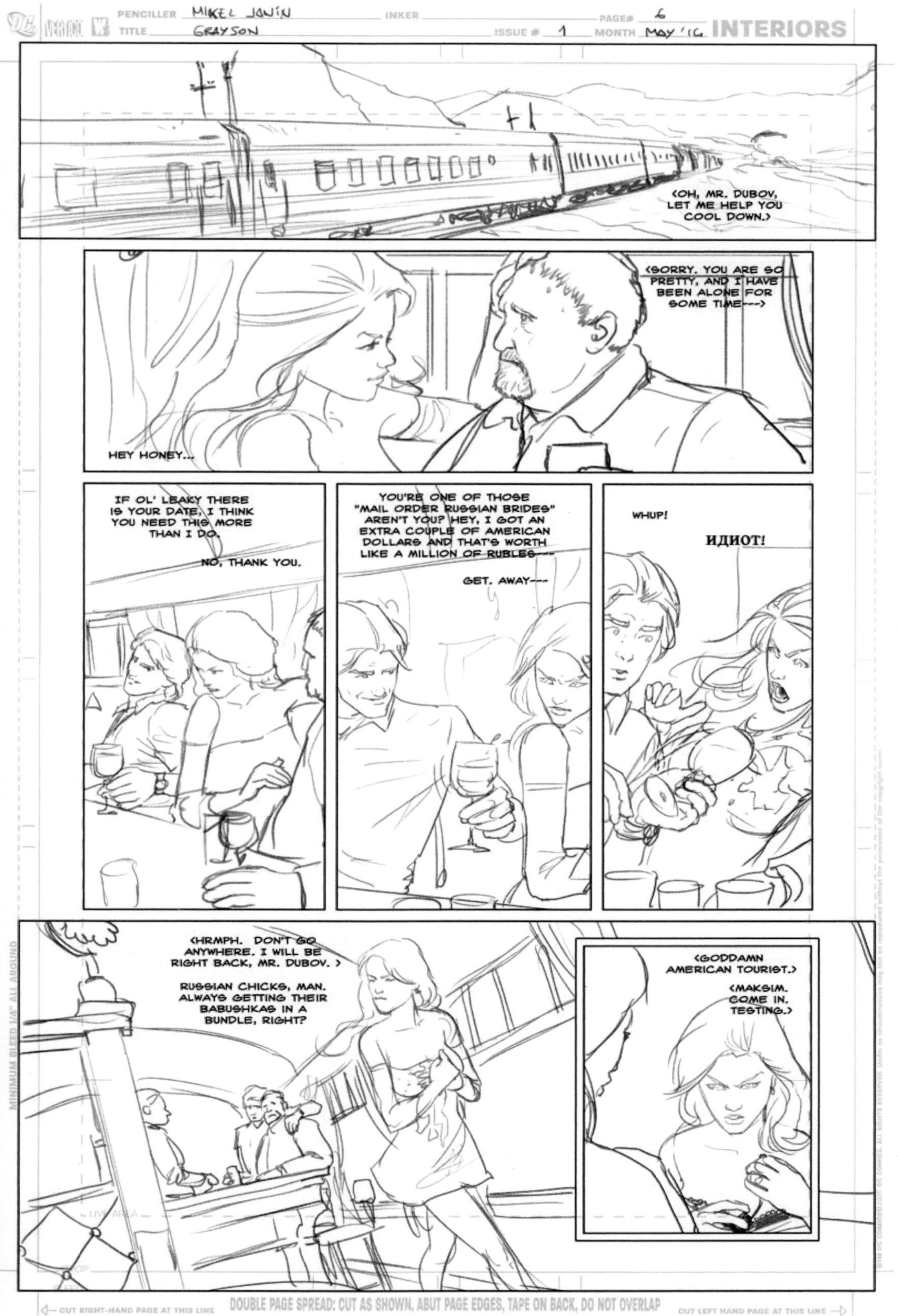
PENCILLER MIKEL JANIN
INKER
PAGE# 6
TITLE GRAYSON
ISSUE # 1
MONTH MAY '16
INTERIORS
<OH, MR. DUBOV, LET ME HELP YOU COOL DOWN.>
<SORRY. YOU ARE SO PRETTY, AND I HAVE BEEN ALONE FOR SOME TIME--->
HEY HONEY...
IF OL' LEAKY THERE IS YOUR DATE, I THINK YOU NEED THIS MORE THAN I DO.
NO, THANK YOU.
YOU'RE ONE OF THOSE "MAIL ORDER RUSSIAN BRIDES" AREN'T YOU? HEY, I GOT AN EXTRA COUPLE OF AMERICAN DOLLARS AND THAT'S WORTH LIKE A MILLION OF RUBLES---
GET. AWAY---
WHUP!
ИДИОТ!
<HRMPH. DON'T GO ANYWHERE. I WILL BE RIGHT BACK, MR. DUBOV.>
RUSSIAN CHICKS, MAN. ALWAYS GETTING THEIR BABUSHKAS IN A BUNDLE, RIGHT?
<GODDAMN AMERICAN TOURIST.>
<MAKSIM. COME IN. TESTING.>
MINIMUM BLEED 1/4" ALL AROUND
CUT RIGHT-HAND PAGE AT THIS LINE
DOUBLE PAGE SPREAD: CUT AS SHOWN, ABUT PAGE EDGES, TAPE ON BACK, DO NOT OVERLAP
CUT LEFT HAND PAGE AT THIS LINE

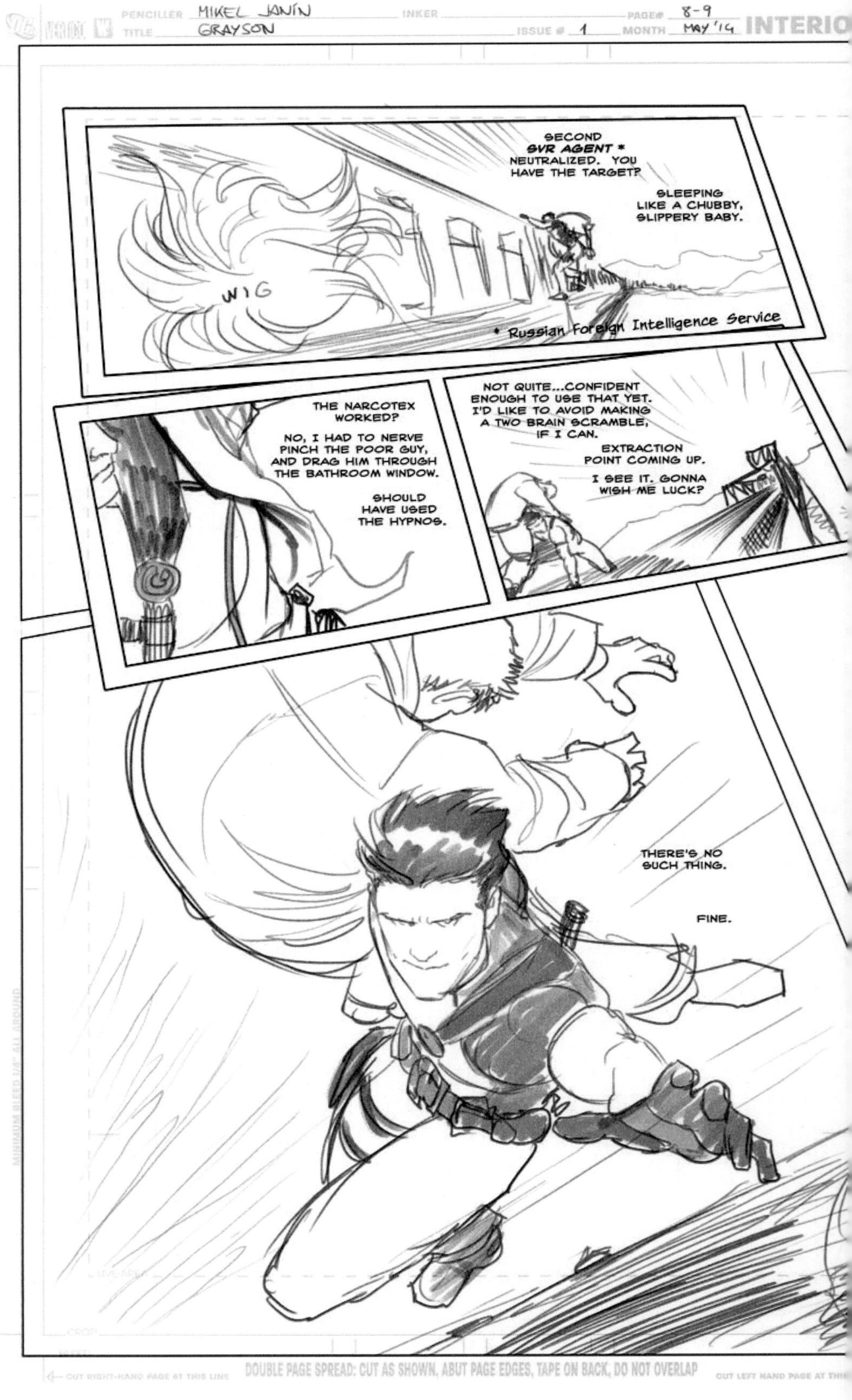
PENCILLER MIKEL JANIN
INKER
PAGE# 8-9
TITLE GRAYSON
ISSUE # 1
MONTH MAY '14
INTERIO
SECOND SVR AGENT * NEUTRALIZED. YOU HAVE THE TARGET?
SLEEPING LIKE A CHUBBY, SLIPPERY BABY.
WIG
* Russian Foreign Intelligence Service
THE NARCOTEX WORKED?
NO, I HAD TO NERVE PINCH THE POOR GUY, AND DRAG HIM THROUGH THE BATHROOM WINDOW.
SHOULD HAVE USED THE HYPNOS.
NOT QUITE...CONFIDENT ENOUGH TO USE THAT YET. I'D LIKE TO AVOID MAKING A TWO BRAIN SCRAMBLE, IF I CAN.
EXTRACTION POINT COMING UP.
I SEE IT. GONNA WISH ME LUCK?
THERE'S NO SUCH THING.
FINE.
DOUBLE PAGE SPREAD: CUT AS SHOWN. ABUT PAGE EDGES, TAPE ON BACK, DO NOT OVERLAP

PENCILLER INKER PAGE#
TITLE ISSUE # MONTH INTERIORS

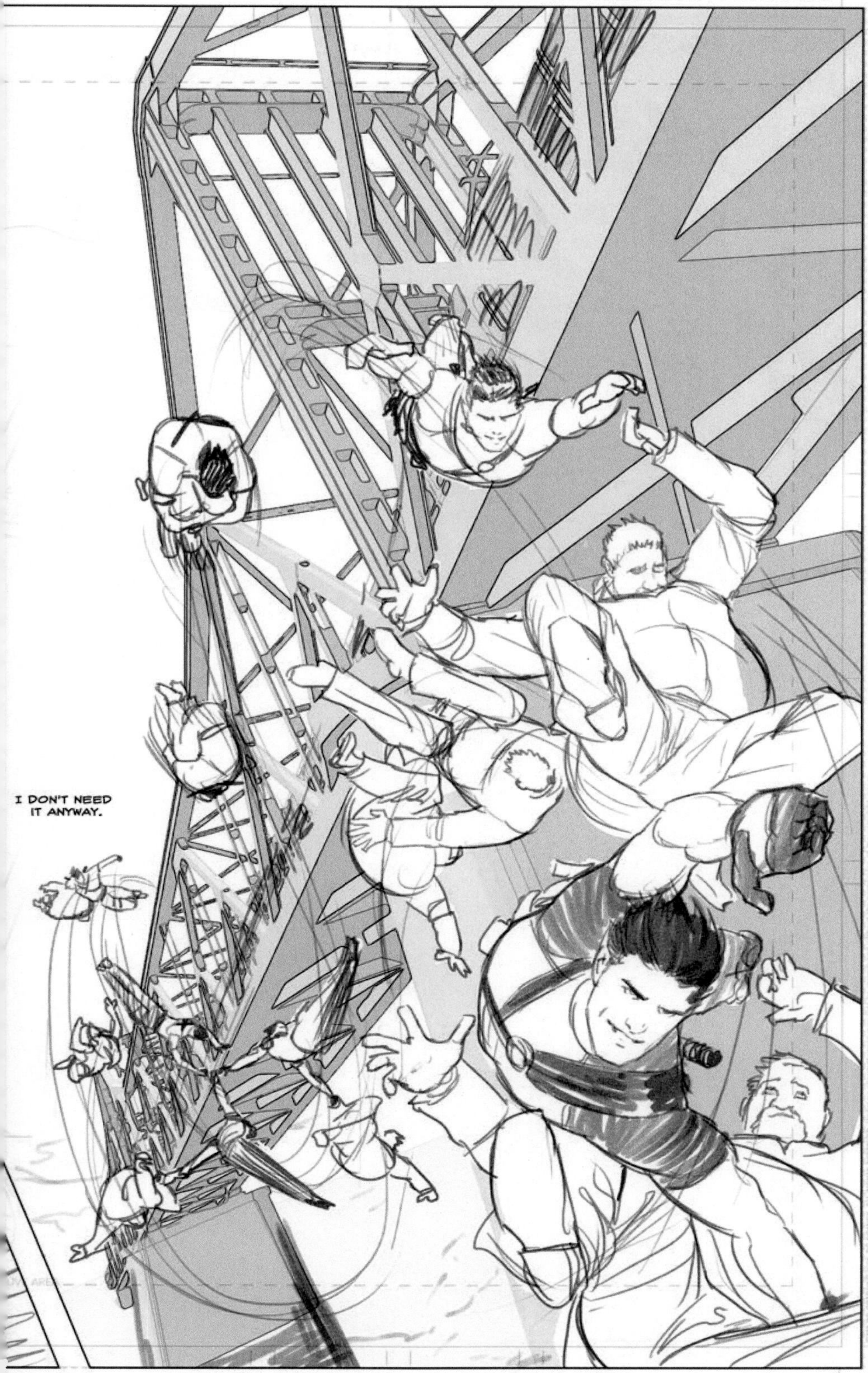
I DON'T NEED IT ANYWAY.

DOUBLE PAGE SPREAD: CUT AS SHOWN, ABUT PAGE EDGES, TAPE ON BACK, DO NOT OVERLAP
CUT LEFT HAND PAGE AT THIS LINE

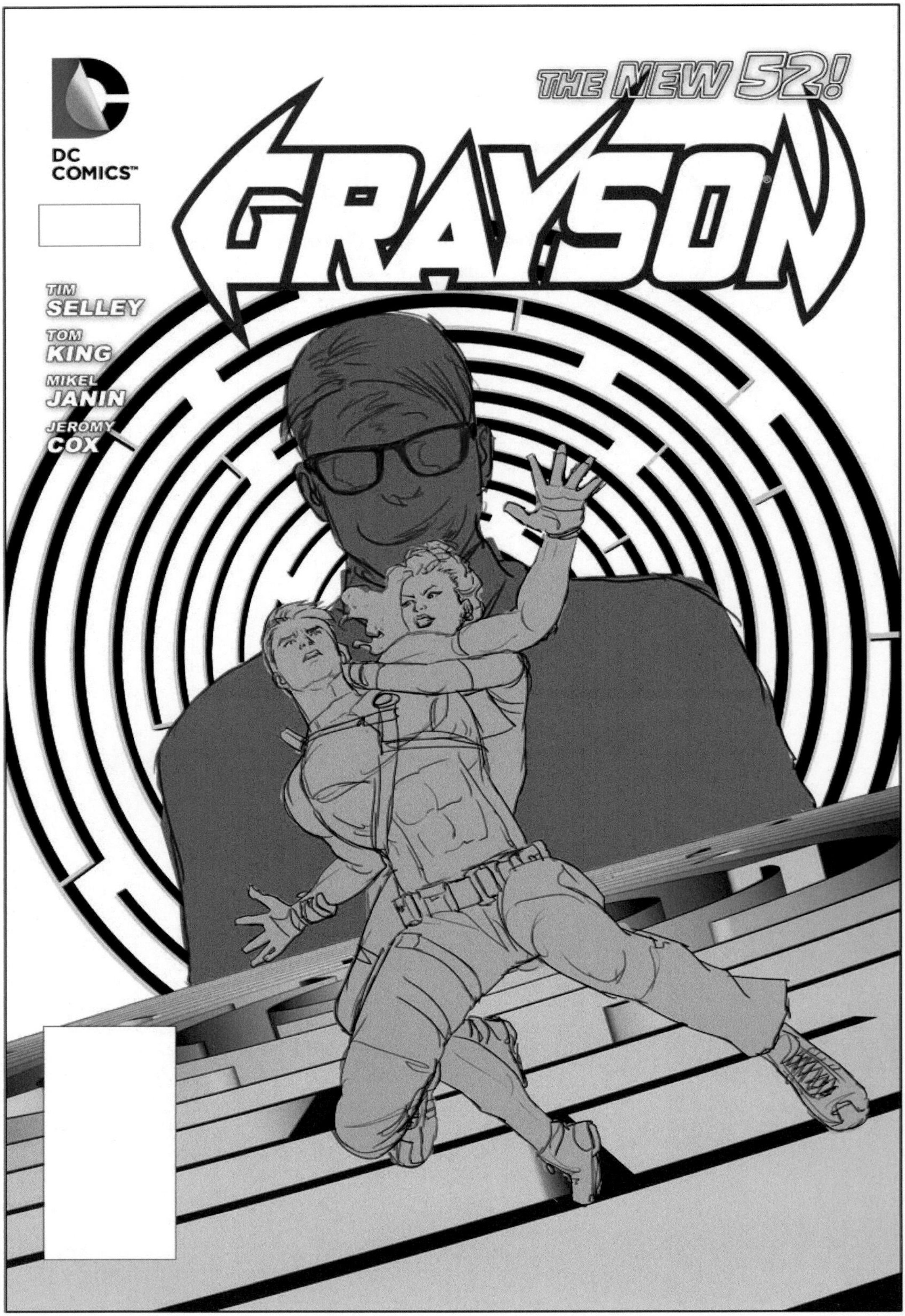
THE NEW 52!
DC COMICS
GRAYSON
TIM SELLEY
TOM KING
MIKEL JANIN
JEROMY COX

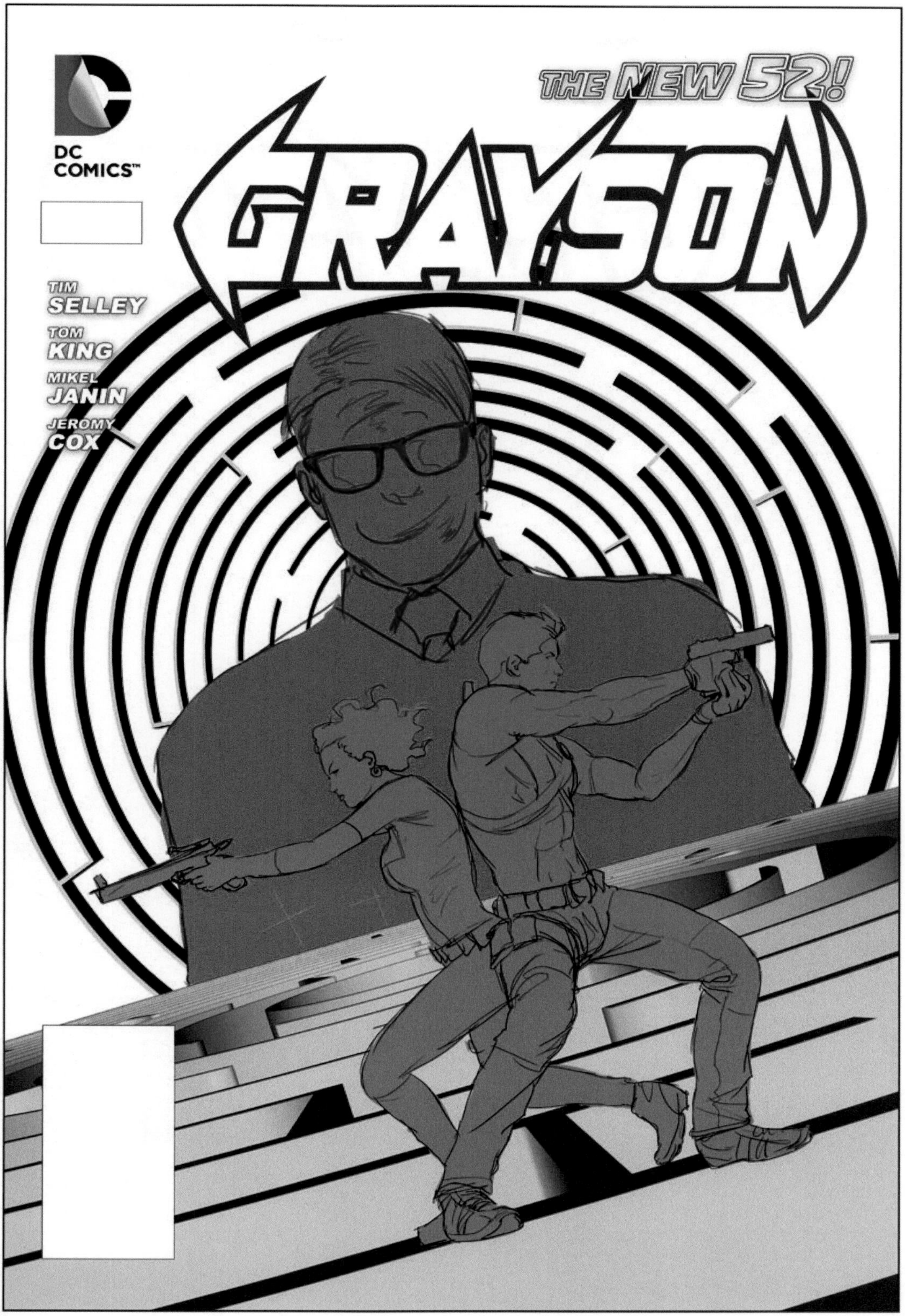
DC COMICS™
THE NEW 52!
GRAYSON
TIM SELLEY
TOM KING
MIKEL JANIN
JEROMY COX

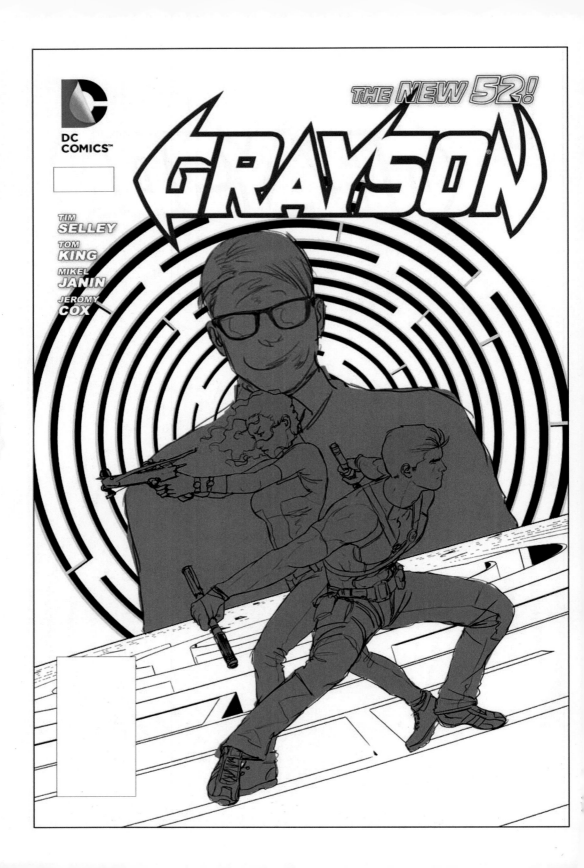

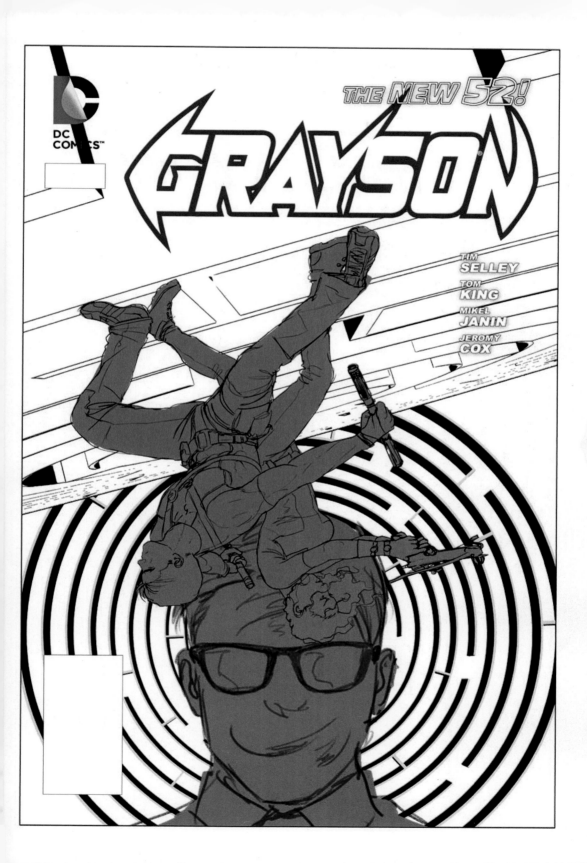